Contents

FOOD AND BEVERAGE SERVICE

NINTH EDITION

JOHN COUSINS
DENNIS LILLICRAP
SUZANNE WEEKES

HODDER
EDUCATION
AN HACHETTE UK COMPANY

Orders: please contact Bookpoint Ltd, 130 Milton Park, Abingdon, Oxon OX14 4SB.
Telephone: (44) 01235 827720. Fax: (44) 01235 400454. Lines are open from 9.00 to 5.00, Monday to Saturday, with a 24-hour message answering service. You can also order through our website www.hoddereducation.co.uk

If you have any comments to make about this, or any of our other titles, please send them to educationenquiries@hodder.co.uk

British Library Cataloguing in Publication Data

A catalogue record for this title is available from the British Library

ISBN: 978 1 471 80795 4

This edition published 2014.

Impression number   10 9 8 7 6 5 4 3 2 1

Year   2014, 2015, 2016, 2017

Copyright © 2014 John Cousins, Dennis Lillicrap, Suzanne Weekes

Hachette UK's policy is to use papers that are natural, renewable and recyclable products and made from wood grown in sustainable forests. The logging and manufacturing processes are expected to conform to the environmental regulations of the country of origin.

Typeset by DC Graphic Design Limited, Swanley Village, Kent.

Printed in Italy for Hodder Education, an Hachette UK Company, 338 Euston Road, London NW1 3BH.

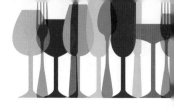

Acknowledgements

The preparation of the ninth edition of this book has drawn upon a variety of experience and literature. We would also like to express our sincere thanks to all the organisations and individuals who gave the assistance and support in the revision of this text. In particular we would like to thank:

Academy of Food and Wine Service, UK; British Airways plc; Burgess Furniture Ltd, London; City and Guilds of London Institute; Croners Catering, Croners Publications; Cutlery and Allied Trade Research Association (CATRA); Anne Dubberley and Julie Bromfield, Petals of Piccadilly, Birmingham; Dunk Ink; Andrew Durkan, Author and Consultant, formally of Ealing College, London; Elia International Ltd, Middlesex; Euroservice UK, Welford, Northants; Foodservice Consultants Society International, UK&I; Professor David Foskett, Author, Consultant and Dean at the London School of Hospitality and Tourism, Hospitality and Leisure, Ealing and also the Operations Team at the School; Simon Girling, Restaurant Manager, The Ritz Hotel, London; Gleneagles Hotel, Auchterarder, Scotland; Hilton Hotels and Resorts; Hunters and Frankau, cigar importers and distributors; IFS Publications; The International Coffee Organisation; International Standards Organisation; Katie Kyrousis, Food and Beverage Services Training Manager, Gleneagles Hotel, Auchterarder, Scotland and WorldSkills Training Manager UK – Restaurant Service; The Langham Hotel, London; Le Columbier Restaurant, London; Louvet Turner Coombe Marketing; Meiko UK Ltd; National Checking Co UK; Maidaid – Halcyon: PalmTEQ Limited UK; The Ritz Hotel, London; The Restaurant Association of Great Britain; Royal Academy of Culinary Arts, UK; Royal Garden Hotel, Joachim Schafheitle, Senior Lecturer, Bournemouth University; Ashley Shaw, House Manager, United Kingdom Bartenders Guild; The Westbury Hotel, London; Six Continents Hotels, London; Louise Smith, Flowers by Louise, Birmingham; Snap-Drape Europe Limited; Sodexo UK and Ireland; Steelite International; The Tea Council; Uniwell Systems (UK) Ltd; Westbury Hotel, London; John Williams, Executive Chef, The Ritz Hotel, London; Ian Whitaker, Chief Executive Cairngorm Mountain; United Kingdom Bartenders Guild, WineSearcher.com and WorldSkills International.

Figures 2.8, 5.2, 5.8, 6.31, 6.32, 6.33, 6.34, 6.35, 6.36, 6.39, 6.40, 6.43, 6.47, 6.48, 6.49, 6.54, 6.55, 6.56, 7.7, 9.7, 10.1, 10.7, 10.16 and 10.17were photographed by Ria Osborne at the University of West London.

Figures 5.9, 6.44 and 6.45 were photographed by Ria Osborne at the Rose and Crown pub, Ealing.

Figures 2.2. 2.4, 3.1, 3.2, 3.9, 3.10, 4.5–4.11, 6.4, 6.5, 6.51, 7.6 and 8.6 were photographed by Andrew Callaghan.

Figures 2.1, 2.3, 2.5–2.7, 2.9, 3.4, 3.11, 5.1, 5.3, 5.4, 5.5, 5.7, 6.3, 6.13–6.15, 6.18, 6.19, 6.38, 6.41, 6.50, 6.52, 6.53, 8.2, 8.5, 8.7, 9.4 and 12.6 were photographed by Carl Drury.

We would also like to thank the following for permission to reproduce copyright photos:

Figure 5.1 © Khoo Eng Yow/Getty Images/iStockphoto/Thinkstock; Figure 5.10 © Jacques PALUT – Fotolia; Figure 5.11 © Galina Peshkova/Getty Images/iStockphoto/Thinkstock

How to use this book and master reference chart

The information in the book can be accessed in three ways:

1 Using the detailed contents list at the front of the book (p.iii)
2 Finding information through the index at the back of the book (p.ix)
3 Using the master reference chart (p.ix).

The master reference chart takes account of the various examining and awarding body recommendations and assessment requirements, especially National Vocational Qualifications. The chart identifies aspects of food and beverage service and indicates the chapter or section where that information is detailed.

Because of the wide variety of hospitality operations, the chart indicates the broad range of knowledge and skills that will be relevant to a range of food service operations. The chart can be used as a checklist when identifying the relevance of a particular aspect to a particular foodservice operation, job or qualification requirement, as well as a means of finding information.

To use the chart, first select the aspect you are interested in from the tasks and duties column. Then note the chapter and/or section identified and go to the indicated page.

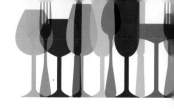

Master reference chart

Tasks and duties	Chapters/sections and page numbers
Industry knowledge	
Define food and beverages	1.1, p.2
Identify the sectors of the foodservice industry	1.1, p.2
Identify variables between different sectors	1.1, p.2/5
Explain the stages of the foodservice cycle	1.2, p.6
Describe examples of foodservice operations	1.2, p.6/8
Identify variables in different foodservice operations	1.2, p.6/9
Identify factors contributing to the meal experience	1.3, p.10
Define customer service	1.4, p.11
Differentiate between levels and standards of service	1.4, p.12
Describe food production methods	1.5, p.14
Distinguish between the service sequence and the customer process	1.6, p.16
Outline the relationship between the different operating systems in a foodservice operation	1.6, p.17
Describe food and beverage service methods	1.6, p.18/19
Identify the main job titles and roles within food and beverage service	1.7, p.20
Personal skills	
Identify factors for success in food and beverage service	2.1, p.27
Develop attributes necessary for food and beverage service	2.2, p.27
Comply with key service conventions and know the reasons for them	2.3, p.30
Work within legal requirements	2.1, p.27
Develop competence in essential technical skills	2.4, p.33
Develop good interpersonal skills	2.5, p.40 and 12.3, p.388
Be able to deal with: ● adults ● children ● those with mobility difficulties ● those with communication difficulties ● customer complaints ● customer incidents	 2.5, p.40 2.5, p.41 2.5, p.42 2.5, p.43 2.5, p.43 2.5, p.44

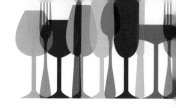

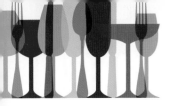

Introduction to the ninth edition

Aim of the book

Food and Beverage Service covers the knowledge and skills necessary for those studying and/or working at a variety of levels in food and beverage service. The book also provides a framework on which to build further studies and to relate further acquired knowledge and experience.

An explanation of how information can be found in the book is given in the section *How to use this book*, p. viii. This section also contains a Master reference chart on pp. ix–xi, which summarises the tasks and duties for staff working in food and beverage service. The chart also identifies where to find information within the book.

In revising this ninth edition we have taken into account recent developments in examining and awarding body recommendations and specifications, in education and training, as well as in the industry at large. The book has been prepared to support the studies of those wishing to be assessed at NVQ/SVQ Levels 1 to 3 in Food and Beverage Service and for a range of other qualifications including those of the City & Guilds Certificate and Diploma in Food and Beverage Service. In addition, the book is intended to support the broader based study requirements in food and beverage service for programmes leading to the award of the National Diploma, the General National Vocational Qualification, the Higher National Diploma, Foundation Degree and undergraduate degree programmes, as well as programmes of the Institute of Hospitality. It is also of value supporting in-company training programmes.

Trends in the foodservice industry

Foodservice operations are continuing to improve and develop, together with advances in quality. The demand for food and beverages away from the home has increased and, with a broader spectrum of the population eating out, customer needs are continuing to diversify.

Food and restaurant styles are also adapting to meet the demands being made by increasingly knowledgeable and value-conscious customers. Menu and beverage list contents are constantly being influenced by trends, fads and fashions, the relationship between health and eating, dietary requirements, cultural and religious influences, the advance of vegetarianism, and customer acceptance, or otherwise, of irradiation and genetically modified foods.

The growing range of foodservice operations has necessitated developments in the approaches to food and beverage service. The traditional view of food and beverage service was as a delivery process, with the customer being considered a passive recipient of the service. More recently this view has changed significantly – and for the better. The customer is now seen as central to the process and as an active participant within it. Increasing competition has meant that both the quality of the service and the perceived value of the experience by customers are the main differentiators between operations that are seeking to attract similar customers.

Consequently, understanding the customer's involvement in the process and identifying the experience they are likely to have, and should expect, have become critical to the business success of foodservice operations.

Expansion of the industry has generally meant greater choice. This, together with potential skill shortages and drives for efficiency, has seen a streamlining of foodservice operations. There is now less emphasis on sophisticated service techniques in some sectors, but more emphasis throughout the industry on sound product knowledge, well-developed interpersonal skills, technical competence and the ability to work as part of a team.

However, service, both in level and standards, still varies greatly throughout the whole range of foodservice operations. While there are many examples of operations that are working with the highest levels of competence, there are also, unfortunately, operations that believe that food and beverage service is something that anyone can do. This is clearly nonsense: only where there are well-developed operating systems, and where the members of staff are trained to work within them, can a foodservice operation work efficiently and effectively. The customer's enjoyment of the meal is also greatly enhanced as the service staff have the confidence and time to be genuinely welcoming.

Any successful foodservice operation requires all elements to work as a whole: service personnel working together with chefs and the wine and drink lists being in harmony with the food. The essential contribution by food and beverage service professionals cannot be underestimated. Michelin Stars or AA Rosettes, for instance, are awarded to restaurants not to individuals. Service managers and service staff, and their skills and professionalism, should therefore have the same focus of attention as any other industry professionals. However, food and beverage service also represents the ultimate paradox: the better it is, the less it is noticed.

Good food and beverage service, in any sector, is achieved where customers' needs are met and where management consistently reinforce and support service staff in the maintenance of clearly identified technical standards and service goals. It is against this background that the revisions for this ninth edition have taken place.

The ninth edition

The content of the book has been structured to follow a logical progression from the underpinning knowledge of food and beverage operations, service areas and equipment, menus and beverages, through to interpersonal and technical service skills, advanced technical skills and then on to key supervisory aspects.

An overview of the foodservice industry is given in Chapter 1. This chapter also provides an identification of the types of operation, sectors, the reasons for eating out, service methods and service staff roles.

Chapter 2 outlines the attributes, skills and knowledge needed by service personnel and especially the need to contribute to the maintenance of a healthy, safe and secure environment.

The next three chapters provide a base of underpinning knowledge about service areas and equipment (Chapter 3); the menu, its construction, example dishes and accompaniments (Chapter 4); and all types of non-alcoholic and alcoholic beverages (Chapter 5).

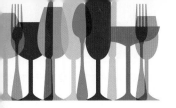

Chapter 6 and Chapter 7 detail essential skills, both interpersonal and technical, and indicate how these are applied to the service sequence for table service (Chapter 6) and counter service (Chapter 7). The application of skills is then further developed for a variety of other service settings: breakfast and afternoon tea (Chapter 8); specialised forms of service (Chapter 9); enhanced service skills (Chapter 10); and events (Chapter 11).

Finally, consideration is given to a number of supervisory aspects (Chapter 12), including legal considerations, sales promotion, customer relations, staffing levels, staff organisation and training, food and beverage pricing and revenue control, beverage control and performance measures.

There are also three annexes which cover: a glossary of cuisine and service terms (Annex A); a cocktail and mixed drink listing giving recipes and methods (Annex B); and information about cigars (Annex C).

Throughout the book we have referred to job titles and job categories such as waiter, supervisor, floor service staff, room attendants, servers and stewards. In all cases these terms, in line with general trends within the industry, refer to both male and female personnel.

The content of the book, while having its origins in classic cuisine and service (the context and the body of knowledge on which modern foodservice operations are based) is also intended to reflect current practice within the industry. Therefore, while the book gives information and describes various aspects of food and beverage service, it should not be seen as a prescriptive book. Clearly the actual operation of the service will be substantially affected by the style and the business needs of the individual operation.

John Cousins, Dennis Lillicrap and Suzanne Weekes

March 2014

John Cousins is a consultant and international authority on food and beverage operations and hospitality management, and is the Director of The Food and Beverage Training Company.

Dennis Lillicrap is a consultant and trainer in food and beverage service. He was formerly Senior Lecturer in Food and Beverage Service at Thames Valley University.

Suzanne Weekes is Senior Lecturer in Hospitality Management and Licensing Law at the London School of Hospitality and Tourism, University of West London.

Chapter 1

The food and beverage industry

1.1 Sectors of the foodservice industry

The international foodservice industry provides millions of meals a day in a wide variety of types of operation.

- **Food** can include a wide range of styles and cuisine types. These can be classified by country, for example, traditional British or Italian; by type of cuisine, for example, oriental; or a particular speciality such as fish, vegetarian or health food.
- **Beverages** include all alcoholic and non-alcoholic drinks. Alcoholic beverages include wines and all other types of alcoholic drink such as cocktails, beers and cider, spirits and liqueurs. Non-alcoholic beverages include bar beverages such as mineral waters, juices, squashes and aerated waters, as well as tea, coffee, chocolate, milk and milk drinks and also proprietary drinks such as Bovril.

Figure 1.1 Multiple food outlets at the Trafford Centre, Manchester (image courtesy of FCSI UK and I)

Within the foodservice industry there are a number of different industrial sectors and these are categorised according to the type of customer demand being met. To help you identify the nature of demand being met within each sector, Table 1.1 provides a list of industry sectors and identifies the prime purpose of the foodservice operations within them. An historical summary is also given together with an identification of both UK and international terminology. This identification of sectors also provides a framework for those studying the food and beverage service industry to which further studies and experience may be related.

Each sector described in Table 1.1 (see page 4) may be further analysed by considering a set of variables that exist in the different sectors (Table 1.2). These variables represent elements that vary in particular sectors and thus provide a basis for examining the different types of foodservice operations within specific sectors. They enable a comprehensive picture of industrial sectors to be compiled and also provide the basis for the comparison of the different sectors.

There are many different industry sectors such as hotels, independent and chain restaurants, popular catering, pubs and wine bars, fast food, leisure attractions and banqueting. There are also sectors where food and beverages are provided as part of another business. These include transport catering, welfare, clubs, education, industrial feeding and the armed forces.

Table 1.2 Variables in foodservice sectors

Historical background	Interpretation of demand/catering concept
Reasons for customer demand	Technological development
Size of sector: • in terms of outlets • in terms of turnover	Influences
	State of sector development
	Primary/secondary activity
Policies: • financial • marketing • catering	Types of outlets
	Profit orientation/cost provision
	Public/private ownership

Some sectors provide food and beverages for profit, whereas others work within the constraints of a given budget, often called *cost provision* (for example, welfare catering and industrial catering). In addition, some sectors provide services to the general public whereas others provide them for restricted groups of people.

It is useful to define these different types of market as follows:
- General market
  - Non-captive: customers have a full choice.
- Restricted market
  - Captive: customers have no choice, for example, welfare.
  - Semi-captive: customers have a choice before entering, for example, marine, airline, trains, some hotels and some leisure activities. The customers could have chosen alternatives to these but, once chosen, have little choice of food and drink other than that on offer.

Taking these definitions into account, a general summary of sectors may be drawn up as shown in Table 1.3. Defining the nature of the market in this way helps us to understand why different methods of organisation may be in operation. For example, in captive markets customers might be asked to clear their own tables, whereas in non-captive markets this is unlikely to be successful.

Table 1.3 Summary of sectors in the foodservice industry

Profit orientated (public or private ownership) (foodservice as main or secondary activity)		Cost provision
Restricted market	**General market**	**Restricted market**
Transport catering	Hotels/restaurants	Institutional catering
Clubs	Popular catering	Schools
Industrial (contract)	Fast food/takeaway	Universities and colleges
Private welfare	Retail stores	Hospitals
	Events/conferences/exhibitions	Armed forces
	Leisure attractions	Prisons
	Motorway service stations	Industrial (in-house)
	Pubs and wine bars	
	ODC (off-premises catering)	

Table 1.1 Sectors of the foodservice industry

Industry sector – UK terminology	Purpose of the foodservice operation	Historical summary	Industry sector – international terminology
Hotels and other tourist accommodation	Provision of food and drink together with accommodation services	Supported by developments in transport and increases in business and leisure-related tourism	*Hotel, motel and other tourist accommodation* Often now referred to as the *lodging industry*
Restaurants including conventional and specialist operations	Provision of food and drink, generally at a high price with high levels of service	Grew out of hotel restaurants (which were originally highly formal) through chefs wishing to start their own businesses	
Popular catering including cafés, pizza, grills, specialist coffee shops, roadside restaurants and steak houses	Provision of food and drink, generally at low/medium price with limited levels of service and often high customer throughput	Has gone through various phases. More recently highly influenced by the USA	*Separate eating and drinking places* Categories usually defined by reference to three criteria:
Fast food including McDonald's and Burger King	Provision of food and drink in highly specialised environment, characterised by high investment, high labour costs and vast customer throughput	Grew from combination of popular catering and takeaway, heavily influenced by USA concepts; highly sophisticated meal packaging and marketing	• level of service, e.g. quick service to full service or fine dining • extent of menu, e.g. limited to full • price range, e.g. low to high
Takeaway including ethnic, spuds, KFC, snacks, fish and chips, sandwich bars, kiosks	Fast provision of food and drink	Developed from a variety of concepts. More recently, influenced by USA and trends in food tastes	
Retail stores	Provision of food and drink as an adjunct to retail provision	Developed originally from prestigious stores wishing to provide food and drink as part of the retailing experience	*Retail market*
Events/banqueting/ conferencing/ exhibitions	Provision of large scale food and drink for events	Originally associated with hotels but has now become major sector in its own right	*Event market*
Leisure attractions such as theme parks, museums, galleries, cinemas and theatres	Provision of food and drink to people engaged in another pursuit	Increases in leisure have made profit from food and drink attractive to leisure and amenity providers	*Leisure market*

Industry sector – UK terminology	Purpose of the foodservice operation	Historical summary	Industry sector – international terminology
Motorway service stations	Provision of food and drink, together with petrol and other retail services, often in isolated locations	Developed in the 1960s with the advent of motorway building. Influenced by USA and became specialised because of government regulations on provision of foodservice operations, retails and fuel as well as location	*Highway (interstate) market*
Industrial catering either in-house operations or through catering/foodservice contractors	Provision of food and drink to people at work	Developed out or recognition that better fed workers work better. Given substantial boost during First and Second World Wars. Further developed by worker unions wanting to preserve conditions and the emergence of professional contract caterers/ foodservice operators	*Business/industry markets*
Welfare catering	Provision of food and drink to people in colleges, universities, the armed forces and to people through established social need	Highly regulated and maintained now through public social conscience	*Social caterer/ foodservice (education, healthcare, institutional and military)*
Licensed trade including public houses, wine bars, licensed clubs and members' clubs	Provision of food and drink in an environment dominated by licensing requirements	Developed from bars and other drinking places with increased regulation and liquor licensing requirements	*Separate drinking places* but also some units included in *Separate eating and drinking places* shown above
Transport catering including railways, airlines and marine	Provision of food and drink to people on the move	Grew out of the need to meet the demands of the travelling public. Originally services were of high levels, reflecting the type of traveller. Eventually changed to meet the needs of a wide range of travellers	*Transportation market*
Outdoor catering (ODC) (or 'off-premises catering' or 'event catering')	Provision of food and drink away from home base; suppliers usually associated with a major event	Developed through the need to provide services at special events. The term ODC is misleading as little of this catering actually takes place outside	*Catering market*

1.2 Food and beverage operations

Food and beverage (or foodservice) operations in the hospitality industry are concerned with the provision of food and drink ready for immediate consumption (but excluding retailing and food manufacturing).

Foodservice operations are concerned with:

1 The *consumer needs and market potential* in the various sectors of the foodservice industry.
2 The *formulation of policy and business objectives* that will guide the choice of operational methods that will be used.
3 The *interpretation of demand* to make decisions on the range and type of food and beverages to be provided, as well as other services, and the service levels and prices to be charged.
4 The *planning and design of facilities* required for the food and beverage operations and the plant and equipment required.
5 The *organisation of provisioning* for food and beverages and other purchasing requirements to meet the needs of food production, beverage provision and the service methods used.
6 Knowledge of the operational and management requirements for the *food production, beverage provision and service processes and methods* and decision making on the appropriateness of the various processes and methods, together with the management and staffing needs in order to meet the requirements of the operation.
7 *Control of costs* associated with the operation of food production, beverage provision and other services and the *control of revenue.*
8 *Monitoring of consumer satisfaction* to continually check on the extent to which the operation is meeting customer needs and achieving customer satisfaction.

The eight elements in this sequence may be referred to as the *foodservice cycle* as re-presented in Figure 1.2. This summarises what food and beverage (or foodservice) operations are concerned with and illustrates that it is not simply about food production, beverage provision or food and beverage service.

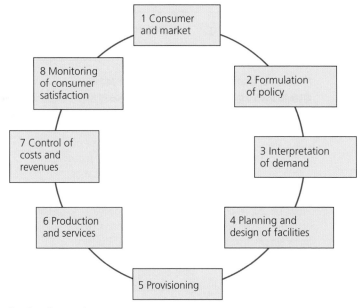

Figure 1.2 The foodservice cycle

The foodservice cycle can be used as a basis to analyse and compare how different foodservice operations work. It provides a standard template or checklist so that information about a specific operation can be collected and organised in a specific way. This can then be compared with the same information collected on other foodservice operations.

The foodservice cycle is also a dynamic model in that it can be used to help understand how an individual operation works. Difficulties in one element of the cycle will cause difficulties in the elements of the cycle that follow. For example, difficulties with purchasing will have effects on food production and service and control. Similarly, difficulties experienced under one element of the cycle will have their causes in preceding elements. For example, difficulties experienced in food and beverage service are often caused by factors such as poor purchasing, inadequate stock control, equipment shortages, poor room layouts or staffing problems.

Types of foodservice operations

Food and beverage (or foodservice) operations include various types of restaurants (bistros, brasseries, coffee shops, first class/fine dining, ethnic, themed), cafés, cafeterias, takeaways, canteens, function rooms, tray service operations, lounge service operations, home delivery operations and room service operations for hotel guests. Examples of the types of operation are given in Table 1.4.

Table 1.4 Examples of types of food and beverage operations

Type of operation	Description
Bistro	Often a smaller establishment, with check tablecloths, bentwood chairs, cluttered decor and friendly informal staff. Tends to offer honest, basic and robust cooking
Brasserie	This is generally a fairly large, styled room with a long bar, normally serving one-plate items rather than formal meals (though some offer both). Often it is possible just to have a drink, coffee or snack. Service provided by waiters, often in traditional style of long aprons and black waistcoats
New wave brasserie (gastrodome)	Slick modern interior design, coupled with similar approaches to contemporary cuisine and service. Busy and bustling and often large and multileveled
Coffee shop	Similar to brasserie-style operations, often themed. May be open all day and serve all meal types from breakfast through to supper
First class restaurant	Usually formal fine dining restaurants with classical preparation and presentation of food and offering a high level of table (silver, guéridon and/or plated) service. Often associated with classic/haute cuisine
Restaurant	Term used to cover a wide variety of operations. Price, level and type of service, decor, styles, cuisines and degree of choice varies enormously across the range of types of operation. Service ranges from full table service to assisted service such as carvery-style operations
International restaurant	Indian, Oriental, Asian, Spanish, Greek, Italian, Creole and Cajun are just some of the many types of cuisine available, with establishments tending to reflect specific ethnic origins. Many of the standard dishes are now appearing within a range of other menu types

Type of operation	Description
Themed restaurant	Often international in orientation, for example, Icelandic hot rock with food prepared and cooked at the table, 'Beni-hana' oriental theme, again with food prepared and cooked at table. Also includes themes such as jungle, rainforest or music/opera, where waiting staff perform as well as serve
International destination restaurant	Often Michelin-starred fine dining restaurants, offering a distinctive personality, cuisine, ambiance, beverages and service. Usually table service at various levels but mostly personal and highly attentive. Generally considered as the home of gastronomy. Expensive but also value laden
Health food and vegetarian restaurants	Increasing specialisation of operations into vegetarianism and/or health foods (though vegetarian food is not necessarily healthy), to meet lifestyle needs as well as dietary requirements
Cafeteria	Primarily self-service with customer choosing selection from a counter or counters in varying designs and layouts. Originally developed for the industrial feeding market but now seen in a variety of sectors
Popular catering and fast-food outlets	Developed from table service teashops and cafés through to steakhouses, and now incorporating snack bars, kiosks, diners, takeaways and cafeterias, with modern-day burger, chicken and fish concepts, and with ethnic foods also being incorporated. Meeting the needs of all-day meal dining (grazing) and also the need for 'grab and go' service, especially for the leisure, industrial and travelling markets
Public houses	Licensed environment primarily for drinking alcoholic beverages. May be simply a serving bar with standing room for customers or may have more plush surroundings incorporating the offer of a variety of foods. These can range from simple plated dishes through to establishments offering full restaurant service (sometimes called gastropubs)
Wine bars	Often a mixture of bar and brasserie-style operation, commonly wine themed, serving a variety of foods

The list of operations in Table 1.4 identifies types of operations but not necessarily the type of customer demand being met. For example, cafeterias may be found in motorway service stations, in airline terminals, at railway stations, in retail catering and in industrial or welfare catering. Therefore, throughout the foodservice industry similar types of operation are found in different types of industry sector.

Variables in foodservice operations

The different operations described in Table 1.4 (see above) indicate very little in terms of methods of organisation adopted and their management. In a similar way to the identifying variables for sectors described in Table 1.2 (p.3), variables can also be identified for different foodservice operations. These variables have been identified from a variety of published sources as well as from experience and can be divided into three groups:

1 organisational
2 customer experience
3 performance measures.

These different groups of variables enable the systematic examination and comparison of types of food and beverage operations. Profiles of differing types of operations can be drawn, based upon the examples of variables identified in Table 1.5. The foodservice cycle also provides a useful checklist when gathering information about a foodservice operation. It helps to organise the information as it is collected and also helps to identify where there are gaps in the information being collected.

Performance measures are further dealt with in Section 12.8, p.423. Customer experience variables are discussed in Section 1.3. The remainder of this book presents further information on a variety of organisational variables.

Table 1.5 Variables in foodservice operations

Organisational variables	
• Nature of market being met	• Capacity
• Legislative controls	• Staff working hours
• Scale of operation	• Staff organisation
• Marketing/merchandising	• Staff capability
• Style of menu and drinks list	• Number of staff
• Range of choice	• Specialised service requirements
• Opening times/service period	• Provisioning and storage methods
• Production methods	• Billing methods
• Type and capability of equipment	• Checking (order taking) methods
• Service methods	• Clearing methods
• Dining arrangements	• Dishwashing methods
• Seating time	• Control method costs/revenue.
• Number of covers available	

Customer experience variables	
• Food and drink available	• Atmosphere (including decor, lighting, air-conditioning, acoustics, noise, size and shape of room, other customers, attitude of staff).
• Level of service and other services	
• Price range/value for money	
• Cleanliness and hygiene	

Performance measure variables	
• Seat turnover/customer throughput	• Sales/profit per sq m (or ft)/per seat
• Customer spend/average check	• Sales analysis
• Revenue per member of staff	• Departmental profit
• Productivity index	• Stock turnover
• Ratio of food and beverage sales to total sales	• Stock holding
	• Complaint levels
	• Level of repeat business.

1.3 The meal experience

There are many different kinds of food and beverage operation, designed to meet a wide range of demand. These different types of operation are designed for the needs people have at a particular time, rather than for the type of people they are. For example, a person may be a business customer during the week, but a member of a family at the weekend; they may want a quick lunch on one occasion, a snack while travelling on another and a meal with the family on another occasion. Additionally, the same person may wish to book a wedding or organise some other special occasion.

The main aim of food and beverage operations is to achieve customer satisfaction. In other words, to meet the customers' *needs*. The needs that customers might be seeking to satisfy include:

● **Physiological**: for example, the need to sate one's appetite or quench one's thirst, or the need for special foods such as diabetic or vegetarian.
● **Economic**: for example, the need for good value; rapid, fast service; a convenient location.
● **Social**: for example, going out with friends or business colleagues; attending a function in order to meet others.
● **Psychological**: for example, the need for enhancement of self-esteem; fulfilling life style needs; the need for variety; as a result of advertising and promotion.
● **Convenience**: for example, as a result of being unable to get home (shoppers, workers) or attending some other event (cinema, theatre); the desire for someone else to do the work; the physical impossibility of catering at home (weddings and other special functions).

Customers may want to satisfy some or all of these needs.

As the reasons for eating out vary, then so do the types of operation that may be appropriate at the time. Differing establishments offer different service, in both the extent of the menu and the price, as well as varying service levels. The choice offered may be restricted or wide.

It is important to recognise that the specific reasons behind a customer's choice will often determine the customer's satisfaction (or dissatisfaction), rather than the food and beverage service by itself. One example is the social need to go out with friends: if one person fails to turn up or behaves in a disagreeable way, then the customer may be dissatisfied with the meal.

If a customer is not able to satisfy his or her needs they will be dissatisfied. The customer may, for instance, be dissatisfied with unhelpful staff, cramped conditions or the lack of choice available. These aspects are the responsibility of the food and beverage operation. However, sometimes the reasons for the customer being dissatisfied might be beyond the operation's control, for example, location, the weather, other customers or transport problems.

Not all customers have a full choice. Those that do are often referred to as the non-captive market; those that don't are often referred to as being part of a captive market.

● **Non-captive markets**: the customer has a choice of eating out opportunities both in terms of the food and drink to be consumed and the type of operation they may wish to go to. While it is true that certain types of catering operations generally attract a certain type of customer, this is by no means true all of the time. The same customers may patronise a variety of different operations depending on the needs they have at a given time, for example, a romantic night out, a quick office lunch or a wedding function.

● **Semi-captive markets**: the availability of choice is also important in this market. Customers may choose, for example, a certain airline or ship or hotel based upon the identification of certain needs they wish to satisfy.
● **Captive markets**: this is where the customer does not have a choice of operation, but there is still a need for satisfaction. For instance, it is generally recognised that better fed workers are more productive and that better fed patients recover quicker. 'Better fed' here, though, does not just refer to the food and drink provided but the whole experience of the meal.

From the food and beverage operator's point of view it is important to recognise that the customer's needs may vary and that food and beverage operators should be aware of factors that might affect the customer's meal experience. Much research has been carried out in recent years identifying these factors. They range from location to the acceptance of credit cards, and from attitudes of staff to the behaviour of other customers. These factors are summarised in Table 1.6.

Table 1.6 Meal experience factors

Factor	Description
Food and beverages on offer	Includes the range of foods and beverages, choice, availability, flexibility for special orders and the quality of the food and beverages
Level of service	The level of service sought will depend on the needs people have at a particular time. For example, a romantic night out may call for a quiet table in a top-class restaurant, whereas a group of young friends might be seeking more informal service. This factor also takes into account the importance to the customer of other services such as booking and account facilities, acceptance of credit cards and the reliability of the operation's product
Level of cleanliness and hygiene	This factor relates to the premises, equipment and staff. Over the last few years this factor has increased in importance in customers' minds. The recent media focus on food production and the risks involved in buying food have heightened awareness of health and hygiene aspects
Perceived value for money and price	Customers have perceptions of the amount they are prepared to spend and relate this to differing types of establishments and operations. Also see notes on price, cost, worth and value in Section 12.5, p.399
Atmosphere of the establishment	This factor takes account of issues such as design, decor, lighting, heating, furnishings, acoustics and noise levels, other customers, the smartness of the staff and the attitude of the staff

1.4 Customer service

Good customer service is often characterised by:
● meeting/exceeding customer expectations
● knowing the benefits/features of the services and products on offer
● being able to listen actively
● being friendly and polite
● being able to adapt methods of communication to meet the individual needs of a range of customers, for example those with language or learning difficulties, health issues, different age groups and cultural differences

- avoiding the use of jargon
- forming professional relationships with customers
- achieving customer satisfaction.

The benefits to the operation include:
- increased sales
- fewer complaints
- attracting new customers through increased reputation
- increases in repeat business and customer loyalty.

For individuals working in food and beverage service the benefits of providing good customer service include:
- recognition – by management for promotion and monetary reward
- achieving job satisfaction, which leads to increased motivation and loyalty.

Defining the customer service of an operation

In order the meet the customer's expectations and to enhance their meal experience, a foodservice operation will determine the level of customer service that the customer should expect within that operation.

Customer service in foodservice operations is a combination of five characteristics:
1 **Service level**: the intensity of or limitations in the personal attention given to customers.
2 **Service availability**: for example, the opening times and variations in the menu and beverage list on offer.
3 **Level of standards**: for example, the quality of the food and beverage items provided, decor, standard of equipment used and level of staffing professionalism.
4 **Service reliability**: the extent to which the product is intended to be consistent and its consistency in practice.
5 **Service flexibility**: the extent to which alternatives are available, and to which there can be variations in the standard products that are offered.

A foodservice operation will determine the *customer service specification* of the operation by taking account of these five customer service factors.

Figure 1.3 A formal restaurant (image courtesy of the Gleneagles Hotel, Scotland)

Use of resources

Although a foodservice operation is designed to provide customer service, it must also be efficient in its use of resources. The three resources used in foodservice operations are:

1 **Materials**: food, beverages and short use equipment (such as paper napkins)
2 **Labour**: staffing costs
3 **Facilities**: premises and plant and equipment.

The management team must always take into account the effect that the level of business has on the ability of the operation, in order to maintain the customer service requirement, while at the same time ensuring productivity in all of the resources being used.

Customer service specification

Within foodservice operations the level of service in a specific operation may be defined as follows:

1 **Technical specification**: refers to the food and beverage items on offer, the portion size or measure, the cooking method, the degree of cooking, the method of presentation, the cover, accompaniments and the cleanliness of items, etc.
2 **Service specification**: refers to two aspects: first, the procedures for service and second, the way in which the procedures are carried out. Procedures include meeting and greeting, order taking, seeking customer comments, dealing with complaints, payment and the special needs of customers. The method in which the service is carried out includes paying attention to the level of staff attentiveness, their tone of voice and body language, etc.

Operations will usually have written statements of both technical and service specification (often called a customer service specification). These may also be detailed in staff manuals that outline expected standards of performance.

Level of service and standards of service

There can be confusion when referring to the levels of service and the standards of service.

- *Level of service* can range from being limited to complex, with high levels of personal attention.
- *Standards of service* are a measure of the ability of the operation to deliver the service level.

Thus an operation might offer low levels of service, such as a fast-food operation, but may do this at a very high standard. Equally, an operation may offer a high level of service, such as a full service restaurant, but may do so with low standards.

Further considerations

Good customer service also depends on the interpersonal skills of the staff (see Section 2.5, p.40) and the attention to issues that affect customer service issues (see Section 12.3, p.388).

Figure 1.4 Informal restaurant (image courtesy of the Gleneagles Hotel, Scotland)

1.5 Food production methods

For a foodservice operation, the production system must be organised to produce the right quantity of food at the correct standard, for the required number of people, on time, using the resources of staff, equipment and materials effectively and efficiently.

As costs of space, equipment, fuel, maintenance and labour continue to rise, more thought and time have to be given to the planning of production systems and kitchen design. The requirements of the production system have to be clearly matched to the type of food that is to be prepared, cooked and served to the required market at the correct price. Allocation of space and the purchase of different types of equipment must be justified and the organisation of the kitchen personnel must also be planned at the same time.

Many modern food production operations are based on the process approach, as opposed to the 'partie' (product approach) system. The process approach concentrates on the specific techniques and processes of food production. This system places importance on the identification of these common techniques and processes across the full range of required dishes. Groupings are not based on the types of dishes or foods (the basis of the 'partie' system) but on the clustering of similar production techniques and processes which apply a range of common skills.

Food production is an operating system and can be managed through a systems approach. A range of different cuisines are able to fit neatly into this approach because the key elements focus on the process and the way the food is prepared, processed (cooked), stored and served. Using this approach, food production systems may be identified using the input/process/output model of systems. Developing this approach further, nine standard production methods can be identified and these are shown in Table 1.7.

Table 1.7 Food production methods

Method	Description
Conventional	Term used to describe production utilising mainly fresh foods and traditional cooking methods
Convenience	Method of production utilising mainly convenience foods
Call order	Method where food is cooked to order either from customer (as in cafeterias) or from waiter. Production area is often open to customer area
Continuous flow	Method involving production line approach where different parts of the production process may be separated (e.g. fast food)
Centralised	Production not directly linked to service. Foods are 'held' and distributed to separate service areas
Cook-chill	Food production storage and regeneration method utilising principle of low temperature control to preserve quality of processed foods
Cook-freeze	Production, storage and regeneration method utilising principle of freezing to control and preserve quality of processed foods. Requires special processes to assist freezing
Sous-vide	Method of production, storage and regeneration utilising principle of sealed vacuum to control and preserve the quality of processed foods
Assembly kitchen	A system based on accepting and incorporating the latest technological development in manufacturing and conservation of food products

In reality, many foodservice operations combine a number of these food production methods to meet the needs of the operation.

1.6 Food and beverage service methods

The service of food and beverages may be carried out in many ways depending on the following factors:

- type of establishment
- time available for the meal
- type of menu presented
- site of the establishment
- type of customer to be served
- turnover of custom expected
- cost of the meal served.

A foodservice operation was traditionally only seen as comprising the three operating systems of:

- food production
- beverage provision
- food and beverage service

Within this view, food and beverage service was primarily designed and managed as a delivery process, with the customer being considered a passive recipient of the service. Only the requirements of the operation itself would determine how the service was designed, planned and controlled. This view has now changed, with the customer being seen as being central to the process and also as an active participant within it. Consequently, understanding the customer's involvement in the process, and identifying the experience they are likely to have and should expect, have become critical to the business success of foodservice operations.

It is also now recognised that food and beverage service itself actually consists of two separate sub-systems, operating at the same time. These are:

- the *service sequence* which is primarily concerned with the delivery of the food and beverages to the customer
- the *customer process* which is concerned with the experience the customer undertakes to be able to order, be served, consume and have the area cleared.

This modern view of a foodservice operation can be summarised in a simple model as shown in Figure 1.5.

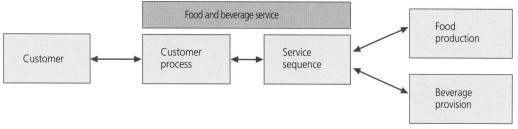

Figure 1.5 Simple model of a foodservice operation

The service sequence

The service sequence is essentially the bridge between the production system, beverage provision and the customer process (or customer experience). The service sequence may consist of eleven or more stages as summarised in Table 1.8.

Table 1.8 Food and beverage service sequence

1 Preparation for service	7 Clearing during service
2 Taking bookings	8 Billing
3 Greeting and seating/directing	9 Dealing with payments
4 Taking food and beverage orders	10 Dishwashing
5 Serving of food	11 Clearing following service
6 Serving beverages	

Each of these stages of the service sequence may be carried out by a variety of methods and these different methods are described throughout the book. The choice of method for the individual stage depends on the factors listed at the start of this section and the process that the customer is to experience.

The customer process

The customer receiving the food and beverage product is required to undertake or observe certain requirements: this is the customer process. Essentially, a customer enters a food service area, orders or selects his or her choice and then is served (the customer may pay either at this point or later). Food and beverages are then consumed, following which the area is cleared.

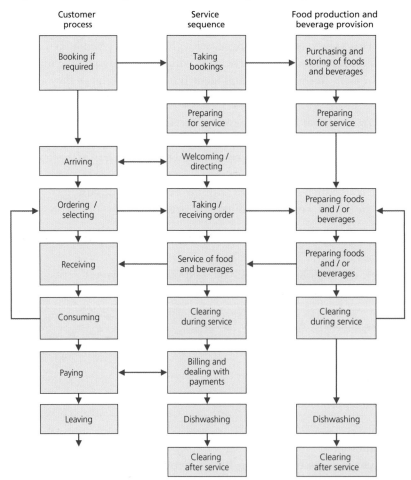

Figure 1.6 Outline of the relationship between different operating systems within a foodservice operation

Bringing these approaches together, it is possible to summarise the relationship between the various systems within a foodservice operation, as shown in Figure 1.6. This model identifies the key stages of a foodservice operation: for the customer, for the food and beverage service staff and for those involved in food production and beverage provision. It also reinforces the existence of the two sub-systems within food and beverage service that must be managed at the same time.

Categorising the different service methods

When considering food and beverage service from a *customer process* perspective, rather than considering it purely as a set of delivery methods, five basic types of customer process can be identified (see Table 1.9).

Table 1.9 Simple categorisation of the customer processes in food and beverage service

Service method	Service area	Ordering/ selection	Service	Dining/ consumption	Clearing
Table service	Customer enters and is seated	From menu	By staff to customer	At laid cover	By staff
Assisted service	Customer enters and is usually seated	From menu, buffet or passed trays	Combination of both staff and customer	Usually at laid cover	By staff
Self-service	Customer enters	Customer selects items onto a tray	Customer carries	Dining area or takeaway	Various
Single point service	Customer enters	Orders at single point	Customer carries	Dining area or takeaway	Various
Specialised or in situ service	Where the customer is located	From menu or predetermined	Brought to the customer	Served where the customer is located	By staff or customer clearing

All modern food and beverage service methods can then be grouped under the five customer processes that are summarised in Table 1.9 as follows.

A **Table service**: the customer is served at a laid table. This type of service, which includes plated service or silver service, is found in many types of restaurant, cafés and in banqueting.

B **Assisted service**: the customer is served part of the meal at a table and is required to obtain part through self-service from some form of display or buffet. This type of service is found in carvery type operations and is often used for meals such as breakfast in hotels. It may also be used for functions.

C **Self-service**: the customer is required to help him or herself from a buffet or counter. This type of service can be found in cafeterias and canteens.

D **Single point service**: the customer orders, pays and receives the food and beverages, for instance at a counter, at a bar in licensed premises, in a fast-food operation or at a vending machine.

E **Specialised service (or service in situ)**: the food and drink is taken to where the customer is. This includes tray service in hospitals or aircraft, trolley service, home delivery, lounge and room service.

A detailed listing of all the modern food and beverage service methods is given in Table 1.10 (below) and listed under each of the groups A to E.

In customer processes A–E, the customer comes to where the food and beverage service is offered and the service is provided in areas primarily designed for that purpose, such as a restaurant or takeaway. In customer process E, the service is provided in another location, where the area is not primarily designed for the purpose, for example, in a guest room, lounge or hospital ward. Additionally, the level of complexity of food and beverage service in terms of staff skills, tasks and duties reduces from Group A (the most complex) to Group D. Group E contains specialised forms of service and these are further considered in Chapter 9.

> **Note:** With the exception of fast-food operations, there is no particular link between a specific service method and a specific food production method. It is also possible that the production and service may be separated by distance or time, or both, as for example in off-premises catering.

Table 1.10 Food and beverage service methods

Group A: Table service		
Service to customers at a laid cover		
Waiter	Silver/English	Presentation and service of food by waiting staff, using a spoon and fork, onto a customer's plate, from food flats or dishes
	Family	Main courses plated (but may be silver served) with vegetables placed in multi-portion dishes on tables for customers to help themselves; sauces offered separately
	Plate/American	Service of pre-plated foods to customers. Now also widely used for banqueting
	Butler/French	Presentation of food individually to customers by food service staff for customers to serve themselves
	Guéridon	Food served onto customer's plate at a side table or trolley; may also include carving, jointing and fish filleting, the preparation of foods such as salads and dressings and flambage
Bar counter		Service to customers seated at a bar counter (often U-shaped) on stools; also found in sushi operations with conveyor belt delivering the food
Group B: Assisted service		
Combination of table service and self-service		
Carvery		Some parts of the meal are served to seated customers; other parts are collected by the customers. Also used for breakfast service and for banqueting

Group C: Self-service

Self-service of customers

Cafeteria	Counter	Customers queue in line formation past a service counter and choose their menu requirements in stages before loading them onto a tray (may include a 'carousel' – a revolving stacked counter, saving space)
	Free-flow	Selection as in counter (above) but in food service area where customers move at will to random service points; customers usually exit area via a till point
	Echelon	Series of counters at angles to the customer flow within a free-flow area, thus saving space
	Supermarket	Island service points within a free-flow area

Note: Some 'call order' production may be included in cafeterias

Group D: Single point service

Service of customers at single point – consumed on premises or taken away

Takeaway	Takeaway	Customer orders and is served from single point, at a counter, hatch or snack stand; customer consumes off the premises; some takeaway establishments provide dining areas
	Drive-thru	Form of takeaway where customer drives vehicle past order, payment and collection points
	Fast food	Term originally used to describe service at a counter or hatch where customers receive a complete meal or dish in exchange for cash or ticket; commonly used nowadays to describe type of establishment offering limited range menu, fast service with dining area, and takeaway facility
Vending		Provision of food service and beverage service by means of automatic retailing
Kiosks		Outstation used to provide service for peak demand or in specific location; may be open for customers to order and be served, or used for dispensing to staff only
Food court		Series of autonomous counters where customers may either order and eat (as in a Bar counter, see above) or buy from a number of counters and eat in separate eating area, or takeaway
Bar		Term used to describe order, service and payment point and consumption area in licensed premises

Group E: Specialised (or in situ)	
Service to customers in areas not primarily designed for service	
Tray	Method of service of whole or part of meal on tray to customer in situ, e.g. at hospital beds; at aircraft seats; at train seats; also used in ODC
Trolley	Service of food and beverages from a trolley, away from dining areas, e.g. for office workers at their desks; for customers at aircraft seats; at train seats
Home delivery	Food delivered to customer's home or place of work, e.g. 'meals on wheels', pizza home delivery, or sandwiches to offices
Lounge	Service of variety of foods and beverages in lounge area, e.g. hotel lounge
Room	Service of variety of foods and beverages in guest bedrooms or in meeting rooms
Drive-in	Customers park their motor vehicle and are served at their vehicles

Note: Banquet/function is a term used to describe catering for specific numbers of people at specific times in a variety of dining layouts. Service methods also vary. In these cases, banquet/function catering refers to the organisation of service rather than a specific service method – see Chapter 11 Events.

1.7 Food and beverage personnel

Typical organisation charts for small and larger hotels are given in Figures 1.7 and 1.8. In both these charts various food and beverage job roles are identified. For food and beverage operations not set within hotels, the organisation often resembles the food and beverage section of the hotel organisation charts. However, different terminology can be used for the various job roles in differing types of establishment. The various job roles in food and beverage service are identified below. In some smaller operations a number of these job roles may be combined.

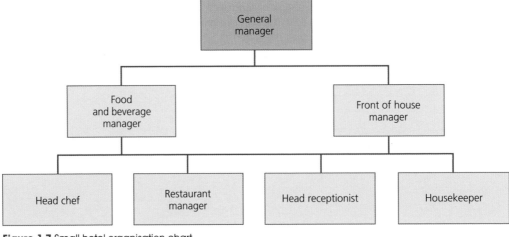

Figure 1.7 Small hotel organisation chart

Food and beverage manager

Depending on the size of the establishment, the food and beverage manager is either responsible for the implementation of agreed policies or for contributing to the setting up of the food and beverage policies. The larger the organisation the less likely the manager is to be involved in policy setting. In general, food and beverage managers are responsible for:

● ensuring that the required profit margins are achieved for each food and beverage service area, in each financial period

● updating and compiling new wine lists according to availability of stock, current trends and customer needs

● compiling, in liaison with the kitchen, menus for the various food service areas and for special occasions

● purchasing of all materials, both food and drink

● ensuring that quality in relation to the price paid is maintained

● determining portion size in relation to selling price

● ensuring staff training, sales promotions and the maintenance of the highest professional standards

● employing and dismissing staff

● holding regular meetings with section heads to ensure all areas are working effectively, efficiently and are well co-ordinated.

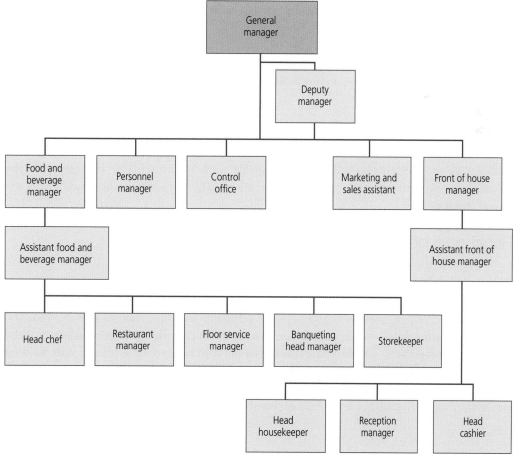

Figure 1.8 Large hotel organisation chart

Food production job roles

Head chef/maître chef de cuisine

The head chef has overall responsibility for the organisation and administration of the food production operation. He or she is responsible for the management of the food production team, often called a kitchen brigade. They also undertake menu planning and development, overseeing the sourcing of produce, settings standards for the operation and ensuring they are maintained.

Second chef/sous-chef de cuisine

The sous-chef is the second in command to the chef de cuisine and will act as head chef when the head is off-duty. He or she may also cover for or assist a chef de partie when required. They often have responsibilities for staff training and staff rotas as well as overseeing stock control. In smaller operations there might not be a sous-chef, while larger operations may have more than one.

Chef de partie/section chef

A chef de partie may also be known as a section chef and is usually in charge of a specific area of food production such as fish, vegetables, roasts, sweets or the larder. In larger kitchens, each chef de partie might have several cooks and/or assistants.

Commis chef

A commis is a junior chef who works under a chef de partie in order to gain experience in the section's work. It is common for commis chefs to work in a number of sections as part of their training.

Kitchen assistants

There are often two types of kitchen assistants. Kitchen hands assist with basic food preparation tasks under the section chef's direction. Stewards work in the scullery and carry out the washing-up and general cleaning duties. In smaller kitchen operations these two duties are often combined.

Food and beverage service job roles

Restaurant manager/supervisor

The restaurant manager or supervisor has overall responsibility for the organisation and administration of particular food and beverage service areas. These may include the lounges, room service (in hotels), restaurants and possibly some of the private function suites. It is the restaurant manager who sets the standards for service and is responsible for any staff training that may be required, either on or off the job. They may make out duty rotas, holiday lists and hours on and off duty and contribute to operational duties (depending on the size of the establishment) so that all the service areas run efficiently and smoothly.

Reception head waiter/receptionist

The reception head waiter or receptionist is responsible for accepting bookings and for keeping the booking diary up to date. They will take reservations and work with the head waiter to allocate these reservations to particular stations. The reception head waiter or receptionist greets customers on arrival and takes them to the table and seats them.

Head waiter/maître d'hôtel/supervisor

The head waiter has overall charge of the staff team and is responsible for seeing that all the pre-preparation duties necessary for service are efficiently carried out. The head waiter will aid the reception head waiter during the service and will possibly take some orders if the station waiter is busy. The head waiter also helps with the compilation of duty rotas and holiday lists and may relieve the restaurant manager or reception head waiter on their days off.

Station head waiter/section supervisor/service captain

For larger establishments the restaurant area is broken down into sections. The station head waiter has overall responsibility for a team of staff serving a number of stations within a section of the restaurant area. Each of the sets of tables (which may be anything from four to eight in number) within the section of the restaurant area is called a *station*. The station head waiter will also assist in taking food and beverage orders and assist with service if required.

Station waiter/chef de rang

The chef de rang or station waiter provides service to one set of tables (between about four and eight) known as a station within the restaurant area. The station waiter will take the food and beverage orders and carry out service at the table with the help of the demi-chef de rang.

Assistant station waiter/demi-chef de rang

The assistant station waiter or demi-chef de rang is the person next in seniority to the station waiter and assists as directed by the station waiter.

Waiter/server/commis de rang

The waiter or commis de rang acts by instruction from the chef de rang. This person mainly fetches and carries, may do some of the service of either vegetables or sauces, offers rolls, places plates upon the table and helps to clear the tables after each course. During the pre-preparation period much of the cleaning and preparatory tasks will be carried out by the commis de rang.

Trainee commis/debarrasseur/apprentice

The trainee commis or debarrasseur is the apprentice or learner who wishes to take up food service as a career. The debarrasseur will carry out many of the tasks during the pre-preparation periods. During the service this person will keep the sideboard well stocked with equipment and may help to fetch and carry items as required for the bar or kitchen. As their skills develop, they will also begin to assist in the service at the table.

Carver/trancheur

The carver or trancheur is responsible for the carving trolley and the carving of joints at the table as required. The carver will plate up each portion and serve with accompaniments as appropriate.

Floor or room service staff/chef d'étage/floor or room waiter

The floor or room service staff are often responsible for a complete floor in an establishment or, depending on the size of the establishment, a number of rooms or suites. Room service of all meals and beverages throughout the day is normally only offered by a first class establishment. In smaller establishments room service may be limited to early morning teas and breakfasts with the provision of in-room mini bars and tea and coffee facilities.

Lounge staff/chef de sale

Lounge service staff may be employed only for lounge service within larger establishments. In a smaller establishment it is usual for members of the food service staff to take over these duties on a rota basis. The lounge staff are responsible for the service of morning coffee, afternoon teas, apéritifs and liqueurs before and after both lunch and dinner and any coffee required after meals. They are responsible for setting up the lounge in the morning and maintaining its cleanliness and presentation throughout the day.

Wine butler/wine waiter/sommelier

The sommelier is responsible for the service of all alcoholic drinks and non-alcoholic bar drinks during the service of meals. The sommelier must also be a good sales person. This employee should have a thorough knowledge of all drink to be served, of the best wines and drinks to go with certain foods, and of the liquor licensing laws in respect of the particular establishment and area.

Bar staff/bar tender/mixologist

The people working within bar areas must be responsible and competent in preparing and serving a variety of wine, drinks and cocktails. They should have a thorough knowledge of all alcoholic and non-alcoholic drinks offered within the establishment, the ingredients necessary for making cocktails and knowledge of the liquor licensing laws to ensure legal compliance. A mixologist is an employee who mixes and serves alcoholic beverages at a bar and is also often used as a name for people who create new mixed drinks. The term can also mean a cocktail maker or simply bartender. Mixology is the art of making mixed drinks.

Barista

The word *barista* is of Italian origin. In Italian, a barista is a male or female bartender who typically works behind a counter, serving both hot and cold beverages as well as alcoholic beverages. Barista does not mean specifically a coffee maker although it is now often used as such. The plural in English is baristas.

Buffet assistant/buffet chef/chef de buffet

The chef de buffet is in charge of the buffet in the room, its presentation, the carving and portioning of food and its service. This staff member will normally be a member of the kitchen team.

Cashier

The cashier is responsible for billing and taking payments or making ledger account entries for a food and beverage operation. This may include making up bills from food and drink checks or, in a cafeteria for example, charging customers for their selection of items on a tray.

Counter assistants

Counter assistants are found in cafeterias where they will stock the counter and sometimes serve or portion food for customers. Duties may also include some cooking of call order items.

Table clearers

Again, table clearers can be found in seating areas where there is no waiter service. These people are responsible for clearing tables using trolleys specially designed for stacking crockery, glassware, cutlery, etc.

Function catering/banqueting staff/events staff

In establishments with function catering facilities there will normally be a number of permanent staff. These will include the banqueting and conferencing manager, one or two assistant managers, one or two head waiters, a dispense person and a secretary to the banqueting and conferencing manager. All other banqueting, conferencing and events staff are normally engaged as required on a casual basis. In small establishments where there are fewer events, the manager, assistant manager and head waiter will undertake the necessary administrative and organisational work.

Staffing requirements

The staffing requirements in various establishments differ for a number of reasons. Table 1.11 gives examples of the food and beverage staffing that might be found in different types of operation.

Table 1.11 Examples of staffing requirements for different types of foodservice operation

Medium class hotel	Cafeteria
Hotel manager	Catering manager
Assistant manager	Supervisors
Head waiter	Assistant supervisors
Waiters	Counter service hands
Wine waiter	Clearers
Cashier	Cashier
Department store	**Industrial foodservice/welfare catering**
Catering manager	Catering manager
Assistant catering manager	Assistant catering manager
Supervisor	Supervisors
Assistant supervisors	Assistant supervisors
Cashier	Waiter
Dispense bar staff	Steward/butler
Wine waiting staff	Counter service staff
Waiting staff	Clearers
	Cashiers
Popular price restaurant	
Restaurant manager/supervisor	
Waiting staff	
Dispense bar assistant	

Chapter 2

Staff attributes, skills and knowledge

2.1 Success in food and beverage service

Today more people than ever are eating outside the home and to meet this demand there is increasing diversity in the nature and type of food and beverages on offer. Because of the expansion of the industry and increasing requirements for improved professionalism in food and beverage service staff, there is even greater need for people to make their careers in this noble profession. In addition, there is a need for improved confidence and performance of staff, through higher standards of knowledge and skills.

Food and beverage service is the essential link between customers and the menu, beverages and other services on offer in an establishment. The server is the main point of contact between the customers and the establishment and plays an important role in a profession with increasing national and international status. The skills and knowledge of food and beverage service, and therefore careers, are transferable between establishments, sectors and throughout the world.

To be successful in food and beverage service requires members of staff to have:
- sound product knowledge
- well-developed interpersonal skills
- a range of technical skills, and
- the ability to work as part of a team.

Working in food and beverage service offers a wealth of opportunity for professional development and advancement – for those committed to the hospitality industry and to working in food and beverage service, a fulfilling, exciting and enjoyable career awaits.

2.2 Attributes of food and beverage service personnel

Appearance and behaviour contribute to the first impression others have of you and are seen as a reflection of the hygiene standards of the establishment and the quality of service to come.

Professional and hygienic appearance
All staff should be aware of the factors listed below and it is their individual responsibility to ensure that they are put into practice:
- Staff should be clean and should use deodorants (but not strong smelling ones).
- Aftershave and perfumes should not be too strong (as this may have a detrimental effect on the customer's palate).
- Sufficient sleep, an adequate and healthy intake of food and regular exercise is essential for good health and the ability to cope with the pressures and stress of work.
- Particular attention should be paid to the hands. They must always be clean, free of nicotine stains and with clean, well-trimmed nails.
- Teeth should be brushed before coming on duty and the breath should be fresh smelling.
- Men should normally be clean-shaven or with any moustache or beard neatly trimmed.
- Women should only wear light make-up. If nail varnish is worn then it should be clear.
- Earrings should not be worn with the possible exception of studs/sleepers.
- Uniform must be clean, starched as appropriate and pressed. All buttons must be present.

- Hair must be clean and well groomed. Long hair must be tied up or back to avoid hairs falling into foods and drinks and to avoid repeated handling of the hair.
- Shoes must be comfortable and clean, and of a plain, neat design. Fashion is not as important here as safety and foot comfort.
- Cuts and burns should be covered with waterproof dressings.
- Any colds or other possible infections should be reported immediately.
- Hands should be washed immediately after using the toilet, smoking or dealing with refuse. Hot water and soap must be used.
- Staff should try to avoid any mannerisms they may have, such as running their fingers through their hair, chewing gum or scratching their face.
- Excessive jewellery should not be worn. The establishment policy should be followed.

Knowledge of food and beverages and technical ability

Staff must have sufficient knowledge of all the items on the menu and wine and drink lists in order to advise and offer suggestions to customers. In addition, they must know how to serve correctly each dish on the menu, what its accompaniments are, the correct cover and the make-up of the dish and its garnish. For beverage service, staff should know how to serve various types of wine and drink, in the correct containers (e.g. glasses, cups) and at the right temperature.

Punctuality

Punctuality is all-important. If staff are continually late on duty it shows a lack of interest in their work and a lack of respect for the management and customers.

Local knowledge

In the interest of customers the staff should have some knowledge of the area in which they work so they may be able to advise customers on the various forms of entertainment offered, the best means of transport to places of interest and so on.

Personality

Staff must be tactful, courteous, good humoured and of an even temper. They must converse with the customer in a pleasing and well-spoken manner, and the ability to smile at the right time pays dividends.

Attitude to customers

The correct approach to the customer is of the utmost importance. Staff must provide service but should not be servile and should be able to anticipate the customer's needs and wishes. A careful watch should be kept on customers during the service (but without staring) to check the progress of the meal. Be attentive but not intrusive at all times during the service sequence.

Cultural awareness

The cultural diversity of customers is increasing and this is reflected in factors such as language, dress and traditions as well as dietary (see Section 4.4, p.97 for more information on specific dietary needs). Members of service staff need to be open-minded, non-judgemental and flexible and able to appreciate and communicate respect for other people's values and beliefs.

Memory

A good memory is an asset to food and beverage service staff. It may help them in various ways in their work if they know the likes and dislikes of customers, where they like to sit in the food service area, what their favourite drinks are, and so on.

Honesty

Trust and respect in the triangle of staff, customer and management relationships lead to an atmosphere at work that encourages efficiency and a good team spirit among the food and beverage service operators.

Loyalty

Staff obligations and loyalty are first to the establishment in which they are employed and its management. Staff therefore need to commit mentally to the ethos of the establishment and be fully aware of their department's aims and objectives.

Conduct

Staff conduct should be impeccable at all times, especially in front of customers. The rules and regulations of an establishment must be followed and respect shown to all senior members of staff. This also applies when staff are off duty but may still be in uniform as they represent the establishment's values and attitudes.

Sales ability

All members of staff reflect the image of the establishment. They are sales people and must therefore have a complete knowledge of all forms of food and drink and their correct service, and so be able to contribute to personal selling and merchandising. (See Section 12.2, p.423 for more information on personal selling and merchandising.)

Sense of urgency

In order for the establishment to generate the maximum amount of business over the service period, with as high a net profit as possible, staff must develop a sense of urgency in their work. This should be promoted by management by displaying a 'do as I do' attitude, leading by example.

Complaints

Staff should have a pleasant manner and demonstrate courtesy and tact, an even temper and good humour. They should never show their displeasure even during a difficult situation. Staff should never argue with a customer and if they are unable to resolve a situation, it should be referred immediately to a senior member of the team who will be able to reassure the customer and put right any fault. Remember, loss of time in dealing with complaints only makes the situation worse.

Contribution to the team

Above all, staff should be able to work as part of a team within and between departments. Being a team member means communicating, co-operating and being reliable so that as a team each member contributes to enable a successful service to be delivered every session.

2.3 Key service conventions

Within food and beverage service there are traditional ways of doing things that have become established over time. These are known as the 'service conventions' and all have some logic behind them. Mostly this is to do with being effective and efficient in carrying out the service. The use of service conventions also ensures standardisation in the service sequence and the customer process (see Section 1.6, p.15, for definitions), both for staff and for customers. Examples of general service conventions and the rationale for them are given in Table 2.1.

Table 2.1 General conventions for food and beverage service

Convention	Rationale
Always work as part of a team	All members of the team should know and be able to do their own job well, to ensure a smooth, well-organised and disciplined operation
Work hygienically and safely	For the protection of other staff and customers from harm and to avoid accidents
Pass other members of staff by moving to the right	Having an establishment rule about each member of staff always moving to the right (or left) avoids confusion and accidents
Avoid contact between fingers and mouth or hair	If contact between fingers and mouth or hair, etc., is unavoidable, then hands must be washed before continuing with service. Always wash hands after using the toilet
Cover cuts and sores	Covering cuts and sores with waterproof plasters or dressings is essential health and safety practice
Use checklists for preparation tasks	Using checklists ensures that all members of staff complete all preparatory tasks in the same way. For example, housekeeping duties, furniture layouts, linen, paper, glassware, tableware, crockery, condiments, accompaniments, table decorations, menus, place cards, table plans, service sideboards/stations and service equipment
Prepare service areas in sequence	Ensure service areas are laid out and housekeeping duties have been completed before the preparation for service begins. This can save time and unnecessary duplication of effort afterwards
Consider using white gloves	In some establishments members of staff wear white cotton gloves when carrying out various preparation tasks. The gloves help to prevent the soiling of clean service items and avoid putting finger marks on cleaned and polished service equipment. White gloves are also sometimes used during service, instead of using service cloths, when serving plated foods that are presented on hot plates
Use a model lay-up	Lay one initial full place setting (cover) to use as a model for all staff to measure against. A place setting is usually about 60 cm wide
Hold glasses or cups at the base or by the handle	This is hygienic practice. Service staff should not hold glasses or cups, etc., by the rim
Hold cutlery in the middle at the sides between the thumb and forefinger	This is safer, makes for more accurate placing of items on the table and helps to prevent finger marking on the clean cutlery items

Convention	Rationale
Lay table place settings (covers) from the inside out	This makes table laying easier. Place a centre to the cover (a table mat or side plate for instance) then lay tableware in order from the inside of the cover outwards. When laying a number of covers it is more efficient to lay each piece of tableware for all covers in sequence, i.e. all side plates, then all side knives, etc.
Use of standard lay-ups	Indicates the type of meals being taken, the sequence of the courses and also what stage customers are at within a meal
Fully or partly lay the table before a meal begins	Most often tables are fully laid before a meal but this may vary, for instance, if the table is likely to become excessively cluttered or where there is not sufficient equipment to fully pre-lay all the tables
Place items on the table consistently	Make sure that any crested or patterned crockery or glassware is always placed the same way round on the table and that it is evenly spaced
Place items low to high	Lower items should be placed near to the customer and taller items behind or to the side of these. This makes items easily accessible by the customer and helps to avoid accidents
Place items according to the customer's position at the table	Items placed on a table should be within reach of the customer. Handles, etc. should be set for the customer's convenience
Use checklists for all aspects of service	These help to ensure that all information is complete and that all managers and staff carry out procedures in the same way
Be aware of customers who may have additional needs	Look out for and be prepared to deal with people with impaired vision, hearing, speech, mobility or language. Also be able to deal with children
Use order notation techniques	Use of such techniques helps any server to identify which member of a party is having a particular item of food or beverage
Avoid leaning over customers	This shows courtesy and respect for physical space. Remember that no matter how clean service staff members are, food and beverage smells do tend to cling to service uniforms
Take food, wine and drink orders through hosts	This is common courtesy – agreement needs to be obtained for any items that are to be served. For larger parties, where there may be a choice, orders may be taken individually but it is useful to confirm what has actually been ordered with the host as this may save any disagreements later
Serve cold food before hot food	When the hot food is served the service is complete and customers can enjoy the meal without waiting for additional items to be served. For the same reason, accompaniments should be automatically offered and served at the same time as the food item
Serve wine before food	Similar to above. Customers will wish to enjoy the wine with their meal. They will not want to wait for the wine service, as their hot food will go cold
Use underplates (liners)	These are used (cold) for four main purposes: to improve presentation on the table; to make carrying of soup plates, bowls and other bowl-shaped dishes easier; to isolate the hand from hot dishes; to allow cutlery to be carried along with the item

Convention	Rationale
Use service salvers or service plates (with napkins or mats on them to prevent items slipping)	Service salvers or service plates are used for five main purposes: to improve presentation of items to be served; to make carrying of bowl-shaped serving dishes easier and more secure (also avoids the thumb of the server being inside a service dish); to allow for more than one serving dish to be carried at a time; to isolate the hand from hot dishes; to allow service gear to be carried along with the item(s)
Hold flats, food dishes and round trays on the palm of the hand	This is safer and ensures that the food items are best presented for the customer. It also makes for easier carrying and avoids the server's thumb or service cloths being seen on the edge of flats, dishes and round trays. If the flats or dishes are hot then the service cloth can be underneath, folded and laid flat onto the palm to protect the hand
Use doilies/dish papers on underplates (liners)	Doilies, dish papers (or linen or paper napkins) on underplates are used to improve presentation, to reduce noise and to prevent the dish from slipping on the underplate. Use doilies for sweet food items and dish papers for savoury food items
Start service from the right-hand side of the host, with the host last	Honoured guests are usually seated on the right of a host. The convention is to serve a table by moving anti-clockwise to each customer, as this ensures that members of the serving staff are walking forwards to serve the next person
Serve women first	Often done if it does not slow the service. Particular care needs to be taken so as not to confuse things when the host is a woman. A host of either gender is still the host and should always be served last. Also be aware that some cultures may require that men are served separately from women, or served first
Silver serve food from the left-hand side of a customer	Ensures that the service dish is nearer the plate for ease of service and to prevent food being spilt onto the person. Customers can more easily see the food being served and make choices if necessary, and members of the service staff are also able to see and control what they are doing
Use separate service gear for different food items	This should be standard. It avoids different food items or sauces being transferred from one dish or plate to another and avoids messy presentation of foods on customers' plates
Serve foods onto plates consistently	For service of the whole main course onto a joint plate, place the main item at the 6 o'clock position with potatoes served next at the 10 past 2 position and vegetables last at the 10 to 2 position (this also follows the UK Royal National Institute for the Blind (RNIB) recommendations). For main courses with potatoes and vegetables and/or salads served on a separate plate or crescent, the main item is placed in the centre of the main plate with the separate plate or crescent of potatoes and vegetables and/or side salad to the left of this
Serve plated foods from the right-hand side of a customer	Plates can be placed in front of the customer with the right hand and the stack of other plated food is then behind the customer's chair in the left hand. If there is an accident, the plates held in the left hand will go onto the floor rather than over the customer. Plated foods should be placed so that the food items are consistently in the same position for all customers
Serve all beverages from the right-hand side of a customer	Glasses are placed on the right-hand side of a cover and the service of beverages follows from this. For individual drinks and other beverages, the tray is held behind a customer's seat in the server's left hand. Other beverages such as coffee and tea are also served from the right. All beverages should also be cleared from the right

Convention	Rationale
Use trays	Use trays to bring foods and beverage items to the service areas and to clear during and following service. Trays can be brought to, or removed from, sideboards or service tables and also to serve plated foods from (or to clear plates onto) with service staff working as a pair
Separate the serving at table from food/drink collection and sideboard/workstation clearing	Ensures that there is always someone in the room to attend to customers and to monitor the overall service, while others are bringing in food and beverage orders or clearing items away from the service station. This approach allows for the training of new staff and ensures that customer contact is primarily through experienced staff
Clear from the right-hand side of a customer	Plates can be removed from in front of the customer with the right hand and the stack of plates is then behind the customer's chair, in the server's left hand. If there is an accident, the plates held in the left hand will go onto the floor rather than over the customer. The exception to this is for side plates, which are on the left-hand side of the cover. These are more easily cleared from the left, thus avoiding stretching in front of the customer
Use checklists for tasks required for clearing after service	In the same way as using checklists for preparatory tasks (see above), using checklists for clearing after service ensures that any member of staff completes all clearing tasks in the same way

2.4 Essential technical skills

There are six essential technical food and beverage service skills. These are identified in Table 2.2 below, together with examples of their application.

Table 2.2 Technical skills and their application

Technical skill	Examples of application
Holding and using a service spoon and fork, and other service equipment	For the service of food at a customer's table, especially for silver service, and for serving at a buffet
Carrying plates	When placing and clearing plates from a customer's table
Using a service salver (round tray)	For carrying glasses, carrying tea and coffee services, as an under liner for entrée dishes and for potato and vegetable dishes
Using a service plate	For carrying items to and from a table, including clean cutlery, clearing side plates and knives, crumbing down and clearing accompaniments
Carrying glasses	Carrying clean glasses by hand or on a salver and for clearing dirty glasses from a service area
Carrying and using large trays	For bringing equipment or food and beverage items to the service area and for clearing used equipment from the service area

These essential technical skills are used specifically for table service and assisted service. However, these skills are also used when providing other forms of service, for example, when carrying trays for room service or using a service salver for bar service.

Holding and using a service spoon and fork

Expertise in this technique can only be achieved with practice. The purpose of the service spoon and fork is to enable the waiter to serve food from a flat or dish onto the customer's plate quickly and to present the food on the plate well.

● The service fork should be positioned above, or on top of, the service spoon.
● The key to developing this skill is the locking of the ends of the service spoon and fork with the small finger and the third finger, as illustrated in Figure 2.1(a).
● The spoon and fork are manoeuvred with the thumb and the index and second fingers (see Figure 2.1(b)). Using this method food items may be picked up from the serving dish in between the service spoon and service fork.
● Alternatively, the service fork may be turned to mould with the shape of the items being served, for example when serving bread rolls (see Figure 2.1(c)).

Figure 2.1 Hand positions for holding a service spoon and fork **(a)** Stage 1; **(b)** Stage 2; **(c)** Stage 3

There are occasions where two service forks may be used, for example when serving fillets of fish, the two forks are held side by side, as this makes the service of this food item easier.

When using a serving spoon and fork for serving at a sweet or cheese trolley or at a buffet or guéridon, the spoon and fork are held one in each hand.

Other service equipment that may be used includes serving tongs, fish slices and gâteaux slices, serving spoons, scoops, small sauce ladles and larger soup ladles.

Figure 2.2 Examples of service equipment

Carrying plates

Clean plates can be carried in a stack using both hands or using a tray. When carrying clean plates that are to be placed on the customer's table, a single hand is used to hold the plates (usually the left hand) and the right hand is used to place the plates at each cover on the customer's table. If the plates are hot then the plates are held with a service cloth placed on the palm of the left hand. A separate service cloth is then used in the right hand to hold the hot plates when placing them in front of the customer.

When carrying plates of pre-plated foods and when clearing plates from a customer's table, a single hand is used to hold the plates (usually the left hand) and the right hand is used to place and remove plates from the customer's table. Special hand positions are used as follows:

● Figure 2.3(a) illustrates the initial hand position for the first plate. Care must be taken to ensure that the first plate is held firmly as succeeding plates are built up from here. The second plate will rest firmly on the forearm and the third and fourth fingers.
● Figure 2.3(b) shows the second plate positioned on the left (holding) hand.

Figure 2.3 Hand positions when clearing plates and carrying pre-plated food **(a)** First plate cleared; **(b)** Second plate cleared

To be able to clear properly ensures efficiency, avoids the possibility of accidents and creates the minimum of inconvenience to customers. Well-developed clearing techniques enable more to be cleared, in less time and in fewer journeys between sideboard or workstation and the customer's table. In addition, clearing properly allows for the stacking of dirties neatly and safely at the sideboard or workstation. (See also Section 6.8 page 248.)

Using a service salver (round tray)

A service salver is a round, often silver or stainless steel tray (but now also can be wood or plastic). A napkin (folded flat) is placed on the tray to help prevent items slipping on the tray as they are being carried. There are also special non-slip mats that can be used instead of napkins. Some trays are made with non-slip surfaces. The service salver may be used to:

● carry clean glasses to, and remove dirty glasses from, a customer's table
● carry clean cutlery to and from a customer's table
● place clean cutlery on the table
● place clean cups and saucers on the table
● provide an underflat when silver serving vegetables.

Carrying clean cutlery

When placing on or removing clean cutlery from a table, the items can be carried on a service salver. This is more efficient, hygienic and safer and generally more professional than carrying these items in bunches in the hands. The blades of the knives should be placed under the arch in the middle of the forks and if carrying sweet spoons and forks, the prongs of the fork should go under the arch in the middle of the spoon. The reason for this is to help hold the items steady on the service salver. Bearing in mind that the handles of the cutlery are generally the heaviest parts, this method prevents them sliding about too much.

Clean cutlery is placed onto the service salver after the final polish and carried to the table on the tray. The cutlery is then placed from the service tray to the table by holding the piece of cutlery between the thumb and forefinger at the side, in order to reduce the possibility of finger marks.

Figure 2.4 Carrying cutlery on a service salver

Carrying cups and saucers

Tea and coffee cups are carried using a service salver, by stacking the saucers, cups and teaspoons separately. Then before placing the cup, saucer and teaspoon on the table, the cup is put onto a saucer, together with a teaspoon, and then the whole service is placed in front of the customer. This is a speedier and safer method (especially when larger numbers are involved) than carrying individual cups, saucers and teaspoons to the table one by one.

As an underflat

When silver serving food dishes, potatoes or vegetables at the table, an underflat should be used to hold either one large vegetable dish or a number of smaller ones, depending on the customer's order. The purpose of using a service salver as an underflat is to:

● add to the presentation of the food being served
● give the waiter more control when using the service spoon and fork to serve from the food dishes onto the customer's plate
● provide greater protection in case of spillage, therefore not detracting from the presentation of the food on the plate or the overall table presentation
● give the waiter added protection against heat and possible spillage on the uniform.

(For more information on silver service see Section 6.5, p.228.)

Using a service plate

A service plate is a joint plate with a napkin upon it. It has a number of uses during the meal service:

- for placing clean cutlery on and removing it from the table
- for clearing side plates and side knives
- for crumbing down after the main course, or any other stage of the meal if necessary
- for clearing accompaniments from the table as and when necessary.

Carrying clean cutlery

When placing on or removing clean cutlery from a table, the items can be carried on a service plate. The reasons for this are the same as given under using a service salver above.

Clearing side plates and knives

When clearing dirty side plates and side knives from the customer's table, the use of a service plate means that the waiter has a larger area on which to stack the side knives and any debris. Using the hand positions shown in Figure 2.2(a) and (b) (p.27), the side plates may be stacked above the service plate and all the debris in a separate pile, together with the side knives laid flat upon the service plate (see Section 6.8, Figure 6.53(a) and (b)). This is a much safer and speedier method, especially when larger numbers are involved.

Clearing accompaniments

The service plate is also used to clear such items as the cruet, cayenne pepper, pepper mill or other accompaniments, which may not already be set on an underplate.

Crumbing down

The service plate is used in the crumbing down process. The purpose here is to freshen up the appearance of the tablecloth prior to laying the sweet covers and serving the sweet. (For further information see Section 6.8, p.248.)

Carrying glasses

There are two basic methods of carrying glasses in the food and beverage service areas: by hand or on a service salver.

Carrying by hand

Wine goblets should be positioned between alternate fingers as far as is possible. The wine goblets should only be carried in one hand, allowing the other hand to remain free to steady oneself in case of emergencies.

Figure 2.3 provides a close up of the wine goblets held in one hand and shows how the base of each glass overlaps the next, allowing the maximum number of glasses to be held in one hand. This method allows wine goblets that are already polished to be handled. They can be carried about the room and set in their correct position on the table without the bowl of the glass being touched. Clean glassware is always handled by the stem and for non-stemmed glassware by the base.

Figure 2.5 Carrying clean glasses by hand

Carrying glasses on a service salver

The method of carrying clean wine goblets about the restaurant using the service salver is illustrated in Figure 2.4.

You can also use a service cloth on the palm of the hand, with the service salver placed upon it. This allows the service salver to be rotated more easily in order to remove each wine goblet in turn by the base and to set it on the table.

Figure 2.5 indicates the use of the service salver for clearing dirty wine goblets from the table. The first dirty wine goblet cleared should be placed on the service salver nearest to the server. As the dirty glasses are cleared, they should be placed on the service salver to ensure a better and more even distribution of weight, to lessen the likelihood of accidents occurring. Again, dirty glassware is always handled by the stem and for non-stemmed glassware by the base. This is more hygienic as it avoids touching where the customer has been drinking from the glass.

Figure 2.6 Carrying clean glasses on a service salver

Figure 2.7 Carrying dirty glasses on a service salver

Carrying glasses using glass racks

Glass racks are usually made of plastic and are often used to carry glasses during the setting up of the restaurant and for functions. These racks enable the transportation of glasses in bulk once they have been washed and polished at a central point. Glass racks are also used for dirty glasses and many can be put through a glass wash machine.

Figure 2.8(a) Carrying clean glasses in a rack

Figure 2.8(b) Carrying dirty glasses in a glass rack

Carrying and using large trays

Trays are used for:

● carrying food from the kitchen to the restaurant
● service in rooms and lounges
● clearing from sideboards/workstations
● clearing from tables (when the customer is not seated at the table)
● carrying equipment.

The correct method of holding and carrying an oblong tray is to position the tray lengthways onto the forearm and to support it by holding the tray with the other hand.

Figure 2.7 shows how to carry an oblong tray. Note the tray is organised so that the heaviest items are nearest the carrier. This helps to balance the tray. Also note that one hand is placed underneath the tray and the other at the side.

Figure 2.9 Carrying a loaded oblong tray

2.5 Interpersonal skills

In a food and beverage operation there is interaction between customers (often referred to as 'external customers') and the food and beverage service staff. Interaction also takes place with people outside the service areas, such as kitchen staff, bill office staff, dispense bar staff and stillroom staff. These are known as 'internal customers'. It is important that the customer can see that the provision of food and beverages and service within an establishment is a joint effort between all departments, with each department understanding the needs of the others in order to meet the customers' demands.

Communication

There are three main types of commutation:

- **Face-to-face**: the skills used here are maintaining eye contact and active listening. Eye contact may differ across cultures; active listening is about head nodding, gestures and repeating back phrases to ensure confirmation of understanding.
- **Telephone communication**: members of staff must be able to use the telephone equipment efficiently and effectively. The communication skills for telephone conversations differ because the member of staff is not face-to-face with the customer. When dealing with a customer on the phone it is import to make sure they are informed when the member of staff is accessing information and if they are to be placed on hold. It is also important to speak clearly and slowly to allow for the possibility that reception on the phone line may not be perfect and in order to adapt your speech to meet the needs of the customer.
- **Written communication**: for example by letter, email, memo and report. Written communication is necessary when a formal response is required. The organisation will provide guidelines to staff on when and how to use written communication.

Dealing with customers

The starting point for all good interpersonal skills is good manners: saying 'please', 'thank you' and 'I beg your pardon'; being pleasant to people; showing that you care about what they want and apologising for anything that has been unsatisfactory, such as having to wait.

When addressing customers, 'Sir' or 'Madam' should be used when the customer's name is not known. If the name is known, then the customer should be referred to as 'Mr Smith' or 'Miss Jones', etc. First names should only be used in less formal operations and where the customer has explicitly indicated that this is acceptable. If the customer has a title, then appropriate use should be made of the correct form of address (for further information on forms of address, see Section 11.4, p.360).

Interpersonal skills in food and beverage service centre on the interactions between the customer and food and beverage service staff. All other interactions are secondary to, and the result of, the prime interaction of customers and staff. This has implications for the way customers are treated. Conversations between customers and staff override conversations between staff. When in conversation with customers, staff should not:

- talk to other members of staff without first excusing themselves from the customer
- interrupt interactions between customers and staff, but should wait until there is a suitable moment to catch the attention of the other member of staff so that they may excuse themselves from the customer first

- serve customers while carrying on a conversation between themselves
- talk across a room, either to each other or to customers.

Customers should always be made to feel that they are being cared for and not that they are an intrusion into the operation.

Further information on customer service is given in Section 1.4, p.11 and on customer relations in Section 12.3, p.388.

Dealing with customers during service

Greetings such as 'Good morning' and 'Good evening' should be used upon receiving customers or when the member of staff first comes into contact with the customer, for example when lounge service staff attend people already seated in the lounge.

The list below identifies examples of interpersonal skills needed at particular points during the service.

- **Showing customers to their table**: always lead and walk with them at their pace.
- **Seating customers**: ladies first, descending in age unless the host is a lady.
- **Handling coats/wraps**: handle with obvious care.
- **Handing menus/wine lists to customers**: offer the list the right way round, open for the customer and wait for the customer to take it.
- **Opening and placing a napkin**: open carefully, do not shake it like a duster, place it on the customer's lap after saying 'excuse me' to the customer.
- **Talking to customers**: only talk when standing next to them and looking at them.
- **Offering water or rolls**: say, for example, 'Excuse me Sir/Madam, may I offer you a bread roll?'
- **Explaining food and beverage items**: use terms the customer understands, not technical terms such as turned vegetable or pane. Use terms that make the item sound attractive such as casserole not stew, creamed or purée potatoes not mashed. Do not use abbreviations, for example, 'veg'.
- **Being culturally aware**: meeting the needs of customers from other cultures will affect the ways in which staff interact with them (see note on cultural awareness in Section 2.2, p.27). In addition staff need to be aware of the dietary requirements of the various religious faiths (see Section 4.4, p.104.)
- **Serving and clearing**: always say 'Excuse me' before serving or clearing and 'Thank you' after you have finished with each customer.
- **Offering accompaniments**: only offer them if you have them at the table. Offering them when they are not at the table usually means 'I will get them if you really want them!'

Other procedures that contribute to good interpersonal skills are highlighted throughout the rest of this chapter. Also see Section 12.3, p.388.

Dealing with children

If children are among the customers arriving in the foodservice area then take the lead in how to care for them from the parents, guardian or accompanying adults. Where applicable, the following factors should be considered.

- Are high chairs/seat cushions required?
- Restrictions on the service of alcohol to minors.

- Are children's meal menus required?
- The portion size required if items are ordered from the standard menu.
- The provision of children's 'give aways', such as crayons, colouring books, etc.
- For the safety of both children and others, staff should be aware of children's movements.
- Should the children be older, then they should be addressed as either 'Sir' or 'Miss'.
- Younger children should be served as promptly as possible as this will lessen the stress on the parents/guardians.

Lost children

Should a child be reported lost, the steps listed below must be taken.

1 A complete description of the lost child should be obtained:
   - male/female
   - name
   - age
   - where last seen
   - clothing worn
   - any predominant features
   - colour of hair
   - whether any accessories were being carried, e.g. a doll.
2 Immediately inform the supervisor/security.
3 Put a constant watch on all entrances/exits.
4 Check all cloakroom/rest areas, play areas and the immediate vicinity where the child has been reported missing.
5 Should nothing result from taking the above actions, immediately inform the police.

Customers with additional needs

Customer mobility

Extra awareness is needed to meet the requirements of customers who may have additional needs, such as mobility difficulties. The following considerations should be given on these occasions.

- Offer wheelchair users places at tables where there is adequate space for manoeuvrability.
- Offer wheelchair users a place out of the main thoroughfare of customer/staff movement.
- Offer wheelchair users a place with easy access to cloakrooms, exits and fire exits.
- Always ensure that menus and wine lists are immediately available to any wheelchair user.
- Never move the wheelchair without asking the customer first.
- Crutches/walking sticks should be placed in a safe but accessible and readily available position.
- Customers with dexterity difficulties may be assisted by first asking the customer how best they can be helped. Assistance may include, for example, ensuring that all items served or placed on to the table are near to the customer, offering to fillet/bone fish and meat items and offering to cut up potato and vegetable items.

Blind and partially sighted customers

Awareness is also required to meet the needs of those customers who may be blind or visually impaired. The following considerations should be taken into account.

- Talk to and treat the customer as you would any other customer.
- Remember it is by touch that blind people 'see' and are made aware that they are involved in what is happening around them.
- If in doubt ask the person directly how they may best be helped.
- Do not talk to their companions as if the person was not there.
- Offer to read menus or wine and drink lists.
- Immediately prior to taking the customer's order, a gentle touch on the hand or arm will attract their attention to you.
- Offer to fillet/bone fish and meat items.
- Offer to cut up potato and vegetable items should it be necessary.
- Never overfill cups, glasses or soup bowls.
- Should you feel it appropriate, use bowls instead of plates for specific food items, but always ask the customer first.
- Ask if you should describe where the food items are on the plate. Use the clock method to explain the location of food on a plate, for example, 6 o'clock for meat, 10 to 10 for vegetables and 10 past 2 for potatoes.

Customers with communication difficulties

Be aware of communication difficulties that may arise when, for example, customers are deaf or hearing impaired or have little understanding of the English language. In such cases the steps shown below may be helpful.

- Speak directly to the customer.
- Stand in such a position that the customer is able to see your face clearly.
- Speak normally but more distinctly.
- Describe food/drink items in simple, precise and plain language.
- Seat customers away from possible excessive noise, as this is uncomfortable for customers wearing hearing aids.
- Always read back the food or drink order received to confirm all requests.
- Listen attentively to what is being said to you to ensure you understand the customer's requirements.

Handling complaints

At some point a customer will make a complaint, for example:

- service was slow
- food when served was cold
- wine served was at the incorrect temperature
- reservation made was not recorded in the booking diary
- server has been inattentive
- wrong dish was brought to the table
- explanation of the menu was inaccurate
- poor attitude of staff.

Should a problem arise and a customer makes a complaint the following steps should be taken.

1 Do not interrupt the customer – let them have their say and make their point.
2 Apologise – but only for the specific problem or complaint.
3 Restate the details of the complaint briefly back to the customer to show you have listened and understood.
4 Agree by thanking the customer for bringing the matter to your attention. This shows you are looking at the problem from the customer's perspective.
5 Act quickly, quietly and professionally and follow the establishment's procedures for handling complaints.

Never:
● lose your temper
● take comments personally
● argue
● lie
● blame another member of staff or another department.

Valid complaints provide important feedback for a foodservice operation and can be used as valuable learning opportunities to improve service.

Dealing with incidents during service

When an unforeseen incident arises it must be dealt with promptly and efficiently without causing more disturbance than is necessary to any of the other customers. Quick action will very often soothe the irate customer and ensure a return visit to your establishment. It is worth remembering at this stage that complaints, of whatever nature, should be referred immediately to the supervisor. Delay will only cause confusion and very often the situation may be wrongly interpreted if it is not dealt with straight away. In the case of accidents, a report of the incident must be kept and signed by those involved.

Listed below are a few of the incidents that may occur and the suggested steps that might be taken in order to put right any fault.

Spillages

If during the service of a course a few drops of sauce or roast gravy have fallen on the tablecloth, the following steps might be taken.

1 Check immediately that none has fallen on the customer being served. Apologise to the customer.
2 If some has fallen on the customer's clothing, allow the customer to rub over the dirtied area with a clean damp cloth. This will remove the worst of the spillage.
3 If it is necessary for the customer to retire to the cloakroom to remove the spillage then the meal should be placed on the hotplate until he or she returns.
4 Depending on the nature of the spillage the establishment may offer to have the garment concerned cleaned.
5 If the spillage has gone on the tablecloth, the waiter should first of all remove any items of equipment that may be dirtied or in the customer's way.
6 The waiter should then mop or scrape up the spillage with either a clean damp cloth or a knife.
7 An old menu card should then be placed on top of the table but under the tablecloth beneath the damaged area.

8   A second menu should be placed on the tablecloth over the damaged area.

9   A clean rolled napkin should then be brought to the table and rolled completely over the damaged area. The menu will prevent any damp from soaking into the clean napkin.

10 Any items of equipment removed should be returned to their correct position on the tabletop.

11 Any meals taken to the hotplate should be returned and fresh covers put down where necessary (see Section 6.2, Figure 6.4(a)–(d), p.209).

12 Again, apologies should be made to the customer for any inconvenience caused.

If a customer knocks over a glass of water accidentally, then the following steps might be taken.

1   Ensure none has gone on the customer.

2   If some of the water has fallen on the customer's clothing then follow steps 2 and 3 above.

3   Where possible, as this form of accident usually involves changing the tablecloth, the party of customers should be seated at another table and allowed to continue their meal without delay.

4   If they cannot be moved to another table then they should be seated slightly back from the table so that the waiter can carry out the necessary procedures to rectify the fault speedily and efficiently.

5   The customers' meals should be placed on the hotplate to keep warm.

6   All dirty items should be removed on a tray to the waiter's sideboard ready to go to the wash-up area.

7   All clean items should be removed and kept on the waiter's sideboard for re-laying.

8   The tablecloth should be mopped with a clean absorbent cloth to remove as much of the liquid as possible.

9   A number of old menus should be placed on the tabletop but underneath the spillage area of the soiled tablecloth.

10 A clean tablecloth of the correct size should be brought to the table. It should be opened out and held as if one were laying a tablecloth during the pre-service preparation period. The table should then be clothed up in the usual manner except that when the clean cloth is being drawn across the table towards the waiter they are at the same time taking off the soiled tablecloth. The soiled tablecloth should be removed at the same time that the clean tablecloth is being laid so that the customers cannot see the bare tabletop at any time. The old menus will prevent any dampness penetrating to the clean tablecloth.

11 When the table has its clean tablecloth on it should be re-laid as quickly as possible.

12 The customers should then be re-seated at the table and the meals returned to them from the hotplate.

Returned food

If, for example, a customer suggests that their chicken dish is not cooked, then the following steps might be taken.

1   Apologise to the customer.

2   The dish should be removed and returned to the kitchen.

3   The customer should be asked if he or she would like another portion of the same dish or would prefer to choose an alternative.

4   The new dish should be collected as soon as possible and served to the customer.

5   Apologies should be made for any inconvenience caused.

The policy of the establishment will dictate whether or not the customer is to be charged for the alternative dish.

Lost property

If, for example, a waiter finds a wallet under a chair that has recently been vacated by a customer, the steps listed below might be taken.

1 A check should be made immediately as to whether or not the customer has left the service area. If he is still in the area, the wallet may be returned to him.

2 If the customer has left the service area, the waiter should hand the wallet to the head waiter or supervisor in charge.

3 The supervisor or head waiter should check with reception and the hall porter to see if the customer has left the building.

4 If the customer concerned is a resident, then reception may ring his room, stating the wallet has been found and can be collected at a convenient time.

5 If the customer is a regular customer, it is possible that the head waiter or receptionist may know how to contact him to arrange for him to collect the wallet.

6 If the customer is a regular customer but cannot be contacted, the wallet should be kept in the lost property office until the customer's next visit.

7 If the owner has not been found or contacted immediately, the head waiter or supervisor should complete a lost property record sheet as shown in Figure 2.10.

8 A copy of the lost property record sheet should go with the wallet to the lost property office where the contents of the wallet must be checked against the list before it is accepted. The details of the find are then entered in a lost property register.

9 Another copy of the record sheet should be given to reception in case any enquiries are received concerning a wallet. Anyone claiming lost property should be passed on to the lost property office.

10 Before the lost property office hands over any lost property, a description of the article concerned and its contents should be asked for to ensure as far as possible that it is being returned to the genuine owner. The office should also see proof of identity of the person claiming ownership.

11 In the case of all lost property, the steps mentioned above should be carried out as quickly as possible as this is in the best interests of the establishment and causes the customer minimum inconvenience. On receipt of lost property, the customer should be asked to sign for the article concerned and to give his address and telephone number.

12 Any lost property unclaimed after three months may become the property of the finder who should claim it through the head waiter or supervisor.

Lost property record sheet	
Date:	Establishment:
Item description:	
Found by:	
Where found:	Time found:
Checked by:	
Where stored:	
Claimed by:	Date:
Contact details:	
Proof of identity seen:	Customer signature:

Figure 2.10 Example of a lost property record sheet

Customer illness

If a customer falls ill in your establishment then the steps below might be taken.

1 As soon as it is noticed that a customer is feeling unwell while in the dining room or restaurant a person in authority should be immediately called.

2 If the customer falling ill is a woman then a female member of staff should attend her.

3 The person in authority must enquire if the customer needs assistance. At the same time he must try to judge whether the illness is of a serious nature or not. If in any doubt it is always better to call for medical assistance.

4 It is often advisable to offer to take the customer to another room to see if they are able to recover in a few minutes. If this happens their meal should be placed on the hotplate until their return.

5 If the illness appears to be of a serious nature, a doctor, nurse or someone qualified in first aid should be called for immediately.

6 The customer should not be moved until a doctor has examined him/her.

7 If necessary the area should be screened off.

8 Although this is a difficult situation to deal with in front of the general public, the minimum fuss should be made and service to the rest of the customers should carry on as normal.

9 The medical person will advise whether an ambulance should be called.

10 The customer may have had a sudden stomach upset and wish to leave without finishing their meal. Assistance should be offered in helping the customer leave the restaurant.

11 Payment for the part of the meal consumed and any ensuing travel costs would be according to the policy of the establishment.

12 It is most important that for all accidents (minor or serious) all details are recorded in an accident book (see page 54). This is in case of a claim against the establishment at a later date.

13 If after a short period of time the customer returns and continues with their meal, a fresh cover should be laid and the meal returned from the hotplate or a new meal served.

Over-consumption of alcohol

If a customer is suspected of having too much to drink the following steps might be taken.

1 If a prospective customer asks for a table and staff believe the client is under the influence of drink, they may refuse them a table, even though there may be one available. It is not always possible, however, to recognise a customer who may prove objectionable later on.

2 If a customer is suspected of being drunk this must first of all be ascertained by the head waiter or supervisor.

3 The customer should then be asked to leave rather than be allowed to become objectionable to other customers.

4 If the customer becomes difficult to handle, then other members of staff may be needed to assist in their removal from the eating area (depending on establishment policy, physical contact should be avoided).

5 If the customer has already consumed part of the meal but is not being objectionable then the remainder of the meal should be served in the normal fashion, but the head waiter or supervisor must ensure no more alcoholic beverages are offered or served.

6 On finishing, the customer should be watched until they have left the premises.

It is always advisable to make out a report of all such incidents. They should also be brought to the immediate attention of the restaurant manager in case of any claim at a later date concerning a particular incident.

Unsatisfactory appearance

If a customer's appearance is not satisfactory according to the policy of the establishment, the following steps might be taken.

1 If a customer's appearance does not meet the dress code policy of the establishment or is likely to give offence to others, then the customer should be asked to correct their dress to the approved fashion required by the establishment.

2 Staff should be made aware of the need for sensitivity towards cultural dress.

3 If the customer will not comply with the request, he or she should be asked to leave.

4 If they have partly consumed a meal then whether they will be charged or not depends on the policy of the house and the discretion of the head waiter or supervisor.

5 A report of the incident must be made and signed by the staff concerned.

Recording incidents

It is advisable that when any incident occurs a report is made out immediately. The basic information that should be found in the report is as follows:

- Place
- Date
- Time
- Nature of incident
- Individual signed reports from those involved

- Action taken
- Name, address and phone number of customer involved
- Names of staff involved.

All reports should be kept in case similar incidents occur at a later date, and for future reference should the need arise.

2.6 Health, safety and security

Maintaining a safe environment

Essentially safety is a civil duty and negligence is a criminal offence. In regard to health, safety and security, staff must:

- understand food hygiene regulations and be aware it is their responsibility to act within the bounds of these regulations
- notify management of any major illnesses
- perform duties in any area concerned with the handling of food in a hygienic manner, paying attention to food and hygiene regulations
- make themselves familiar with all escape routes and fire exits in the building
- ensure that fire exits remain clear at all times
- participate in fire evacuation drills and practices
- take reasonable care for the health and safety of themselves and of others and ensure that health and safety regulations are followed
- report to heads of department or duty managers any hazards which may cause injury or ill-health to customers and/or staff.

Avoiding hazards

Employees have a responsibility to themselves, work colleagues and customers to be aware of hazards that may arise when working. Many accidents occur through carelessness or lack of thought, for example:

- not wearing the appropriate protective clothing such as an apron
- not wearing sensible (i.e. stable and properly fitted) shoes
- delay in clearing spillages or picking up items of equipment that have fallen on the floor
- being unaware of customers' bags placed on the floor
- items of equipment stored incorrectly
- broken glass or crockery not wrapped up sufficiently before being placed in the bin
- forgetting to unplug electrical appliances prior to cleaning
- putting ashtray debris into rubbish bins containing paper (a fire hazard)
- forgetting to switch off and unplug an appliance after use or at the end of the service
- not being observant with table lamps or lit candles on a buffet
- over-filling coffee pots, soup tureens, glasses, etc.
- using cups, glasses, soup bowls, etc., for storing cleaning agents
- stacking trays incorrectly
- carrying a mix of equipment on a tray, such as cutlery, crockery and glassware
- carpet edges turned up
- faulty wheels on trolleys or castors on sideboards
- being unaware of customers' walking sticks and crutches
- inadequate space for the safe service of food and drink because of bad planning
- lack of knowledge in carrying out certain tasks, such as opening a bottle of sparkling wine.

Procedure in the event of an accident

All employers must be able to provide first aid should such a need arise. In the event of an accident the first course of action should be to call for the assistance of a trained and qualified first aid person.

Under the terms of the Health and Safety at Work Act employers must keep a record of all accidents that occur in the workplace. If you are involved in or witness an accident you will be required to give information and/or to complete an accident form. For this reason it is wise to make notes on the incident as soon as you are able. The information should include:

- the location of the accident
- the time of the accident
- a statement of the event
- details of witnesses
- treatment administered.

Procedure in case of fire

All employees should be given fire drill training during their induction programme. This initial training should then be followed up by regular training sessions on the procedures to be followed in the event of fire. This training should include:

- fire procedures in the employee's specific area of work
- fire drill instructions for both customers and staff
- the location of fire points (safe places where staff and customers should assemble after an evacuation) nearest to employee's particular area of work
- the location of fire exits
- the correct type of fire extinguisher to be used in relation to the type of fire (see Table 2.3).
- an identification of the employee's specific responsibilities in the event of fire.

In the event of the fire alarm ringing employees must be aware of the following rules.
1 Follow the fire instructions as laid down for the establishment.
2 Usher all customers and staff out of the work area promptly and calmly.
3 Pay special attention to customers with special needs such as those with mobility problems.
4 Walk quickly but do not run. Display a sense of urgency.
5 Do not panic; remain calm as composure will be imitated by others.
6 Proceed as promptly as possible to the nearest assembly point.
7 Ensure that someone watches to see that there are no stragglers.
8 Follow the exit route as laid down in the establishments fire instructions.
9 Never use a lift.
10 Never re-enter the building until told it is safe to do so.
11 Do not waste time to collect personal items.

Table 2.3 Fire extinguishers and their uses

Contents	Water	Foam	CO_2	Dry powder	Wet chemical
Label colour*	White on red	Cream on red	Black on red	Blue on red	Yellow on red
Electrical suitability	Dangerous – electrically conductive		Safe – non-electrically conductive		
Suitable for	Solids	Some liquids	Electrical – Do not use in a confined space	Liquid	Liquid especially cooking fats and oils
Unsuitable for	Oil	Electrical	Solids	Very little	Solids

* Under European Union standards the body of every extinguisher must be coloured red. However, a colour zone is used to indicate what the extinguishing medium is – the colours used for these mediums are the ones given here and they are the same as the previous whole-body colour coding system.

Employees have a responsibility to assist in fire prevention, control and safety.

They must therefore ensure that:
● fire exits are not obstructed
● fire-fighting equipment is not damaged or misused
● no smoking rules are observed at all times
● as far as is possible all electrical and gas equipment is switched off
● all doors and windows are closed when not being used for evacuation purposes
● fire doors are not locked or wedged open
● sufficient ashtrays/stands are available for the disposal of cigarette ends and used matches
● the procedure for making an emergency fire call is known.

Cleaning programmes

Maintaining clean work areas and equipment is important to:

- control the bacteria that cause food poisoning
- reduce the possibility of physical and chemical contamination
- reduce the possibility of accidents (e.g. slips on a greasy floor)
- create a positive image for customers, visitors and employees
- comply with the law
- avoid attracting pests to the kitchen.

The cleaning schedule should include the following information:

- **What** is to be cleaned.
- **Who** should do it (name if possible).
- **How** it is to be done and how long it should take.
- **When** it is to be done, i.e. time of day.
- **Materials** to be used, including chemicals and their dilution, cleaning equipment required and protective clothing to be worn.
- **Safety precautions** that must be taken.
- **Signatures** of the cleaner and the supervisor checking the work, along with the date and time.

All food and beverage service staff should be made aware of the importance of cleaning programmes to reduce the build-up of dust, bacteria and other forms of debris. For this reason, as well as safety and hygiene considerations, full attention must be given by all concerned to cleaning tasks and when they should be carried out. Regular maintenance also makes the service area look attractive and projects a positive image of the establishment.

A cleaning programme should be set up for any cleaning tasks that must be done in a particular area. Some tasks are done daily, even twice daily, for instance, the washing and polishing of crockery before each service period. Other tasks might be done weekly, monthly or every six months. Certain items of equipment will need cleaning immediately after each service period is finished.

Examples of cleaning tasks are shown in Table 2.4.

Table 2.4 Cleaning tasks

Immediately after use	Carving trolley
	Sweet trolley
	Copper pans
	Refrigerated trolleys
	Flare lamps
Daily	Vacuuming
	Damp dusting chairs
	Polishing sideboard tops
	Cleaning brasses

Weekly	Silver cleaning
	Cleaning pictures
	Defrosting fridges
	Wiping down doorframes and all high ledges
	Washing cellar/crockery store floors
Monthly plus	Shampoo carpets
	Dry clean curtains
	Maintenance checks on still-set, chilling units, fridges and air-conditioning systems
	Clean all lighting

Points to note:
- Always use the correct cleaning materials for the task in hand.
- Clean frequently.
- Rinse all surfaces well.
- Dusters should only be used for dusting and no other cleaning tasks.
- Use cleaning procedures that are adequate and efficient.
- Cloths used for cleaning toilets must not be used for any other purpose.
- Clean and store equipment safely and in its correct place.
- Do not use cleaning cloths for wiping down food preparation surfaces.
- Ensure vacuum cleaners are emptied on a regular basis.
- Consider safety at all times to reach high points, for example, use a stepladder.

Maintaining a secure environment

Depending upon the nature of the establishment, the security measures that are laid down may vary considerably. Staff must be aware of the security measures that relate to their own work environment as well as those outlined below.
- The importance of wearing some form of recognised identity badge.
- Being observant and reporting 'suspicious' persons and/or packages.
- Not discussing work duties with customers or outside of the workplace.
- Allowing bags, packages and one's person to be searched upon request when either entering or leaving the workplace.
- Being aware of the security procedures for the establishment in the event that sudden and urgent action needs to be taken.
- Ensuring external fire doors are kept shut but not locked, nor left ajar in error.
- Ensuring that all areas have been vacated when responsible for 'locking up' duties. All toilets/cloakrooms must be carefully checked and at the same time all windows and doors should be checked to ensure they are locked.
- Keys should only be handled by someone in authority. A signing out book should be available when staff request keys.
- Keys should never be left unattended.
- When handling cash, all large denomination notes should be checked carefully as well as all cheque and credit card payments, to prevent fraud, the passing of illegal notes and the acceptance of altered credit cards.
- Being alert and observant at all times and not hesitating in reporting anything suspicious to the immediate superior.

Dealing with a suspicious item or package

All employees should be constantly alert for suspicious items or packages.

- If an object is found then it must immediately be reported to the security officer, manager or supervisor.
- Do not touch or attempt to move the object.
- If there are customers in the immediate vicinity, discreetly attempt to establish ownership of the object.
- If the ownership is established then ask the customer to keep the object with them or hand it in for safe keeping.
- If no immediate ownership is established, then the area should be cleared and the authorities notified without delay.

Dealing with a bomb threat

Immediate action needs to be taken as a bomb could go off at any moment. As a result staff should:

- be aware of and follow establishment policy with regard to bomb threats and evacuation procedures
- evacuate the immediate work area
- search the work area to ensure it is cleared, if this is their responsibility
- evacuate the premises and usher all customers/staff through the nearest usable exits to specified assembly areas
- count all persons present to determine their safety and minimise the risk of accidents.

Chapter 3

Food and beverage service areas and equipment

3.1 Design and purchasing factors

A customer's first impression on entering the service area is of great important and their business may be gained (or lost) on this alone. The creation of atmosphere by the right choice of decor, furnishings and equipment is therefore a major factor that contributes to the success of the foodservice operation. A careful selection of items in terms of shape, design and colour enhances the overall decor or theme and contributes towards a feeling of harmony. The choice of furniture and its layout and the linen, tableware, small equipment and glassware will be determined by factors such as:

- the type of clientele expected
- the site or location of the establishment
- the layout of the food and beverage service area
- the type of service offered
- the funds available.

The general points to be considered when purchasing equipment for a food and beverage service area are:

- flexibility of use
- type of service being offered
- type of customer
- design
- colour
- durability
- ease of maintenance
- stackability
- cost and funds available
- availability in the future – replacements
- storage
- rate of breakage, i.e. crockery
- shape
- psychological effect on customers
- delivery time.

Front-of-house service areas are some of the busiest of a foodservice establishment, especially during the service periods. It is therefore important that these areas are well designed for operational purposes and that department heads ensure that all members of staff know exactly what their duties are and how to carry them out efficiently and effectively.

The service areas behind the scenes are known as back-of-house areas. These areas include the stillroom, hotplate (or pass) area and the wash-up. The back-of-house service areas are usually between the kitchen and food and beverage service or front-of-house areas. They are important parts of the design of a foodservice operation, acting as the link between kitchen or food preparation areas and the restaurant or food and beverage service areas. They are also meeting points for staff of various departments as they carry out their duties and so a well-designed layout is essential to ensure an even flow of work. The back-of-house areas must also be efficiently organised, stocked with well-designed equipment and appropriately supervised.

3.2 Stillroom

The stillroom provides items of food and beverages required for the service of a meal that are not catered for by the other major departments in a foodservice operation, such as the kitchen, larder and pastry. The duties performed in this service area will vary according to the type of meals offered and the size of establishment concerned.

Staffing

In a large establishment a stillroom supervisor is in charge of the stillroom. Depending on its size and the duties to be performed, the stillroom supervisor may have a number of staff under their control. The person in charge is responsible for the compilation of work rotas for all stillroom staff so that all duties are covered and the area is staffed throughout the whole of the service period. The stillroom supervisor is also responsible for ordering supplies from the main dry goods store and the effective control of these items.

Because of the number of hours that the stillroom has to remain open and to ensure it is run efficiently, staff may be required to work on a shift basis.

Figure 3.1 Example of a stillroom.

Equipment

The equipment found in a stillroom is fairly standard and there tends to be a considerable amount needed because of the wide range of food items offered and the need to ensure their proper storage, preparation and presentation. The following are examples of items that might be needed.
- Refrigerator for storage of milk, cream, butter, fruit juices, etc.
- Hot and cold beverage-making facilities.
- Large double sink and draining board for washing-up purposes.
- Dishwasher of a size suitable for the stillroom but large enough to ensure efficient turnover of equipment.
- Salamander or toasters.
- Sandwich toaster.
- Bread slicing machine.
- Worktop and cutting board.
- Storage space for small equipment such as crockery, glassware and cutlery and tableware.
- Storage cupboard for all dry goods held in stock and for paper items like doilies and napkins.
- Coffee grinding machine to ensure the correct grind of coffee for the brewing method.
- Ice maker.

Provisions

As a basic guide, the following food items would normally be dispensed from the stillroom.

- All beverages such as coffee, tea, chocolate, tisanes, Bovril, Horlicks, Ovaltine and other drinks.
- Assorted fruit juices: orange, tomato, pineapple and grapefruit.
- Milk, cream and alternatives.
- Sugars: loose, pre-wrapped portions, brown coffee crystals, Demerara, etc., and alternatives.
- Preserves: marmalade, cherry, plum, raspberry, strawberry, apricot and honey. For the purpose of control and to reduce wastage, many establishments now offer pre-portioned jars or pots of jams or preserves at breakfast and for afternoon tea, rather than a preserve dish.
- Butter: either passed through a butter pat machine, curled or pre-wrapped portions and also butter alternatives.
- Sliced and buttered brown, white and malt bread.
- Rolls, brioche and croissants.
- Bread substitute items: gluten free, rye, rice crackers, etc.
- Dry crackers, digestive and water biscuits for service with cheese; sweet biscuits for service with early morning and afternoon teas and coffees.
- Assorted breakfast cereals: cornflakes, Weetabix, muesli and so on. In many establishments cereals of all types are offered in pre-wrapped, portion-controlled packets.
- Toasted scones and teacakes.
- Pastries, gâteaux and sandwiches.

Control

There are two main ways of controlling goods to be issued from the stillroom.

1 If a foodservice area requires items such as butter, sugar, preserves, etc., in bulk, a requisition signed by a supervisor is required before the stillroom will issue the items.
2 Upon receipt of a waiter's check, tea, coffee or any other beverage required in the necessary portions will be dispensed.

3.3 Hotplate

The hotplate or pass is the meeting point between the service staff and the food preparation staff. Active co-operation and a good relationship between the members of staff of these two areas help to ensure that the customer receives an efficient and quick service of their meal.

The hotplate itself should be stocked with all the crockery necessary for the service of a meal. This may include some or all of the following items:

- soup plates
- fish plates
- joint plates
- sweet plates
- consommé cups
- platters
- soup cups.

The food flats and serving dishes required for service are often placed on the top of the hotplate to warm through and used as required. The hotplate is usually gas or electrically operated and should be lit or switched on well in advance of the service to ensure all the necessary crockery and silver is sufficiently heated before the service commences.

Figure 3.2 Example of a hotplate area

Aboyeur or barker

The aboyeur, or barker, is in charge, and controls the hotplate (or pass) during the service period. As an aid to the food service staff the aboyeur would control the 'off board', which tells the waiter immediately of any menu item that is not available (off). It should be sited in a prominent position for all to see.

The aboyeur will initially receive the food check from the waiter. Written food orders must be legible to the aboyeur so that there is no delay in calling up a particular dish. The aboyeur checks that none of the dishes ordered are off the menu. Then the order from the various 'corners' (or 'parties' or 'sections') of the kitchen is called up, as each particular dish is required. If a dish required has to be prepared and cooked to order, then it is important that the aboyeur orders this to be done before the waiter comes to the hotplate to collect it. This ensures there will be no major delay for the waiter who is going to serve the dish or for the customer who is waiting for the next course to be served. When a food check is finished with it is placed into a control box. This box is often kept locked and can only be opened by a member of staff from the control department who, for control purposes, marries the copy of the food check from the kitchen with the copy the cashier has and the duplicate copy of the bill.

With the modern use of an EPOS (electronic point of sale) system the electronic order can be sent directly from the restaurant to each section of the kitchen and the aboyeur is the co-ordinator for the dishes to arrive on the pass at the same time, checking for quality before releasing the plate to the waiting staff. The control department then uses the EPOS information to control sales and revenue. (For an example of a radio-controlled electronic system for order taking and communication, see Section 6.3, p.215 and Figure 6.20, p.215.)

Hotplate language and terminology

To ensure there is no delay in any food dish reaching the hotplate, the aboyeur should call it up, allowing time for preparation, cooking and presentation. Various special kitchen terms are used to warn the food preparation staff working in various corners to get ready certain dishes. Because of a multi-national work force, many establishments now use one single specified language within a kitchen. This is often the language of the country, such as English in the UK. All members of staff need to know the system for their own establishment.

Examples of traditional kitchen terms are:
- **Le service va commencer**: general warning to kitchen that service is about to commence.
- **Ça marche trois couverts**: indication to the kitchen of the number of covers on the table, in this case three covers.
- **Poissonnier, faites marcher trois soles Véronique**: example of fish section informed of the order required, in this case three sole Véronique.
- **Poissonnier, envoyez les trois soles Véronique**: when the order is required at the hotplate by the waiter, the aboyeur calls it up. In this example it is the fish section being told to bring the order for the three sole Véronique.
- **Oui**: the reply given by the chef de partie (section chef) to the order called out by the aboyeur.
- **Bien soigné**: the term called out by the aboyeur before the actual order when an extra special order is required.
- **Dépêchez-vous**: the words used to hurry up an order.
- **Arrêtez**: the term used to cancel an order.
- Foods requiring special degrees of cooking are given the following terms:
  - Omelette baveuse: soft inside.
  - Steak grillé:
    - bleu: (rare) surfaces well browned, inside raw
    - saignant: underdone
    - à point: medium
    - bien cuit: cooked right through, well done.

Whatever system is used all food service staff should be familiar with the specific terms being used in the production area in order to appreciate exactly what is going on at the hotplate and in the food production areas, to ensure quick and efficient service.

3.4 Wash-up

The wash-up must be sited so that staff can work speedily and efficiently when passing from the food service areas to the kitchens. Servers should stack trays of dirties correctly within the service area, with all the correct sized plates together and tableware stacked on one of the plates with the blades of the knives running under the arches of the forks. All glassware that has not had grease or fat in it should be taken to a separate glass wash-up point, often in the bar.

The wash-up service area should be the first section in the stillroom when the waiter enters from the service area. Here all the dirty plates are deposited, stacked correctly and all the tableware placed in a special wire basket or container in readiness for washing. The server must place any debris into the bin or bowl provided. All used paper, such as napkins, doilies or kitchen paper, should be put in separate waste bins to ensure proper recycling.

Dishwashing methods

There are four main methods of dishwashing for foodservice operations and a summary of these is shown in Table 3.1.

Table 3.1 Summary of dishwashing methods (based on a chart from Croner's Catering)

Method	Description
Manual	Soiled ware washed by hand or brush machine
Automatic conveyor	Soiled ware loaded in baskets, mounted on a conveyor by operators for automatic transportation through a dishwashing machine
Flight conveyor	Soiled ware loaded within pegs mounted on a conveyor, by operators for automatic transportation through a dishwashing machine
Deferred wash	Soiled ware collected together, stripped, sorted and stacked by operators for transportation through a dishwashing machine at a later stage

Manual

The dirty crockery is placed into a tank of hot water containing a soap detergent. After washing, the plates are placed into wire racks and dipped into a second sterilising tank containing clean hot water at a temperature of approximately 75 °C (179 °F). The racks are left for two minutes and then lifted out and the crockery left to drain. If sterilised in water at this temperature the crockery will dry by itself without the use of drying-up cloths. This is more hygienic. After drying, the crockery is stacked into piles of the correct size and placed on shelves until required for further use.

Automatic

Many larger establishments have dishwashing machines. These are necessary because of the high usage of crockery. Instructions for use of a dishwashing machine are supplied by the manufacturer, together with details of detergent to be used and in what quantity. These directions should be strictly adhered to.

Debris should be removed from the crockery before it is placed into the wire racks. The racks are then passed through the machine, the crockery being washed, rinsed, and then sterilised in turn. Having passed through the machine the crockery is left to drain for two to three minutes and is then stacked and placed on shelves until required for further use. As with the tank method, the plates do not require drying with tea cloths. Developments of this method include the automatic conveyor and the flight conveyor dishwashing methods, as described in Table 3.1.

Figure 3.3 Dishwashing area with flight conveyer to left of picture and tray washer on right of picture (image courtesy of Meiko UK)

3.5 Colour and lighting considerations

Colour

The restaurant surroundings can contribute a great deal towards the price–quality relationship in the minds of potential customers. What may be suitable for a fast-food operation would be entirely unsuitable for a restaurant operation catering for an executive market. Bright illumination may be found in bars with light colours on the walls, but foodservice areas are better with dimmer illumination and warmly coloured walls, as these give a more relaxed and welcoming atmosphere. Colour should also contribute to a feeling of cleanliness.

The colour scheme used in the foodservice area should help to reflect the character of the operation. There is also an association between colour and the presentation of the food that must be considered. Colour schemes generally regarded as most useful in allowing food presentation to shine include pink, peach, pale yellow, light green, beige, blue and turquoise. These colours reflect the natural colours found in well-presented foodstuffs.

Just as decor and light play an important role, so table accessories need to be carefully chosen as slip cloths, serviettes and place mats all help to make the environment more attractive.

Lighting

A well-designed colour scheme can easily be spoilt by a badly planned lighting system and therefore the two aspects should be considered together at the design stage.

Modern designs tend towards a versatile system of lighting by which a food and beverage service area may have bright lighting at lunchtime and a more diffused form of lighting in the evening. It is also an advantage to be able to change the colouring of the lighting for special functions.

Restaurants have many choices available to them. The three main light sources to be found are low voltage directional down lighters and surface mounted fittings, low energy lamps and light emitting diodes (LED) luminaires.

Low voltage halogen lighting is warmer in colour but less efficient to operate than low energy bulbs of an equivalent wattage. It can however be easily directed to specific spots such as a particular table or area. Low voltage diachroic lamps overcome many of the colour problems found when using mains voltage incandescent lamps, which create a yellow light when dimmed. One disadvantage of halogen lighting is the amount of heat generated by the lamps.

The main virtue of low energy lighting is its lower operating cost, but it is often criticised for giving a dull and lifeless illumination. Food may be made to look appealing by using blue-white light from fixtures, but the blue-white glow may also detract from a warm romantic atmosphere. It is generally not used where directional lighting is needed, as it is not easily focused or controlled.

LED lighting is a relatively new idea. Originally used as a low energy, low temperature warning light in televisions and other electrical equipment, it has now become more widely used in general lighting. Its advantages are many. It produces a directional crisp light which is ideal for highlighting a particular item. LED luminaires have an extremely long life, often running into tens of thousands of hours. Colours can be changed in an instant by varying the input voltage, so one luminaire can produce several different colours or a mixture of colours. Its low operating temperature makes it safe to use where a customer may touch the luminaire, for example when up lighting a column from below at floor level.

A balance is usually needed between the low running costs of low energy lamps and superior light quality from low voltage halogen lighting and LEDs. This balance will depend upon both the budget for the installation and the running costs of the overall lighting scheme.

The foodservice area needs more than proper decor lighting. Functional lighting is a must, giving proper illumination for chefs to prepare food, staff to serve it and customers to order and eat it. Functional lighting may amount to as much as 75 per cent of a restaurant's total lighting system. In the dining room two basic areas require functional lighting: the table and the room as a whole. The aim therefore is to mix the right blend of decor and functional lighting at the lowest possible cost.

Table lighting is most flattering to customers when it shines down from the ceiling and is then reflected back from a horizontal surface. Halogen down lighters serve the purpose well here. Care must be taken, however, to ensure that the bulbs used do not give off too bright a light, as this will create too much contrast between dark and light spots. Clean and well-polished silver, glassware and crockery on a dining table, or a well-polished reflective tabletop in the lounge, will bounce light gently upwards, acting as a softener to overhead lights. Positioning of these down lights is absolutely critical to avoid lighting the tops of customers' heads. Tabletop lighting can add atmosphere and create ambience and includes candles, gaslights and shaded electric lighting. These low level lights are the most flattering of all, as they reduce facial shadows by infilling dark areas caused by down lights.

Functional lighting in the dining room must serve a number of purposes.
- Fixtures directing light onto ceilings and walls should indicate to customers the dimensions of the room, together with any special attractions, such as pictures and old oak beams. Low voltage diachroic lamps are best suited for this purpose.
- The lighting should project a subdued atmosphere, with contrasts between bright and dark areas and tabletops capturing much of the light, while ceilings and upper walls remain dark.
- It may be necessary to feature special areas of a dining room, such as a buffet or self-service salad bar.

The food and beverage service area needs to have a good mix of decor and functional lighting. Brighter lights subconsciously tell customers to eat more quickly and leave and are therefore the recommended way to illuminate an establishment that requires fast turnover and high volume throughput.

3.6 Bar

The bar may be situated within a food and beverage service area and dispense wine or other alcoholic drinks that are to be served to a customer consuming a meal or using a lounge area. However, in many establishments, because of the planning and layout, wine and other alcoholic drinks for consumption with a meal are sometimes obtained from bars situated outside the food and beverage service area itself – in other words, from one of the public bars. All drinks dispensed must be checked for and controlled in some way (see Section 6.4, p.236 and Section 12.7, p.452).

Equipment

To provide an efficient service of the different types of drinks requested by customers, the bar must have available all the equipment required for making cocktails, decanting wine, serving wine correctly, making non-alcoholic fruit cocktails and so on. The equipment should include the items described below.

Main items

- **Cocktail shaker**: the ideal utensil for mixing ingredients that will not normally blend together well by stirring. A three-part utensil.
- **Boston shaker**: consists of two cones, one of which overlaps the other to seal in the mix. Made of stainless steel, glass or plated silver. The mix is strained using a Hawthorn strainer.
- **Mixing glass**: like a glass jug without a handle, but has a lip. Used for mixing clear drinks, which do not contain juices or cream.
- **Strainer**: there are many types, the most popular being the Hawthorn. This is a flat spoon-shaped utensil with a spring coiled round its edge. It is used in conjunction with the cocktail shaker and mixing glass to hold back the ice after the drink is prepared. A special design is available for use with liquidisers and blenders.
- **Bar spoon**: for use with the mixing glass when stirring cocktails. The flat 'muddler' end is used for crushing sugar and mint in certain drinks.
- **Bar liquidiser or blender**: used for making drinks that require puréed fruit.
- **Drink mixer**: used for drinks that do not need liquidising, especially those containing cream or ice cream. If ice is required, use only crushed ice.

Other items

Examples include:

- assorted glasses
- ice buckets and stands
- wine baskets
- water jugs
- cutting board and knife
- coasters
- cork extractor
- ice pick
- small ice buckets and tongs
- ice crushing machine
- drinking straws
- cocktail sticks
- carafes
- wine and cocktail/drinks lists
- coloured sugars
- glass cloths, napkins and service cloths
- mini whisk
- sink unit
- refrigerator
- ice making machine
- glass washing machine
- optics/spirit measures
- wine measures
- cooling trays
- bottle opener
- muslin and funnel
- lemon squeezing machine
- swizzle sticks
- strainer and funnel
- service salvers
- wine knife and cigar cutter (where legislation allows smoking)
- bin
- hot beverage maker
- juice press.

Food items

Examples include:

- olives
- Worcestershire sauce
- salt and pepper
- nutmeg
- assorted bitters: peach, orange, angostura
- caster sugar
- eggs
- mint
- orange
- coconut cream
- Maraschino cherries
- Tabasco sauce
- cinnamon
- cloves
- cube sugar
- Demerara sugar
- cream
- cucumber
- lemon
- lime
- salted nuts/crisps
- gherkins
- silver skin onions.

Figure 3.4(a) Examples of cocktail bar equipment: (1) cocktail shaker, (2) Boston shaker, (3) mixing glass with bar spoon, (4) Hawthorn strainer, (5) jug strainer insert, (6) mini whisk, (7) straws, (8) ice crusher, (9) juice press, (10) ice bucket and tongs

Figure 3.4(b) Examples of bar equipment: (1) bottle coaster, (2) Champagne star cork grip, (3) wine bottle holder, (4) vacu-pump, (5, 7, 9, 12) wine bottle openers, (6, 10) Champagne bottle stoppers, (8) wine funnel, (11) wine bottle foil cutter, (13) Champagne cork grip, (14) wine cork extractor

Figure 3.4(b) (continued) (15) appetiser bowls and cocktail stick holder, (16) measures on drip tray, (17) cutting board and knife, (18) cigar cutters, (19, 21) bottle stoppers, (20) bottle pourers, (22) crown cork opener, (23) mini juice press

Planning the bar

When planning a bar, whether a fixed bar or a temporary bar for a function, there are certain factors that must be given prime consideration and these are described below.

Siting

A major factor is the siting of the bar. The position should ensure the bar achieves the greatest possible number of sales.

Area

The bar staff must be given sufficient area or space in which to work and move about. There should be a minimum of 1 m (3 ft 3 in) from the back of the bar counter to the storage shelves and display cabinets at the rear of the bar.

Layout

During initial planning, careful consideration must be given to the layout of the bar. Adequate storage for the stock and equipment listed above must be provided in the form of shelves, cupboards and racks. Everything should be easily to hand so that bar staff do not have to move about more than necessary to provide a quick and efficient service.

Figure 3.5 Back bar fitting (image courtesy of Williams Refrigeration)

Plumbing and power

It is essential to have hot and cold running water for glass washing. Power is necessary for the cooling trays, refrigerators and ice making machines.

Safety and hygiene

Great care must be observed to ensure that the materials used in the make-up of the bar are hygienic and safe. Flooring must be non-slip. The bar top should be of a material suited to the general decor that is hard wearing, easily wiped down and has no sharp edges. The bar top should be of average working height – approximately 1 m (3 ft 3 in) – and a depth (across the top from the bar to the service side) of about 0.6 m (20 in).

3.7 Furniture

Furniture must be chosen according to the needs of the establishment. Examples of various dining arrangements are shown in Table 3.2.

Table 3.2 Dining arrangements (based on a chart from Croner's Catering)

Type	Description of furniture
Loose random	Freestanding furniture positioned in no discernible pattern within a given service area
Loose module	Freestanding furniture positioned within a given service area to a pre-determined pattern, with or without the use of dividers to create smaller areas within the main area
Booth	Fixed seating (banquette), usually high backed, used to create secluded seating
High density	Furniture with minimum dimensions and usually fixed, positioned within a given service area to create maximum seating capacity
Module	Seating incorporates tables and chairs constructed as one and may be fixed to the floor
In situ	Customers served in areas not designed for service, e.g. aircraft and hospital beds
Bar and lounge areas	Customers served in areas not primarily designed for food and beverage service

Materials and finishes

By using different materials, designs and finishes of furniture and by their careful arrangement, the atmosphere and appearance of the service area can be changed to suit different occasions.

Various types of wood and wood grain finishes are available, each suitable to blend with a particular decor. Wood is strong and rigid and resists wear and stains. It is a popular material for chairs and tables in most food and beverage service areas but is not ideal for canteens, some staff dining rooms and cafeterias.

Although wood predominates, more metals (mainly aluminium and aluminium-plated steel or brass) are gradually being introduced into dining furniture. Aluminium is lightweight, hardwearing, has a variety of finishes, is easily cleaned and costs are reasonable. Nowadays a wooden-topped table with a metal base may be found, together with chairs with lightweight metal frames and plastic finishes for the seat and back.

Formica or plastic-coated tabletops may be found in many cafeterias and staff dining rooms. These are easily cleaned, hardwearing and eliminate the use of linen. The tabletops come in a variety of colours and designs suitable for all situations. Place mats may take the place of linen.

Chairs

Chairs come in an enormous range of designs, materials and colours to suit all situations and occasions. Because of the wide range of styles available, chairs vary in height and width, but as a guide, a chair seat is 46 cm from the ground, the height from the ground to the top of the back is 1 m and the depth from the front edge of the seat to the back of the chair is 46 cm.

Plastics and fibreglass are now used extensively to produce dining room chairs. These materials are easily moulded into a single-piece seat and back to fit the body contours, with the legs usually being made of metal. The advantages are that these are durable, easily cleaned, lightweight, may be stacked, are available in a large range of colours and designs and are relatively inexpensive. They are more often found in bars, lounges and staff dining rooms than in a first class hotel or restaurant.

The main considerations when purchasing chairs should be size, height, shape and the variety of seating required, for example, banquette (fixed bench seating as shown in Figure 3.6), armchairs, straight-backed and padded chairs, to give the customer a choice. Remember when purchasing chairs that the height of the chair must allow enough room for the diner to sit comfortably at the table. A leather or wool fabric is much better to sit on than PVC or man-made fibres which tend to become uncomfortable around the back and seat.

Figure 3.6 Restaurant area with traditional seating and with banquette seating shown on right of picture (image courtesy of Dunk Ink UK)

Tables

Tables come in three main shapes: round, square and rectangular. An establishment may have a mixture of shapes to give variety or tables of all one shape depending on the shape of the room and the style of service being offered. Square or rectangular tables will seat two to four people and two tables may be pushed together to seat larger parties, or extensions may be provided in order to cope with special parties, luncheons, dinners and weddings, etc. By using these extensions correctly a variety of shapes may be obtained, allowing full use of the room and enabling the maximum number of covers in the minimum space. The tabletop may have a plastic foam back or green baize covering which is heat resistant and non-slip so the tablecloth will not slide about as it would on a polished wooden top table. This type of covering also deadens the sound of crockery and tableware being laid. As a guide tables are approximately the following sizes:

Square
- 76 cm (2 ft 6 in) square to seat two people
- 1 m (3 ft) square to seat four people

Round
- 1 m (3 ft) in diameter to seat four people
- 1.52 m (5 ft) in diameter to seat eight people

Rectangular
- 137 cm x 76 cm (4 ft 6 in x 2 ft 6 in) to seat four people, extensions being added for larger parties

Sideboards

The style and design of a sideboard (or workstation) varies from establishment to establishment and is dependent upon:
- the style of service and the food and beverages on offer
- the number of service staff working from one sideboard
- the number of tables to be served from one sideboard
- the amount of equipment it is expected to hold.

It is essential that the sideboard is of minimum size and portable so that it may be easily moved if necessary. If the sideboard is too large for its purpose it is taking up space, which could be used to seat more customers. Some establishments use smaller fixed sideboards and also use tray jacks (movable folding tray stands, as illustrated in Figure 3.7) when serving and clearing.

Figure 3.7 Example of a tray jack

The material used in the make-up of the sideboard should blend with the rest of the decor. The top of a sideboard should be of a heat resistant material that can be easily washed down. After service the sideboard is either completely emptied out or restocked for the next service. In some establishments the waiters are responsible for their own equipment on their station. If sideboards are restocked after service, the sideboard will also carry its own stock of linen. Thus, in this example a sideboard has everything necessary to equip a particular waiter's station or set of tables.

Figure 3.8 Examples of sideboards (images courtesy of Euroservice UK)

The actual lay-up of a sideboard depends on its construction (the number of shelves and drawers for tableware, etc.) and on the type of menu and service offered. The lay-up of the sideboard will vary according to the needs and style of service and presentation of the establishment. However, within an establishment it is preferable that all sideboards should be laid up in the same way so that staff become used to looking for a certain item in a certain place and thus facilitating speedy service. For examples of the items that may be found in a sideboard see Section 6.2, p.193.

3.8 Linen

There are many qualities of linen in present day use, from the finest Irish linen and cotton to synthetic materials such as nylon and viscose. The type of linen used will depend on the class of establishment, type of clientele and cost involved, and the style of menu and service to be offered. The main items of linen normally to be found are described below.

Tablecloths
- 137 cm x 137 cm (54 in x 54 in) to fit a table 76 cm (2 ft 6 in) square or a round table 1 m (3 ft) in diameter
- 183 cm x 183 cm (72 in x 72 in) to fit a table 1 m (3 ft) square
- 183 cm x 244 cm (72 in x 96 in) to fit rectangular shaped tables
- 183 cm x 137 cm (72 in x 54 in) to fit rectangular shaped tables

Slip cloths
- 1 m x 1 m (3 ft x 3 ft) used to cover a slightly soiled tablecloth.

Napkins (serviettes)
- 46–50 cm (18–20 in) square if linen
- 36–42 cm (14–17 in) square if paper

Buffet cloths
- 2 m x 4 m (6 ft x 12 ft) – this is the minimum size; longer cloths will be used for longer tables

Waiter's cloths or service cloths
- Servers use these as protection against heat and to help to keep uniforms clean.

Tea and glass cloths

- These are used for drying items after washing; tea cloths should be used for crockery and glass cloths for glassware. The best are made of linen or cotton and are lint free.

Use and control of linen

Linen should be used only for its intended purpose in the restaurant and not for cleaning purposes, as this often results in permanent soiling which will render the item unusable in the future.

Linen should be stored on paper-lined shelves, the correct sizes together, and with the inverted fold facing outward, which facilitates counting and control. If the linen is not stored in a cupboard it should be covered to avoid dust settling on it.

The stock of clean linen is usually issued upon receipt of a requisition signed by a responsible person from the service department. A surplus linen stock is usually held in the food service area in case of emergency.

At the end of each service the dirty linen should be counted, recorded and sent to the issuing department to be exchanged for clean. Because of the high cost of laundering, where a tablecloth is perhaps only a little grubby, a slip cloth can be placed over it for the succeeding service.

A range of disposable linen, including napkins, place mats and tablecloths, are available in varying colours and qualities. There are also now reversible tablecloths with a thin polythene sheet running through the centre that prevents any spillages from penetrating from one side to the other. Although the expense of such items may seem high, there are many advantages and comparable laundry charges may well be higher. For more information on disposables, see Section 3.12 (p.83).

3.9 Crockery

The crockery must blend in with the general decor of the establishment and also with the rest of the items on the table. An establishment generally uses one design and pattern of crockery, but when an establishment has a number of different service areas it is easier, from the control point of view, to have a different design in each service area. Nowadays manufacturers produce a range of patterns and styles and will guarantee a supply for a period of ten years in order to be able to replace breakages, etc.

When purchasing crockery the general points previously identified in Section 3.1 (p.55) should be borne in mind. Other factors to consider are described below.
- Every item of earthenware should have a complete cover of glaze to ensure a reasonable length of life.
- Crockery should have a rolled edge to give added reinforcement at the edge. (Note that hygiene is most important – chipped crockery can harbour germs.)
- The pattern should be under rather than on top of the glaze. However, this demands additional glaze and firing. Patterns on top of the glaze will wear and discolour very quickly. Crockery with the pattern under the glaze is more expensive but will last longer.
- Crockery must be dishwasher-proof.

Some manufacturers stamp the date, month and year on the base of the item. From this, the life of the crockery can be determined with some accuracy. Crockery that is produced as being suitable for the foodservice industry is often referred to as 'hotelware'. Manufactures also tend to give trade names to their hotelware to indicate strength or durability. Some examples of these names are:

- Vitreous
- Vitresso
- Vitrock
- Ironstone
- Vitrex
- Vitrified
- Steelite.

Foodservice crockery

There are various classifications of foodservice crockery. Although referred to as crockery here (and throughout the book), all glazed tableware was traditionally referred to as china. Items include:

- flatware, for example, plates and saucers and serving flats
- cups and bowls, for example, tea and coffee cups, soup and sweet bowls and serving dishes
- hollow-ware, for example, pots and vases.

Types of crockery

Bone china

This very fine, hard china is expensive. Decorations are only found under the glaze. It can be made to thicker specifications for hotel use. The price of bone china puts it out of reach of the majority of everyday caterers and only a few of the top-class hotels and restaurants use it. Metalised bone china has been developed specially for the hospitality industry. It contains added metallic oxides to make it much stronger than bone china.

Hotel earthenware

Vitrified (or vitreous) earthenware is produced in the United Kingdom in vast quantities. It is the cheapest but least durable hotelware although it is much stronger than regular domestic earthenware. There is a standard range of designs and patterns in varying colours.

Domestic weight earthenware is lighter and thinner than hotel earthenware (or vitrified hotelware). Because of its short life, lack of strength and possible high breakage rate it is not regarded as suitable for commercial use.

Stoneware

This is a natural ceramic material traditionally made in the United Kingdom and fired at a very high temperature, about 1,200 °C–1,315 °C (2,200 °F). It is shaped by traditional handcrafting techniques so there are a wide variety of shapes and finishes available, from matt to a high gloss glaze. It is non-porous and extremely durable with high thermal and shock resistance. The price is slightly higher than earthenware due to its long-life guarantee.

Porcelain

This is of a different composition with a semi-translucent body, normally cream/grey, and has a high resistance to chipping.

Crockery sizes

A wide range of crockery items are available (see Figure 3.9(a)) and their exact sizes will vary according to the manufacturer and the design produced. As a guide, the sizes are as follows:

- Side plate: 15 cm (6 in) diameter
- Sweet plate: 18 cm (7 in) diameter
- Fish plate: 20 cm (8 in) diameter
- Soup plate: 20 cm (8 in) diameter
- Joint plate: 25 cm (10 in) diameter
- Cereal/sweet bowl: 13 cm (5 in) diameter
- Breakfast cup and saucer: 23–28 cl (8–10 fl oz)
- Teacup and saucer: 18.93 cl (6 $\frac{2}{3}$ fl oz)
- Coffee cup and saucer (demi-tasse): 9.47 cl (3½ fl oz)
- Teapot: 28.4 cl (½ pint)
  56.8 cl (1 pint)
  85.2 cl (1½ pint)
  113.6 cl (2 pint)

Other items of crockery required include:

- consommé cup and saucer
- soup bowl/cup
- platter (oval plate)
- salad crescent
- egg cup
- butter dish
- teapot

- hot water jug
- coffee pot
- milk jug
- cream jug
- hot milk jug
- sugar basin
- salt and pepper pots.

Although crockery has been the traditional medium for presenting and serving food, there is now an increasing trend to use contemporary styles of glassware instead. Figure 3.9(b) gives examples of both traditional crockery and also contemporary styled glassware that can be used as alternatives to crockery.

Figure 3.9(a) Selection of crockery – traditional style

Figure 3.9(b) Selection of contemporary tableware

Storage

Crockery should be stored on shelves in piles of approximately two dozen. Any higher may result in their toppling down or damage to plates at the bottom of the stack because of the weight bearing down on them. Crockery should be stored at a convenient height for placing on and removing from the shelves without fear of accidents occurring. If possible crockery should be kept covered to prevent dust and germs settling on it.

3.10 Tableware (flatware, cutlery and hollow-ware)

Tableware includes all items of flatware, cutlery and hollow-ware and may be classified as follows:
- flatware in the catering trade denotes all forms of spoon and fork, as well as serving flats
- cutlery refers to knives and other cutting implements
- hollow-ware consists of any other item, apart from flatware and cutlery, for example, teapots, milk jugs, sugar basins and serving dishes.

Manufacturers produce varied patterns of flatware, hollow-ware and cutlery in a range of prices to suit all demands. There are also patterns of flatware and cutlery that are scaled down to three-quarters the normal size specifically for tray service.

Although traditionally flatware included spoons and forks and cutlery referred to knives, the modern usage of these terms has changed. All spoons, forks and knives used as eating implements are now referred to as cutlery. The term 'cutlery' is therefore used throughout the rest of this book.

The majority of foodservice areas use either plated silverware or stainless steel. Once again, the points mentioned previously concerning purchasing should be borne in mind. In addition, when purchasing flatware and cutlery it is important to consider:
- the type of menu and service offered
- the maximum and average seating capacity
- the peak demand period turnover
- the washing-up facilities and their turnover.

Figure 3.9 Examples of cutlery (left to right: fish fork, sweet (small) fork, joint fork, fish knife, small (side) knife, joint knife, coffee spoon, tea spoon, soup spoon, sweet spoon, table (service) spoon).

Silver

Manufacturers will often quote 20-, 25- or 30-year plate. This denotes the length of life a manufacturer may claim for their plate subject to fair or normal usage. The length of life of silver also depends upon the weight of silver deposited. There are three standard grades of silver plate – full standard plate, triple plate and quadruple plate.

In silver-plated tableware two grades have been specified:
1   Standard for general use.
2   Restaurant thicker grade for restaurant use and marked with an 'R'.

The minimum thickness of silver plating quoted should give a life of at least 20 years, depending on usage.

The hallmark on silver indicates two things: the two symbols represent the standard of silver used and the Assay office responsible. The two letters are the maker's mark and the date letter.

Plain cutlery and flatware is more popular than patterned for the simple reason that it is cheaper and easier to keep clean. The best investment is knives with handles of hard soldered silver plate, nickel or good stainless steel. Handles are an important factor in cutlery. Plastic materials, however, are much cheaper and usually satisfactory.

Silver cleaning methods

All the service silver should be cleaned on a rota basis. It is the duty of the head plate person to ensure that this is carried out and that all silver is cleaned regularly. Obviously items that are in constant use will require more attention. The head plate person will also put on one side any articles of silver that are broken or that require buffing up or re-plating, so that they may be sent to the manufacturer for any faults to be corrected.

There are various methods of silver cleaning and the method used generally depends on the size and class of establishment. The main methods used are summarised in Table 3.3.

Table 3.3 Summary of silver cleaning methods

Method	Description
Silver dip	Items to be cleaned are completely immersed in dip in a plastic bowl for a very short time, rinsed in clean water and polished with a tea cloth. This is a very quick method but is hard on metal if left in dip too long
Burnishing machine	Items to be cleaned are placed in a drum containing ball bearings, soap powder and water. The drum rotates and the tarnish is rubbed off. All items are rinsed in hot water and dried with a tea cloth
Polvit	Items to be cleaned are placed in an enamel or galvanised iron bowl within which is the Polvit aluminium metal sheet containing holes, together with some soda. At least one piece of silver needs contact with the Polvit. Boiling water is poured onto the silver being cleaned. A chemical reaction causes the tarnish to be lifted. After three to four minutes remove silver and rinse in boiling water. Drain and then polish with a clean, dry tea cloth
	A simpler version of this may be used for silver fork tips that have become tarnished. An aluminium saucepan on the stove, half filled with gently boiling water, can be used to put fork tips into for a short time. The forks need to touch each other and the side of the saucepan at the same time for the chemical reaction to take place. This easily removes the tarnishing and is less harmful to the silver than using silver dip

Method	Description
Plate powder	Pink powder is mixed with a little methylated spirit to a smooth paste. The smooth paste is rubbed well onto the tarnished silver with a clean piece of cloth. The article is left until the paste has dried which is then rubbed off with a clean cloth. The article must be rinsed well in very hot water and given a final polish with a clean dry tea cloth. For a design or engraving use a small toothbrush to brush the paste into the design and a clean toothbrush to remove it. This method is both time-consuming and messy, but produces very good results. (Information based on that obtained from the Cutlery and Allied Trades Research Association (CATRA).)

Stainless steel

Stainless steel tableware is available in a variety of grades. The higher priced designs usually incorporate alloys of chromium (which makes the metal stainless) and nickel (which gives a fine grain and lustre). Good British flatware and cutlery is made of 18/8 or 18/10 stainless steel – this is 18 per cent chromium and 8 per cent nickel. It should be noted however that the harder the metal used for the cutting edge the more difficult it is for the manufacturer to gain a sharp edge due to the metal's hardness.

Stainless steel is finished by different degrees of polishing:
- high polish finish
- dull polish finish
- light grey matt, non-reflective finish.

Stainless steel resists scratching far more than other metals and may therefore be said to be more hygienic. Although it does not tarnish it can stain. Special cleaning products for stainless steel can be used to keep stainless steel looking clean and polished, for example there is a commercial powder that is applied with a wet sponge or cloth and rubbed on the surface before being rinsed off.

Table knives require attention to keep the sharpness of the blade. Table knives are normally sharpened, according to the recommendations of the Cutlery and Allied Trades Research Association (CATRA), to approximately a 60 ° edge angle (compared to the 30 ° for the Chef's knife). Traditionally table knives were sharpened with a plain edge (that is, without serrations, scallops or indentations on the edge). Today many knives found in the foodservice industry have much thicker blades and the cutting edges are serrated. There is a well-established myth that for a table knife to work well it must be serrated. However, a serrated knife simply tears the meat piece rather than cutting it.

Specialised service equipment

There is an almost unlimited range of flatware, cutlery and hollow-ware in use in the catering industry today. These items are those necessary to give efficient service of any form of meal at any time of the day. Everyone is familiar with the knife, fork, spoon, flats, vegetable dishes and lids, entrée dishes and lids, soup tureens, teapot, hot water jugs, sugar basins and so on that we see in everyday use. Over and above these, however, there are a number of specialist items of equipment provided for use with specific dishes. Some of these more common items of specialist equipment are shown in Table 3.4, together with a brief note of the dishes that they may be used for.

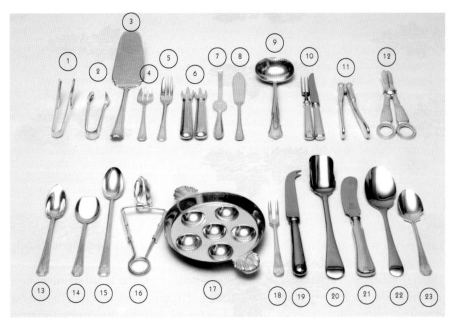

Figure 3.11 Specialised service equipment as listed in Table 3.4

Table 3.4 Items of specialised equipment and their use

Equipment	Use
1 Asparagus holder	Used to hold asparagus spears when eating
2 Sugar tongs	Required for cube sugar
3 Pastry slice	Sweet trolley – serving portions of gâteau
4 Oyster fork	Shellfish cocktail/oysters
5 Pastry fork	Afternoon tea
6 Corn-on-the-cob holders	One to pierce each end of the cob
7 Lobster pick	To extract the flesh from the claw
8 Fish knife	To break the fish and push it onto the fork
9 Sauce ladle	Service from sauce boat
10 Fruit knife and fork	Dessert – cover
11 Nutcrackers	Dessert – fruit basket
12 Grape scissors	To cut and hold a portion of grapes
13 Grapefruit spoon	Grapefruit halves
14 Ice cream spoon	For all ice cream dishes served in coupes
15 Sundae spoon	Ice cream sweet in a tall glass
16 Snail tongs	Used to hold the snail shell
17 Snail dish	Dish is round with two ears, having six indentations to hold a portion (6) of snails
18 Snail fork	Used to extract the snail from its shell

Equipment	Use
19 Cheese knife	Cheese board
20 Stilton scoop	Service of Stilton cheese
21 Butter knife	To serve a butter portion
22 Gourmet spoon	Sauce spoon for cover
23 Preserve spoon	Used with preserve/jam dish

Storage

In larger establishments the silver room (also known as the plate room) is a separate service area in which a complete stock of tableware required for the service of meals, together with a slight surplus stock in case of emergency, is stored. Tableware for banqueting service may be of a different design and kept specifically for that purpose within the banqueting department. In smaller establishments it is often combined with the wash-up area.

Large tableware items such as flats, salvers, soup tureens and cloches are often stored on shelves, with all the flats of one size together and so on. All shelves should be labelled showing where each different item goes. This makes it easier for control purposes and for stacking; heavier items should go on lower shelves and smaller and lighter items on higher shelves as this helps to prevent accidents. All tableware, together with the smaller items such as cruets, butter dishes, special equipment, table numbers and menu holders, can be stored in drawers lined with green baize. This helps to prevent noise and stops the various items sliding about and scratching when in the drawer.

Theoretically all tableware should be stored in a room or cupboard that can be locked, since it constitutes a large part of the capital investment of the foodservice operation. Cutlery may be stored in cutlery trolleys or trays ready for use, which can also be locked in a store.

Staffing

For large operations there may be a head plate person with a number of staff under them. In smaller establishments duties are often combined with the wash-up. It would then be the duty of either the washing-up staff or the waiting staff to ensure that all the service tableware is kept clean.

3.11 Glassware

Well-designed glassware combines elegance, strength and stability, and should be fine rimmed and of clear glass. All glassware should be clean and well-polished.

Glassware contributes to the appearance of the table and the overall attraction of the service area. There are many standard patterns available to the foodservice operator. Most manufacturers now supply hotel glassware in standard sizes for convenience of ordering, availability and quick delivery. Modern drinking glasses take many new forms and shapes, although all are primarily designed to meet the needs of the range of drinks offered. Examples of drinking glasses and their use are shown in Figure 3.12.

Cocktail glasses: for cocktails generally and smaller: for Pink Lady and White Lady

The saucer: for Champagne cocktails and Daisies. Not really used much now

The tulip: all Champagne and sparkling wines and also for Buck's Fizz and the Grasshopper

The flute: for sparkling wines generally and also for Brandy Alexander and Kir Royale

Paris goblet: in various sizes and used for wines, waters and beers. Also used for Cobblers, Pina Colada and Green Blazer

Worthington: for bottled beers, soft drinks and for Pimms, Coolers and long drinks such as Fruit Cups

Rocks/Old Fashioned glass: also known as whisky glass, often used for any spirits and mixers. Also used for drinks such as Old Fashioned and Negroni

Highball/Collins glass: used for spirits and mixers and for Highballs, John Collins, Tom Collins, Mint Julep, Tequila Sunrise and Spritzers

Brandy balloon: small for brandies and for B & B and brandy and liqueur-based cocktails, for frappés and for liqueurs. Larger for long drinks such as Pimms

Sour glass: for spirits and mixers and for sours and as an alternative to rocks glass

Martini Cocktail glass: for Dry, Medium and Sweet Martinis and Manhattans but also used for other cocktails

Slim Jim: for spirits and mixers and for sours and as an alternative to highball glass

Copita (sherry): mainly for sherry but also used for sweet wines

Elgin: traditional glass used for sherry in single and double measure (Schooner) sizes. Also in smaller version used for liqueurs

Port or sherry (dock) glass: used for both ports and sherries and also for sweet wines

Lager/pilsner: different sizes used for bottled and draught lager beers

Beer (straight): traditional beer glass in different sizes for half and full measures of any beers and also beer based mixed drinks

Beer (dimple): traditional beer glass in different sizes for half and full measures of any beers and also beer based mixed drinks, including Black Velvet and also Pimms

Figure 3.12 Examples of drinking glasses and their uses

A wine glass should be plain and clear so that the colour and brilliance of a wine can be clearly seen. It should have a stem for holding the wine glass so that the heat of one's hand does not affect the wine on tasting. There should be a slight incurving lip to help hold the aroma and it should be large enough to hold the particular wine being tasted. Although standard goblets can be used for a range of wines there are various glass shapes that are traditionally associated with certain wines. Examples of these are shown in Figure 3.13.

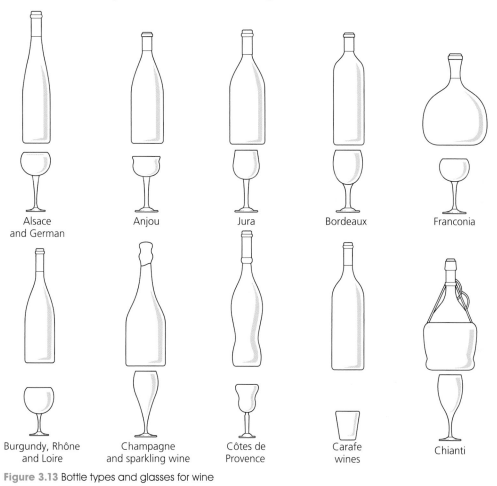

Figure 3.13 Bottle types and glasses for wine

Type and sizes of glassware

Glass is produced from sand (silicon dioxide), which is combined with other substances to produce particular characteristic properties. The mixture is heated to a very high temperature, which forms a molten mass. This glass is either blown or moulded to different shapes and then allowed to cool and solidify. The various types of glass used in the hospitality industry are described below. Examples of sizes for drinking glasses are shown in Table 3.5.

Table 3.5 Examples of sizes for glassware

Glass	Size
Wine goblets	14.20, 18.93, 22.72, 28 cl (5, 6⅔, 8, 10 fl oz)
Flûte/tulip	18–23 cl (6–8 fl oz)
Saucer champagne	18–23 cl (6–8 fl oz)
Cocktail glasses	4–7 cl (2–3 fl oz)
Sherry, Port	5 cl (1.75 fl oz)
Highball	23–28 cl (9–10 fl oz)
Lowball	18–23 cl (6–8 fl oz)
Worthington	28–34 cl (10–12 fl oz)
Lager glass	28–34 cl (10–12 fl oz)
Brandy balloon	23–28 cl (8–10 fl oz)
Liqueur glass	2.5 cl (0.88 fl oz)
Tumbler/Slim Jim	28.40 cl (½ pint)
Beer	25–50 cl (½–1 pint)

Soda lime glass

This glass contains sand, soda ash and limestone as the principal ingredients. It is used for everyday relatively inexpensive glassware.

Lead crystal

This form of glass includes sand, red lead and potash, which produces a slightly softer glass of high brilliance. The surface can be left plain or can be cut to produce prismatic effects and sparkle.

Borosilicate glass

This is glass made with the addition of borax, which increases its hardness and heat resistance. This type of glass is used for flame ware.

Tempered and toughened glass

This glass has additional treatments to make it more resistant to the effects of heat. It is mostly used as ovenware glass, but the treatment is also used to produce glassware that needs to withstand heavy usage.

Glassware decoration

The surface of glassware may be decorated by:
- cutting to produce patterns or badging
- sand-blasting to texture the surface
- acid-etching to make patterns or to add badging
- engraving using grinding wheels to add patterns
- surface printing with patterns from transfers.

As well as being used for drinking glasses, jugs and vases, etc., contemporary glassware is now used as an alternative to crockery for the presentation and service of food (see Section 3.9, p.71).

Storage and cleaning

Drinking glasses are normally stored in a glass pantry and should be placed in single rows on thin plastic grid matting, upside down to prevent dust settling in them. Plastic racks made specifically for the purpose of stacking and storing glasses are another alternative. Such racks are also a convenient method of transporting glassware from one point to another, reducing breakages. Tumblers and other straight-sided glassware should not be stacked inside one another as this may result in breakages and can cause accidents to staff.

Most day-to-day glassware used in the industry can be washed using dishwashers, although this is not recommended for some types of glassware. This includes lead crystal and other forms of fine glassware, which should be hand washed. Over time most glassware will become milky in appearance and will then need to be replaced. Finer glassware will become like this very quickly, unless hand washed.

Glass decanters should also be hand washed. They can also be cleaned using a proprietary denture cleaner. An alternative product contains small ball bearings that are put into the decanter with warm water and a small amount of detergent. The decanter is then moved so that the ball bearings move around inside it. Afterwards the decanter is emptied though a filter so as to reclaim the ball bearings for use another time. The decanter is then thoroughly rinsed in hot water. After cleaning and rinsing, decanters should be stood upside-down on special stands made for the purpose, or on plastic or wooden dowels set into a wooden base (to prevent the decanters falling over). This ensures that the decanters drain and dry fully and no limescale deposits build up inside.

3.12 Disposables

There has been considerable growth in the use of disposables or 'throw-aways' as they are sometimes called and this is due to a number of factors:
- the need to reduce costs
- the difficulty of obtaining labour for washing up
- to reduce the high cost of laundering
- improved standards of hygiene
- breakage cost minimisation
- reduction in storage space required
- changes in cooking and storage technology, for example, cook/chill and cook/freeze
- the needs of transport caterers on trains, boats and planes
- the development of fast-food and takeaway operations
- increased customer acceptability.

Although many establishments use disposables to cut costs, they must be attractive, presentable and acceptable to the client and help to attract customers. The choice of which disposables to use may be determined by:

- necessity because of operational needs for:
  - outdoor catering
  - automatic vending
  - fast food
  - takeaways
- cost considerations such as:
  - traditional forms of service equipment
  - cost of laundry
  - wash-up costs.

Types of disposables

The main varieties of disposables are generally used as follows:

- storage and cooking purposes
- service of food and beverages, for example, plates, knives, forks, cups
- decor – napkins, tablecloths, slip cloths, banquet roll, place mats
- hygiene – wipes
- clothing, such as aprons, chef hats, gloves
- packaging – for marketing and presentation purposes.

Normal restaurant linen may be replaced by disposable serviettes, place mats, tray cloths, tablecloths and coasters, etc. Today, most forms of disposables can be of various colours, patterned or have the house-style motto or crest reproduced on them. The vast range of colours available also allows for changes in a service area with different colours being used for each meal.

Throwaway packs of knives, forks and spoons are more convenient and hygienic where the turnover of custom is very high over very short periods of time. This might apply in industrial canteens and transport catering. Throwaway packs eliminate delays at service points where the speed of washing-up is inadequate.

A considerable advance in the range of disposables available has been the introduction of disposables whose approximation to crockery tableware is very close. For instance, they may have a high quality, overall finish and a smooth, hard, white surface. Plates are strong and rigid with no tendency to bend or buckle and a plasticising ingredient ensures that they are greaseproof and moisture-proof, even against hot fat and gravy. Oval meal plates, snack trays and compartmentalised plates are all available to the caterer.

Environmental issues

When purchasing disposable items it is important to consider products that are environmentally friendly. With the development of new materials many disposable products are now totally compostable and biodegradable, as they are made from renewable resources such as:

- sugar cane fibre off cuts – very similar to conventional paper products and used for bowls, plates and cups
- clear polylactic acid (PLA) from carbon stored in plants such as corn and used for cups, containers and straws. Unsuitable for hot liquids but can be frozen
- cornstarch cutlery, made from a starch-based polymer and chalk
- bamboo ware, used to make plates, bowls, cups and cutlery from reconstituted bamboo.

Advantages of disposables

- **Equipment and labour**: disposables reduce the need for washing-up equipment, staff and materials.
- **Hygiene**: usage improves the standard of hygiene in an establishment.
- **Time**: disposables may speed up service, for example, for fast food.
- **Properties**: disposables have good heat retention and insulation properties.
- **Marketing**: disposables can be used as a promotional aid.
- **Capital**: usage reduces the amount of capital investment.
- **Carriage**: they are easily transported.
- **Cost**: disposables may be cheaper than hiring conventional equipment.

Disadvantages of disposables

- **Acceptability**: customer acceptability may be poor.
- **Cost**: disposables can be more expensive than some conventional equipment.
- **Storage**: back-up quantities are required.
- **Supply**: there is heavy reliance on supply and delivery time.
- **Environment**: unless they are made from renewable resources and are completely biodegradable they have a negative impact on the environment.

3.13 Automatic vending

In the broadest sense, automatic vending may be defined as selling by automation. It is a form of automatic retailing using one of the following methods of payment:
- coin
- banknote
- money card
- token
- free vend.

Vending can be used to provide either services and facilities or consumables, for example:

- service and facilities:
  - TV time
  - gas
  - water
  - electricity
  - shoe cleaning
  - car parking
  - toilets
  - baggage store
- consumables:
  - hot and cold beverages
  - meals
  - confectionery
  - tobacco
  - alcoholic drinks.

Types of foodservice vending machine

Within foodservice operations, automatic vending mainly is used for the supply of food and beverages, both hot and cold. Vending machines are found in canteens, factories, offices, industrial concerns, railway stations, garages, motorway service stations, schools, hospitals, leisure centres and hotels. Vending machines used for foodservice operations include the following.

● Merchandiser: customer can view the products on sale, for example, confectionery machines. Can be used for refrigerated drinks (bottles and cans) and pre-packaged meals and snacks. Can also be used for hot meals and snacks through internal heating.
● Hot beverage vendor: mixes the powdered ingredients with hot water to produce the product.
● In-cup system: ingredients are already in individual cups to which hot water is added.
● Cold beverage vendor: by use of post-mix syrup and water (carbonated or non-carbonated).
● Micro-vend system: provides a range of hot or cold foods from which the customer may make a selection and heat in an accompanying microwave oven.

The number and type of machines required will depend on their location, type and number of people they are providing a service for, cost factor and the variety of food and beverage items required.

Figure 3.14 Examples of foodservice vending machines

The machines required might be installed either individually or in small groups, to supplement the conventional catering establishment or to cover a small sales demand that does not warrant the expense of employing extra labour and plant. The opposite to this would be the installation of a complete vending service where demand is highly volatile, space is limited and the use of staffed operations would be uneconomical.

General factors that should be considered prior to purchasing foodservice vending equipment may be summarised as follows:

● Cup sales: may be one to two drinks per person per day when charged but could double if offered free.
● Ingredient capacity: related to required periods of restocking.
● Number of selectors (items) available: this will often relate to the demand (anticipated number of customers).
● Hygiene: ease of cleaning.
● Extraction efficiency: for heat/steam systems.
● Restocking: ease of filling.
● Maintenance: regular servicing contract.

- **Physical dimension/acceptability**: whether the machine will fit into the environment and blend in with the decor.
- **Siting**: as close as is feasible to those using the machine, that is, either on the work floor or in a food service area so as to maximise use.
- **Weight (floor loading)**: ease of moving for cleaning and siting purposes.
- **Availability of services**: power and plumbing.
- **Capital available**: whether the machine should be leased or purchased.
- **Training**: whether staff can be trained easily to replenish, clean and maintain machines.
- **Policy**: there must be clear guidelines linked to failure of a machine and insurance cover.

Advantages of foodservice vending

The machines themselves may be used in conjunction with the conventional kitchen production. At the same time they relieve some of the pressure of work on the counter hands and cashier by taking some of the customers away from the counter and to the machines. This is especially true where only hot or cold beverages are required together with a limited range of snacks for a certain percentage of those being catered for. Other advantages are:

- **round-the-clock service**: automatic vending machines can provide a 24-hour service
- **low cost**: automatic vending machines are cheaper to operate than conventional methods of service
- **food cost control**: this is a great advantage because automatic vending allows for strict portion control
- **economy of labour**: results in a reduction in the foodservice wages bill
- **natural tea break**: with the advent of these machines the fixed tea break has given way to the natural tea break, which can increase staff productivity
- **fresh beverages**: while a main meal may be served, if beverages are available by machine then they are fresh and taken as and when required
- **variety**: automatic vending machines offer a variety of hot and cold snacks and beverages, all contained within a space considerably smaller than would be necessary for conventional forms of production and service
- **reduced wastage**: as long as customer demand has been correctly gauged, wastage can be reduced to a minimum
- **ease of maintenance**: a member of the permanent staff should be trained to replenish and clean the vending machines daily.

Disadvantages of vending

There are disadvantages to automatic vending in relation to the total operation that should be considered before making a final decision on usage, including:

- **speed of service**: for a beverage this is approximately 10 seconds; a cafeteria operator would be faster. Conventional systems are more suitable for large-scale operations
- **quality**: although quality has improved for both the product and its packaging, customer resistance still exists
- **human presence**: there may be very little, if any, human presence. Manufacturers have researched this problem and attempted to overcome it with attractively designed and colourful machines
- **electricity**: vending machines are subject to power failure and power surges

- **maintenance**: automatic vending machines require daily servicing and cleaning. Depending upon the style of operation, the machines may require servicing and cleaning twice a day
- **vandalism**: most modern machines are robust, but can be vandalised resulting in loss of revenue through lack of available service
- **breakdown**: it can take vital service hours to repair a vending machine.

Cleaning of vending machines

Automatic vending machines are neither self-cleaning nor self-maintained and human assistance is therefore required. Regular maintenance is required if vending machines are to run smoothly and without the problems of mechanical breakdown. The type of vending machine and the service demand upon it will determine its service requirements.

Daily cleaning and replenishment is nearly always required, although demand may necessitate additional daily visits for cleaning and replenishment.

Staff should be trained to clean and replenish vending machines. Key factors to be considered are shown below.

- Clean at times when demand is lowest to avoid unnecessary loss of sales.
- Avoid electrical accidents by using the minimum amount of water while cleaning and preferably disconnect the machine from the mains supply.
- Read the supplier's recommendations carefully and use only nominated cleaning agents.
- Ensure the temperature controls are functioning correctly.
- Ensure all sales items are clearly visible and operating instructions are easy to follow.
- When replenishing the machine, check the sell-by dates and put older items to the front.
- Ensure all packaging and labelling is correct.
- Check slow moving sales items very carefully for the correct use-by dates and any deterioration in the commodity.
- Refill appropriate containers with the relevant powders for the products being sold.
- Ensure as appropriate that cups, plates and napkins are available in the machines.
- Always wipe down the complete outside of the vending machine to project an image of good hygiene.

> **Note:** At all times extreme care must be taken concerning the various aspects of hygiene and food safety when food and beverages are being served in this way.

Chapter 4

The menu, menu knowledge and accompaniments

4.1 Purpose of the menu

Originally the bill of fare (English) or menu (French) was not presented at the table. Banquets generally consisted of two courses, each made up of a variety of dishes, anything from 10 to 40 in number. The first set of dishes were placed on the table before the diners entered – hence the word 'entrée' – and, when consumed, these dishes were removed or relieved by another set of dishes – hence the words 'relevés' or 'removes'. This style of service was referred to as *service à la française*.

The word 'menu' dates back to the eighteenth century, although the custom of making a list of the courses for a meal is much older. Modern menus first appeared during the early nineteenth century, in the Parisian restaurants of the Palais-Royal. At this time, France, and later other countries, adopted the style of service referred to as *service à la russe*. In this system of service one course is served after another throughout the meal.

The menu is primarily a selling aid. The design of the menu should be appealing and interesting to the customer so it encourages them to view its contents. Clear information that is easily found and followed will make the customer feel more at home and will assist in selling the menu.

Design considerations of the menu include:
- size and shape
- artwork/colour
- ease of handling
- logical flow of information.

Other considerations are:
- providing a clear and accurate description of the dishes
- clear indication of pricing
- stating whether a service charge is included or not
- the inclusion of dietary information.

Menus can be presented in a variety of ways. These include:
- single laminated cards
- fold out cards with inserts from the size A5 and above
- iPads
- chalk boards
- white boards
- printed signs, sometimes illuminated from behind
- projections onto table tops.

4.2 Classic menu sequence

Over the last 100 or so years the sequence of the European menu has taken on a classical format or order of dishes. This format is used to lay out menus as well as to indicate the order of the various courses. Although the actual number of courses on a menu, and dishes within each course, will depend on the size and class of the establishment, most follow the classic sequence. This sequence is as follows:

1 **Hors d'oeuvres**: Traditionally this course consisted of a variety of compound salads (see p.112) but now includes such items as pâtés, mousses, fruit, charcuterie and smoked fish.

2 **Soups (potages)**: Includes all soups, both hot and cold.

3 **Egg dishes (oeufs)**: There are a great number of egg dishes beyond the usual omelettes, but these have not retained their popularity on modern menus.

4 **Pasta and rice (farineux)**: Includes all pasta and rice dishes. May be referred to as farinaceous dishes.

5 **Fish (poisson)**: This course consists of fish dishes, both hot and cold. Fish dishes such as smoked salmon or seafood cocktails are mainly considered to be hors d'oeuvres dishes and therefore would be served earlier in a meal.

6 **Entrée**: Entrées are generally small, well garnished dishes which come from the kitchen ready for service. They are usually accompanied by a rich sauce or gravy. Potatoes and vegetables are not usually served with this course if it is to be followed by a main course. If this is the main meat course then it is usual for potatoes and vegetables to also be offered. Examples of this type of dish are tournedos, noisettes, sweetbreads, garnished cutlets or filled vol-au-vent cases.

7 **Sorbet**: Traditionally sorbets (sometimes now called granites) were served to give a pause within a meal, allowing the palate to be refreshed. They are lightly frozen water ices, often based on unsweetened fruit juice, and may be served with a spirit, liqueur or even Champagne poured over. Russian cigarettes also used to be offered at this stage of a meal.

8 **Relevé**: This refers to the main roasts or other larger joints of meat which would be served together with potatoes and vegetables.

9 **Roast (rôti)**: This term traditionally refers to roasted game or poultry dishes.

10 **Vegetables (légumes)**: Apart from vegetables served with the Relevé or Roast courses, certain vegetables (e.g. asparagus and artichokes) may be served as a separate course, although these types of dishes are now more commonly served as starters.

11 **Salad (salade)**: Often refers to a small plate of salad that is taken after a main course (or courses) and is quite often simply a green salad and dressing.

12 **Cold buffet (buffet froid)**: This course includes a variety of cold meats and fish, cheese and egg items together with a range of salads and dressings.

13 **Cheese (fromage)**: Includes a range of cheeses and various accompaniments, including biscuits (water, Ryvita, digestive, cream crackers), breads, celery, grapes, apples and chutneys. This course can also refer to cheese-based dishes such as soufflés.

14 **Sweets (entremets)**: Refers to both hot and cold puddings.

15 **Savoury (savoureux)**: Sometimes simple savouries, such as Welsh rarebit or other items on toast, or in pastry, or savoury soufflés, may be served at this stage.

16 **Fruit (dessert)**: Fresh fruit, nuts and sometimes candied fruits.

17 **Beverages**: Traditionally this referred to coffee but nowadays includes a much wider range of beverages, including tea, coffee (in both standard and de-caffeinated versions) as well as other beverages such as tisanes, milk drinks (hot or cold) and proprietary drinks such as Bovril, Horlicks or Ovaltine. These are commonly available throughout the day, with a choice of milks, creams (including non-dairy creamers) and sugars (including non-sugar sweeteners).

Note: Although listed here to indicate the sequence for meals, beverages are not counted as a course as such and therefore should not be included when the number of courses for a meal is stated. Thus if a meal is stated as having four courses, this means that there are four food courses and that the beverages at the end are an addition to these.

The classic menu sequence outlined above is based on a logical process of taste sensations. This classic sequence also provides the guide for the compilation of both à la carte and table d'hôte menus (see below for definitions), as is evident in many examples of modern menus. However, a number of courses are often now grouped together. At its most simple this might comprise:

● starters – courses 1 to 4
● main courses – courses 5, 6 and 8 to 12
● afters – courses 13 to 16
● beverages – course 17

This sequence is also used as a guide for the compilation and determination of the order of courses for event and special party menus.

This sequence shows the cheese course after the main course and before the sweet course. However, the sweet course is still sometimes offered before the cheese course.

> **Note:** The modern European classic menu sequence outlined here is derived from traditional European (mainly Franco-Russian, Swiss and English) cuisine and service influences. The menu structure and menu sequence can change considerably within the various world cuisines. Menu terms also vary, for instance in the USA a main course is commonly called an entrée and sweets are commonly called dessert. The term 'dessert' is also now becoming more commonly used to denote sweets generally.

4.3 Classes of menu

Menus may be divided into two classes, traditionally called table d'hôte (table of the host) and à la carte (from the card).

Table d'hôte menu

The key characteristics of the table d'hôte menu are:
● the menu has a fixed number of courses
● there is a limited choice within each course
● the selling price is fixed
● the food is usually available at a set time.

À la carte menu

The key characteristics of the à la carte menu are:
● the choice is generally more extensive
● each dish is priced separately
● there may be longer waiting times as some dishes are cooked or finished to order.

Some menus offer combinations of these two classes, with a number of menu items being offered together at a set price and other menu items being priced separately.

Sometimes the term 'menu du jour' is used instead of the term 'table d'hôte menu'. Another menu term used is 'carte du jour' (literally 'card of the day') or 'menu of the day', which can also be a fixed meal with one or more courses for a set price. A 'prix fixe' (fixed price) menu is similar.

A 'tasting menu' ('menu degustation') is a set meal with a range of courses (often between 6 and 10). These tasting menus are offered in restaurants where the chef provides a sample of the range of dishes available on the main menu. These tasting menus can also be offered with a flight (selection) of wines (sometimes this can be a different wine for each course). For all classes of menu the price of the meal might also include wine or other drinks.

Figure 4.1 Example of a table d'hôte menu (courtesy of The Ritz Hotel, London)

THE RITZ RESTAURANT

ARTS DE LA TABLE

BRESSE CHICKEN £
Demi-Deuil En Vessie
Serves two people

COTE DE VEAU £
Truffled Creamed Potatoes and Madeira Sauce
Serves two people

VENISON WELLINGTON £
Celeriac and Truffle Sauce
Serves two people

LEG OF BABY LAMB £
Truffle Pomme Dauphinois and
Artichoke Barigoule
Serves two people

Please allow a minimum of 30 minute preparation time

MENU SURPRISE

To be served for the whole table

SIX SEASONAL COURSES £
Designed by Chef John Williams

Any dietary requirements can be catered for,
please ask your waiter for assistance
Tobias Brauweiler Head Sommelier offers a
choice of classic or fine wines by the glass

Menu with Classic Wine Selection £155 per pers
Menu with Fine Wine Selection £185 per pers

Price includes Value Added Tax and Service

THE RITZ RESTAURANT

FIRST COURSES

SALAD OF QUAIL £22
Watercress and Wild Mushrooms

LOBSTER £24
Cucumber, Beetroot and Caviar

CELERIAC VELOUTE £18
Quail Egg and Black Diamond

DRESSED CRAB ROLL £22
Avocado and Charentais Melon

TERRINE OF GOOSE LIVER £23
Spiced Port, Pears and Hazelnut Cake

SALT BAKED CELERIAC £24
Smoked Brisket and Truffle

VAR SALMON £24
Avocado and Grapefruit Sabayon

LANGOUSTINE £24
Cauliflower and Spiced Apple

Price includes Value Added Tax and Service

Figure 4.2 Example of an á la carte menu (courtesy of The Ritz Hotel, London)

THE RITZ RESTAURANT

MAIN COURSES

DOVER SOLE £
Pumpkin, Mushrooms and Shellfish Sauce

NATIVE LOBSTER £
Carrot Fondant, Ginger and Lime

TURBOT £
Fennel, Walnuts and Brown Butter Sauce

TOURNEDOS OF BEEF £
Smoked Celeriac and Truffle Sauce

LOIN OF LAMB £
Herb Crust, Artichoke and Smoked Garlic

VENISON £
Red Cabbage, Celeriac and Duck Liver

BRESSE DUCK £
Chestnut, Orange and Brussels Sprouts

PIGEON £
Lovage, Pomme Anna and Apple

Price includes Value Added Tax and Service

THE RITZ RESTAURANT

DESSERTS

CHOCOLATE SOUFFLÉ £14
Vanilla Chantilly and Hazelnut Ice Cream

TRUFFLED CHESTNUT MONT BLANC £20

APPLE PARFAIT £16
Vanilla and Calvados Ice Cream

VANILLA YOGHURT PARFAIT £15
Rhubarb, Ginger and Warm Doughnut

HAZELNUT SEMI-FREDDO £17
Chocolate and Vanilla

VANILLA BRÛLÉE £14
Pear and Date

LEMON BERGAMOT £16
White Chocolate and Yoghurt

CRÊPES SUZETTE £36
Serves two people
Please place your order at the beginning of the meal
Our maitre d'hotel will be delighted to prepare them
at your table

BRITISH CHEESE £16
Selection from Trolley

Price includes Value Added Tax and Service

ALL DAY DINING

STARTERS

Pomodoro tomato, red pepper and pesto soup	£8.50
Spicy corn fed chicken and coriander velouté with ginger wonton	£8.25
Smoked organic Scottish salmon Old England	£16.00
Parma Ham, white balsamic and mango	£12.00

SALADS & SANDWICHES

Classic Blue Fin Tuna Nicoise	£13.00
℣ Salad with avocado, tomato and asparagus	£14.00
Classic Caesar Salad	10.00
with corn fed chicken	£13.50
with Tiger prawns and avocado	£15.00
Confit duck salad with saladaise potatoes	£14.50
Crotin goats cheese, poached pear, chicory and walnut salad	£14.00
100% pure Angus beef burger with hand cut chips	£16.00
Croque Madame - baked chicken, Gruyère cheese with fried free range egg	£15.50
Croque Monsieur ham and Gruyère cheese	£15.50

℣ Club with corn fed chicken, and hand cut chips

Baked Ruben on rye pastrami, sauerkraut, Savora mustard and Montgomery cheddar

Angus beef steak sandwich with Pomodoro tomatoes, onion rings and iceberg lettuce

All sandwiches served on either bloomer, rye bread or sliced white a

MAIN

Pink Paris mushroom risotto	£16.75
Deep fried plaice fillets and chips with mushy peas	£17.00
Seared Scottish Salmon, spring onion mashed potatoes and grain mustard sauce	£18.50
Tiger prawn penne pasta, garlic and crispy shallots	£18.00
Tomato tart, goats cheese, roquette and confit onions	£17.50
Rump of English lamb with thyme and seasonal vegetables	£20.50

FROM THE GRIDDLE

Corn fed chicken Supreme 160g	£17.00
Angus rib eye steak 175g / 225g	£20.00 / £24.00
Castle of Mey sirloin steak 175g / 225g	£21.50 / £25.50

All griddle mains are served with a baked Pomodoro tomato with confit onions, field mushroom and gaufrette potatoes with either béarnaise, red wine or green peppercorn sauce

SIDE ORDERS

Petit pois, spring onion and mint	£3.75
Green beans and shallots	£3.75
Potatoes chipped, mashed or buttered	£3.75
Market vegetables	£3.75
Green salad with tomato and cucumber	£3.75

All prices are inclusive VAT. A discretionary 12.5% service charge will be added to your bill.

Figure 4.3 Example of All Day Dining menu (part of the Palm Court menu, courtesy of The Langham Hotel, London)

Other types of menus

There are many other types of menu found in the various sectors of the hospitality industry. Examples of these are:

- Breakfast menus and afternoon tea menus – refer to Chapter 8, p.294.
- Floor/room service menus, lounge service menus, hospital tray service menus, airline tray service menus and rail service menus – refer to Chapter 9, p.305.
- Event menus – refer to Chapter 11, p.385/392.

4.4 Menu development

Although the content of the menu is traditionally based on classic cuisine it is continually being updated by the latest food trends and fashions. Customers today are far more aware of different food commodities and cooking methods because of exposure to media such as television, the internet and food-related publications.

Principal influences on extent and style of menus

Decisions on the extent and style of the menu will take account of:

- the location of the establishment, both in terms of access for customers and for obtaining deliveries
- the available kitchen space and equipment. If space is limited then the storage, preparation and service of menu items will be restricted and a smaller menu will need to be put in place
- the knowledge and ability of kitchen staff to ensure they can produce the menu to the desired standard
- the level of service being offered
- the opening times of the operation
- the number of covers to be served in a specific time.

Principal influences on content

Customer demand is affected by a greater understanding of:

- the relationship between health and eating
- dietary requirements (these can be both medical and lifestyle choices)
- cultural and religious influences
- vegetarianism
- ethical influences
- seasonality and locally sourced foods.

Health and eating

The key issue in the relationship between health and eating is having a healthy diet. This means eating a balanced diet rather than viewing individual foods as somehow healthier or less healthy. Customers are increasingly looking for the availability of choice that will enable them to achieve a balanced diet as well as specific information on methods of cooking used, for example, low fat or low salt methods. General consensus suggests that the regular diet should be made up of at least on-third based on a range of bread, cereals, rice and potatoes; one-third based on a variety of fruit and vegetables; and the remainder based on dairy foods, including low fat milk, low fat meats and fish and small amounts of fatty and sugary food.

Figure 4.4 indicates the recommended daily intake for the different food groups. This is usually presented as five food groups. However, sometimes fruits and vegetables are classified as two separate groups, making six groups in total. This food pyramid shows these six food groups.

Figure 4.4 Diagram of recommended daily intake for different food groups

Because of these influences there is now a greater emphasis on offering alternatives such as low fat milks (for example, skimmed or semi-skimmed), non-dairy creamers for beverages, alternatives to sugar such as sweeteners, sorbets alongside ice creams, and polyunsaturated fat and non-animal fats as alternatives to butter. These influences have also affected cooking ingredients and methods, with the development of lower fat dishes, lighter cuisine and attractive and decent alternatives for non-meat eaters, including greater use of animal protein substitutes such as Quorn and tofu.

Dietary requirements

Customers may have a range of dietary requirements based on medical and/or on lifestyle choices. There are a variety of medical conditions, including allergies, which are more common than was previously understood. Customers may therefore require a certain diet for medical reasons (including the prevention of allergic reactions). Such customers will need to know about the ingredients used in a dish since eating certain ingredients may make them very ill and may even be fatal.

To aid the customer in making an appropriate choice, menu items that are suitable for a vegetarian diet may be identified with a 'V' and those containing nuts may be identified with an 'N' next to their description. Although such customers will usually know what they can and cannot eat, it is important that when asked, a server is able to accurately describe the dishes so that the customer can make the appropriate choice.

The server should *never* guess and if in doubt, should seek further information. Some examples of dietary requirements are given in Table 4.1.

Table 4.1 Examples of dietary requirements

Allergies	Food items that are known to cause allergies include the gluten in wheat, rye and barley (known as coeliac), peanuts and their derivatives, sesame seeds and other nuts such as cashew, pecan, brazil and walnuts, as well as milk, fish, shellfish, eggs and tropical fruits. Sometimes these foods can cause anaphylactic shock resulting in the lips, tongue or throat swelling dramatically over a very short period of time. The result can be fatal so prompt medical treatment is needed in such cases
Diabetic	This refers to the inability of the body to control the level of insulin within the blood. An appropriate diet may include foods listed in the low cholesterol section below and the avoidance of dishes with high sugar content
Low cholesterol	Diets will include polyunsaturated fats and may include limited quantities of animal fats. Other items eaten may include lean, poached or grilled meats and fish, fruit and vegetables and low fat milk, cheese and yoghurt
Low sodium/salt	This requires a reduction in the amount of sodium or salt consumed. Diets will include low sodium/salt foods and cooking with very limited or no salt

Cultural and religious dietary influences

Various faiths have differing requirements with regard to the dishes/ingredients that may be consumed and these requirements often also cover preparation methods, cooking procedures and the equipment used. Examples are given in Table 4.2 below.

Table 4.2 Dietary requirements according to the various faiths

Hindus	Do not eat beef and rarely pork. Some Hindus will not eat any meats, fish or eggs. Diet may include cheese, milk and vegetarian dishes
Jews	Only 'clean' (kosher) animals may be consumed. Jews do not eat pork or pork products, shellfish or animal fats and gelatine from beasts considered to be unclean or not slaughtered according to the prescribed manner. There are restrictions placed on methods of preparation and cooking. The preparation and eating of meat and dairy products at the same meal is not allowed
Muslims	Will not eat meat, offal or animal fat unless it is halal (i.e. lawful, as required under Islamic Dietary Law) meat. Will not consume alcohol, even when used in cooking
Sikhs	Do not eat beef or pork. Some will keep to a vegetarian diet. Others may eat fish, mutton, cheese and eggs. Sikhs will not eat halal meat
Rastafarians	Will not eat any processed foods, pork or fish without fins (e.g. eels). Will not consume tea, coffee or alcohol
Roman Catholics	Few restrictions on diet. Usually will not eat meats on Ash Wednesday or Good Friday. Some keep with the past requirement for no meat to be eaten on Fridays. Fish and dairy products may be eaten instead

Vegetarianism

Vegetarianism may derive from cultural, religious, moral, ethical or physiological considerations. It is therefore important that food descriptions are accurate.

The various forms of vegetarianism are summarised in Table 4.3 below.

Table 4.3 Forms of vegetarianism

Vegetarians: semi	Do not eat red meats, or all meats other than poultry, or all meats. Diet will include fish and may include dairy produce and other animal products
Vegetarians: lacto-ovo	Do not eat meat, fish or poultry but may drink milk, eat milk products and eggs
Vegetarians: lacto	Do not eat meat, fish, poultry and eggs but may drink milk and eat milk products
Vegans	Do not eat any foods of animal origin. Diet will mainly consist of vegetables, vegetable oils, cereals, nuts, fruits and seeds
Fruitarians	More restricted form of vegetarianism. Excluded are all foods of animal origin together with pulses and cereals. Diet may include mainly raw and dried fruit, nuts, honey and olive oil

Ethical influences

Customers have become increasingly aware of ethical issues, such as:
- ensuring sustainability of foods consumed
- fair trade
- the acceptability or otherwise of genetically modified foods or irradiated foods
- reducing food packaging and food waste
- reducing the effects of food production and transportation on the environment generally.

Seasonality and locally sourced foods

There is a trend towards using more seasonal and locally sourced food and beverage items, when the quality, taste, freshness and nutritional value are all at their peak and when supplies are more plentiful and cheaper. For foodservice businesses, the benefits can include:
- improved menu planning, as suppliers can give information in advance on what they are able to provide
- more reliable products and service, with greater flexibility to respond to customer needs
- increased marketing opportunities through making a feature of using locally sourced food and beverage items and through special promotions related to local and seasonal food and beverage specialities
- support for training of staff from local suppliers.

Legal considerations of food service are summarised in Section 12.1, p.381 and information about how to meet customer needs is given in Section 12.2, p.383.

4.5 Menu and service knowledge

Knowledge about the product is at the core of successful food and beverage service. This knowledge enables the server to advise the customer of the content of dishes, the methods used in making the dishes and to ensure that the customer is provided with an appropriate service lay-up and the correct accompaniments.

The rest of this chapter provides information on the lay-ups, accompaniments and service for a selection of menu items by course. Additional information is contained in Annex A: Glossary of cuisine and service terms (p.427).

There are a number of dishes where traditional accompaniments are normally served. Accompaniments offered with certain dishes are mainly to assist in improving the flavour or to counteract richness. There are also traditions indicating the appropriate lay-up or cover for certain dishes. The sections that follow contain guides to these lay-ups and accompaniments. However, these guides are not intended to be prescriptive, as changes are constantly taking place and new accompaniments are tried. Also, the desire for healthier eating has led to a number of changes, for example, alternatives to butter such as Flora are often provided and frequently bread is not buttered in advance, thereby allowing the customer to choose his or her requirements. The availability of lower fat milks, non-dairy creamers and non-sugar sweeteners is also now standard.

For the lay-up the most important consideration is to aid eating. The use of fish knives and forks, for instance, is becoming less fashionable (the original reason for these Victorian items was as much to do with people wanting to show that their silver was new, rather than inherited, as it was to do with being able to keep these items separate from other items). Small (demi-tasse) coffee cups are now seen less often in restaurants although these cups are still used for espresso.

Main cooking methods

Food production (cooking) may be carried out in a variety of ways. The main cooking methods are described below.

- **Baking:** cooking in either a fan oven or conventional oven. Often referred to as 'dry' cooking.
- **Boiling:** cooking food in a simmering liquid.
- **Braising:** slow cooking in minimum liquid in a casserole dish with a lid.
- **Deep frying:** cooking by placing into deep fat held at a temperature of about 175–190 °C (350–375 °F).
- **Grilling:** quick and dry method of cooking food by radiant heat, either over heated charcoal or under electric or gas salamanders.
- **Microwave:** cooking or re-heating food using high frequency power in a microwave oven powered by electricity.
- **Poaching:** cooking in a minimum amount of liquid held at simmering point.
- **Roasting:** cooking with convected dry heat in the oven.
- **Shallow frying:** cooking in the minimum amount of heated fat or oil.
- **Steaming:** cooking heat is transferred from the water vapour (steam) to the food being cooked.
- **Stewing:** Very slow cooking of food items in their own juices and using the minimum amount of liquid, such as stock, in the process.
- **Water bath:** technique of vacuum packing ingredients and cooking them at low temperatures in a water bath. This is a slow and gentle process where moisture is not expelled and flavour is retained.

Sauces

Although there appears to be a wide variety of sauces, they are almost always variations on the same base sauces, as described in Table 4.4.

Table 4.4 Base sauces

Fond brun	Basic brown meat sauce
Velouté	White sauce using fish, meat, poultry or vegetable stock
Allemande	A velouté thickened with cream and egg yolks
Béchamel	Savoury white sauce made with milk
Tomato sauce	Made with fresh, tinned or puréed tomatoes
Mayonnaise	Cold sauce made from egg yolks, oil, vinegar, salt, pepper and mustard
Hollandaise	Hot sauce made from melted butter, egg yolks, shallots, vinegar and seasonings
Vinaigrette	Cold sauce made from mixing oil, vinegar and a selection of seasonings

These sauces provide the base for other sauces, by adding a variety of different ingredients. For example:

- cheese to a béchamel sauce to create a Mornay sauce
- whipped cream to a Hollandaise sauce to create sauce Mousseline
- tarragon and other herbs added to Hollandaise to make Béarnaise
- gherkins, capers, and fines herbes to mayonnaise to form tartare sauce.

Other food items

There are a variety of food items which support the service of a range of dishes. Some of these items have specific uses for particular dishes and others are used generally across a number of dishes. Table 4.5 below gives examples of food items used in food and beverage service.

Table 4.5 Food items used to support a range of dishes

Item	Description	Use
Aïoli/ailloli	Garlic mayonnaise	Cold fish dishes and as a salad dip, e.g. for crudités
Apple sauce	Purée of cooking apples, slightly sweetened, served hot but more usually cold	Roast pork, roast duck and roast goose
Balsamic vinegar	Aromatic vinegar, acid product made from sweet grape wine, aged in oak	Dressings
Cayenne	Hot, red pepper (actually a species of powdered capsicum)	Oysters, smoked salmon
Chilli sauce	Hot sauce, mostly Chinese made	With Chinese-style foods
Chilli vinegar	Vinegar flavoured with chillies	Oysters

Item	Description	Use
Chutney	Generic name for Indian sauces. Common varieties are sweet mango or hot mango, also Piccalilli and others such as the proprietary Branston Pickle	Indian chutneys for Tandoori and other Indian dishes. Other chutneys for cold meats, with cheeses and Ploughman's lunch
Cider vinegar	Acid product made from cider	Can be used in salad dressings. Viewed by some as a product for the health conscious
Cocktail gherkins	Small gherkins	Appetisers or garnish for charcuterie
Cocktail onions	Small, pearl onions	Appetisers or garnish for charcuterie
Cocktail sauces	Manufactured sauces of mayonnaise with added flavourings, e.g. tomato	Seafood cocktails
Corn oil	Light-flavoured oil made from corn	Dressings
Cranberry sauce	Sauce made from cranberries, usually available as a proprietary sauce. Can be served hot or cold	Roast turkey
Croûtons	Small cubes of fried or toasted bread	Garnish for soups and also used in some salad dishes, e.g. Caesar salad
Cucumbers, pickled	Pickled cucumbers	For meats, salad dishes, charcuterie and cheese
Cumberland sauce	Sweet-and-sour sauce including orange and lemon juice and zest, redcurrant jelly and port. Can be kitchen made or proprietary bottled	Game dishes and for charcuterie
Dill pickle	Pickled gherkins or cucumbers flavoured with dill	Meats, salad dishes, charcuterie and cheese
French dressing	Dressing made from oil and usually wine vinegar or lemon juice, with seasoning. Mustards and herbs may be added	Salads
Gherkins	Small pickled cucumbers	Charcuterie
Ginger	Spicy root used in many forms. Ground ginger is most common in restaurants	Melon
Groundnut oil	Bland oil made from groundnuts	Dressings
Horseradish sauce	Hot-tasting sauce made from horseradish root, usually available as proprietary sauce, often needs creaming down	Roast beef and Chicken Maryland and also for cold smoked fish dishes when creamed down
HP Sauce	Brown proprietary, spicy, vinegar-based sauce	Cold meats and other dishes
Indian pickles	Unsweetened hot pickles, featuring limes, mango, brinjals, etc.	Accompaniment for Indian (and other) savoury dishes
Kasundi	Hot Indian pickle featuring chopped mango	Accompaniment for Indian (and other) savoury dishes

Item	Description	Use
Ketchup, tomato	Sauce of tomato pulp, vinegar and sweetening. Usually available as a proprietary sauce	Grills, fish, burgers
Lemon	Citrus fruit (slices, segments or halves)	Infinite variety of uses, especially smoked fish, fried fish and a range of drinks including tea
Lime	Citrus fruit (slices, segments or halves)	Similar to lemon above
Malt vinegar	Acid product of brewed malted barley	Dressings and traditionally (in UK) for chips
Mayonnaise	Made from combination of oil and egg yolks, flavoured with vinegar, herbs and seasoning	Dressing for poached fish and sauce for salads
Mint jelly	Sweetish jelly made with mint. Proprietary versions often used	Roast lamb, as an alternative to mint sauce. Also offered with roast mutton
Mint sauce	Vinegar-based sauce with chopped mint and sweetening. Proprietary versions usually used	Roast lamb
Mustard, English	Generally the hottest. Available as powder for making up or as proprietary bottled, sometimes with other ingredients such as whole seeds	Roast beef, boiled beef, grills, cold meats, pâtés and as ingredient in dressings, e.g. vinaigrette
Mustard, other	Wide variety including French, au poivre, vert, Bordeaux, Meaux, Dijon, Douce, German (senf)	Cold meats, grills, dressings
Mustard sauce	Warm sauce, generally kitchen made, but also available as proprietary sauce	Traditionally grilled herring but is used for other meat and fish dishes
Oil (general)	Many varieties, usually low in unsaturated fats	Dressings and increasingly for cooking
Olive oil	Oil made from olive pressings (cholesterol free)	Dressings
Olives	Black or green fruit lightly pickled in brine	Appetisers but also garnish for food and drinks, or chopped as flavouring
Onions – pickled	Small onions pickled in malt vinegar (brown) or white vinegar (silver skin)	Cold meats, Ploughman's lunch
Oriental vinegars	Several varieties	Give character to dressings and food dishes
Paprika	Powdered, mild, red capsicum	Garnish on and in seafood cocktails
Parmesan	Italian hard cheese (grated or shredded)	Used in soups, e.g. minestrone and for pasta dishes
Parsley	Chopped or sprig	Garnish on wide variety of dishes. Sometimes deep fried with fried fish
Pepper	Ground white pepper	Traditional form of pepper in table shaker

Item	Description	Use
Peppercorns	Green are usually pickled in brine and soft	In food dishes
	White and black	Black used for the table in pepper mills but sometimes mixed
Piccalilli	Mixed pickle in thickened, spiced sauce (predominantly turmeric and sugar)	Cold meats, Ploughman's lunch, buffet, snacks
Piri-piri	Hot chilli sauce of Portuguese/African origin	Prawns, crayfish, chicken
Redcurrant jelly	Proprietary sauce	Traditionally offered with hare. Also traditionally offered with roast mutton but now often offered with roast lamb
Rouille	Provençale sauce made from pounded chillies, garlic and breadcrumbs (or cooked potatoes) blended with olive oil and fish stock	Used as accompaniment to boiled fish and fish soups such as bouillabaisse. If served with chicken bouillabaisse then chicken stock is used
Salt, refined	Ground table salt	Traditionally used as salt in table cellar or shakers
Salt, sea	Salt derived from evaporated sea water	Seasoning, especially with boiled beef and used in table grinders
Soya oil	Oil made from crushed soya bean	Dressings
Soy sauce	Clear, dark brown sauce, usually Chinese, made from soy beans	Chinese and sometimes other dishes
Sunflower oil	Light textured and flavoured oil from sunflower seeds	Dressings
Tabasco sauce	Hot, spicy, pepper proprietary sauce	Oysters, clams, other seafood and in other dishes
Tartare sauce	Mayonnaise-based sauce with addition of chopped gherkins, capers and lemon juice	All deep fried fish
Vinaigrette	Combination of oil and vinegar or lemon juice with seasoning. May also include mustards and herbs	Dressings
Wasabi	Finley grated root of the Wasabia japonica plant. Extremely strong flavour. Sometimes called Japanese horseradish	Used in paste form as condiment with sushi, sashimi and other oriental dishes
Wine vinegar	Acid product of wine, red or white	Dressings
Worcestershire sauce	Maceration of blend of spices and fruit in vinegar. Often known by the maker's brand name 'Lea and Perrins'	Tomato juice, Irish stew, Scotch broth, seafood cocktails and in dressings. Also used as a flavouring in a variety of other dishes

4.6 Hors d'oeuvres and other appetisers

Traditionally, hors d'oeuvres were a selection of salads, fish and meats (see Figure 4.5 and Table 4.6). The selection was served onto a cold fish plate and the cover was a fish knife and fork. The cover nowadays is more likely to be dictated by the type of food being served and its presentation. Oil and vinegar were also traditionally offered but this has become less common because such foods are usually already well dressed. Buttered brown bread is also offered less often, thereby allowing the customer a choice of breads and butter or alternatives.

Figure 4.5 Plated appertiser

Table 4.6 Example of common hors d'oeuvre items

Canapés	These are slices of bread with the crusts removed, cut into a variety of shapes, then toasted or fried in oil or butter and garnished. Garnishes can include smoked salmon, foie gras, prawns, cheese, asparagus tips, tomato, egg, capers, gherkins, salami and other meats
Eggs	These can be poached, presented in aspic or mayonnaise or hard-boiled, cut in two and garnished or stuffed with various fillings, which include the yolk
Fish	May include items such as anchovies, herring (fresh or marinated), lobster, mackerel (marinated, smoked or fresh), smoked eel (filleted or sliced) and prawns (plain, in cocktail sauce or in a mousse)
Meats	Includes items such as pâtés, ham (raw, boiled or smoked) and salamis of all varieties
Salads	Plain or compound. Examples of plain salads include fish and meat salads, cucumber salad, tomato salad, potato salad, beetroot salad, red cabbage and cauliflower. Compound salads include Russian (mixed vegetables in mayonnaise); Andalouse (celery, onions, peppers, tomatoes, rice and vinaigrette); Italienne (vegetable salad, cubes of salami, anchovy fillets and mayonnaise); and Parisienne (slices of crayfish, truffles, Russian salad and bound with mayonnaise and aspic)

Table 4.7 Examples of other appetisers

Asparagus (Asperges)	Fresh asparagus can be eaten hot with, for example, melted butter or Hollandaise sauce or cold with vinaigrette or mayonnaise. It is useful to place an upturned fork under the right-hand side of the plate to tip the plate so that the sauce will form in a well at the bottom of the plate towards the left-hand side. Can be eaten using a side knife and fork, an asparagus holder or the fingers. If with the fingers, then a finger bowl containing lukewarm water and a slice of lemon and a spare napkin should be offered
Avocado (Poire d'avocat)	Generally served in halves with a salad garnish on a fish plate. Can be served with vinaigrette (now more likely to be made with a wine vinegar), which is served separately, or with prawns in a cocktail sauce. There are also special dishes to hold half an avocado. Brown bread and butter is less common now. Alternative methods of presentation are also found, for example, where the avocado is sliced and fanned out. A side knife and sweet fork are then laid
Caesar salad	Salad of cos (or Romaine) lettuce, dressed with vinaigrette or other similar dressing (originally containing near-raw egg), garlic, croûtons and grated (or shaved) parmesan cheese. There are a number of variations to these ingredients. Side knife and sweet fork are laid. Sometimes this salad is served in a bowl
Caviar (Caviare)	The cover laid is a caviar knife (broad blade knife) or side knife on the right-hand side of the cover. Served onto a cold fish plate and accompaniments include blinis (buck wheat pancakes) or hot breakfast toast, butter, segments of lemon, chopped shallots and chopped egg yolk and egg white. Portion size is usually up to about 30 g (1 oz)
Charcuterie	This can include a selection of meat (mainly pork) items including Bayonne ham, salamis, smoked ham, Parma ham and also pâtés and terrines. Cover is a side knife and sweet fork or a joint knife and fork if taken as a main course. Accompaniments are peppermill and cayenne pepper, gherkins and sometimes onions. Occasionally a small portion of potato salad is offered. Bread is usually offered but brown bread and butter is now less common
Corn on the cob (Maïs naturel)	These are usually served with special holders which are like small swords or forks. Three wooden cocktail sticks in each end can be used, but avoid trying to use two sweet forks as it is possible to painfully catch teeth on the prongs. Although special dishes are available, a soup plate can be used to provide a reservoir for the melted butter or Hollandaise sauce. A peppermill is offered. A finger bowl containing lukewarm water and a slice of lemon and spare napkin is advisable
Fresh fruit	Either served on a plate or in a bowl. Eaten with a side knife and sweet fork (fruit knife and fork if available) if served on a plate and sweet spoon and fork if served in a bowl. Usually no accompaniment is offered although some people may like caster sugar. Both caster sugar and ground ginger are offered with melon if served alone. (For guéridon preparations of fruit see p.380)
Fruit cocktails	Usually served in a glass or some form of bowl. These are eaten with a teaspoon and caster sugar is offered, especially if grapefruit is included in the cocktail
Fruit juices	Usually served in a glass. Sometimes caster sugar is offered in which case a teaspoon should be given to stir in the sugar. For tomato juice, salt and Worcestershire sauce (shaken) are offered, and again a teaspoon should also be given to aid mixing in these accompaniments
Globe artichokes (Artichaut)	This vegetable is usually served whole as a starter. The edible portion of the leaves is 'sucked off' between the teeth after being dipped in a dressing (for example, vinaigrette if served cold or melted butter or Hollandaise sauce if served hot). The leaves are held with the fingers. The heart is finally eaten with a side knife and sweet fork. A finger bowl containing lukewarm water and a slice of lemon and a spare napkin are essential. There are special dishes for this vegetable, but a fish plate with a small bowl for the dressing will also suffice. In this case a spare plate for the discarded leaves will be needed. Alternatively a joint plate may be used

Gravlax (Gravadlax)	Salmon pickled with salt, sugar and dill. Usually eaten with a fish knife and fork or a side knife and sweet fork. Traditional accompaniments are a slightly sweetened sauce of mustard and dill and often half a lemon (which may be wrapped in muslin to prevent the juice squirting onto the customer when the lemon is squeezed). A variety of unbuttered breads are often offered, with butter and alternatives served separately
Mousses and pâtés	Normally these are eaten using a side knife and sweet fork. Hot, unbuttered breakfast toast or bread is offered. Butter or alternatives may be offered and other accompaniments appropriate to the dish itself, for example, lemon segments with fish mousses, although lemon is often offered with meat-based pâtés
Niçoise salad	There are a number of versions of this salad. Generally it includes boiled potatoes, whole French beans, tomatoes, hard-boiled eggs (quartered or sliced), stoned black olives, flakes of tuna fish and anchovy fillets. This salad is usually made up and plated. Vinaigrette is often offered
Other salads	Salads can be made up and served plated or constituted at the guéridon. Dressings vary. Cover is usually related to the main ingredient, i.e. fish knife and fork for fish-based salads but a side knife and sweet fork may be used for all. For guéridon service of salads see Section 10.5 (p.341)
Oysters (hûitres)	Cold oysters are usually served in one half of the shell on a bed of crushed ice in a soup plate. An oyster fork is usually offered and placed on the right hand side of the cover, but a small sweet fork can also be used. Oysters are usually eaten by holding the shell in one hand and a fork in the other. A finger bowl containing lukewarm water and a slice of lemon and an extra napkin may be offered. Accompaniments include half a lemon and the oyster cruet (cayenne pepper, pepper mill, chilli vinegar and Tabasco sauce). Traditionally brown bread and butter is also offered
Potted shrimps	A fish knife and fork or a side knife and sweet fork should be laid. Accompaniments include hot, unbuttered, breakfast toast (there is plenty of butter already in this dish), cayenne pepper, a peppermill and segments of lemon
Seafood cocktails (Cocktail de crevettes)	These are usually made up and served in a seafood cocktail holder, glass or bowl. A teaspoon and small fork/oyster fork are often laid for eating. Sometimes the cutlery is placed on the underplate and set on the table with the dish. Accompaniments are a lemon segment, peppermill, sometimes cayenne pepper and traditionally brown bread and butter, although this is less common now
Smoked salmon (saumon fumé)	Usually eaten with a fish knife and fork or a side knife and sweet fork. Traditional accompaniments are half a lemon (which may be wrapped in muslin to prevent the juice squirting onto the customer when the lemon is squeezed), cayenne pepper, peppermill and brown bread and butter. Nowadays a variety of unbuttered bread may be offered with butter and alternatives served separately. Oil is sometimes offered and also chopped onions and capers
Other smoked fish	As well as the accompaniments offered with smoked salmon, creamed horseradish has become a standard offering with all other smoked fish including trout, mackerel, cod, halibut and tuna
Snails (escargots)	Snail tongs are placed on the left and a snail fork on the right. The snails are served in an escargot dish, which has six or twelve indentations. French bread is offered for mopping up the sauce. Half a lemon (which may be wrapped in muslin to prevent the juice squirting onto the customer when the lemon is squeezed) may also be offered, and a finger bowl containing lukewarm water and a slice of lemon and an extra napkin is laid as part of the cover

Service of hors d'oeuvres and other appetisers

Many of these dishes are served plated but they may also be silver served. Some may also be prepared and served in the room, for example, caviar, pâté, seafood cocktails, smoked salmon, salads and dressings, and melon.

When the dishes are plated the cover is usually a small knife and fork. Sometimes fish knives and forks are presented with fish dishes. For other dishes usually the lay-up depends of the types of food being presented, for example, a prawn cocktail is often presented with a small fork and a teaspoon/oyster fork.

4.7 Soups

Soups are divided into a number of categories, including consommés, veloutés, crèmes, purées, potages, bisques (shellfish base soups) and broths. Examples of these are shown in Table 4.8. There are also various national soups and examples of these are shown in Table 4.9.

Table 4.8 Types of soup and service methods

Consommé	Clarified soup made from poultry, beef, game or vegetable bouillon. Usually served in consommé cups with a sweet spoon. These soups were once drunk from the cup using the handles and the spoon was provided to help in eating the garnish. The tradition continues in the use of the cup but it is now presented at the table on a consommé saucer or underplate. The handles on some styles of cups have become merely representative ears. Warmed Sherry or sometimes Madeira might be added to the consommé in the restaurant just before serving. Although consommé is usually served hot it can also be served cold or jellied (en gelée)
Veloutés, crèmes and purées	These soups are usually eaten from a soup plate on its underplate and with a soup spoon, although it is common now to see soup bowls of varying designs. Traditionally croûtons were only offered with purées and Cream of Tomato soup, but they are now commonly offered with a range of soups
Potages, broths and bisques	These are usually served in soup plates, set on underplates and eaten with a soup spoon, but again bowls of varying designs are also used. Bisques are soups with a shellfish base

Table 4.9 Examples of national soups

Batwinia (Russian)	Purée of spinach, sorrel, beetroot and white wine, with small ice cubes served separately. Served very cold
Bortsch (Polish)	Duck-flavoured consommé garnished with duck, diced beef and turned root vegetables. The accompaniments are sour cream, beetroot juice and bouchées filled with duck pâté. A soup plate is often used, as there are a large number of accompaniments
Bouillabaisse (French)	This is really a form of fish stew. Although a soup plate and soup spoon is used, it is common for a side knife and sweet fork to also be laid as part of the cover. Thin slices of French bread, dipped in oil and grilled (sippets), are offered as well as rouille (see Annex A: Glossary of cuisine and service terms, p.491)
Cherry (German)	Bouillon consisting of cherry purée, cherry juice and red wine, served with stoned cherries and sponge finger biscuits

Chowder (USA)	Chowders are thick soups usually containing seafood, potatoes and cream or milk. The most well-known is New England clam chowder made with potatoes, onion, bacon or salt pork, flour and clams. Served with clam cakes, which are deep fried balls of buttery dough with chopped clam inside
Cock-a-leekie (Scottish)	Veal and chicken consommé garnished with shredded leeks and chicken. Served with prunes. These may have been put into the soup plate at the service point
Gazpacho (Spanish)	A cold, tomato-based soup. It contains tomatoes, onions, breadcrumbs, peppers, cucumber, garlic, ice water, sugar and spices. Croûtons, diced cucumber, peppers, tomato and onion may all be offered as accompaniments. Served chilled in soup plates on underplates and eaten with a soup spoon
Kroupnich (Russian)	Barley and sections of poultry offal garnished with small vol-au-vents stuffed with poultry meat
Mille fanti (Italian)	Consommé with a covering of breadcrumbs, Parmesan cheese and beaten eggs
Minestrone (Italian)	Vegetable paysanne soup with pasta. Traditional accompaniments are grated Parmesan cheese and grilled flûtes
Miso (Japanese)	Miso is a paste made from fermented soya beans. The soup is made by adding this paste to dashi soup stock. The stock itself is made from bonito flakes and konbu seaweed. Ingredients that provide contrasts such as spring onion and the delicate tofu, and those that float and sink such as potatoes and seaweed, may be paired together and offered as a garnish at the last moment
Petit Marmite (French)	Beef and chicken-flavoured soup garnished with turned root vegetables and dice of beef and chicken. Served in a special marmite pot, which resembles a small casserole. This marmite pot sits on a dish paper on an underplate. A sweet spoon set on the right-hand side of the cover is used to eat this soup, as it is easier to get this spoon into the small pot. Accompaniments are grilled flûtes, poached bone marrow and grated (shaved) Parmesan cheese. Sometimes the bread and cheese are done as a croûte on top of the soup before serving at the table
Potage Germiny (French)	Consommé thickened before service with egg yolks and cream. Cheese straws are offered
Shchi (Russian)	Bortsch consommé, garnished with sauerkraut. Beetroot juice and sour cream are offered separately
Soupe à l'oignon (French)	French onion soup, often served in a consommé cup or soup bowl. Can be served with grilled flûtes and grated (shaved) Parmesan cheese but is often topped with a slice of French bread gratinated with cheese

Service of soup

Most soups are plated although they may also be silver served. Soups are usually eaten from a soup plate, placed on an underplate, and eaten with a soup spoon. However, it is common today to see soup bowls of varying modern designs, together with their underplate.

Consommé is traditionally served in a consommé cup on a consommé saucer and set on a fish plate. Traditionally eaten with a sweet spoon but a soup spoon is now more common. Consommé may be finished in the room by the addition of warmed (flambéed) sherry.

4.8 Egg dishes

Egg dishes as separate courses have become less common in recent years. Omelettes have retained their popularity while dishes such as oeuf en cocotte occasionally feature on menus. The egg dishes listed in Table 4.10 have specific service requirements.

Figure 4.6 Oeuf en cocotte

Table 4.10 Egg dishes and service requirements

Oeuf sur la plat	The egg is cooked in the oven in the oeuf sur la plat dish and is then served to the customer in this dish on an underplate. A sweet spoon and fork are used but a side knife may be given, depending on the garnishes. A sur la plat dish is a small, round, white earthenware or metal dish with two ears
Oeuf en cocotte	The egg is cooked in the cocotte dish and served in this dish with various garnishes. The dish is placed on a doily on an underplate and a teaspoon is used to eat the food. A cocotte dish is a small round earthenware dish with straight sides, about the size of a small teacup
Omelettes	As an egg course an omelette, with various savoury fillings, is eaten with a joint fork and is served onto a hot fish plate. The joint fork is placed on the right-hand side of the cover. Should the omelette be eaten as a main course it would be served onto a hot joint plate, the cover being a joint knife and fork, as potato and vegetables or salad would accompany this dish. Omelettes are often plated but may be served from a flat using two joint forks, two fish knives or a slice. The ends may also be trimmed as part of this service
Savoury soufflés	These are usually served in the ramekin dish they are baked in. This is placed on an underplate and the cutlery laid is a teaspoon and/or a small (sweet) fork

4.9 Pasta and rice dishes

Pasta and rice dishes are also referred to as farinaceous dishes and include all pastas such as spaghetti, macaroni, nouilles and ravioli and rice dishes such as pilaff or risotto. Also included are dishes such as Gnocchi Piedamontaise (potato), Parisienne (choux paste) and Romaine (semolina).

Figure 4.7 Pasta dish

Accompaniments

Grated Parmesan cheese is normally offered with all these dishes. Sometimes the Parmesan cheese is shaved from a large piece rather than grated.

Service of pasta and rice dishes

Most pasta and rice dishes are now served plated but may occasionally be silver served, for example gnocchi, pilaff or risotto.

For spaghetti, a joint fork should be laid on the right-hand side of the cover and a sweet spoon on the left. For all other farinaceous dishes a sweet spoon and fork are used, with the sweet spoon on the right and the fork on the left.

4.10 Fish dishes

A wide variety of fish and shellfish are available today. They provide a good source of protein and may be cooked and presented in many ways. The general accompaniments for fish dishes are shown in Table 4.11. Fish dishes with special service requirements are listed in Table 4.12.

Figure 4.8 Fish dish

Table 4.11 General accompaniments for fish dishes

Hot fish dishes with a sauce	Usually no accompaniments
Hot fish dishes without a sauce	These often have Hollandaise or another hot butter-based sauce offered. Lemon segments may also be offered
Fried fish which has been bread crumbed (à l'Anglaise)	These dishes often have tartare sauce or another mayonnaise-based sauce offered, together with segments of lemon
Fried or grilled fish dishes, not bread crumbed	These dishes are usually offered with lemon. Sometimes sauces such as Hollandaise or tartare are offered
Deep fried fish which has been dipped in batter (à l'Orly)	A (kitchen-made) tomato sauce is sometimes offered together with segments of lemon. Proprietary sauces can also be offered, as can vinegar if chips are being served
Cold poached fish dishes	Usually mayonnaise or another mayonnaise-based sauce such as Sauce Vert is offered, together with segments of lemon

Table 4.12 Fish dishes with special service requirements

Grilled herring (hareng grillé)	Served as a starter on a hot fish plate. A fish knife and fork was traditionally laid to complete the cover, but now more commonly a side knife and small/sweet fork completes the place setting. Usually served with a mustard sauce
Whitebait (blanchailles)	Served as a starter on a hot fish plate and traditionally eaten with a fish knife and fork. Nowadays more commonly a side knife and small/sweet fork would complete the cover. Accompaniments are cayenne pepper, peppermill, segments of lemon and brown bread offered with butter or alternatives
Mussels (moules marinière)	Usually served in a soup plate or bowl on an underplate with brown bread and butter, or more commonly now a variety of breads offered with butter or alternatives. Cayenne pepper may be offered. A fish knife and fork, or a side knife and small/sweet fork and sweet spoon are often laid for eating. A plate for the debris is usually placed on the table with a finger bowl containing lukewarm water and a slice of lemon together with a spare napkin
Cold lobster (homard froid)	Cover is a fish knife and fork or a side knife and small/sweet fork and a lobster pick together with a spare debris plate and a finger bowl, filled with lukewarm water and a slice of lemon together with a spare napkin. Lemon and sauce mayonnaise are the usual accompaniments
Sushi and sashimi	Wasabi and soy sauce

Service of fish dishes

Most main courses are plated but may also be silver served. Some can be finished and served in the room, for example, filleting sole or removing the black outer skin and bone from a cutlet of salmon.

For a fish course as a starter then often a fish knife and fork is laid, but a small knife and sweet fork may be used instead.

Traditionally, main course fish dishes were eaten with a fish knife and fork but this practice is declining. More often now a joint knife and fork are laid.

Oriental dishes are often serviced with chopsticks and sometimes a ceramic spoon. A sweet spoon might also be set.

4.11 Meats, poultry and game

Roast meats

In all cases roast gravy is offered. For dishes where the roast is plain (not roasted with herbs, for instance) the accompaniments are shown in Table 4.13.

Table 4.13 Accompaniments for plain roast meats

Roast beef (boeuf rôti)	Horseradish sauce, French and English mustards and Yorkshire pudding
Roast lamb (agneau rôti)	Traditionally mint sauce, although redcurrant jelly is sometimes also offered.
Roast mutton (mouton rôti)	Traditionally redcurrant jelly, although mint sauce is sometimes also offered. An alternative traditional accompaniment is a white onion sauce
Roast pork (porc rôti)	Apple sauce and sage and onion stuffing
Veau rôti	A thickened roast gravy and lemon, parsley and thyme stuffing

Boiled meats

Accompaniments for boiled meets are listed in Table 4.14.

Table 4.14 Accompaniments for boiled meats

Boiled mutton (mouton bouilli)	Caper sauce is traditionally served
Salt beef (silverside)	Turned root vegetables, dumplings and the natural cooking liquor
Boiled fresh beef (boeuf bouilli)	Turned root vegetables, natural cooking liquor, rock salt and gherkins
Boiled ham (jambon bouilli)	Parsley sauce or white onion sauce

Other meat dishes

Figure 4.9 Grilled steak

Table 4.15 Accompaniments for other meat dishes

Irish stew	This stew is often served in a hot soup plate and a sweet spoon is offered together with the joint knife and fork. The sweet spoon would be positioned outside the joint knife to the right of the cover. Accompaniments are Worcestershire sauce and pickled red cabbage
Curry (kari)	Served on a hot joint plate and eaten with a sweet spoon and joint knife and fork. The sweet spoon would be positioned outside the joint knife to the right of the cover. General accompaniments are poppadums (crisp, highly seasoned pancakes), Bombay Duck (dried fillet of fish from the Indian Ocean) and mango chutney. Also offered is a Curry Tray, which will have items such as diced apple, sultanas, sliced bananas, yoghurt and desiccated coconut as part of the selection available
Mixed grill and other grills	These dishes may be garnished with cress, tomato, straw potatoes and parsley butter. Various mustards (French and English) and sometimes proprietary sauces (tomato ketchup and brown sauce) are offered as accompaniments. The cover is a hot meat plate and a joint knife and fork
Steaks	Accompaniments and cover are as for mixed grill. Sometimes a steak knife (serrated cutting edge) replaces the joint knife. Sauce Béarnaise is offered with Chateaubriand (double fillet) and sometimes with other grilled steaks

Poultry, furred and feathered game

Figure 4.10 Roast chicken

Table 4.16 Accompaniments for poultry and furred and feathered game

Poultry	
Roast chicken (poulet rôti)	The accompaniments are bread sauce, roast gravy, parsley and thyme stuffing, game chips, grilled bacon rolls and watercress. Sage and onion stuffing is also served
Roast duck (caneton rôti)	Sage and onion stuffing, apple sauce and roast gravy are served
Wild duck (caneton sauvage rôti)	Roast gravy and traditionally an orange salad with an acidulated cream dressing is offered as a side dish
Roast goose (oie rôti)	Sage and onion stuffing, apple sauce and roast gravy
Roast turkey (dinde rôti)	Cranberry sauce, chestnut stuffing, chipolata sausages, game chips, watercress and roast gravy are the usual accompaniments
Furred game	
Jugged hare	Heart-shaped croûtons, forcemeat balls and redcurrant jelly
Venison (venaison)	Cumberland sauce and redcurrant jelly
Feathered game	
When roasted	The accompaniments for all feathered game such as partridge (perdreau), grouse (lagopède) and pheasant (faisan) are fried breadcrumbs, hot liver pâté spread on a croûte on which the meat sits, bread sauce, game chips, watercress and roast gravy

Service of meats poultry and game

Most main courses are plated although they may also be silver served. Some can also be prepared and served in the room, for example, meats carved at the table, steaks cooked at the table and the preparation of such dishes as Steak Diane. The cover is a joint knife and fork and a hot meat plate. Sometimes steak knives are offered. For oriental dishes, chopsticks and sometimes a ceramic spoon are usually offered. A sweet spoon and fork might also be set.

4.12 Potatoes, vegetables and salads

A wide variety of potatoes and vegetables, including salads, may be served with various main dishes and courses.

Figure 4.11 Potatoes and vegetables

Potatoes

There are four categories: floury, firm, waxy and salad potatoes, all of which have different uses. Potatoes are from the tuber family, which also includes items such as sweet potato, yams and Jerusalem artichoke.

Vegetables

Vegetables fall into a number of categories:

- **Roots**: such as carrots, parsnips, salsify and beetroot.
- **Bulbs**: such as onions and fennel.
- **Leaf**: such as chicory, spinach, cress and the various lettuces.
- **Brassicas**: such as broccoli, cabbage, cauliflower and pak choi.
- **Stems and shoots**: including asparagus, bean sprouts, celery, samphire and globe artichokes.
- **Fruiting**: including aubergine, avocado, cucumber, peppers and tomatoes.
- **Plantains**: such as ackee and breadfruit.
- **Mushrooms and fungi**: including field mushrooms, chanterelles, morels and truffles.

Salads

There are two main types of salad:

- **Plain salads**, which consist of two main types. These may be either green salads made up of green leaf ingredients or vegetable salads made up of one main vegetable ingredient which will dominate the overall flavour of the dish. Plain salad may often be served with a main course or as a separate course after a main course. Various types of dressings are either included in the salad or offered separately.
- **Compound salads**, which may be a plain salad plus other ingredients, such as meat, fish and mushrooms, or a combination of a number of ingredients, mixed together using specific dressings or sauces.

Table 4.17 Examples of salads

D'orange	Lettuce hearts, in sections, filleted orange, freshly made acidulated cream dressing
Endive	Hearts of lettuce, endive, sauce vinaigrette
Française	Lettuce hearts, sections of skinned tomato, hard-boiled egg, with vinaigrette offered separately
Japonaise	Lettuce, bananas, apple, tomatoes all in dice, shelled walnuts, fresh cream offered separately
Lorette	Corn salad, julienne of beetroot, raw celery heart and vinaigrette offered separately
Mimosa	Lettuce hearts, filleted orange, grapes skinned and stoned, sliced banana, sprinkled with egg yolk, acidulated cream dressing offered separately
Niçoise	French beans, tomato quarters, sliced potatoes, anchovies, capers, olives, vinaigrette
Russian	Macedoine of separately mixed cooked root vegetables including potato, often decorated with other ingredients such as tomatoes, eggs, anchovies, lobster, ham and tongue, and bound in mayonnaise sauce
Saison	Lettuce hearts plus other salad vegetables in season, vinaigrette offered separately
Verte	Lettuce hearts, vinaigrette offered separately

Service of potatoes vegetables and salads

Most often potatoes and vegetables are pre-plated, but may also be silver served onto the main plate alongside the main dish. No additional cutlery is required.

Potatoes, vegetables or salads can be separately pre-plated or silver served onto a side plate or crescent-shaped dish, separate from the main plate. This is positioned at the top left-hand corner of the cover. A separate sweet fork for the salad and service spoons and forks for the potatoes and vegetables may be offered.

Potatoes, vegetables or salads may also be placed on the table in multi-portion serving dishes from which the customers can serve themselves, using service spoons and forks (family service).

When a salad is served separately as a first course or after the main course the cover is:
- a cold fish plate or bowl such as a soup plate on an underplate
- a small (side) knife and sweet fork.

All salads should be served chilled, crisp and attractive in appearance. Remember a salad is not complete without a well-made salad dressing or sauce, such as vinaigrette or mayonnaise. For examples of salad dressings see Section 10.5, p.312.

For the preparation and service of salads and dressings at the guéridon, see Section 10.5, p.344.

- **Baked potato**: a baked potato (pomme au four) may be accompanied by cayenne pepper, peppermill and butter (or substitutes). Butter is not now automatically put on the top of the potato, but is offered separately, together with alternatives.

4.13 Cheese

Cheeses are distinguished by flavour and categorised according to their texture. They differ from each other for a number of reasons, mainly arising through variations in the making process. Differences occur in the rind and how it is formed and in the paste and the cooking process (relating here to both time and temperature). Cheeses also vary because the milk used comes from different animals such as cows, sheep and goats. The texture of cheese depends largely on the period of maturation.

Dependent upon use, cheeses may be purchased either whole or pre-portioned. Cheese should be stored:
- in a cool, dark place, with good air circulation or in a refrigerator
- with its original wrapping, otherwise it should be wrapped in either greaseproof paper, cling film or aluminium foil to prevent any drying out
- away from food items that absorb flavours/odours, such as dairy produce.

The recognised categories of cheese are:
- fresh
- soft
- semi-hard
- hard
- blue.

Examples of cheeses commonly available within each of the five categories are listed in Table 4.18.

Table 4.18 Examples of cheeses within the five categories

Fresh cheese	
Cottage	Unripened low fat, skimmed milk cheese with a granular curd. Originated in the USA and now has many variations
Cream	Similar to cottage cheese but is made with full fat milk. There are a number of different varieties available, some made from non-cow's milks
Mozzarella	Italian cheese made from buffalo milk but may now also be made from cow's milk
Ricotta	Italian cheese made from the whey of cow's milk. A number of other Italian varieties are available, made from sheep's milk
Soft cheese	
Bel Paese	This light and creamy Italian cheese has a name that means 'beautiful country' and was first produced in 1929
Brie	Famous French cheese made since the eighth century. Other countries now make this style of cheese, distinguishing it from the original French Brie by the addition of the name of the country or county of origin, e.g. German Brie, Somerset Brie
Camembert	Famous French cheese which is stronger and often more pungent than Brie
Carré de l'est	A soft cheese produced in France that is made from pasteurised cow's milk, and packed in square boxes. Like Camembert, it softens on ripening and is darker in colour than Brie. When ripe it has a mild flavour
Feta	Greek cheese made from both goat's and sheep's milk
Liptauer	Hungarian cheese spread made from sheep and cow's milk. Often found with various additions, such as onions, mustard or spices
Munster	French Vosges cheese similar to Camembert in shape but with an orange-red rind. American, German and Swiss versions are also available
Stracchino	Italian cheese originally from Lombardy. A soft, delicate cheese which now has a number of varieties
Semi-hard cheese	
Caerphilly	Buttermilk-flavoured cheese with a soft paste. Some people will find it almost soapy. Originally a Welsh cheese but now manufactured all over Britain
Cantal	French cheese from the Auvergne, similar to Cheddar
Cheddar	Classic British cheese now made all over the world and referred to as, for example, Scottish cheddar, Canadian cheddar
Cheshire	Crumbly, slightly salty cheese, available as either white or red. It was originally made during the twelfth century in Cheshire but is now made all over Britain
Derby	English Derbyshire cheese now more often known by the sage-flavoured variety, Sage Derby
Edam	A Dutch cheese that is similar to, but harder than, Gouda. It has a fairly bland, buttery taste and a yellow or red wax coated rind. It is sometimes flavoured with cumin
Emmenthal	The name of this Swiss cheese refers to the Emme Valley. It is similar to Gruyère, although it is softer and slightly less tasty

Esrom	Similar to the French Port Salut, this Danish cheese has a red rather than yellow rind
Gloucester/Double Gloucester	Full-cream, classic English cheeses originally made only from the milk of Gloucestershire cows
Gouda	Buttery textured, soft and mild flavoured well-known Dutch cheese with a yellow or red rind
Gruyère	Mainly known as a Swiss cheese, but both the French and Swiss varieties can legally be called by this name. It has small pea-size holes and a smooth, relatively hard texture. The French varieties may have larger holes
Jarlsberg	Similar to Emmenthal, this Norwegian cheese was first produced in the late 1950s. It has a yellow wax coating
Lancashire	Another classic English cheese similar to Cheshire (white Cheshire is sometimes sold as Lancashire)
Leicester	Mild flavoured and orange-coloured English cheese
Monterey	Creamy, soft American cheese with many holes. A harder version known as Monterey Jack is suitable for grating
Pont l'Evêque	Similar to Camembert, but square in shape, this French cheese originates from Normandy
Port Salut	Mild flavoured cheese with a name meaning 'Port of Salvation', referring to the abbey where exiled Trappist monks returned after the French Revolution
Tilsit	Strong flavoured cheese from the East German town of the same name where it was first produced by the Dutch living there. Now available from other parts of Germany
Wensleydale	Yorkshire cheese originally made from sheep or goat's milk but now made from cow's milk. This cheese is the traditional accompaniment to apple pie

Hard cheese

Kefalotyri	Literally Greek for 'hard cheese', this is a tasty cheese from Greece which is suitable for grating
Parmesan	Classic Italian hard cheese, more correctly called Parmigiano Reggiano. It is also known as the grated cheese used in and for sprinkling over Italian dishes, especially pasta, and also minestrone
Pecorino	Made from sheep's milk and used for grating or as a table cheese. Comes from southern Italy. Also available with added peppercorns as Pecorino Pepato from Sicily
Provolone	Smoked cheese made in America, Australia and Italy. Now made from cow's milk but originally from buffalo milk. Younger versions are softer and milder than the longer kept and more mature varieties

Blue cheese

Bleu d'Auvergne	Strong, spicy, full-flavoured cow's milk blue cheese from the Auvergne, with a lingering finish and a salty tang. Has a natural rind and the cheese is creamy and moist with a sharp aroma. Invented in 1845 by farmer Antoine Roussel, who used a needle to make holes in the cheese to allow air inside, facilitating mould veins to develop in the cheese
Blue de Bresse	Fairly soft and mild flavoured French cheese from the area between Soane-et-Loire and the Jura
Blue Cheshire	One of the finest of the blue cheeses which only becomes blue accidentally, although the makers endeavour to assist this process by pricking the cheese and maturing it in a favourable atmosphere

Danish Blue	One of the most well-known of the blue cheeses. Softish and mild flavoured, it was one of the first European blue cheeses to gain popularity in Britain
Dolcelatte	Factory-made version of Gorgonzola. The name is Italian for 'sweet milk' and the cheese is fairly soft with a creamy texture and greenish veining
Dorset Blue	A strong, hard-pressed cheese, being close textured and made from skimmed milk. It is straw-coloured with deep blue veins, rather crumbly and has a rough rind
Gorgonzola	Softish, sharp flavoured, classic Italian cheese with greenish veining, which is developed with the addition of mould culture
Roquefort	Classic, sheep's milk cheese from the southern Massif Central in France. The maturing takes place in caves which provide a unique humid environment which contributes to the development of the veining
Stilton	Famous and classic English cheese made from cow's milk. So called because it was noted as being sold in the Bell Inn at Stilton by travellers stopping there. According to legend it was first made by a Mrs Paulet of Melton Mowbray. Traditionally served by the spoonful but nowadays usually, and perhaps preferably, it is portioned. The pouring of port on to the top of a whole Stilton, once the top rind had been removed, was also popular but this practice has declined. The White Stilton has also become popular and is slightly less flavoursome than the blue variety

Service of cheese

If not plated, the cheese board or trolley will be presented to the customer containing a varied selection of cheeses in ripe condition together with sufficient cheese knives for cutting and portioning the different cheeses (see Figure 4.12 for examples of the methods for presenting, cutting and portioning). If cheese is wrapped in foil this must be removed by the waiter before serving. The waiter should remove the cheese rind if it is not palatable (edible). This is not necessary in the case of Camembert and Brie as the rind of these two French cheeses is palatable.

Cover
The cover for cheese is:
- side plate
- side knife
- sometimes a small/sweet fork.

Accompaniments
Accompaniments set on the table prior to the cheese being presented and served may include:
- cruet (salt, pepper, and mustard)
- butter or alternative
- celery served in a celery glass part filled with crushed ice, on an underplate
- radishes (when in season) placed in a glass bowl on an underplate with teaspoon
- caster sugar for cream cheeses
- assorted cheese biscuits (cream crackers, Ryvita, sweet digestive, water biscuits, etc.) or various breads.

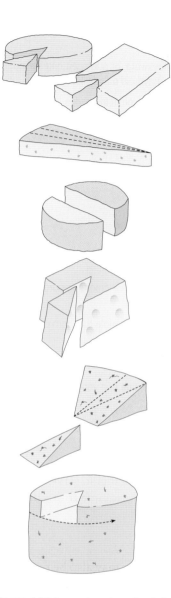

Round and square cheeses can be presented whole and then portioned by being cut into triangular pieces. Note that with square or oblong cheeses one of the cuts is at an angle.

Brie or similar type cheeses may be either presented whole or cut into triangular slices and then portioned by being sliced (much like a cake) as required.

Small soft cheeses such as goat's cheeses may be presented whole and then portioned by being cut in half or quarter as the customer requests.

Flattened or pyramid shaped cheeses may be presented whole and then portioned by being cut into small triangles by keeping one side of each cut at an angle.

Largish wedges of blue cheeses can be cut from a cylinder or half cylinder of cheese for presentation, and these wedges are then cut into smaller wedges for service. Other cheeses bought in cylinders or half cylinders can be cut and presented for service and then portioned in the same way.

A cylinder (truckle) or half cylinder of cheese may also be presented whole and then portioned by individual wedges being cut from it. In order to do this the cheese is first cut around at about 25 to 30 cm. This is also an alternative to the tradition of Stilton being portioned by scooping the cheese out from the top of the cylinder after removing the top rind.

Figure 4.12 Examples of methods for cutting cheeses

4.14 Sweets

Most sweets are generally served onto sweet plates or are pre-plated. Puddings and various hot dishes can be pre-plated onto or served into sweet plates or bowls. The lay-up is usually the sweet spoon and fork. Often the customer may require a sugar sifter. Various items may require different lay-ups, for instance a sundae spoon, ice cream spoon or teaspoon. The main consideration is always to aid eating.

The range of possible sweets is very extensive and varied. Examples of types of sweet dishes are listed in Table 4.19.

Table 4.19 Examples of types of sweet dishes

Bavarois, mousses, syllabubs	Either served in individual dishes or glassware, or portioned and served. Examples are: Bavarois au framboise, Bavarois au vanille
Charlottes	Moulds lined with sponge and filled with bavarois in various flavours and sometimes with fruits
Coupes and sundaes	Usually ice cream and various fruit combinations, served in coupe dishes or sundae dishes
Creams	Such as Chantilly (sweetened whipped cream flavoured with vanilla), custard (Sauce Anglaise) and dishes such as Egg Custard or Crème Brûlée
Fritters (beignets)	Such as beignets de banane, beignet de pomme
Fruit dishes	Such as fruit salads, poached fruits (Compôte) and baked apples
Gâteaux	Au chocolat, au café
Ices (ice cream, frozen yoghurt) and sorbets (water ices)	Presented in various forms, including bombs (ice cream preparations made into bomb shapes using moulds)
Omelettes	With a variety of fillings and flavourings, for example rum, jam or apple
Pancakes	With a variety of fillings, for example cherries or other fruits
Pies, flans and other pastries	Examples include flan aux poires, Bakewell tart, Dutch apple tart
Puddings	Including Bread and Butter, Cabinet, Diplomate and various fruit puddings
Soufflés	Hot or cold. Includes soufflé au citron, soufflé au café, soufflé au fromage

There are no particular accompaniments to sweets and the choice of whether to serve on a plate or in a bowl is often dependent on the texture of the sweet dish, for example fruit salad in a bowl and gâteau portions on a sweet plate.

Service of sweets

Many sweet dishes are plated and some may also be silver served. They may also be portioned and served from a sweet trolley in the room. Other sweet dishes may be prepared and served in the room from the guéridon trolley, for example crêpes suzette, peach flambé and banana flambé. Other considerations are as follows.

● With portioned items such as gâteaux, flans or pies, then the cut face, or point of the cut item, is placed facing the customer.
● The serving of sauces such as custard and whipped cream can be from sauce boats (ladled or spooned not poured) or there may be individual portion jugs. Alternatively, a sauceboat may be left on an underplate on the table for the customers to help themselves.
● If sauces are served then it is usual not to serve these over the item but around it – unless the customer specifically requests it.

For most sweets the cover is a sweet spoon and fork. For other dishes, the lay-up will depend of the type of food being presented, for example sweets presented in a coupe are often eaten with a teaspoon.

There are no particular accompaniments to sweets. Often the customer may require a sugar sifter or, depending on the nature of the sweet selected, sauces such as custard or sauce Anglaise (rich custard) may be offered. Alternatives to this might be Chantilly cream, single cream or double whipped cream.

4.15 Savouries

On the lunch and dinner menu a savoury may generally be served as an alternative to a sweet. In a banquet it may be a separate course served in addition to either a sweet or cheese course. Examples of savouries are given in Table 4.20.

Table 4.20 Examples of savouries

On toast	Usually shaped pieces of toast with various toppings such as anchovies, sardines, mushrooms, smoked haddock and the classic Welsh rarebit (a mature cheese, egg yolk and béchamel sauce mixture, bound together, spread on toast and grilled) or Buck rarebit (Welsh rarebit with a poached egg on the top)
Canapés or croûtes	Shaped pieces of bread about 6 mm (¼″ inch) thick, brushed with melted butter and grilled, or may be shaped shallow fried bread. Examples include: ● Scotch woodcock (scrambled egg, topped with a trellis of anchovies and studded with capers) ● Croûte Diane (chicken livers wrapped in streaky bacon) ● Croûte Derby (ham purée garnished with a pickled walnut) ● Devils on horseback (prunes wrapped in bacon) ● Angels on horseback (poached oysters wrapped in bacon) ● Canapé Charlemagne (shrimps in a curry sauce) ● Canapé Quo Vadis (grilled roes garnished with small mushrooms)
Tartlettes	Round pastry cases with various fillings such as mushrooms, or cheese soufflé mixtures with various garnishes, or prawns or other fish in various sauces
Barquettes	Filled boat-shaped pastry cases, similar to tartlettes
Bouchées	Filled small, round puff pastry cases. A small edition of a vol-au-vent
Omelettes	Two- and three-egg omelettes with various flavours/fillings such as parsley, anchovy, cheese or fines herbes (mixed herbs)
Soufflés	Made in a soufflé dish with various flavours such as mushroom, spinach, sardine, anchovy, smoked haddock or cheese
Flans	Either single or portioned savoury flans such as Quiche Lorraine

Service of savouries

Savouries are usually served plated although occasionally they may be silver served. The cover is a hot fish plate and a small/side knife and sweet fork. Should the savoury take the form of an individual savoury soufflé then it would be eaten from the dish in which it is cooked using either a teaspoon or a sweet spoon and fork. The accompaniments are:
● salt and pepper
● cayenne pepper
● pepper mill
● Worcestershire sauce (usually only with meat savouries).

4.16 Dessert (fresh fruit and nuts)

Dessert may include all types of fresh fruits and nuts according to season, although the majority of the more popular items are now available all the year round. Some of the more popular items are dessert apples, pears, bananas, oranges, tangerines, black and white grapes, pineapple and assorted nuts such as Brazils. Sometimes a box of dates may appear in the fruit basket.

The dessert is usually dressed up in a fruit basket by the larder section and may be used as a central piece on a cold buffet until required.

Cover, accompaniments and service

Cover
The cover to be laid for dessert is normally:
- fruit plate
- fruit knife and fork – traditionally interlocked on the fruit plate
- spare napkin
- one finger bowl, on a side plate at the top right-hand corner of the cover, containing lukewarm water and a slice of lemon which may be used for rinsing fingers
- one finger bowl, on a side plate and containing cold water for rinsing the grapes. It will be placed at the top left-hand corner of the cover
- nut crackers and grape scissors, to be placed on the fruit basket
- spare side plate for shells and peel.

Accompaniments
The following accompaniments should be set on the table:
- caster sugar holder on a side plate
- salt for nuts.

Service
The fruit basket/fruit bowl is presented to the customer who makes his or her choice of a portion of fresh fruit or nuts. If the customer chooses nuts, the nutcrackers would be removed from the fruit basket, placed on a side plate and left on the table at the head of the cover.

If grapes are chosen then the waiter rests the fruit basket on the table, at the left-hand side of the customer, and supporting it with one hand cuts off the selected portion of grapes with the aid of the grape scissors. These will grip the stem once the portion has been cut and removed from the main bunch, and thus by holding the portion with the grape scissors they may be rinsed in the finger bowl at the top left-hand corner of the cover and placed on the fruit plate.

If guéridon service is being used, the procedure will be the same but takes place from the guéridon or trolley.

Should the customer require any other fresh fruit he or she will make their selection from the fruit basket/fruit bowl and place the desired fresh fruit onto their fruit plate. If they request their choice of fresh fruit to be peeled, cored, sliced or segmented this will be carried out by the waiter from the guéridon or trolley and on completion will be presented attractively on the fruit plate or, if requested, flambéed and then served onto the customer's fruit plate from the flambé pan. The guéridon preparation of fruit is described in Section 10.12, p.349.

Chapter 5

Beverages – non-alcoholic and alcoholic

5.1 Tea

Tea was discovered by accident over 5000 years ago, when leaves from a tea bush accidentally dropped into some boiling water and delicately flavoured the liquid. Tea was originally drunk for its medicinal benefits and it was not until the 1700s that it began to be consumed as the delicious beverage that we know today.

Figure 5.1 Tea plantation

Tea is prepared from the leaf bud and top leaves of a tropical evergreen bush called *camellia sinensis*. It produces what is regarded as a healthy beverage, containing approximately only half the caffeine of coffee and at the same time it aids muscle relaxation and stimulates the central nervous system.

The tea leaf itself contains a number of chemicals including amino acids, vitamins, caffeine and catechins. The latter is a type of antioxidant which in green tea is thought to be more effective in preventing certain cancers such as liver cancer. Green and black teas may also protect against cardiovascular disease.

The leaf particle size is referred to as grades. The main ones are:
- **Pekoe (pecko)**: the delicate top leaves
- **Orange pekoe**: a rolled leaf with a slim appearance
- **Pekoe dust**: the smallest particle of leaf size.

In between these grades there are a set of grades known as fannings. In tea terminology, 'flush' refers to a picking, which can take place at different times of the year.

Tea producing countries

Tea is grown in more than 25 countries around the world. The crop benefits from acidic soil, a warm climate and where there is at least 130 cm of rain a year. It is an annual crop and its flavour, quality and character is affected by its location, altitude, type of soil and climate. The main tea producing countries are described below.

China

This is the oldest tea growing country and is known for speciality blends such as Keemun, Lapsang Souchong, Oolongs and green tea.

East Africa (Kenya, Malawi, Tanzania and Zimbabwe)

This area produces good quality teas, which are bright and colourful and used extensively for blending purposes. Kenya produces teas which are easily discernible and have a reddish or coppery tint and a brisk flavour.

India

India is the largest producer of tea, producing about 30 per cent of the world's tea. Best known are the teas from Assam (strong and full bodied), Darjeeling tea (delicate and mellow) and also Nilgiri, which is second only to Assam and produces teas similar to those of Sri Lanka.

Indonesia

Teas produced here are light and fragrant with bright colouring when made and are used mainly for blending purposes.

Sri Lanka (formerly Ceylon)

Teas here are inclined to have a delicate, light lemon flavour. They are generally regarded as excellent afternoon teas and also lend themselves to being iced.

All teas are fermented (oxidised) during the process of manufacture, which gives them their black colour. The one exception is China green tea.

Tea products available

Most teas used are blended teas sold under proprietary brands or names. Other teas, sometimes called speciality or premium teas, are sold by the name of the specific tea (see Table 5.1 Service of tea below). The word 'blend' indicates that a named tea may be composed of a variety of different teas to produce one marketable tea, which is acceptable to the average consumer taste. For instance, what is sometimes termed a standard tea may contain somewhere in the region of 15 different teas, some of which would almost certainly include Indian tea for strength, African tea for colour and China tea for flavour and delicacy.

Tea may be purchased in a variety of forms depending on requirements such as:
- volume of production
- type of establishment
- clientele
- the occasion
- method of service
- storage facilities available
- cost.

The different means of purchasing are:
- **Bulk**: this is leaf tea (also called loose tea), which allows the traditional method of serving.
- **Tea bags**: these are heat-sealed and contain either standard or speciality teas. They come in one-cup, two-cup, pot-for-one or bulk brew sizes up to several litres.
- **String and tag**: this comes as a one-cup teabag with string attached and a tag that remains outside the cup or teapot for easy and quick identification of the tea by the customer.

● **Envelopes**: this is again a string and tag teabag but in an envelope for hygienic handling. It is used for trays for in-room tea and coffee-making facilities.
● **Instant**: instant tea granules.
● **Pods**: these are specially designed individual portions of tea that are used in proprietary tea and coffee makers. Each pod makes one portion of tea and the pod is then disposed of.

Storage

Tea should be kept:
● in a dry, clean and covered container
● in a well-ventilated area
● away from excess moisture
● away from any strong smelling foods as it very quickly absorbs strong odours.

Making tea

The type of tea used will, of course, depend on the customer's choice, but most establishments carry a varied stock of Indian, Ceylon, China and speciality teas, together with a variety of tisanes (fruit flavoured teas and herbal infusions) available upon request.

The quantities of dry tea used per pot or per gallon may vary slightly with the type of tea used, but as an approximate guide the following may be used:
● 42.5–56.7 g (1½–2 oz) dry tea per 4.546 litres (1 gallon)
● ½ litre (1 pint) of milk will be sufficient for 20–24 cups
● ½ kilogram (1 lb) sugar for approximately 80 cups.

When brewing smaller amounts in the stillroom, such as a pot for one or two, it is often advisable to install a measure for the loose tea. This ensures standardisation of the brew and control on the amount of loose tea being used. Alternative methods of pre-portioning tea may also be used, such as tea bags.

When making tea in bulk and calculating quantities of tea required for a party, allow approximately ⅙ litre (⅓ pint) per cup or 24 cups per 4.546 litres (1 gallon). If breakfast cups are used, capacity approximately ¼ litre (½ pint), then allow only 16 cups to 4.546 litres (1 gallon).

Because tea is an infusion the flavour is obtained by allowing the tea to brew. To achieve good results, a few simple rules can be applied:
● Heat the pot before putting in the dry tea so that the maximum heat can be obtained from the boiling water.*
● Measure the dry tea exactly.
● Use freshly boiled water*.
● Make sure the water is boiling on entering the pot.
● Allow the tea to brew for 3–6 minutes (depending on the tea) to obtain maximum strength from the brew.
● Remove the tealeaves at the end of the brewing period if required, but especially if making the tea in multi-pot insulated urns.
● Ensure all the equipment used is scrupulously clean.

* Recommended time and water temperatures for brewing different teas can vary. Based on 3g of tea per 250ml of water, examples are: 180 seconds at 95 °C for black tees, 180 seconds at 75 °C, for green teas and 300 seconds at 65 °C for white teas. For oolong teas it is 6g to 250ml for 60 seconds at 85 °C.

Table 5.1 lists the ways of serving various teas.

Table 5.1 Service of teas

Afternoon tea	Usually a blend of delicate Darjeeling tea and high-grown Ceylon tea to produce a refreshing and light tea. As the name of the blend suggests, this tea is suitable for afternoon tea but may also be taken at any time. Served with milk or lemon and sugar offered separately
Assam	Rich, full and malty flavoured tea, suitable for service at breakfast, usually with milk. Sugar would be offered separately
China	Tea made from a special blend of tea that is more delicate in flavour and more perfumed than any other tea. Less dry tea is required than for making Indian or Ceylon tea. Traditionally China tea is rarely served with milk. It is made in the normal way and is best made in a china pot. China tea is normally drunk on its own, but may be improved, according to taste, by the addition of a slice of lemon. Slices of lemon would be offered on a side plate with a sweet fork. Sugar may be offered separately
Darjeeling	Delicate tea with a light grape flavour and known as the 'Champagne of teas'. Usually served as an afternoon or evening tea with either lemon or a little milk if preferred. Sugar may be offered separately
Earl Grey	Blend of Darjeeling and China tea, flavoured with oil of Bergamot. Usually served with lemon or milk. Sugar would be offered separately
English Breakfast	Often a blend of Assam and Kenya teas to make a bright, flavoursome and refreshing tea. Usually served as a breakfast tea but may be offered at any time. Usually served with milk but can also be taken with lemon. Sugar is offered separately
Iced tea	This is strong tea that is made, strained and well chilled. The tea is then stored chilled until required. It is traditionally served in a glass, such as a tumbler. A slice of lemon may be placed in the glass and some additional lemon slices served separately as for Russian tea. Sugar may be offered
Indian or Ceylon Blend	Indian or Ceylon Blend tea may be made in either china or metal teapots. These teas are usually offered with milk. Sugar is offered separately
Jasmine	Green (unoxidised) tea that is dried with Jasmine Blossom and produces a tea with a fragrant and scented flavour
Kenya	Consistent and refreshing tea usually served with milk. Sugar would be offered separately
Lapsang Souchong	Smoky, pungent and perfumed tea, delicate to the palate and may be said to be an acquired taste. Usually served with lemon. Sugar would be offered separately
Multi-pot	There are many occasions when tea has to be produced in bulk. Such occasions might be a reception tea, tea breaks in an industrial catering concern or at functions catering for large numbers. In these instances tea may be made in multi-pots/urns, which may be described as teapots or urns, varying in capacity from 1 to 25 litres (1 to 5 gallons). These containers have infusers which hold the required quantity of tea leaves for the size of pot/urn being used. The infuser would be placed in the pot/urn and freshly boiled water added. The mix would then be allowed to brew for a number of minutes – a maximum of 10 minutes for a 25-litre urn – and the infuser is then removed to ensure a good quality product is served. The quantity of tea made should always relate to the number to be served – this will ensure minimum delay in the service and minimum wastage

Russian or lemon tea	Tea that is brewed from a special blend similar to China tea, but is also often made from either Indian or Ceylon tea. It is made in the normal way and is usually served with a slice of lemon. The tea is served in quarter litre (half pint) glasses, which stand in a silver holder with a handle and on a side plate with a teaspoon. A slice of lemon may be placed in the glass and a few slices of lemon served separately. Sugar would be served separately.
Sri Lanka	Makes a pale golden tea with a good flavour. Ceylon Blend is still used as a trade name. Served with lemon or milk. Sugar would be offered separately
Tisanes	These are fruit flavoured teas and herbal infusions which are often used for medicinal purposes and are gaining in popularity with trends towards healthier eating and drinking. Often these do not contain caffeine. Examples are:

Herbal teas	Fruit teas
• camomile	• cherry
• peppermint	• lemon
• rosehip	• blackcurrant
• mint	• mandarin orange

These teas are usually made in china pots or can be made by the cup or glass. Sometimes served with sugar

Characteristics of good tea

Tea should have:

- good flavour
- good aroma
- good colour when milk or cream are added – not grey
- good body.

Reasons for bad quality tea

- Water not fresh
- Water has not reached boiling point
- Infusion time too long or too short
- Stale or old tea has been used
- Too much or too little tea used
- Dirty equipment
- Tea re-heated
- Brewed tea being kept too long before use or kept at wrong temperature.

For further information on the service of tea see Section 6.7, p.244.

5.2 Coffee

Coffee trees were cultivated about 1000 years ago in the Yemen. The first commercial cultivation of coffee is thought to have been in the Yemen district of Arabia in the fifteenth century. By the middle of the sixteenth century coffee drinking had spread to Sudan, Egypt, Syria and Turkey. Venetian traders first brought coffee to Europe in 1615 and the first coffee house in England was opened in Oxford in 1650. The drinking of coffee spread from Britain to America, and after the Boston Tea Party in 1773, the North American palate changed from drinking tea as a beverage to coffee.

Figure 5.2 Coffee beans

The trees that produce coffee are of the genus *Coffea*, which belongs to the *Rubiaceae* family. There are somewhere in the region of 50 different species, although only two of these are commercially significant. These are known as *Coffea arabica* and *Coffea camephora*, which is usually referred to as *Robusta*. Arabica accounts for some 75 per cent of world production.

The coffee tree is an evergreen shrub, which reaches a height of two to three metres when cultivated. The fruit of the coffee tree is known as the 'cherry' and these are about 1.5 cm in length and have an oblong shape. The cherry usually contains two coffee beans. The coffee tree will not begin to produce fruit until it is 3–5 years old and it will then usually yield good crops for up to 15 years.

The coffee bean goes through various stages while it is being processed. These are:
- harvesting
- wet processing (washing, fermenting and drying)
- dry processing (laid out on mats in the sun)
- sorting
- grading
- grinding
- packaging.

Coffee producing countries

Coffee is a natural product grown in many countries of the tropical and sub-tropical belt in South and Central America, Africa and Asia. It is grown at different altitudes in different basic climates and in different soils and is viewed as an international drink consumed throughout the world. Brazil is the world's largest grower of coffee, Columbia is second, the Ivory Coast third and Indonesia fourth.

Coffee products available

The different means of purchasing coffee are:

- **Bulk**: (either as beans or in vacuum packs of pre-ground beans) allowing for the traditional methods of making and serving.
- **Coffee bags**: these are heat-sealed and come in one-cup, two-cup, pot-for-one or bulk brew sizes up to several litres.
- **Instant**: instant coffee granules, available in sizes from one cup to pot size.
- **Individual filters**: vacuum packed and containing one portion.
- **Pods**: these are specially designed individual portions of pre-ground coffee that are used in proprietary coffee and tea makers. Each pod makes one portion of coffee and the pod is then disposed of.

The blend

Companies who sell coffee have their own blending experts whose task it is to ensure that the quality and taste of their particular coffee brand is consistent, despite the fact that the imported beans will vary from shipment to shipment.

Samples of green coffee beans are taken from bags in the producing countries and the port of arrival. The samples are sent to prospective buyers whose experts roast, brew and taste samples to test their quality before deciding on the type of blend for which the particular coffee is suitable.

The roasting

Most brands of coffee sold in shops are, in fact, a blend of two or more batches of beans. Because they have no smell or taste, green beans have to be roasted in order to release the coffee aroma and flavour. The roasting process should give a uniform colour. The outputs from different roastings are used to form different blends.

The common degrees of roasting are:

- **light or pale roastings**: suitable for mild beans to preserve their delicate aroma.
- **medium roastings**: give a stronger flavour and are often favoured for coffees with well-defined character.
- **full roastings**: popular in many Latin countries, they have a bitter flavour.
- **high roasted coffee**: accentuates the strong bitter aspects of coffee, although much of the original flavour is lost.

Commercial coffee roasters can either convert the beans into instant (soluble) coffee or prepare them for sale as roasted or ground beans. The higher the roast, the less acidity and the more bitterness there is in the coffee.

Certain coffees also have flavourings added, either in the blend or during the process of making. Examples of these include:

- **Turkish coffee**: vanilla
- **French coffee**: chicory
- **Viennese coffee**: fig.

The grind

Roasted coffee must be ground before it can be used to make the brew. Coffee is ground to different grades of fineness to suit the many different methods of brewing. The most suitable grinds for some common methods of brewing coffee are:

Method	Grinding grade
Cafetière	Medium
Espresso	Very fine
Filter/Drip	Fine to medium
Jug	Coarse
Percolator	Medium
Turkish	Pulverised
Vacuum infusion	Medium fine to fine

Storage

Some tips for storing coffee:
- Store in a well-ventilated storeroom.
- Use an airtight container for ground coffee to ensure that the oils do not evaporate, causing loss of flavour and strength.
- Keep coffee away from excess moisture.
- Do not store near any strong smelling foods or other substances, as coffee will absorb their odours.

Making coffee

Methods of brewing can vary, ranging from instant coffee brewed by the cup, through to $1\frac{1}{2}$–3 litre (3–6 pints) units and up to machines that may produce large quantities for functions. Coffee beans may be purchased and then ground according to requirements. The beans should not be ground until immediately before they are required as this will ensure the maximum flavour and strength from the oils within the coffee bean. If ground coffee is purchased it normally comes in vacuum-packed packets in order to maintain its qualities until use. These packets contain set quantities to make 4.5 litres (1 gallon) and 9 litres (2 gallons) and so on.

When making coffee in bulk 283.5–340 g (10–12 oz) of ground coffee is sufficient to make 4.5 litres (1 gallon) of black coffee. Assuming that cups with a capacity of $\frac{1}{3}$ pint will be used then 283.5–340 g (10–12 oz) of ground coffee is sufficient to provide 24 cups of black coffee or 48 cups if serving half coffee and half milk. When breakfast cups are used then 16 cups of black coffee or 32 cups of half coffee and half milk will be available. At a dinner where demi-tasse cups are used, capacity is 48 cups of black coffee or 96 cups half black coffee and half milk.

The rules to be observed when making coffee in bulk are as follows:
- Use freshly roasted and ground coffee.
- Buy the correct grind for the type of machine in use.
- Ensure all equipment is clean before use.
- Use a set measure of coffee to water: 283.5–340 g per 4.5 litres (10–12 oz per gallon).
- Add boiling water to the coffee and allow to infuse.

- The infusion time must be controlled according to the type of coffee being used and the method of making.
- Control the temperature since to boil coffee is to spoil coffee (it will develop a bitter taste).
- Strain and serve.
- Offer milk (hot or cold) or cream separately and sugar and alternatives.
- The best serving temperatures are 82 °C (180 °F) for coffee and 68 °C (155 °F) for milk.

Characteristics of good coffee

Coffee should have:

- good flavour
- good aroma
- good colour when milk or cream are added – not grey
- good body.

Reasons for bad quality coffee

- Water not fresh.
- Water has not reached boiling point.
- Insufficient or too much coffee used.
- Infusion time too short or too long or at wrong temperature.
- Coffee not roasted correctly.
- Stale or old coffee used.
- Incorrect grind of coffee used for equipment in operation.
- Coffee kept too long before use or kept at wrong temperature.
- Dirty equipment.
- Sediment remaining in storage or serving compartment.

Coffee making methods

Coffee may be made in many ways and the service depends on the method used. A description of the various methods is given below.

Instant

This may be made in individual coffee or teacups, or in large quantities. It involves mixing soluble coffee solids with boiling water. When making instant coffee in bulk, approximately 71 g (2½ oz) to each 4.5 litres (1 gallon) of water should be allowed. This form of coffee may be made very quickly, immediately before it is required, by pouring freshly boiled water onto a measured quantity of coffee powder. Stir well.

Saucepan or jug method

This is an American method of making coffee, more often used in the home than in a catering establishment. A set measure of ground coffee is placed in a saucepan or jug and the required quantity of freshly boiled water is poured onto the coffee grounds. This should then be allowed to stand for a few minutes to extract the full flavour and strength from the ground coffee. It is then strained and served.

La cafetière (coffee or tea maker)

La cafetière, or jug and plunger method, makes coffee simply and quickly by the infusion method and to order. This ensures that the flavour and aroma of the coffee are preserved. La cafetière comes in the form of a glass container with a lip held in a black, gold or chrome finished holder and sealed with a lid which also holds the plunger unit in position.

This method involves simply adding boiling water to the ground coffee, stirring and then placing the plunger unit and lid in position. A guideline to the quantity of coffee to be used might be:

- 2 level sweet spoonfuls for the 3 cup size
- 6 level sweet spoonfuls for the 8 cup size
- 9 level sweet spoonfuls for the 12 cup size.

Infusion time is from 3 to 5 minutes. During this time the coffee grains will rise to the top of the liquid. After this if the plunger is moved slightly the coffee grains will fall to the bottom of the glass container. When the grains have fallen it is easier to push the plunger down.

Percolator method

This method is used more in the home than commercially. A set quantity of coffee grounds is placed in the percolator, which is then filled with freshly drawn water. The water, upon reaching boiling point, rises up through a tube and percolates the coffee grounds, extracting the full flavour, colour and strength. Hot or cold milk, cream and sugar may be added to taste. This method of making coffee is in decline.

Vacuum infusion ('Cona')

This traditional method of making coffee has considerable visual appeal in the restaurant and has the advantage that the coffee served is always fresh as only limited quantities are made at one time.

Banks of these machines may be used for varying requirements, housing two, three, four or five containers at one time. They are compact and portable and very easy to keep clean. The method of making the coffee is fairly simple but is best supervised for safety reasons and to ensure the best results and a consistent standard.

The filters in this vacuum-type equipment are usually made of metal or plastic, but sometimes glass. The bowls are either glass or metal.

In this method of making coffee the lower bowl is filled with cold water or, to speed up the operation, freshly heated but not boiled water, up to the water level. The upper bowl is then set in the lower bowl, making sure it is securely in place. The filter is placed in the upper bowl, ensuring it is securely fitted, and the required quantity of ground coffee is added according to the amount of water being used. The water is then heated.

As the water reaches boiling point it rises up the tube into the upper bowl, mixing with the ground coffee. As it rises in the upper bowl, it is often best to stir the mixture gently to ensure that all coffee grounds infuse with the liquid, as sometimes the grounds are inclined to form a cap on top of the liquid and therefore do not fully infuse. At the same time, care must be taken that the filter is not knocked as this may cause grains to pass into the lower bowl.

On reducing the heat, the coffee liquid passes back into the lower bowl leaving the grounds in the upper bowl. The upper bowl and filter are then removed and washed ready for re-use. The coffee in the lower bowl is ready for use and should be served at a temperature of approximately 82 °C (180 °F).

Filter (café filtre)

This is a method originating from and traditionally used in France and may be made individually in the cup or in bulk. The filter method produces excellent coffee. Fresh boiled water is poured into a container with a very finely meshed bottom, which stands on a cup or pot. Within the container is the required amount of ground coffee. The infusion takes place and the coffee liquid falls into the cup/pot below. Filter papers may be used to avoid the grounds passing into the lower cup, but this will depend on how fine or coarse is the ground coffee being used. There are now many electronic units available of differing capacities. Cold water is poured into a reservoir and is brought to boiling point and then dripped onto the ground coffee.

Pour through filter method

This is an excellent method of making filter coffee, which has increased in popularity over the past few years. Many of these pour through filter machines are available for purchase or to hire from a number of the main coffee suppliers.

The principle behind this method is that when the measured quantity of freshly drawn water is poured into the top of the pour through filter machine this water displaces the hot water already in the machine. This hot water infuses with the ground coffee and runs into the serving container as a coffee liquid ready for immediate use. It takes approximately 3–4 minutes to make one brew.

When coffee is made by this method, ensure that:
- the machine is plugged in and switched on at the mains
- the brew indicator light is on. This tells the operator that the water already held in the machine is at the correct temperature for use
- the correct quantity of fresh ground coffee, which will usually come in the form of a vacuum-sealed pack, is used. A fresh pack should be used for each new brew of filter coffee being made
- a new clean filter paper is used for each fresh brew.

Individual filter

This is an alternative way of making bulk filter coffee. It is a plastic, disposable, individual filter, bought with the required amount of coffee already sealed in the base of the filter. Each individual filter is sufficient for one cup and after use the whole filter is thrown away. The advantage of this method is that every cup may be made to order. It appeals to customers as they are able to see that they are receiving entirely fresh coffee and it also has a certain novelty value.

When making a cup of coffee by this method, the individual filter is placed onto a cup. Freshly boiled water is then poured into the individual filter to the required level. The liquid then infuses with the ground coffee within the individual filter and drips into the cup. A lid should be placed over the water in the filter to help retain the temperature. Time of making is approximately 3–4 minutes.

Espresso

This method is Italian in origin. The machines used in making this form of coffee can provide cups of coffee individually in a matter of seconds, some machines being capable of making 300–400 cups of coffee per hour.

Figure 5.3 Espresso machine

The method involves passing steam through the finely ground coffee and infusing under pressure. The advantage is that each cup is made freshly for the customer. Served black, the coffee is known as espresso and is served in a small cup. If milk is required, it is heated for each cup by a high-pressure steam injector and transforms a cup of black coffee into a Cappuccino. As an approximate guide, from 12 kg (1 lb) of coffee used, 80 cups of good strength coffee may be produced. The general rules for making coffee apply here, but with this special and delicate type of equipment extra care should be taken in following any instructions.

Still-set

This method normally consists of a small central container into which the correct sized filter paper is placed. A second, fine-meshed metal filter with a handle is then placed on the filter paper and the ground coffee placed on top of this. There is an urn on either side of varying capacities according to requirements. The urns may be 4½, 9, 13 or 18 litres (1, 2, 3 or 4 gallons) in size.

These still-sets are easy to operate, but must be kept very clean at all times and regularly serviced. The urns should be rinsed before and after each brew until the water runs clear. This removes the thin layer of cold coffee that clings to the side of the urn that, if left, will spoil the flavour and aroma of the next brew.

Boiling water is passed through the grounds and the coffee passes into the urn at the side. Infusion should be complete in 6–8 minutes for 4½ litres (1 gallon) of coffee, using medium ground coffee. The milk is heated in a steam jacket container. It should be held at a constant temperature of 68 °C because if held at too high a temperature or boiled or heated too soon, on coming into contact with the coffee it will destroy its flavour and taste. At the same time, the milk itself becomes discoloured. The coffee and milk should be held separately, at their correct temperatures ready for serving.

Figure 5.4 Modern still-set

Decaffeinated

Coffee contains caffeine, which is a stimulant. Decaffeinated coffee is made from beans after the caffeine has been extracted. The coffee is made in the normal way.

Iced coffee

Strong black coffee should be made in the normal way. It is then strained and chilled well until required. It may be served mixed with an equal quantity of cold milk for a smooth beverage, or with cream. It is served in a tall glass, with ice cubes added and with straws. Cream or milk is often served separately and sugar offered.

Turkish or Egyptian coffees

These are made from darkly roasted mocha beans, which are ground to a fine powder. The coffee is made in special copper pots, which are placed on top of a stove or lamp, and the water is then allowed to boil. The sugar should be put in at this stage to sweeten the coffee, as it is never stirred once poured out. The finely ground coffee may be stirred in or the boiling water poured onto the grounds. The amount of coffee used is approximately one heaped teaspoonful per person. Once the coffee has been stirred in, the copper pot is taken off the direct heat and the cooling causes the grounds to settle. It is brought to the boil and allowed to settle twice more and is then sprinkled with a little cold water to settle any remaining grains. The coffee is served in small cups. While making the coffee it may be further flavoured with vanilla pods but this is optional.

Figure 5.5 illustrates ways in which coffee may be made. Examples of modern coffee service styles are given in Table 5.2.

Figure 5.5 Coffee brewing methods (clockwise from top): pour through filter machine, single filter, Turkish/Greek/Arabic coffee, jug and plunger/cafetière

Table 5.2 Examples of modern coffee service styles

Filter (filtre)	Traditional method of making coffee. Often served with hot or cold milk or cream
Cafetière	Popular method of making and serving fresh coffee in individual or multi-portion jugs. Often served with hot or cold milk or cream
Espresso	Traditional short strong black coffee
Espresso doppio	Double espresso served in larger cup
Café crème	Regular coffee prepared from fresh beans, ground fresh for each cup, resulting in a thick cream coloured, moussy head
Espresso ristretto	Intense form of espresso, often served with a glass of cold water in continental Europe
Americano	Espresso with added hot water to create regular black coffee. May also be regular black coffee made using filter method
Espresso macchiato	Espresso spotted with a spoonful of hot or cold milk or hot milk foam
Espresso con panna	Espresso with a spoonful of whipped cream on top
Cappuccino	Espresso coffee topped with steamed frothed milk, often finished with a sprinkling of chocolate (powdered or grated)
Caffè (or café) latté	Shot of espresso plus hot milk, with or without foam
Flat white	Double shot of espresso topped with frothed milk which has been stirred together with the flat milk from the bottom of the jug, to create a creamy rather than frothy texture
Latte macchiato	Steamed milk spotted with a drop of espresso
Caffè mocha (or mochaccino)	Chocolate compound (syrup or powder) followed by a shot of espresso. The cup or glass is then filled with freshly steamed milk topped with whipped cream and cocoa powder
Iced coffee	Chilled regular coffee, sometimes served with milk or simply single espresso topped up with ice cold milk
Turkish/Egyptian	Intense form of coffee made in special jugs with finely ground coffee

| Decaffeinated | Coffee with caffeine removed. Can be used as alternative to prepare the service styles listed above |
| Instant coffee | Coffee made from processed powder (often freeze dried). Regular and decaffeinated styles are available |

Figure 5.6 Examples of insulated jugs and dispensers for coffee and tea service (images courtesy of Elia®)

Irish and other speciality coffees

Speciality coffees are often completed and served at the table using the following equipment:

- service salver
- tray cloth or napkin
- 20 cl (7 fl oz) stemmed glass on a side plate
- teaspoon
- jug of double cream
- 25 ml measure
- coffee pot
- sugar basin of coffee sugar with a teaspoon
- bottle of the spirit or liqueur being used.

The procedure for making Irish coffee is as follows:

- A Paris goblet or other suitable stemmed glass of about 20 cl (7 fl oz) capacity is used.
- Brown sugar is added first (a certain amount of sugar is always required when serving this form of coffee, as it is an aid to floating the double cream on the surface of the hot coffee).
- One measure of Irish whiskey added.
- The teaspoon is then placed in the goblet before the coffee is poured into the glass. This is so the spoon will help to conduct the heat and avoid cracking the bowl of the glass as the hot, strong black coffee is poured in.
- The coffee should then be stirred well to dissolve the sugar and to ensure the ingredients are blended. The liquid should now be within 2½ cm (1 in) of the top of the glass. The liquid may still be swirling but not too much, as this will tend to draw the cream down into the coffee as it is poured.
- The double cream should be poured slowly over the back of a teaspoon onto the surface of the coffee until it is approximately 1.9 cm (¾ in) thick. The coffee must not be stirred: the best flavour is obtained by drinking the whiskey-flavoured coffee through the cream.
- When the Irish coffee has been prepared, the glass should be put on a doily on a side plate and placed in front of the customer.

Figure 5.7 Tray laid for the service of Irish coffee

Other forms of speciality, or liqueur, coffees include:

Café Royale or Café Parisienne: Brandy   **Russian coffee**: Vodka

Jamaican coffee or Caribbean coffee: Rum   **Highland coffee**: Scotch Whisky

Monk's coffee: Benedictine   **Seville coffee**: Cointreau

Calypso coffee: Tia Maria   **Swiss coffee**: Kirsch

5.3 Chocolate

Chocolate and cocoa come from the fruit of the plant *Theobroma cacao*, in the form of beans containing up to 25–30 white seeds. This cocoa plant is grown in countries as far afield as Mexico, Central and South America, West Africa and Asia.

Production process

The seeds are fermented, dried and shipped abroad where they are then roasted and blended before being pressed, ground and sieved for use as powdered or solid products. They then become cocoa powder, drinking chocolate, eating chocolate and couverture chocolate used for decorating purposes.

Figure 5.8 Hot chocolate served in a glass

Beverage preparation

This beverage is very popular and may come sweetened or non-sweetened and as a powder or soluble granules. It may be mixed with hot water or hot milk. Whipped cream from a whipped cream dispenser, marshmallows or a sprinkling of powdered chocolate may be added upon request. There are also flavoured chocolates available such as ginger, hazelnut and chilli. The Continental style chocolate is of a thicker consistency while the American chocolate is lighter. Usually offered as large, medium or small and served in a tall glass or mug.

Product characteristics

The characteristics of these beverages vary according to the exact ingredients used and in what proportions. This has an impact on:

- flavour
- consistency
- sweetness/bitterness
- milkiness/smoothness
- overall presentation.

Some products on the market only have to be mixed with hot water as dried skimmed milk and milk proteins are among the ingredients making up the product.

Storage of chocolate products

Drinking chocolate products come in individual vacuum sealed packs or pods for use with electronic beverage making machines or in containers of varying sizes to suit demand and turnover. When not in use the containers should be kept air tight, in cool, dry and well-ventilated conditions and away from excess moisture and sunlight.

Incorrect beverage making procedures

Problems arising with the quality of the beverage produced may be due to:

- incorrect amount of drinking chocolate (powder or granules) to liquid (water or milk), affecting consistency and strength
- the temperature of the liquid used is not sufficient to dissolve the powder or granules
- poor storage has affected the commodity being used
- dirty equipment and no regular cleaning or maintenance.

5.4 Other stillroom beverages

Other beverages may be offered for service and are often made in the stillroom. These include drinks such as cocoa, Horlicks, Ovaltine and Bovril. They should be prepared and served according to the maker's instructions.

If milk shakes are requested, then the following basic ingredients are required:

- chilled milk
- syrups (flavourings) (for example flavourings see p.156)
- ice cream.

Milk shakes are often served with a straw in a tall glass after making in a mixer or blender.

5.5 Checking and cleaning beverage making equipment

All equipment used to make and serve hot beverages must be kept spotlessly clean and sterilised at regular intervals. Standards of health, safety and hygiene must be maintained as well as ensuring that the product meets the customer's expectations. Checklists are essential to ensure continuity of the cleaning process as staff will change due to shift work and they all need to work to the same level of competence.

Common faults in hot beverage making equipment might be:
- lack of power – fuses
- lack of pressure – no steam
- leaks
- filter basket scaled up
- blocked pipes due to build-up of coffee grounds
- dirty small equipment due to faulty dishwasher
- limescale build up.

Large equipment such as dishwashers, glass washing machines, still-sets, espresso machines and pour through machines should all be maintained on a regular monthly/three-monthly schedule and according to the maker's instructions. Where applicable, equipment should be sterilised on a daily basis. Cleaning may require the equipment to be stripped down, soaked, seals checked, new washers fitted, stains and excess limescale build up removed and temperature gauges checked to ensure they are functioning correctly. If these checks are not carried out regularly then this in turn can affect all small equipment and the product you wish to produce.

Daily checks on espresso machines at the start of service include:
1 steam valves opened
2 steam wand/s clean
3 seals on group handles clean and undamaged
4 steam pressure
5 exterior of machine clean and polished.

On a daily basis all small equipment needs to be checked for cracks, chips, lids not fitting correctly, no broken hinges, teapot spouts not chipped. Anything not in order should be put on one side to be mended as soon as possible.

Small equipment covers the following items:
- teacups
- tea saucers
- coffee cups
- coffee saucers
- hot milk jugs
- cold milk jugs
- hot water pots
- coffee pots
- teapots
- sugar bowls
- sugar tongs
- slop basins
- tea strainers
- side plates
- service salvers
- trays
- teaspoons.

5.6 Non-alcoholic bar beverages (soft drinks)

The drinks covered in this section are 'non-alcoholic' and contain no alcohol. These drinks are also often referred to as 'soft drinks' with alcoholic drinks sometimes being referred to as 'hard' drinks.

Non-alcoholic dispense bar beverages may be classified into five main groups:
1   aerated waters
2   natural spring/mineral waters
3   squashes
4   juices
5   syrups.

Aerated waters

These beverages are charged (or aerated) with carbonic gas. Artificial aerated waters are by far the most common. The flavourings found in different aerated waters are obtained from various essences.

Examples of these aerated waters are:
● **Soda water**: colourless and tasteless
● **Tonic water**: colourless and quinine flavoured
● **Dry ginger**: golden straw-coloured with a ginger flavour
● **Bitter lemon**: pale, cloudy yellow-coloured with a sharp lemon flavour.

Other flavoured waters are:
● 'Fizzy' lemonades
● Orange
● Ginger beer
● Cola, etc.

Aerated waters are available in bottles and cans and many are also available as post-mix. The term post-mix indicates that the drink mix of syrup and the carbonated (filtered) water is mixed after (post) leaving the syrup container, rather than being pre-mixed (or ready mixed) as in canned or bottled soft drinks. The post-mix drinks are served from hand-held dispensing guns at the bar. These have buttons on the dispensing gun to select the specific drink. The key advantage of the post-mix system is the saving on storage space, especially for a high turnover operation. Dispensing systems need regular cleaning and maintenance to ensure that they are hygienic and working properly. Also, the proportions of the mix need to be checked regularly: too little syrup and the drinks will lack taste; too much syrup and the flavours become too strong.

Figure 5.9 Post-mix dispenser gun

Natural spring waters/mineral waters

The European Union has divided bottled water into two main types: mineral water and spring water.

● Mineral water has a mineral content (which is strictly controlled).
● Spring water has fewer regulations, apart from those concerning hygiene.

Waters can be still, naturally sparkling or carbonated during bottling.

Bottle sizes for mineral and spring waters vary considerably from, for example, 1.5 l to 200 ml. Some brand names sell in both plastic and glass bottles, while other brands prefer either plastic or glass bottles depending on the market and the size of container preferred by that market.

Table 5.3 Examples of varieties of mineral water

Name	Type	Country
Appollinaris	Naturally sparkling	Germany
Badoit	Slightly sparkling	France
Buxton	Still or carbonated	England
Contrex	Still	France
Evian	Still	France
Perrier	Sparkling and also fruit flavoured	France
San Pellegrino	Carbonated	Italy
Spa	Still, naturally sparkling and also fruit flavoured	Belgium
Vichy	Naturally sparkling	France
Vittel	Naturally sparkling	France
Volvic	Still	France

Table 5.4 Examples of varieties of spring water

Name	Type	Country
Ashbourne	Still or carbonated	England
Ballygowen	Still or sparkling	Ireland
Highland Spring	Still or carbonated	Scotland
Llanllry	Still or sparkling	Wales
Malvern	Still or carbonated	England
Strathmore	Still or sparkling	Scotland

Natural spring waters are obtained from natural springs in the ground, the waters themselves being impregnated with the natural minerals found in the soil and sometimes naturally charged with an aerating gas. The potential medicinal value of these mineral waters, as they are sometimes termed, has long been recognised by the medical profession. Where natural spring waters are found, there is usually what is termed a spa, where the waters may be drunk or bathed in according to the cures they are supposed to effect. Many of the best-known mineral waters are bottled at the springs (bottled at source).

Recently there has been a shift in consumer demand for bottled waters. The reasons for this include:

- environmental and sustainability concerns. In some cases demand has reduced considerably. Regular utility tap water, from safe commercial supplies, has become more popular in food service operations and customers increasingly expect this to be available, chilled or served with ice
- the emergence of commercial filter systems being used by food service operations. Utility supplied tap water is filtered at the establishment and then offered either as chilled still or sparking water in branded carafes or bottles, for which the establishment makes a charge.

Squashes

A squash may be served diluted with water, soda water or lemonade. Squashes are also used as mixers for spirits and in cocktails, or used as the base for such drinks as fruit cups. Examples are:

- orange squash
- lemon squash
- grapefruit squash
- lime juice.

Juices

The main types of juices held in stock in the dispense bar are:

- bottled, canned or in cartons:
  - orange juice
  - pineapple juice
  - grapefruit juice
  - tomato juice.

- fresh:
  - orange juice
  - grapefruit juice
  - lemon juice.

Apart from being served chilled on their own, these fresh juices may also be used in cocktails and for mixing with spirits.

Syrups

The main uses of these concentrated, sweet, fruit flavourings are as a base for cocktails, fruit cups or mixed with soda water as a long drink. The main ones used are:

cassis (blackcurrant)   gomme (white sugar syrup)
cerise (cherry)   grenadine (pomegranate)
citronelle (lemon)   orgeat (almond).
framboise (raspberry)

Syrups are also available as 'flavouring agents' for cold milk drinks such as milk shakes.

Information on the service of non-alcoholic bar beverages may be found in Section 6.7, p.244.

Other non-alcoholic beverages

Milkshakes
These are made from:
- chilled milk
- syrups (concentrated flavourings)
- ice cream.

Smoothies
Smoothies are made in a blender and have become increasingly popular. The ingredients required might include fresh fruit or vegetables, the latter being sweetened if necessary. Also frozen fruit, frozen yogurt, fruit juices, milk and honey may be used in a recipe. Crushed ice is often used to ensure the product is well chilled on serving. Pre-made bottled or carton versions are also available.

Natural vegetable juices
Often known as 'health drinks', these include carrot juice and beetroot juice.

5.7 Wine and drinks lists

The function of the wine and drinks list is similar to that of the menu and is a selling aid. Careful thought is needed in its planning, design, layout, colour and overall appearance to ensure it complements the style of the establishment. The design considerations of the wine and drinks list are similar to those of food menus (see Section 4.1, p.90). Adequate information, easily found and followed, will make the customer feel more at home and will assist in selling the wines and drinks on offer.

Service staff should have a good knowledge of all the wines and drinks available and of their main characteristics. They should also have a good knowledge of wines or other drinks that are most suitable to offer with different foods (matching food to wine and other drinks is discussed in Section 5.16, p.184).

Types of wine and drinks lists

Bar and cocktail lists

These may range from a basic standard list offering the common apéritifs such as sherries, vermouths, bitters, a selection of spirits with mixers, beers and soft drinks, together with a limited range of cocktails, through to a very comprehensive list offering a good choice in all areas. The actual format and content will be determined by the style of operation and clientele that the establishment wishes to attract, for example, the emphasis may be on:

- cocktails: traditional or fashionable
- malt whiskies
- beers
- New World wines
- non-alcoholic drinks.

A list of cocktails, their recipes and service notes is given in Annex B, p.500.

Restaurant wine lists

These may take various formats such as:

- a full and very comprehensive list of wines from all countries, with emphasis on the classic areas such as Bordeaux/Burgundy plus a fine wine/prestige selection
- a middle-of-the-road, traditional selection, for example, some French, German and Italian wines, together with some New World wines
- a small selection of well-known or branded wines – a prestige list
- predominantly wines of one particular country.

Figure 5.10 Traditional wine list

Figure 5.11 iPad based wine list

After meal drinks lists (digestifs)

These lists are often combined with the wine list – although occasionally they are presented as a separate liqueur list. The list should offer a full range of liqueurs, together with possibly a specialist range of brandies and/or a specialist range of malt whiskies. Vintage and Late Bottled Vintage (LBV) port may also be offered here. In addition a range of speciality liqueur/spirit coffees might also be included (such as those identified in Section 5.2, p.132).

Banqueting and event wine lists

The length of the list will generally depend on the size and style of operation. In most instances there is a selection of popular wine names/styles on offer. There would be a range of prices from house wines to some fine wines to suit all customer preferences. In some instances the banqueting wine list is the same as the restaurant wine list.

For further information see Chapter 11 Events (p.355).

Room service drinks lists

There may be a mini bar in the room or the room service menu may offer a choice from a standard bar list. The range of wines offered is usually limited and prices will vary according to the type of establishment.

Contents of wine and drinks lists

The contents of wine and drinks lists are commonly listed in the order in which they may be consumed:

1 Apéritifs – which alongside sparkling and still wines can include a range of aromatised wines (p.166), fortified wines (p.165) and natural spring and mineral waters (p.147).
2 Cocktails (p.155).
3 Spirits (p.172) and associated mixers such as aerated waters (p.146).
4 Wines – sparkling (p.163) and still (p.163).
5 Beers (p.177), cider (p.179), aerated waters and squashes (p.146).
6 Digestifs – which as well as liqueurs (p.175) may also include various spirits (p.172), such as brandy (p.173), malt whiskies (p.175), and also ports, other fortified wines, sweet table wines, and vins doux naturels (p.172).
7 Speciality coffees (p.142).

Listing of wines

Wines are usually listed in three main ways:

1 By place of origin (geographical)
2 By type
3 By grape.

Geographical listing for wines

The traditional approach is to list wines by geographical area. Within this approach the wines are presented country by country or region, such as for instance France, or Australasia (which includes Australia and New Zealand), and then within that area by area. It is also usual to have the wines presented under each country, region or area with white wines first, followed by rosé wines and then red wines. Using this approach the listing of wines within a wine list might be:

1 Champagne and sparkling
2 France
3 Germany
4 Italy
5 Spain
6 Portugal
7 England
8 Other European wines
9 Australia
10 The Americas (USA and South America)
11 Australasia
12 South Africa
13 Other world wines
14 House wines

Listing wines by type

A modern approach is to have wines listed by type:
- Sparkling wines
- White wines
- Rosé wines
- Red wines
- Dessert (sweet) wines.

The wines can then be listed under each type of wine in three main ways:
1 Country by country
2 Region by region (similar to the geographical listing described above)
3 By the style of the wine.

If wines are to be listed by type and by style, then they could be presented under the following headings:
- Sparkling wines
- Rosé wines
- White wines:
  - grapey whites
  - grassy-fruity whites
  - richer whites
- Red wines:
  - fruity reds
  - claret-style reds
  - herby spicy reds.

To help customers choose a wine and to enable staff to make recommendations, it is also useful for each of the groups of wines to be listed in order from the lighter wines to the more full wines. Table 5.16 on pp.185–186 gives examples of wines by type, by style, and from light to full.

Listing wines by grape

If wines are to be listed by grape then one approach could be to list the grapes in alphabetical order as follows:

White grapes
- Chardonnay
- Chenin blanc
- Gewürztraminer
- Pinot Blanc
- Pinot Gris/Pinot Grigio
- Riesling
- Sauvignon Blanc
- Sémillon
- Other white grapes

Red grapes
- Cabernet Sauvignon
- Gamay
- Merlot
- Pinot Noir
- Sangiovese
- Shiraz/Syrah
- Tempranillo
- Zinfandel
- Other red grapes

Under each heading the wines made with that grape are listed, as well as the principal blends that are made with that grape as the predominant grape. When wines are listed under the headings 'Other white grapes' or 'Other red grapes', then the grape(s) of the wine should also be listed next to the name of the wine.

Again, to help the customer choose a wine and to aid staff in making recommendations, it is useful for each of the groups of wines to be listed in order from the lighter wines to the more full wines (see Table 5.16, pp.185–186).

General information

It is usual to give information on wine and drinks lists that help the customer in making decisions and also the staff in making recommendations. This information is shown below.

Wines

- Bin number
- Name of wine
- Country and area of origin
- Quality indication (e.g. AOC, Qmp, etc.)
- Shipper
- Château/estate bottled
- Varietal (grape type(s))
- Vintage
- Alcoholic strength
- ½ bottle, bottle, magnum
- Price
- Supplier
- Descriptive notes as appropriate.

Other drinks

- Type of drink, for example juices, whisky, gin, sherry.
- Brand name if appropriate, for example Martini.
- Style (sweet, dry, etc.).
- Description, for example for cocktails.
- Alcoholic strength as appropriate.
- Descriptive notes as appropriate.

Alcoholic strength

Although there are various types of alcohol, the two main ones are methyl alcohol (methanol) and ethyl alcohol (ethanol). Methanol is used for various industrial purposes but is a dangerous poison when drunk; alcoholic beverages are drinks that contain ethanol. Alcoholic beverages are divided into three general classes: beers, wines and spirits.

The two main scales of measurement of alcoholic strength may be summarised as:
1   OIML Scale (European): range 0% to 100% alcohol by volume.
2   American Scale (USA): range 0° to 200° – similar to the Sikes Scale which was previously used in the UK, but has a scale of 200° rather than 175°.

The Organisation Internationale Métrologie Légale (OIML) Scale (previously called Gay-Lussac Scale) is directly equal to the percentage of alcohol by volume in the drink at 20 °C. It is the universally accepted scale for the measurement of alcohol. The 'by volume' measurement indicates the amount of pure alcohol in a liquid. Thus, a liquid measured as 40% alcohol by volume will have 40% of the contents as pure alcohol (under the American Scale alcoholic strength of 80° equals 40% by volume). The alcoholic content of drinks, by volume, is now almost always shown on the label. Table 5.5 gives the approximate alcoholic strength of a variety of drinks.

Table 5.5 Approximate alcoholic strength of drinks (OIML scale)

0%	Non-alcoholic
not more that 0.05%	Alcohol-free
0.05–0.5%	De-alcoholised
0.5–1.2%	Low alcohol
1.2–5.5%	Reduced alcohol
3–6%	Beer, cider, FABs* and 'alcopops'** with any of these being up to 10%
8–15%	Wines, usually around 10–13%
14–22%	Fortified wines (liqueur wines) such as sherry and port, aromatised wines such as vermouth, vins doux naturels (such as Muscat de Beaumes-de-Venise) and Sake***
37.5–45%	Spirits, usually at 40%
17–55%	Liqueurs, very wide range

* FABs is a term used to describe flavoured alcoholic beverages, for example Bacardi Breezer (5.4%).

** 'Alcopops' is a term used to describe manufactured flavoured drinks (generally sweet and fruity) which have had alcohol such as gin added to them. They are also known as alcoholic soft drinks or alcoholic lemonade. Usually 3.5% to 5% but can be up to 10%.

*** Sake is a strong (18%), slightly sweet, form of beer made from rice.

5.8 Cocktails and mixed drinks

England, Mexico, America and France all claim to have originated the cocktail and while there are many stories, no one knows their authenticity. However, it was in the USA that cocktails first gained in popularity. At this stage, the cocktail was as much a pre-mixed stimulant mixture for taking on sporting occasions as it was a bar drink. Figure 5.12 shows some examples of cocktails.

Figure 5.12 Cocktails (illustration courtesy of Six Continents Hotels)

A modern cocktail is normally a short drink of up to about 10 cl (3½–4 oz) – anything larger often being called a 'mixed drink' or 'long drink'. However, the term cocktail is now generally recognised to mean all types of mixed drinks. Table 5.6 gives the range of drinks that can be included under the heading cocktails.

Table 5.6 Types of cocktails

Blended drinks	Made using a liquidiser
Champagne cocktails	For example, Bucks Fizz, which has the addition of orange juice
Cobblers	Wine and spirit-based, served with straws and decorated with fruit
Collins	Hot weather drinks, spirit-based, served with plenty of ice
Coolers	Almost identical to the Collins but usually containing the peel of the fruit cut into a spiral; spirit- or wine-based
Crustas	May be made with any spirit, the most popular being brandy; edge of glass decorated with powdered sugar and crushed ice placed in glass
Cups	Hot weather, wine-based drinks
Daisies	Made with any spirit; usually served in tankards or wine glasses filled with crushed ice
Egg Noggs	Traditional Christmas drink; rum or brandy and milk-based; served in tumblers
Fixes	Short drink made by pouring any spirit over crushed ice; decorated with fruit and served with short straws

Fizzes	Similar to a Collins; always shaken and then topped with soda; must be drunk immediately
Flips	Similar to Egg Noggs, containing egg yolk but never milk; spirit, wine or sherry-based
Frappés	Served on crushed ice
Highball	American; a simple drink that is quickly prepared with spirit and a mixer
Juleps	American; containing mint with claret, Madeira or bourbon whiskey base
Pick-Me-Ups	To aid digestion
Pousse-Café	Layered mix of liqueurs and/or spirits using differences in the specific densities of drinks to create layers – heaviest at the bottom, lightest at the top
Smashes	Smaller version of a julep
Sours	Always made with fresh juices to sharpen the flavour of the drink
Swizzles	Take their name from the stick used to stir the drink; 'swizzling' creates a frost on the outside of glass
Toddies	Refreshers that may be served hot or cold; contain lemon, cinnamon and nutmeg

Making cocktails

The art of making a good cocktail is to blend all the ingredients together so that upon tasting no single ingredient is predominant. Making cocktails has become very popular and the professionalism of cocktail making is increasing. Cocktail making is often now called mixology and cocktail makers are called mixologists.

The four main methods for making cocktails and mixed drinks are described below.

Shaken

Ice is placed in a standard cocktail shaker or a Boston shaker together with the ingredients so as to combine the ingredients and chill them down. The lid is then placed on the cocktail shaker and then shaken hard until the outside is very cool and condensation has formed. The mixture is then strained into a serving glass using a Hawthorne strainer to remove the ice and other solid ingredients.

Stirred

The ice and ingredients are placed into a mixing glass and then gently stirred with a bar spoon to mix the ingredients and chill them down. The mixture is then strained into the serving glass using a Hawthorn strainer to remove the ice and other solid ingredients.

Built

The drink is created in the serving glass by putting the ingredients and the ice into a service glass, one after the other. Drinks made in this way often including the process of muddling – crushing together ingredients, such as fruit, leaves and sugar, at the bottom of a glass before adding other ingredients. Muddling is carried out using the flat end of a bar spoon as the muddler (see Section 3.6, p.62 for a picture of a bar spoon) or another specially designed tool.

Layered

Liquids, which can be alcoholic and non-alcoholic, that have different specific densities are floated one on top of the other in the serving glass. These drinks can also be referred to as poured drinks.

Another term that is sometimes used in relation to cocktail making is 'throwing'. This technique involves the long pouring of the ingredients of a cocktail between two mixing glasses, for example in a Martini to aerate the drink which enhances the flavour of the gin. Long pouring (pouring from a height) is also sometimes used when putting various liquids into a shaker, mixing glass or the serving glass. More recently smoothies have become popular and are often seen as health drinks. These are made in a blender. In addition to fresh fruit or vegetables they are sometimes sweetened and the recipe may also include crushed ice, frozen fruit, honey or frozen yogurt. Pre-made bottled or carton versions are also available.

Non-alcoholic cocktails are also popular and apply the same methods and skills that are used for the alcoholic varieties. More often non-alcoholic cocktails are now referred to as 'mocktails'.

> **Note**: For examples of bar equipment see Section 3.5, p.61. Examples of glassware used for serving cocktails are shown in Section 3.11, Figure 3.12 (p.80).
>
> Also see notes on the service of cocktails in Section 6.6, p.233.
>
> For a list of cocktail recipes and methods see Annex B, p.427.

5.9 Bitters

Bitters are used either as apéritifs or for flavouring mixed drinks and cocktails. The most popular varieties are listed in Table 5.7.

Table 5.7 Popular varieties of bitters

Amer Picon	A very black and bitter French apéritif. Grenadine or Cassis is often added to make the flavour more acceptable. Traditionalists add water in a proportion 2:1
Angostura bitters	Takes its name from a town in Bolivia. However, it is no longer produced there but in Trinidad. Brownish red in colour, it is used in the preparation of pink gin and the occasional cocktail and may be regarded as mainly a flavouring agent
Byrrh	(Pronounced beer.) This is a style of bitters made in France near the Spanish border. It has a base of red wine and is flavoured with quinine and herbs and fortified with brandy
Campari	A pink, bittersweet Italian apéritif that has a slight flavour of orange peel and quinine. Serve in an 18.93 cl (6⅔ fl oz) Paris goblet or Highball glass. Use one measure on ice and garnish with a slice of lemon. Top up according to the customer's requirements with soda or iced water
Fernet Branca	The Italian version of Amer Picon. Best served diluted with water or soda. Good for hangovers!
Underberg	A German bitter that looks like, and almost tastes like, iodine. It may be taken as a pick-me-up with soda
Other bitters	Orange and peach bitters are used principally as cocktail ingredients. Other well-known bitters are Amora Montenegro, Radis, Unicum, Abbots, Peychaud, Boonekamp and Welling. Many are used to cure that 'morning after the night before' feeling. Cassis or Grenadine is sometimes added to make the drink more palatable

5.10 Wine

Wine is the alcoholic beverage obtained from the fermentation of the juice of freshly gathered grapes. The fermentation takes place in the district of origin, according to local tradition and practice.

Only a relatively small area of the world is wine producing. This is because the grape will only provide juice of the quality necessary for conversion into a drinkable wine where two climatic conditions prevail:

- sufficient sun to ripen the grape
- winters that are moderate yet sufficiently cool to give the vine a chance to rest and restore its strength for the growing and fruiting season.

These climatic conditions are found in two main wine producing zones, which lie between the latitudes 30° and 50° north of the equator and 30° and 50° south of the equator.

Three-quarters of the world's wine is produced in Europe (often referred to as 'Old World') and just under half in the EU. France and Italy produce the most wine, with Italy being the next largest producer followed by Spain and Germany, and Portugal. Outside Europe (often referred to as 'New World'), the largest producer is the USA followed by Australia, Argentina, Chile and South Africa.

Vinification

The process central to vinification (wine making) is fermentation – the conversion of sugar by yeast to alcohol and carbon dioxide. This process is also necessary to the making of all alcoholic beverages – not only for still, sparkling and fortified wines, but also spirits, liqueurs and beers (although some variations and further processes will be applied for different types of beverages).

Vine species

The process of cultivating grapes is known as 'viticulture'. The vine species that produces grapes suitable for wine production, and which stocks most of the vineyards of the world, is named *Vitis vinifera*. Most varieties now planted in Europe and elsewhere have evolved from this species through cross-breeding, to suit local soils and climates. The same grape in different regions may be given a different name, for example, Grenache in the Rhône region is also known as Garnacha, which produces fine Spanish wines. There are a number of grapes that have become known as having distinctive characteristics. Examples of these principal grapes of the world, and their general characteristics, are given in Table 5.8.

Table 5.8 Principal white and red grapes used for wine making

White grapes	Where grown	General characteristics of the wine
Chardonnay	Worldwide	The white grape of Burgundy, Champagne and the New World. Aromas associated with chardonnay include ripe melon and fresh pineapple. The fruity, oaky New World wines tend to be buttery and syrupy, with tropical fruits and richness. In Burgundy the wines are succulent but bone-dry, with a nutty intensity. Chablis, from the cooler northern Burgundy, gives wines that have a sharp, steely acidity that may also be countered by the richness of oak. Also one of the three grapes for Champagne

White grapes	Where grown	General characteristics of the wine
Chenin blanc	Loire, California and South Africa (known as Steen)	Variety of styles: bone-dry, medium-sweet, intensely sweet or sparkling wines, all with fairly high acidity making the wines very refreshing. Aroma association tends to be apples
Gewürztraminer	Alsace, Australia, Chile, Eastern Europe, Germany, New Zealand, USA	One of the most pungent grapes, making wines that are distinctively spicy, with aromas like rose petals, grapefruit and tropical fruits such as lychees. Wines are aromatic and perfumed and are occasionally off-dry
Muscat	Worldwide	Mainly sweet, perfumed wines, smelling and tasting of grapes and raisins and made in styles from pale, light and floral to golden, sweet and orangey, or brown, rich and treacly. Often fortified (as in the French *vins doux naturels,* e.g. Muscat des Beaumes-de-Venise). Also principal grape for sparkling Asti
Pinot Blanc/ Weissburgunder	Alsace, Eastern Europe, northern Italy, Germany, USA	Dry, neutral, fresh and fruity wines with the best having appley and soft spicy and honeyed aromas
Pinot Gris/Pinot Grigio/Ruländer/ Tokay-Pinot Gris	Alsace, Canada, Germany, Hungary, Italy, New Zealand, Slovenia, USA	Generally full bodied spicy white wines, often high in alcohol and low in acidity. Wines are crisp and neutral in Italy and aromatic and spicy in Alsace and elsewhere, with a hint of honey. Also used to make golden sweet wines, especially from Alsace
Riesling	Alsace, Australia, Canada, Germany, New Zealand, South Africa, USA	Range of wines from the steely to the voluptuous, always well perfumed, with good ageing potential. Aromas tend towards apricots and peaches. Germany makes the greatest Riesling in all styles. Piercing acidity and flavours ranging from green apple and lime to honeyed peaches, to stony and slate-like. Styles can range from bright and tangy to intensely sweet
Sauvignon Blanc	Worldwide	Common aroma association with gooseberries, the wines are green, tangy, fresh and pungent. When made with oak, it can be a different wine: tropical fruits in the Californian examples, while the Bordeaux classic wines are often blended with Sémillon and begin with nectarine hints and then become more nutty and creamy with age. May be called Blanc Fumé
Sémillon	Mainly Bordeaux but also Australia and New Zealand	Lemony, waxy dry whites; when oaked they can gain flavours of custard, nuts and honey. Luscious golden sweet wines when grapes are affected by *Botrytis Cinera* (Noble Rot), e.g. Sauternes
Viognier	Rhône Valley and southern France, Australia, USA	Rhône wines, e.g. Condrieu, are aromatic, with hints of apricots and spring flowers; wines from other areas tend to be less perfumed

Red grapes	Where grown	General characteristics of the wine
Cabernet Sauvignon	Worldwide	Principal grape of Bordeaux, especially in the Médoc. New World wines deliver big wines with upfront blackcurrant fruit; Bordeaux wines need time to mature. Generally benefits from being blended, e.g. with Merlot, Cabernet Franc, Syrah, Tempranillo, Sangiovese. Also used to make aromatic rosé wines

Red grapes	Where grown	General characteristics of the wine
Gamay	Beaujolais, Loire, Savoie, Switzerland and USA	The grape of Beaujolais, making light and juicy wines. Characteristic pear drop aroma association indicating wine made using macération carbonique method. Makes lighter wine in the Loire Valley in central France and in Switzerland and Savoie. Known as 'Napa Gamay' in California
Grenache/ Garnacha	Southern France and Rhône, Australia, Spain, USA	Makes strong, fruity but pale wines, and fruity rosé wines. Important grape as part of blends, e.g. for Châteauneuf-du-Pape in the Rhône and for Rioja in Spain. Characteristics of ripe strawberries, raspberries and hints of spice
Malbec	South-West France, Argentina	French wines tend to be plummy and tannic. In Bordeaux it is used for blending. Argentinean wines tend to be rich and perfumed
Merlot	Worldwide	Principal grape of Saint-Emilion and Pomerol in France. Aromas tend towards plums and damsons. The wines are low in harsh tannins and can be light and juicy, smooth and plummy or intensely blackcurrant
Nebbiolo	Italy	One of Italy's best red grapes, used in Barolo and Barbaresco. Fruity and perfumed wines with a mixture of tastes and flavours of black cherry and sloes, tar and roses. Aroma association tends towards prunes. Traditionally tough and tannic when young, with good plummy flavours as they develop
Pinot Noir/ Spätburgunder/ Pinot Nero	Worldwide	Principal grape of Burgundy's Côte d'Or. Aromas can be of strawberries, cherries and plums (depending on where grown). Silky and strawberry-like; simple wines have juicy fruit; the best mature wines, such as the great red wines of Burgundy, are well perfumed. Loire and German wines are lighter. Also one of the three grapes of Champagne and used elsewhere (e.g. California and Australia) for making white, sparkling or red and very pale pink wines
Sangiovese	Italy, Argentina, Australia, USA	Principal grape of Chianti. Also known as Brunello and Moreluno. Mouth-watering, sweet-sour red fruit in young wines, reminiscent of juicy cherries, which intensifies in older wines
Shiraz/Syrah	Worldwide	Warm, spicy, peppery wines with aromas of raspberries; French Syrah tends to be smoky, herby and packed with red fruits (raspberries, blackberries or blackcurrants); Australian Shiraz has sweeter black cherry fruit and often black chocolate or liquorice aromas. Very fruity rosé wines are also made
Tempranillo	Spain, Portugal, Argentina	Early ripening, aromatic Rioja grape (Ull de Liebre in Catalonia, Cencibel in La Mancha, Tinto Fino in Ribera del Duero, Tinta Roriz in Douro and Aragonez in southern Portugal). Wines are light and juicy with hints of strawberries and plums, silky and spicy with hints of prunes, tobacco and cocoa. Wines in cooler climates are more elegant and those in warmer climates are more beefy
Zinfandel (Pimitivo in Italy)	California, Italy	Aromas of blackberries, bramble and spice. In California wines have blackberry flavours, which are sometimes slightly metallic. Can be structured and lush and also used to make the pale pink 'blush' white wine. Genetically linked and known as Primitivo in Southern Italy, where it makes big, rustic wines

The grape

The grape consists of a number of elements:

- **Skin** – which provide tannins and colour
- **Stalk** – which provides tannins
- **Pips** – provide bitter oils
- **Pulp** – contains sugar, fruit acids, water and pectins.

The yeast required for the fermentation process is found on the outside of the grape skin in the form of a whitish bloom.

The colour in wine comes mainly from the skin of the grape and is extracted during the fermentation process. Red wine can only be made from red grapes. However, white wine can be made from white or red grapes, provided that, in the case of red grapes, the grape skins are removed before fermentation begins.

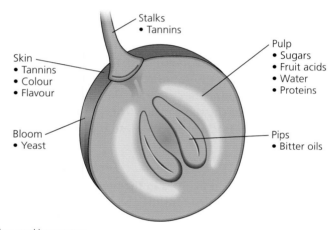

Figure 5.13 The wine making grape

Factors that influence the quality and final taste of wine

The same vine variety, grown in different regions and processed in different ways, will produce wines of differing characteristics. The factors that affect the quality and final taste of wines are:

- climate and microclimate
- method of wine making – vinification
- nature of the soil and subsoil
- luck of the year – vintage
- vine family and grape species
- ageing and maturing process
- method of cultivation – viticulture
- method of shipping or transportation
- composition of the grape(s)
- storage temperature.
- yeast and fermentation.

Wines may be identified as vintage wines. These are wines grown and made in a particular year and this is stated on the bottle. Non-vintage wines are those where the bottle may contain wines from different years. No date will be shown on the bottle.

Pests and diseases

The vine is subject to pests and diseases in the form of birds, insects, fungi, viruses and weeds. The main ones are described below.

Phylloxera vastatrix

A louse-like, almost invisible aphid, which attacks the roots of the vine. Phylloxera arrived in Europe in the mid-1800s almost by accident, transported on American vines imported into various European countries from the eastern states of North America. It ravaged many of the vineyards of Europe at this time. The cure was to graft the European vine onto resistant American rootstocks. This practice has since become standard throughout the world wherever *Vitis vinifera* is grown.

Grey rot or pourriture gris

This fungus attacks the leaves and fruit of the vine during warm damp weather. It is recognised by a grey mould. The fungus imparts an unpleasant flavour to the wine.

Noble rot or pourriture noble (*Botrytis cinerea*)

This is the same fungus in its beneficent form, which may occur when humid conditions are followed by hot weather. The fungus punctures the grape skin, the water content evaporates and the grape shrivels, thus concentrating the sugar inside. This process gives the luscious flavours characteristic of Sauternes, German Trockenbeerenauslese and Hungarian Tokay Aszu.

Faults in wine

Faults occasionally develop in wine as it matures in the bottle. Nowadays, through improved techniques and attention to detail regarding bottling and storage, faulty wine is a rarity. Some of the more common causes of faulty wine are given below.

Corked wines

These are wines affected by a diseased cork caused through bacterial action or excessive bottle age. TCA (trichloroanisole) causes the wine to taste and smell foul. This is not to be confused with cork residue in wine, which is harmless.

Maderisation or oxidation

This is caused by bad storage leading to too much exposure to air, often because the cork has dried out. The colour of the wine browns or darkens and the taste slightly resembles that of Madeira, hence the name. The wine tastes 'spoilt'.

Acetification

This is caused when the wine is over exposed to air. The vinegar microbe develops a film on the surface of the wine and acetic acid is produced, making the wine taste sour, resembling wine vinegar (vin vinaigre).

Tartare flake

This is the crystallisation of potassium bitartrate. These crystal-like flakes, sometimes seen in white wine, may cause anxiety to some customers as they spoil the appearance of the wine, which is otherwise perfect to drink. If the wine is stabilised before bottling, this condition should not occur.

Excess sulphur dioxide (SO_2)

Sulphur dioxide is added to wine to preserve it and keep it healthy. Once the bottle is opened, the smell will disappear and, after a few minutes, the wine is perfectly drinkable.

Secondary fermentation

This happens when traces of sugar and yeast are left in the wine in the bottle. It leaves the wine with an unpleasant, prickly taste that should not be confused with the pétillant or spritzig characteristics associated with other styles of healthy and refreshing wines.

Foreign contamination

Examples include splintered or powdered glass caused by faulty bottling machinery or re-used bottles which previously held some kind of disinfectant.

Hydrogen sulphide (H_2S)

The wine smells and tastes of rotten eggs and should be thrown away.

Sediment, lees, crust or dregs

This is organic matter discarded by the wine as it matures in the cask or bottle. It can be removed by racking, fining or, in the case of bottled wine, by decanting.

Cloudiness

This is caused by suspended matter in the wine, which disguises its true colour. It may also be caused by extremes in storage temperatures.

Classification of wine types

Still (or light) wine

This is the largest category. The alcoholic strength may be between 9% and 15% by volume. The wines may be:
- **Red**: produced by being fermented in contact with grape skins (from which the wine gets its colour). Normally dry wines.
- **White**: usually produced from white grapes, but the grape juice (must) is usually fermented away from the skins. Normally dry to very sweet.
- **Rosé**: can be made in three ways: from black grapes fermented on the skins for up to 48 hours; by mixing red and white wines together; or by pressing grapes so that some colour is extracted. Rosé wine may be dry or semi-sweet. Rosé wines are called 'blush' wines in the USA when made wholly from red grapes.
- **Sparkling wines**: available from France, Spain (Cava), Italy (Prosecco), Germany (Sekt) and many other countries.

The most famous sparkling wine is Champagne, which is made in an area of north-eastern France. It is created by the secondary fermentation in the bottle (known in Champagne as *méthode champenoise* and elsewhere as *méthode traditionelle*).

Effervescent wines made outside this area are called vins mousseux or sparkling wines. A summary of the four methods for making sparkling wines is given in Table 5.9.

Table 5.9 Key differences in methods of production of sparkling wines

Method	Fermentation and maturation	Removal of sediment
Méthode traditionelle	In bottle	By the processes of remuage and dégorgement (moving the sediment to the neck of the bottle and then opening the bottle to remove it, topping up the bottle with more wine and then resealing)
Méthode transvasement or transfer method	In bottle	By transfer under pressure to a vat and then filtering before rebottling
Charmat or méthode cuve close	In tank	By filtration process
Méthode gazifié or carbonation method	Sometimes termed 'impregnation', where carbon dioxide is injected into a vat of still wine that has been chilled and which is then bottled under pressure. Least expensive method	

Sweetness in sparkling wine

The dryness or sweetness of the wine is indicated on the label:

- **Extra brut** – very dry
- **Brut** – dry
- **Sec** – medium dry
- **Demi-sec** – medium sweet
- **Demi doux** – sweeter
- **Doux** – luscious.

Other sparkling wine terms

- French
  - **Vin mousseux**: sparkling wine other than Champagne.
  - **Méthode traditionelle**: sparkling, made by the traditional method.
  - **Pétillant/perlant**: slightly sparkling.
  - **Crémant**: less sparkling than mousseux.
- German
  - **Spritzig**: slightly sparkling.
  - **Flaschengarung nach dem traditionellen Verfahren**: sparkling wine made by the traditional method.
  - **Sekt**: sparkling (also used to mean the wine itself).
  - **Schaumwein**: sparkling of lesser quality than Sekt.
  - **Perlwein**: slightly sparkling.

- Italian
  - o **Prosecco**: name of the northern Italian village, where the grape is believed to have originated; the term is now often used as the generic name for Italian sparkling wines.
  - o **Frizzante**: semi-sparkling.
  - o **Spumante**: sparkling.
  - o **Metodo classico/tradizionale**: sparkling wine made by the traditional method.
- Portuguese
  - o **Espumante**: sparkling.
  - o **Vinho verde**: meaning 'green wine', slightly sparkling.
- Spanish
  - o **Espumosos**: sparkling.
  - o **Metodo tradicional**: sparkling, made by the traditional method.
  - o **Cava**: sparkling, made by the traditional method, also used as generic name for Spanish sparkling wines.

Organic wines

These wines, also known as 'green' or 'environmentally friendly' wines, are made from grapes grown without the aid of artificial insecticides, pesticides or fertilisers. The wine itself will not be adulterated in any way, save for minimal amounts of the traditional preservative, sulphur dioxide, which is controlled at source.

Alcohol-free, de-alcoholised and low alcohol wines

These wines are made in the normal way and the alcohol is removed either by hot treatment – distillation – which unfortunately removes most of the flavour as well, or, more satisfactorily, by a cold filtration process, also known as reverse osmosis. This removes the alcohol by mechanically separating or filtering out the molecules of alcohol through membranes made of cellulose or acetate. At a later stage, water and a little must are added, thus attempting to preserve much of the flavour of the original wine.

The definitions for these wines are:
- **alcohol-free**: maximum 0.05% alcohol
- **de-alcoholised**: maximum 0.50% alcohol
- **low alcohol**: maximum 1.2% alcohol.

Vins doux naturels

These are sweet wines that have had their fermentation muted by the addition of alcohol in order to retain their natural sweetness. Muting takes place when the alcohol level reaches between 5% and 8% by volume. They have a final alcoholic strength of about 17% by volume. One of the best known is Muscat de Beaumes-de-Venise, named after a village in the Côtes du Rhône where it is made. The wine is fortified with spirit before fermentation is complete so that some of the natural sugar remains in the wine. It is usually drunk young.

Fortified (liqueur) wines

Fortified wines such as sherry, port and Madeira have been strengthened by the addition of alcohol, usually a grape spirit. These are now known within the EU as liqueur wines or vins de liqueur. Their alcoholic strength may be between 15% and 22% by volume. Examples are:
- **Sherry** (from Spain) 15–18% – Fino (dry), Amontillado (medium), Oloroso (sweet).
- **Port** (from Portugal) 18–22% – ruby, tawny, vintage character, late bottled vintage, vintage.

- **Madeira** (made on the Portuguese island of Madeira) 18% – Sercial (dry), Verdelho (medium), Bual (sweet), Malmsey (very sweet).
- **Marsala** (dark sweet wine from Marsala in Sicily) 18%.
- **Málaga** (from Málaga, Andalusia, Spain) 18–20%.

Aromatised wines

These are flavoured and fortified wines.

Vermouths

The four main types of vermouth are:

- **Dry vermouth**: often called French vermouth or simply French (as in Gin and French). It is made from dry white wine that is flavoured and fortified.
- **Sweet vermouth/bianco**: made from dry white wine, flavoured, fortified and sweetened with sugar or mistelle.
- **Rosé vermouth**: made in a similar way to Bianco, but it is less sweet and is coloured with caramel.
- **Red vermouth**: often called Italian vermouth, Italian or more often 'It' (as in Gin and It). It is made from white wine and is flavoured, sweetened and coloured with a generous addition of caramel.

Other aromatised wines

- **Chamberyzette**: made in the Savoy Alps of France. It is flavoured with the juice of wild strawberries.
- **Punt-e-mes**: from Carpano of Turin. This is heavily flavoured with quinine and has wild contrasts of bitterness and sweetness.
- **Dubonnet**: made in France and is available in two varieties: blonde (white) and rouge (red) and is flavoured with quinine and herbs.
- **St Raphael**: red or white, bittersweet drink from France flavoured with herbs and quinine.
- **Lillet**: popular French apéritif made from white Bordeaux wine and flavoured with herbs, fruit peel and fortified with Armagnac brandy. It is aged in oak casks.
- **Pineau des Charentes**: although not strictly an aromatised or fortified wine, Pineau des Charentes has gained popularity as an alternative apéritif or digestif. It is available in white, rosé or red and is made with grape must from the Cognac region and fortified with young Cognac to about 17% alcohol by volume.

Quality control for wines

The majority of the world's wine-makers must ensure that their products conform to strict quality regulations covering such aspects as the location of the vineyards, what variety of grape is used, how the wine is made and how long it is matured.

Many countries now give the name of grape varieties on the wine label. Within the EU, if a grape variety is named on the label then the wine must contain at least 85 per cent of that variety. For EU wines, any number of grapes may be listed as part of descriptive text, but only a maximum of two may appear on the main label. For most countries outside of the EU, the wine must contain 100 per cent of the named variety, although there are exceptions. These include Australia and New Zealand who are permitted 85 per cent and the USA who are permitted 75 per cent. Australia allows up to five varieties, provided each is at least 5 per cent of the blend.

European Union

European Union directives lay down general rules for quality wines produced in specified regions (QWPSR) or, in French, vin de qualité produit en regions determinés (VQPRD) for example:

France

- **Vin de table**: this is ordinary table wine in the cheapest price range.
- **Vin de pays**: the lowest official category recognised. Wines of medium quality and price, made from certain grapes grown within a defined area. The area must be printed on the label. A minimum alcohol content is specified.
- **Vin delimité de qualité supérieure (VDQS)**: a quality wine just below appellation-controlled standard. Area of production, grape varieties, minimum alcohol content, cultivation (viticulture) and wine making (vinification) methods are specified.
- **Appellation d'origine contrôlée (AC or AOC)**: quality wine from approved areas. Grape varieties and proportions, pruning and cultivation method, maximum yield per hectare, vinification and minimum alcohol content are specified.

Germany

- **Deutscher Tafelwein**: wine made from one of the four German wine regions designated for table wine (Rhein and Mosel, Bayern, Neckar and Oberrhein). It is often blended. A minimum alcohol content is specified.
- **Landwein**: quality wine from one of 19 designated districts. A minimum alcohol content is specified.
- **Qualitätswein bestimmter Anbaugebiete (QbA)**: quality wine in medium price range (includes Liebfraumilch) from one of the 13 designated regions (Anbaugetieten). It must carry an Amtliche Prüfungsnummer (control number).
- **Qualitätswein mit Prädikat (QmP)**: quality wines with distinction. They have no added sugar. The Prädikat (distinction) describes how ripe the grape was when it was harvested – generally the riper the grape, the richer the wine. There are six categories:
    1 **Kabinett**: Made from grapes harvested at the normal time, usually October, but in a perfect state of ripeness.
    2 **Spätlese**: Made from late harvested grapes.
    3 **Auslese**: Made from selected bunches of ripe grapes.
    4 **Beerenauslese**: Made from selected ripe grapes affected by noble rot.
    5 **Eiswein**: Made from ripe grapes left on the vine to be picked and pressed when frozen.
    6 **Trockenbeeranauslese**: Made from selected single grapes heavily affected by noble rot.
- **Erstes Gewächs** (first growth), **Grosses Gewächs** (great growth) and **Erste Lage** (top site): new higher-level quality designations of wines from the finest vineyards. All classifying regions use the same **Verband Deutscher Prädikatsweingüter** (VDP) logo for these super-premium wines.

> **Note**: Some German wines labels carry the terms Trocken (dry) or Halbtrocken (medium dry) or Lieblich (medium sweet). The two newer classifications of dry wines are: Classic and Selection (which meets additional quality criteria).

Italy
- **Vino da tavola**: ordinary table wine, unclassified.
- **Vino tipico/Vino da tavola con indicazione geographics (IGT)**: wine from a defined area.
- **Denominazione de origine contrallata (DOC)**: quality wine from an approved area. Grape varieties, cultivation and vinification methods and maximum yields are specified.
- **Denominazione di origine controllata e garantia (DOCG)**: guaranteed quality wines from approved areas. Grape variety and proportions, maximum yield, vinification methods, pruning and cultivation and minimum alcohol content are specified.

Spain
- **Vino de mesa**: ordinary table wine.
- **Vino de tierra**: wines from specified regions
- **Denominación de origen (DO)**: quality wines from specified regions.
- **Denominación de origen calficada (DOCa)**: a DO with a consistent track record for quality.

Spanish wines may also have the term *Reserva* on the label. For red wines this indicates a wine that has aged for at least one year in oak casks and two years in the bottle; for white and rosé wines this indicates a wine aged for at least two years, including six months in oak casks. The other term is *Gran reserva*: for red wines this indicates a wine that has been aged for at least two years in oak casks and three years in the bottle; for white and rosé wines this indicates a wine that has been aged for at least four years, including at least six months in oak casks.

Portugal
- **Vinho de mesa**: ordinary table wine from no particular region and may be a blend from several regions.
- **Vinho regional**: quality table wine from a particular place within a specified region.
- **Denominação di origin controlada (DO)**: quality wines from specified regions. The quality and authenticity of the wine is guaranteed.

Estate bottled
The following terms indicate that the wine was bottled on the estate.
- Mise en bouteille au domaine or Mise du domaine (France).
- Erzeugerabfullung or Aus eigenem Lesegut (Germany).
- Imbottligliato all'origine or Imbottigliato al'origine nelle cantine della fatoria dei: bottled at source in the cellars of the estate of (Italy).
- Embottelado or Engarrafado de origen (Spain).
- Engarrafado na origem (Portugal).

Other terms used in France:
- **Mise en bouteille au château**: means the wine was bottled at the château (literally means castle) printed on the label. It is seen mostly on wines from Bordeaux.
- **Mise en bouteille dans nos caves**: means the wine was bottled in the cellars of the company or person (négociant) whose name usually appears on the label.
- **Mise en bouteille par**: indicates that the wine was bottled by the company, or individual, whose name appears after these words.

Countries outside the EU

Developments in the international wine business, especially in the New World, have led to a more marketing-led approach to wines. Simpler information is given on the labels and also on detailed back labels, including the identification of grape varieties (or the use of the Californian term 'varietals') and straightforward advice on storage, drinking and matching the wine with food.

Although most countries have a category for wines that is similar to EU Table Wine, this is mainly sold locally. On the international markets the wines are classified as Wine with Geographical Description. Each country has its own system for dividing its vineyard areas into regions, zones, districts and so on, and controlling the use of regional names. Where regions, vintages and varieties are named on the label, these wines may also have a small proportion of wine from other regions, vintages and varieties blended with them. All countries have their own legislation covering production techniques and use of label terms to prevent consumers from being misinformed.

- **Argentina**: has a system of DOCs (Controlled Denominations of Origin) but it is common for wines to be labelled by region.
- **Australia**: the Label Integrity Scheme controls regional, varietal and vintage labelling. The Authentication of Origin scheme denotes that if a wine region is mentioned then at least 80 per cent of the wine must come from that source. In addition, a system of regional appellations is being established which is designed to lead to greater geographical descriptions.
- **Chile**: has a system of regional DOs (denominations of origin) in which regions are divided into sub-regions.
- **New Zealand**: does not have a hierarchical structure of regional terms, although some regional names, for example, Wairau Valley or Gimblett Gravels, are more specific than others such as Marlborough or Hawkes Bay.
- **South Africa**: the Wine of Origin (WO) scheme in South Africa controls regional labelling of wines, as well as varietal and vintage details on wine bottles. Estates are also included in the WO scheme and estate wines must only include grapes grown by the named estate.
- **USA**: the American Viticulture Areas (AVAs) is a guarantee of source – at least 85 per cent must come from within that area – but not of quality or method of production. Regional terms can range from naming a state or a single vineyard. One increasingly popular term used in California is 'coastal', which allows for blending across almost all the Californian vineyards lying up to 100 km inland of the Pacific.

Reading a wine label

The EU has strict regulations that govern what is printed on a wine bottle label. These regulations also apply to wine entering the EU. In addition, standard sized bottles of light (or still) wines bottled after 1988, when EU regulations on content came into force, must contain 75 cl, although bottles from previous years, containing 70 cl for example, will still be on sale for some years to come.

In addition to the various quality terms described on pp.167–168 and the sparkling wine terms given on p.171, examples of taste and colour terms that appear on wine labels are given in Table 5.10.

Table 5.10 Examples of wine label terms indicating colour and taste

Term	France	Germany	Italy	Spain	Portugal
Wine	vin	view	vino	vine	vinho
Dry	sec	trocken	secco	seco	seco
Medium	demi-sec	halbtrocken	abboccato	abocado	semi-seco
Sweet	doux/moelieaux	süß	dolce	dulce	doce
White	blanc	weißwein	bianco	blanco	branco
Red	rouge	rotwein	rosso	tinto	tinto
Rosé	rosé	rosé	rosato	rosado	rosado

The label on a bottle of wine can give a lot of useful information about that wine. The language used will normally be that of the country of origin. The information always includes:

● the name of the wine
● the country where the wine was made
● alcoholic strength in percentage by volume (% vol)
● contents in litres, cl or ml
● the name and address or trademark of the supplier.

It may also include:

● the varietal(s) (name of the grape(s) used to make the wine)
● the year the grapes were harvested, called the vintage, if the wine is sold as a vintage wine
● the region where the wine was made
● the property where the wine was made
● the quality category of the wine
● details of the bottler and distributor.

Examples of the kind of information that is given on various wine labels are shown in Figure 5.14.

France

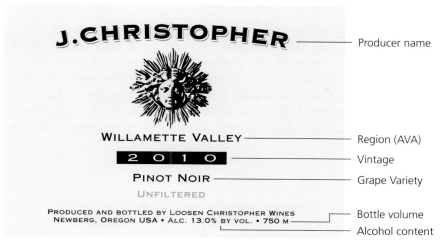

USA

Figure 5.14 Guide to example wine labels (images courtesy of: Wine-searcher.com - The Search Engine for Wines)

Closures for wine bottles

There are now four main types of closures for wine bottles.

Natural corks

These closures are made from whole pieces of cork. Each is individual and unique and there can be quality variation. However, natural cork has a high degree of elasticity and compressibility and can mould itself around tiny imperfections in the neck of the bottle. It is well proven for the long-term storage of wines. Natural cork is however susceptible to trichloroanisole (TCA) (see corked wine, p.169). If the cork dries out or is loose fitting the bottle can leak and the wine can become oxidised through being exposed to the air.

Technical (or composite) corks

These are agglomerate corks made from small pieces of natural cork moulded into a cork shape and held with food-grade glue. The better quality closures are agglomerate with solid cork discs at either end. The solid end is the only part that comes into contact with the wine. However, as with natural cork, it is susceptible to TCA. The opening process is similar to natural corks.

Synthetics (plastics)

These are synthetic closures that may be used for wines that are to be drunk within about 18 months of bottling. After this time synthetic closures may lose their elasticity, resulting in the risk of the seal being broken and the wine becoming oxidised through exposure to the air. Although not susceptible to TCA, there are some risks of the closure taking up fruit flavours from the wine or adding plastic flavours to the wine. The opening process is similar to traditional corks, although this type of closure can be more difficult to extract than cork and re-inserting the closure into the neck of the bottle is also difficult.

Screw caps

Various makes of screw cap and linings are used which are easy to open and reseal. The closure provides a tight seal for the bottle and TCA is unlikely. However, these closures are relatively new and the longer-term effects on wines for laying down (ageing) are yet to be determined. The opening procedure is to hold the whole length of the seal in the opening hand and to hold the base of the bottle in the other hand. The closure is held firmly in the opening hand with more pressure, from the thumb and first finger, around the cap itself. The bottle is then sharply twisted using the hand holding the base. There will be a click and then the upper part of the screw top can be removed.

5.11 Spirits

Production

All spirits are produced by the distillation of an alcoholic beverage. The history of distillation goes back over 2000 years when it is said that stills were used in China to make perfumes, and by Arabs to make spirit-based drinks.

The principle of distillation is that ethyl alcohol vaporises (boils) at a lower temperature (78 °C) than water (100 °C). Thus, where a liquid containing alcohol is heated in an enclosed environment the alcohol will form steam first and can be taken off, leaving water and other ingredients behind. This process raises the alcoholic strength of the resulting liquid.

There are two main methods of producing spirits:
1 The pot still method, which is used for full, heavy flavoured spirits such as brandy.
2 The patent still method (also referred to as the 'column still' or 'continuous still' or the 'Coffey still' after its inventor), which produces the lighter spirits such as vodka.

Bases for spirits

The bases used in the most common spirits are listed in Table 5.11. In each case the base is made into a fermented liquid (alcoholic wash) before distillation can take place.

Table 5.11 Bases for spirits

Spirit	Base
Whisky, gin and vodka	Barley, maize or rye (i.e. beer)
Brandy	Wine
Calvados	Cider
Rum	Molasses
Tequila	Pulque

Types of spirit

Aquavit

Made in Scandinavia from potatoes or grain and flavoured with herbs, mainly caraway seeds. To be appreciated fully, Aquavit must be served chilled.

Arrack

Made from the sap of palm trees. The main countries of production are Java, India, Ceylon and Jamaica.

Brandy

Brandy may be defined as a spirit distilled from wine. The word brandy is more usually linked with the names Cognac and Armagnac, but brandy is also made in almost all wine-producing areas.

Eau de vie

Eau de vie (water of life) is the fermented and distilled juice of fruit and is usually water-clear in appearance. The best eau de vie comes from the Alsace area of France, Germany, Switzerland and Eastern Europe. Examples are:

- **Calvados**: from apples and often known as apple brandy (France)
- **Himbergeist**: from wild raspberries (Germany)
- **Kirschwasser**: (Kirsch) from cherries (Alsace and Germany)
- **Mirabelle**: from plums (France)
- **Quetsch**: from plums (Alsace and Germany)
- **Poire William**: from pears (Switzerland and Alsace)
- **Slivovitz**: from plums (Eastern Europe)
- **Fraise**: from strawberries (France, especially Alsace)
- **Framboise**: from raspberries (France, especially Alsace).

Gin

The term 'gin' is taken from the first part of the word Genièvre, which is the French term for juniper. Juniper is the *principal botanica* (flavouring agent) used in the production of gin. The word 'Geneva' is the Dutch translation of the botanical, juniper. Maize is the cereal used in gin production in the United Kingdom. However, rye is the main cereal generally used in the production of Geneva gin and other Dutch gins.

Malted barley is an accepted alternative to the cereals mentioned above. The two key ingredients (botanicals) recognised for flavouring purposes are juniper berries and coriander seeds.

Types of gin are:

- **Fruit gins**: as the term implies, these are fruit flavoured gins that may be produced from any fruit. The most popular are sloe, orange and lemon.
- **Geneva gin**: this is made in Holland by the pot still method alone and is generally known as 'Hollands' gin.
- **London Dry Gin**: this is the most well-known and popular of all the gins. It is unsweetened.

- **Old Tom**: this is a sweet gin made in Scotland. The sweetening agent is sugar syrup. As the name implies, it was traditionally used in a Tom Collins cocktail.
- **Plymouth Gin**: this has a stronger flavour than London Dry and is manufactured by Coates in Devon. It is most well-known for its use in the cocktail Pink Gin, together with the addition of Angostura bitters.

Grappa

An Italian-style brandy produced from the pressings of grapes after the required must – unfermented grape juice – has been removed for wine production. It is similar in style to the French marc brandy.

Marc

Local French brandy made where wine is made. Usually takes the name of the region, for example, Marc de Borgogne.

Pastis

Pastis is the name given to spirits flavoured with anis and/or liquorice, such as Pernod. The spirit is made in many Mediterranean countries and is popular almost everywhere. It has taken over from absinthe, once known as the 'Green Goddess'.

Rum

This is a spirit made from the fermented by-products of sugar cane. It is available in dark and light varieties and is produced in countries where sugar cane grows naturally, for example, Jamaica, Cuba, Trinidad, Barbados, Guyana and the Bahamas.

Schnapps

A spirit distilled from a fermented potato base and flavoured with caraway seed. The main countries of production are Germany and Holland.

Tequila

A Mexican spirit distilled from the fermented juice (pulque) of the agave plant. It is traditionally drunk after a lick of salt and a squeeze of lime or lemon.

Vodka

A highly rectified (very pure) patent still spirit. It is purified by being passed through activated charcoal, which removes virtually all aroma and flavour. It is described as a colourless and flavourless spirit.

Whisk(e)y

Whisky or whiskey is a spirit made from cereals: Scotch whisky from malted barley; Irish whiskey usually from barley; North American whiskey and Bourbon from maize and rye. The spelling *whisky* usually refers to the Scotch or Canadian drink and *whiskey* to the Irish or American.

- **Scotch whisky**: this is primarily made from barley, malted (hence the term malt whisky) then heated over a peat fire. Grain whiskies are made from other grains and are usually blended with malt whisky.
- **Irish whiskey**: this differs from Scotch in that hot air rather than a peat fire is used during malting, thus Irish whiskey does not gain the smoky quality of Scotch. It is also distilled three times (rather than two as in the making of Scotch) and is matured longer.
- **Canadian whisky**: this is usually a blend of flavoured and neutral whiskies made from grains such as rye, wheat and barley.
- **American whiskey**: this is made from various mixtures of barley, maize and rye. Bourbon is made from maize.
- **Japanese whisky**: this is made by the Scotch process and is blended.

5.12 Liqueurs

Liqueurs are defined as sweetened and flavoured spirits. They should not be confused with liqueur spirits, which may be whiskies or brandies of great age and quality. For instance, a brandy liqueur is a liqueur with brandy as a basic ingredient, while a liqueur brandy may be defined as a brandy of great age and excellence.

Production

Liqueurs are made by two basic methods:

1 Heat or infusion method: best when herbs, peels, roots, etc., are being used, as heat can extract their oils, flavours and aromas.
2 Cold or maceration method: best when soft fruits are used to provide the flavours and aromas.

The heat method uses a pot still for distillation purposes while the cold method allows the soft fruit to soak in brandy in oak casks over a long period of time.

For all liqueurs a spirit base is necessary and this may be brandy, rum or a neutral spirit. Many flavouring ingredients are used to make liqueurs and these include:

- aniseed
- apricots
- blackcurrants
- caraway seeds
- cherries
- cinnamon
- coriander
- kernels of almonds
- nutmeg
- rind of citrus fruit
- rose petals
- wormwood.

Types of liqueurs

Table 5.12 lists some of the more popular liqueurs. The service of liqueurs is discussed in Section 6.6, p.233.

Table 5.12 Popular liqueurs

Liquer	Colour	Flavour/spirit base	Country of origin
Abricotine	Red	Apricot/brandy	France
Avocaat	Yellow	Egg, sugar/brandy	Holland
Anisette	Clear	Aniseed/neutral spirit	France, Spain, Italy, Holland
Amaretto	Golden	Almonds	Italy
Archers	Clear	Peaches/Schnapps	UK
Arrack	Clear	Herbs, sap of palm trees	Java, India, Sri Lanka, Jamaica
Bailey's Irish Cream	Coffee	Honey, chocolate, cream, whiskey	Ireland
Bénédictine DOM	Yellow/green	Herbs/brandy	France
Chartreuse	Green (45% abv) Yellow (55% abv)	Herbs, plants/brandy	France
Cherry Brandy	Deep red	Cherry/brandy	Denmark
Cointreau	Clear	Orange/brandy	France
Crème de cacao	Dark brown	Chocolate, vanilla/rum	France
Disaronno	Amber	Almonds with herbs and fruits soaked in apricot kernel oil	Italy
Drambuie	Golden	Heather, honey, herbs/whisky	Scotland
Frangelico	Golden	Hazelnut	Italy
Galliano	Golden	Herbs/berries/flowers/roots	Italy
Grand Marnier	Amber	Orange/brandy	France
Glayva	Golden	Herbs, spice/whisky	Scotland
Kahlúa	Pale chocolate	Coffee/rum	Mexico
Kümmel	Clear	Caraway seed/neutral spirit	East European countries
Malibu	Clear	Coconut/white rum	Caribbean
Maraschino	Clear	Maraschino cherry	Italy
Parfait amour	Violet	Violets, lemon peel, spices	USA
Sambuca	Clear	Liquorice/neutral spirit	Italy
Southern Comfort	Golden	Peaches/oranges/whiskey	United States
Strega (The Witch)	Yellow	Herbs/bark/fruit	Italy
Tia Maria	Brown	Coffee/rum	Jamaica
Van der hum	Amber	Tangerine/brandy	South Africa

5.13 Beer

Beer in one form or another is an alcoholic beverage found in all bars and areas dispensing alcoholic beverages. Beers are fermented drinks, deriving their alcoholic content from the conversion of malt sugars into alcohol by brewer's yeast. The alcoholic content of beer varies according to type and is usually between 3.5% and 10% alcohol by volume.

Types of beer

Bitter: Pale, amber-coloured beer served on draught. May be sold as light bitter, ordinary bitter or best bitter. When bottled it is known as pale ale or light ale depending on alcoholic strength.

IPA (India Pale Ale): Heavily hopped strong pale ale, originally brewed in the UK for shipping to British colonies. The modern style is a light coloured, hoppy ale.

Abbey-style: Ale brewed in the monastic tradition of the Low Countries but by secular brewers, often under licence from a religious establishment.

White beer: Traditional beers made with a high proportion of wheat, sometimes known as wheat beers.

Mild: Can be light or dark depending on the colour of the malt used in the brewing process. Generally sold on draught and has a sweeter and more complex flavour than bitter.

Burton: Strong, dark, draught beer. This beer is also popular in winter when it is mulled or spiced and offered as a winter warmer.

Old ale: Brown, sweet and strong. Can also be mulled or spiced.

Strong ale: Colour varies between pale and brown and taste between dry and sweet. Alcoholic content also varies.

Barley wine: Traditionally an all-malt ale. This beer is sweet and strong and sold in small bottles or nips (originally ⅓ of a pint, now 190 ml).

Stout: Made from scorched, very dark malt and generously flavoured with hops. Has a smooth malty flavour and creamy consistency. Sold on draught or in bottles and was traditionally not chilled (although today it often is). Guinness is one example.

Porter: Brewed from charred malt, highly flavoured and aromatic. Its name comes from its popularity with market porters working in Dublin and London.

Lager: The name comes from the German *lagern* (to store). Fermentation takes place at the bottom of the vessel and the beer is stored at low temperatures for up to six months and sometimes longer. Sold on draught, in a bottle or can.

Trappist beer: Beer brewed in Trappist monasteries, usually under the supervision of monks. Six Belgian breweries produce this beer, which is strong, complex and un-pasteurised, and often includes candy sugar in the recipe.

Pilsner: Clear, pale lagers (originally from Pilsen, hence the name). Modern styles are characterised by a zesty hop taste and bubbly body.

Smoked beers: Beers made with grains that have been smoked as part of the malting process. Various woods are used, including alder, cherry, apple, beech or oak. Sometimes the process uses peat smoke.

Fruit beers and flavoured beers: Variety of beers with additional flavourings such as heather or honeydew, or fruit beers, which have fresh fruits such as raspberry or strawberry introduced during the making process to add flavour.

Reduced alcohol beer: There are two categories of beer with reduced alcohol levels:
1 Non-alcoholic beers (NABs) which must contain less than 0.5% alcohol by volume.
2 Low alcohol beers (LABs) which must contain less than 1.2% alcohol by volume.

The beer is made in the traditional way and then the alcohol is removed.

Cask-conditioning beers: Cask-conditioned ale is ale that has its final fermentation in the cask (or barrel) from which it is dispensed.

Bottle-conditioned beers: Also known as sediment beers, bottle-conditioned beers tend to throw a sediment in the bottle while fermenting and conditioning takes place. These beers need careful storage, handling and pouring. Only available in bottles.

Draught beer in cans: These draught-flow beers have an internal patented system that produces a pub-style, smooth creamy head when poured from the can. A range of beers are available in this format.

Faults in beer

Although thunder has been known to cause a secondary fermentation in beer, thereby affecting its clarity, faults can usually be attributed to poor cellar management. The common faults are given below.

Cloudy beer

This may be due to too low a temperature in the cellar or, more often, may result from the beer pipes not having been cleaned properly.

Flat beer

Flat beer may result when a wrong spile has been used – a hard spile builds up pressure, a soft spile releases pressure. When the cellar temperature is too low, beer often becomes dull and lifeless. Dirty glasses, and those that have been refilled for a customer who has been eating food, will also cause beer to go flat.

Sour beer

This may be due to a lack of business resulting in the beer being left on ullage for too long. Sourness may also be caused by adding stale beer to a new cask or by beer coming in contact with old deposits of yeast that have become lodged in the pipeline from the cellar.

Foreign bodies

Foreign bodies or extraneous matter may be the result of production or operational slip-ups.

Mixed beer drinks

A selection of beverages based on beer is given below:

- Mild and bitter
- Stout and mild
- Brown and mild
- Light and mild
- Shandy: draught bitter or lager and lemonade or ginger beer

- Black velvet: Guinness and champagne
- Black and tan: half stout and half bitter
- Lager and lime
- Lager and blackcurrant.

5.14 Cider and perry

Cider is an alcoholic beverage obtained through the fermentation of apple juice, or a mixture of apple juice and up to 25 per cent pear juice. Perry is similarly obtained from pear juice and up to 25 per cent apple juice.

Cider and perry are produced primarily in England and Normandy, but may also be made in Italy, Spain, Germany, Switzerland, Canada, the USA, Australia and New Zealand. The English areas of production are the counties of Devon, Somerset, Gloucester, Hereford, Kent and Norfolk where the best cider orchards are found.

Cider

The characteristics of the apples that are required for making cider are:

- the sweetness of dessert apples
- the acidity of culinary apples
- the bitterness of tannin to balance the flavour and help preserve the apple.

Main types of cider

Draft

This is unfiltered. Its appearance, while not cloudy, is also not 'star-bright'. It may have sugar and yeast added to give it condition. Draft cider may be completely dry (known as 'scrumpy') or sweetened with sugar. It is marketed in oak casks or plastic containers.

Keg/bottled

This cider is pasteurised or sterile filtered to render it star-bright. During this stage, one or more of the following treatments may be carried out:

- it may be blended
- it may undergo a second fermentation, usually in a tank, to make it sparkling
- it may be sweetened
- its strength may be adjusted
- it will usually be carbonated by the injection of carbon dioxide gas.

The characteristics of keg and bottled ciders are:

- **Medium sweet (carbonated)**: 4% vol alcohol.
- **Medium dry (carbonated)**: 6% vol alcohol.
- **Special (some carbonated)**: 8.3% vol alcohol – some special ciders undergo a second fermentation to make them sparkling.

Perry

Perry is usually made sparkling and comes into the special range. It may be carbonated or the sparkle may come from a second fermentation in sealed tanks. In the production of perry the processes of filtering, blending and sweetening are all carried out under pressure.

Perries were traditionally drunk on their own, chilled and in saucer-shaped sparkling wine glasses. Today the tulip-shaped sparkling wine glass is more commonly used.

5.15 Tasting techniques

The wine waiter, or sommelier, must have an extensive knowledge of the contents of the wine list. In addition, he or she should have a good knowledge of the characteristics of the different wines and other drinks offered. To develop these skills and knowledge a professional approach to tasting must be adopted. The details below mainly relate to wine tasting but the techniques are similar for a range of other drinks.

Professional tasting

The tasting, or evaluation, of wine and other drinks is carried out to:
- develop learning from experience
- help in the assessment of the quality of a wine in terms of value (the balance between price and worth) when making purchasing decisions
- monitor the progress of a wine which is being stored, to determine the optimum selling time and as part of protecting the investment
- assist in the description of a wine when explaining its qualities or deficiencies to customers
- provide a personal record of wines tasted, which helps to reinforce the experience and the learning.

To appreciate the tasting of wine to the full it should be carried out in an environment that supports the wine evaluation process. That is with:
- no noise to distract the taster
- good ventilation to eliminate odours
- sufficient light (daylight rather than artificial if possible), preferably north facing in the northern hemisphere (south facing in the southern hemisphere), as the light is more neutral
- a white background for tables so as not to affect the perception of the colour of the wine
- a room temperature of about 20 °C (68 °F).

The tool of the taster is the glass, which must be the correct shape. A wine glass with a stem and of sufficient capacity should be chosen (see Figure 5.15). The glass should be fairly wide but narrowing at the top. This allows the elements making up the bouquet to become concentrated and thus better assessed. The wine tasting glass should never be filled to more than one-third capacity. This allows the taster to swirl the wine round the glass more easily. It goes without saying that the tasting glass should be spotlessly clean.

Figure 5.15 Wine taster's glass (International Standards Organisation)

Professional approach

The purpose of the wine tasting is to attempt to identify characteristics that describe the wine, which are then used to assess its quality. When undertaking professional tasting it is important to be logical in the approach and to always follow the same sequence. The professional tasting, or evaluation, of wines includes three key stages:

1 recording the details of each individual wine
2 looking at, smelling and tasting the wine
3 recording the findings.

Approaching the process in this way ensures the development of confidence and the ability to make sound judgements.

Recording wine details

To ensure a complete record of the tasting of each wine, it is important to record the following details:

- name of wine
- country and area of origin
- quality indication (e.g. AOC, Qmp, etc.)
- shipper
- château/estate bottled varietal(s) (grapes)
- alcohol level
- ½ bottle, bottle, magnum
- price
- supplier.
- vintage

Looking at, smelling and tasting the wine

When tasting the wine there are two sets of factors to be considered. The first are to do with assessing and evaluating the characteristics of the wine and making a judgement about its quality. The second are to do with identifying taste and aroma associations.

Professional wine tasting is really an analysis and evaluation of qualities of the wine by the senses. This includes:

- looking at the wine to assess its clarity, colour and intensity, and the nature of the colour by identifying the specific shade of white, rosé or red
- smelling, or nosing, the wine to assess the condition of the wine, the intensity of aroma or bouquet, and to identify other aroma characteristics. Taste is 80 per cent smell!
- tasting the wine to assess the sweetness/dryness, acidity, tannin, body, length and other taste characteristics

- touch, to feel the weight of the wine in the mouth, the temperature, etc.
- hearing, to create associations with the occasion
- drawing conclusions about the evaluation (summing up) and making a judgement of the quality of the wine (poor, acceptable, good, outstanding).

Examples of the terms that might be used as part of the evaluation of the wine are given in Table 5.13.

Table 5.13 Examples of wine evaluation terms

Sight	**Clarity**: clear, bright, brilliant, gleaming, sumptuous, dull, hazy, cloudy
	Colour intensity: pale, subdued, faded, deep, intense
	White wine: water clear, pale yellow, yellow with green tinges, straw, gold, deep yellow, brown, Maderised
	Rosé wine: pale pink, orange-pink, onion-skin, blue-pink, copper
	Red wine: purple, garnet, ruby, tawny, brick-red, mahogany
Smell (nose, aroma, bouquet)	**Condition**: clean – unclean
	Intensity: weak – pronounced
	Other aroma descriptors: fruity, perfumed, full, deep, spicy, vegetal, fine, rich, pleasant, weak, nondescript, flat, corky
Taste	**Sweetness/dryness**: bone dry, dry, medium dry, sweet, medium sweet, sweet, luscious
	Acidity: low – high
	Tannin: low – high
	Body: thin, light, medium, full-bodied
	Length: short – long
	Other taste descriptors: fruity, bitter, spicy, hard, soft, silky, floral, vegetal, smooth, tart, piquant, spritzig/petillant (slightly sparkling)
Conclusion	**Summing up**: well-balanced, fine, delicate, rich, robust, vigorous, fat, flabby, thick, velvety, harsh, weak, unbalanced, insipid, for laying down, just right, over the hill
	Overall quality/value: poor – acceptable – good – outstanding

Tasting technique

After assessing the clarity, colour and smell, take a small amount of the wine in the mouth together with a little air and roll it around so that it reaches the different parts of the tongue. Now lean forward so that the wine is nearest the teeth and suck air in through the teeth. Doing this helps to highlight and intensify the flavour. (Fortified wines, spirits and liqueurs are often assessed by sight and smell without tasting.)

When tasting the following should be considered:
- The taste-character of the wine is detected in different parts of the mouth but especially by the tongue: sweetness at the tip and the centre of the tongue, acidity on the upper edges, saltiness on the tip and at the sides, sour at the sides and bitterness at the back.
- Sweetness and dryness will be immediately obvious.

- Acidity will be recognised by its gum-drying sensation, but in correct quantities acidity provides crispness and liveliness to a drink.
- Astringency or tannin content, usually associated with red wines, will give a dry coating or furring effect, especially on the teeth and gums.
- Body, which is the feel of the wine in your mouth, and flavour, the essence of the wine as a drink, will be the final arbiters as to whether or not you like it.
- Aftertaste is the finish the wine leaves on your palate.
- Overall balance is the evaluation of all the above elements taken together.

> **Note**: It is important that you make up your own mind about the wines you taste. Do not be too easily influenced by the observations of others.

General grape and wine characteristics

There are a number of grapes that have distinctive characteristics. Examples of these grapes are listed in Table 5.8 (pp.158–160) and information on their general characteristics is also given. The type and style of various specific wines is identified, and listed from light to full, in Table 5.16 on pp.185–186.

As well as describing and assessing the quality of the wine, many people also find it useful to apply a range of aroma and taste associations. Some examples of common aroma and taste associations are given in Table 5.14.

Table 5.14 Common aroma and taste associations

White grapes		Red grapes	
Chardonnay	ripe melon, fresh pineapple, tropical fruits, nutty	Cabernet Sauvignon	blackcurrants
Chenin Blanc	apples	Nebbiolo	roses, prunes, black cherries, sloes
Gewürztraminer	rose petals, grapefruit, tropical fruits, e.g. lychees	Merlot	plums, damsons, blackcurrants
Muscat	grapes/raisins	Pinot Noir	strawberries, cherries, plums (depending on where grown)
Riesling	apricots, peaches, lime	Syrah/Shiraz	raspberries, blackberries, blackcurrants
Sauvignon Blanc	gooseberries, tropical fruits (when sweet – grapes, custard, nuts, honey)	Zinfandel	blackberries, bramble, spice
Other aroma and taste associations can include pine trees, resin, vanilla, coffee, tea, herbs, smoke, toast, leather, cloves, cinnamon, nutmeg, ginger, mint, truffles, oak, figs, lilac and jasmine			

Recording the findings

Whenever wine is being evaluated a written record should be kept. These notes should be made at each stage of the process, otherwise it is possible to become muddled and confused. The process of writing down the findings helps to reinforce the discipline of the approach and leads, over time, to the development of greater confidence and skill, and also provides a record of wine tastings over time.

5.16 Matching food with wine and other drinks

Food and its accompanying wine/drink should harmonise well together, with each enhancing the other's performance. However, the combinations that prove most successful are those that please the individual.

When considering possible food and wine partnerships all guidelines have exceptions. For example, although fish is usually served with white wine, some dishes, for example heavily sauced salmon, red mullet, or a fish such as lamprey (which is traditionally cooked in red wine) can be successfully accompanied by a slightly chilled red Saint-Emilion, Pomerol or Mercury. The key issue in not having red wine with fish comes from the reaction of oily fish, such as mackerel, with red wine to produce a metal taste in the mouth. The general guidelines on matching wine and food are summarised in Table 5.15 and possible food and drink/wine combinations are shown in Table 5.17.

Table 5.15 General guidelines for matching wine and food

Characteristic	Food considerations
Acidity	Can be used to match, or to contrast, acidity in foods, for example, crisp wines to match lemon or tomato, or to cut through creamy flavours
Age/maturity	As wine ages and develops it can become delicate with complex and intricate flavours. More simple foods, such as grills or roasts, work better with older wines than stronger tasting foods, which can overpower the wines
Oak	The more oaked the wine then the more robust and flavoursome the foods need to be. Heavily oaked wines can overpower more delicate foods
Sweetness	Generally the wine should be sweeter than the foods or it will taste flat or thin. Sweet dishes need contrast for them to match well with sweeter wines, for example, acids in sweeter foods can harmonise with the sweetness in the wines. Savoury foods with sweetness (e.g. carrots or onions) can match well with ripe fruity wines. Blue cheeses can go well with sweet wines. Also sweeter wines can go well with salty foods
Tannin	Tannic wines match well with red meats and semi-hard cheeses (e.g. cheddar). Tannic wines are not good with egg dishes and wines with high tannin content do not work well with salty foods
Weight	Big, rich wines go well with robust (flavoursome) meat dishes, but can overpower lighter flavoured foods

Some general guidelines when selecting and serving wines are given below.
- Dry wines should be served before sweeter wines.
- White wines should be served before red wines.
- Lighter wines should be served before heavier wines.
- Good wines should be served before great wines.
- Wines should be at their correct temperature before serving.
- Wine should always be served to customers before their food.

When making recommendations, it is useful to be able to identify the type and style of the wine required and the extent to which the wine should be light or full. Table 5.16 sets out a range of wines by type and style and from light at the top of the chart to full towards the bottom.

Table 5.16 Examples of wines by type, by style, and from light to full

	Sparkling	White wines		
	White	**Grapey whites**	**Grassy-fruity whites**	**Richer whites**
LIGHT	Dry Champagne; Saumur; Vouvray; Touraine	Yugoslav Riesling; Tafelwein; Liebfraumilch; Grüner Veltliner	Frascati; Soave; Muscadet	Bordeaux and Loire Sauvignon
	Clairette de Die; Frizzante	Alsace; Bulgarian and Hungarian Riesling; Mosel Kabinett; German Trocken	Orvieto; Muscadet sur lie; Van de Pays de Gascogne	Sancerre; Pouilly Blanc Fumé; New Zealand Sauvignon
	Cuve Close; Deutsche Sekt	Australian Dry Muscat; Alsace Muscat; Alsace Pinot Blanc	Pinot Blanco; Italian Chardonnay; Pinot Grigio	Lighter Californian and New Zealand Chardonnay; St Veran
	Crémant d'Alsace; Cava; Blanquette de Limoux	English wines; Rhine Kabinett; Mosel Spätlese	Chenin Blanc (South Africa and France); Mâcon Blanc; Chablis; Penedès White	Pouilly Fussé; St Aubin; Top class dry white Bordeaux
	Crémant de Bourgogne; Champagne Blanc de Blancs	Australian, Californian, Alsace and New Zealand Riesling; Alsace and New Zealand Gewürztraminer	Rioja (new style); Mâcon Villages (Lugny, etc.)	Grand Cru Chablis; Puligny and Chassagne Montrachet; Mersault; Californian Fumé; Gavi di Gavi
	Saumur demi-sec; Cava semi-secco; demi-sec Champagne	Rhine Spätlese and Auslese; Alsace Verdange Tardive	Vouvray (medium); Vinho Verde	White Rhône; Dão; White Rioja (old style); Retsina
	Vintage Champagne; Australian and Californian sparkling	Trockenbeeren-auslese; Eiswein; Muscat de Beaumes-de-Venise	Californian medium white; French medium white	Corton Charlemagne; Australian Sémillon; Le Montrachet
FULL	Rich Champagne; Mocasto; Asti Spumanti	Tokay; Setúbal; Australian Muscats	Barsac; Sauternes; Australian late picked Sémillon	Australian Chardonnay; Richer Californian Chardonnay

Rosé wines	Red wines		
	Fruity reds	**Claret-style reds**	**Herby-spicy reds**
Anjou Rosé; Cabernet d'Anjou	Beaujolais Nouveau; Côtes du Rhône Nouveau; Vino Novello	Red Loire (Cabernet Franc); Grave de Friuli; Yugoslav Cabernet	Valpolicella; Bardolino; Chianti
Spanish Rosé; Rosé de Provence; Chiaretto di Bardolino	Beaujolais; Beaujolais Villages; Mâcon Rouge	Southern French Cabernet Sauvignon; Côtes du Duras; Côtes de Buzet; Bergerac	Côtes du Rhône; Vins de Pays; Syrah de l'Ardeche
Chilean Rosé; Rosé de la Loire; Bordeaux Rosé	Bourgogne Rouge; Bourgogne Passe tout grains; Cru Beaujolais	Bordeaux Rouge; Bulgarian Cabernet Sauvignon	Gigondas; Dolcetto; Brunello de Montalcino; Chianti Classico
Alsace Pinot Noir; Sancerre Rosé; Jura Rosé	Sancerre Rouge; Côtes de Beaune; Beaune Villages; Rioja	Médoc; New Zealand Cabernet; Côtes du Bourg	Dão; Barbera; Barberesco; Bairrada
Portuguese Rosé	Beaune; Côtes de Nuits Villages; Navarra	Bordeaux Crus Classés; Spanish, Italian and the lighter Californian Cabernet Sauvignon	Châteauneuf-du-Pape; Australian Cabernet Sauvignon; Cabernet Shiraz; Zinfandel; Cahors; Barolo
Rosé Champagne; Rosé Saumur; Rosé Cava	Volnay; Reserva Rioja; Gran Reserva Rioja	Californian and Bulgarian Merlot; Saint-Emilion; Pomerol	Traditional East European, Greek and North African wines
Blanc de Noirs; Californian Blush	Pomard; Aloxe Corton; Nuits St Georges	Chilean, South African and Lebanese Cabernet Sauvignon	Côte Rôtie; Nebbiolo d'Alba
Tavel Rosé; Lirac Rosé; Californian Rosé	Gevery Chambertin; Californian and Australian Pinot Noir	Australian and fuller Californian Cabernet Sauvignon	Hermitage; Australian Shiraz; Amarone della Valpolicella

LIGHT

FULL

Beers and food

Recently there has been an increasing trend to offer beers with food, either alongside or as an alternative to wines. As with wines it is a question of trial and error to achieve harmony between particular beers and foods. Generally the considerations for the pairing of beers and foods are similar to those for matching wines with foods, as shown in Table 5.15 and Table 5.17, and in particular, taking account of acidity, sweetness/dryness, bitterness, tannin, weight and the complexity of the taste.

Making recommendations to customers

A few general pointers are set out below that may be followed when advising the customer on which beverage to choose to accompany a meal (see also Table 5.17). However, it must be stressed that customers should at all times be given complete freedom in their selection of wines or other drinks.

- Apéritifs are alcoholic beverages that are drunk before the meal. If wine will be consumed with the meal, then the apéritif selected should be a grape (wine-based) rather than a grain (spirit-based) apéritif, since the latter can potentially spoil or dull the palate.
- The apéritif is usually a wine-based beverage. It is meant to stimulate the appetite and therefore should not be sweet. Dry and medium dry sherries, dry vermouths and Sercial or Verdelho Madeira are all good examples of apéritifs.
- Starter courses are often best accompanied by a dry white or dry rosé wine.
- National dishes should normally be complemented by the national wines of that country, for example, Italian red wine with pasta dishes.
- Fish and shellfish dishes are often most suited to well-chilled dry white wines.
- Red meats such as beef and lamb blend and harmonise well with red wine.
- White meats such as veal and pork are acceptable with medium white wines.
- Game dishes require the heavier and more robust red wines to complement their full flavour.
- Sweets and desserts are served at the end of the meal and here it is acceptable to offer well-chilled sweet white wines that may come from the Loire, Sauternes, Barsac or Hungary. These wines harmonise best with dishes containing fruit.
- The majority of cheeses blend well with port and other dry robust red wines. Port is the traditional wine harmonising best with Stilton cheese.
- The grain- and fruit-based spirits and liqueurs all harmonise well with coffee.

Table 5.17 Food and wine/drink combinations

Appetisers	
Hors d'oeuvres	Sometimes combinations can be difficult because of overpowering dressings on salad items. However, fino or manzanilla sherry, Sancerre, Pinot Grigio, Sauvignon Blanc or Gewürztraminer can be tried. Depending on the dishes, the lighter red wines may make a good combination with the foods. Beers that might be considered include smoked beers and Japanese beers
Soups	These do not really require a liquid accompaniment but sherry or dry port or Madeira could be tried, as can traditional English ales. Consommés and lobster or crab bisque can be enhanced by adding a glass of heated sherry or Madeira before serving
Terrines, pâtés and foie gras	Beaujolais or a light, young red wine, white wines from Pinot Gris or Sauvignon Blanc grapes and also some sweet white wines, especially Sauternes or demi-sec Champagne for foie gras. Fruit beers and English porters might also be tried
Omelettes and quiches	Difficult for wine but an Alsatian Riesling or Sylvaner could be tried, as could white (wheat) beers
Farinaceous dishes (pasta and rice)	Classically Italian red wines such as Valpolicella, Chianti, Barolo, Santa Maddalena or Lago di Caldaro; most lagers or IPA (India Pale Ale)
Fish	
Oysters and shellfish	Dry white wines: Champagne, Chablis, Muscadet, Soave and Frascati; also white beers, Guinness or other stouts
Smoked fish	White Rioja, Hock, white Graves, Verdicchio, smoked beers and Japanese beers
Fish dishes with sauces	Fuller white wines such as Vouvray, Montrachet or Yugoslav Riesling; white beers
Shallow fried or grilled fish	Vinho Verde, Moselle, Californian Chardonnay, Australian Sémillon or Chardonnay; most lagers or IPA and English porter, especially with scallops
White meats	**The type of wine/drink to serve is dependent on whether the white meat (chicken, turkey, rabbit, veal or pork) is served hot or cold**
Served hot with a sauce or savoury stuffing	Either a rosé such as Anjou or light reds like Beaujolais, New Zealand Pinot Noir, Californian Zinfandel, Saint-Julien, Bourg and Burgundy (e.g. Passe-tout-grains) and Corbières; white beers
Served cold	Fuller white wines such as Hocks, Gran Viña Sol, Sancerre and the rosés of Provence and Tavel; white beers
Other meats	
Duck and goose	Big red wines that will cut through the fat: Châteauneuf-du-Pape, Hermitage, Barolo and the Australian Cabernet Shiraz; most beers
Roast and grilled lamb	Medoc, Saint-Emilion, Pomerol and any of the Cabernet Sauvignons; most beers
Roast beef and grilled steaks	Big red Burgundies, Rioja, Barolo, Dão and wines made from the Pinot Noir grape; most beers and especially flavoured beers (e.g. heather or honeydew)
Meat stews	Lighter reds, Zinfandel, Côtes du Rhône, Clos du Bois, Bull's Blood, Vino Nobile di Montepulciano; Belgian Abbey-style and Trappist beers, flavoured beers (e.g. heather or honeydew), darker beers

Hare, venison and game	Reds with distinctive flavour: Côte Rôtie, Bourgeuil, Rioja, Chianti, Australian Shiraz, Californian Cabernet Sauvignon, Chilean Cabernet Sauvignon, and also fine red Burgundies and Bordeaux reds; Belgian Abbey-style and Trappist beers
Oriental foods, Peking duck, mild curry, tandoori chicken, shish kebab	Gewürztraminer, Lutomer Riesling, Vinho Verde, Mateus Rosé or Anjou Rosé; most lagers and IPA
Cheese	The wine from the main course is often followed through to the cheese course, although it is also worth considering the type of cheese being served
Light, cream cheeses	Full-bodied whites, rosés and light reds; beers generally
Strong, pungent (even smelly) and blue-veined varieties	Big reds of Bordeaux and Burgundy, or tawny, vintage or vintage-style ports and also the luscious sweet white wines; beers generally, especially fruit beers
Sweets and puddings	Champagne works well with sweets and puddings. Others to try are the luscious Muscats (de Beaumes-de-Venise, de Setúbal, de Frontignan, Samos), Sainte-Croix-du-Mont, Sauternes, Banyuls, Monbazillac, Tokay, wines made from late-gathered individual grapes in Germany, and also the Orange Muscats and speciality drinks such as Vin de Frais (fermentation of fresh strawberries) both of which can go well with chocolate. Fruit beers (which can also be especially good with chocolate), porters, and Belgian-style strong golden ales can all pair well with various sweets and puddings
Dessert (fresh fruit and nuts)	Sweet fortified wines, sherry, port, Madeira, Málaga, Marsala, Commandaria; white beers
Coffee	Cognac and other brandies such as Armagnac, Asbach, Marc, Metaxa, Grappa, Oude Meester, Fundador; good aged malt whiskies; Calvados, sundry liqueurs and ports; Champagne; white beers

5.17 Safe, sensible drinking

The majority of the population who drink alcohol do so for many reasons: to quench a thirst, as a relaxant or simply because it is enjoyable. A small amount of alcohol does no harm and can even be beneficial. However, the more you drink and the more frequently you drink, the greater the health risks. Alcohol depresses the brain and nerve function thereby affecting one's judgement, self-control and skills. The four general stages of becoming drunk are:

● Stage 1: Happy (relaxed, talkative and sociable).
● Stage 2: Excited (erratic and emotional; movement and thinking affected).
● Stage 3: Confused (disorientated, loud, out of control).
● Stage 4: Lethargic (unable to stand, talk or walk).

Most of the alcohol consumed passes into the bloodstream from where it is rapidly absorbed. This absorption may be slowed down somewhat if drink is accompanied by food but the amount of alcohol consumed will be the same. The liver must then burn up almost all the alcohol consumed, with the remainder being disposed of in urine or perspiration. It takes approximately one hour for the liver to burn up one unit of alcohol; if the liver has to deal with too much alcohol over a number of years, it will inevitably suffer damage.

Sensible limits

So what are the sensible limits to avoid damage to health? Of course, not drinking alcohol cuts out any risk. However, medical opinion in the UK has set the limit at 21 units spread throughout the week for men and 14 units spread throughout the week for women (excluding pregnant women). Drinking in excess of these limits is likely to be damaging to health.

One unit of is equal to 10 millilitres (liquid) or 8 grams (weight) of alcohol. This is roughly equivalent to:

- ½ pint of ordinary beer or lager
- one glass of wine (125 ml)
- one glass of sherry (50 ml)
- one measure of vermouth or other apéritif (50 ml)
- one measure of spirits (25 ml).

However it is important to note:

- Some extra strength lagers and beer have two or three times the strength of ordinary beers.
- Many low calorie drinks may contain more alcohol than their ordinary equivalents.
- There are about 100 calories in a single unit of alcohol. The amount of calories quickly adds up and can lead to weight gain. Replacing food with alcohol as a source of calories denies the body essential nutrients and vitamins.

Calculating alcohol intake

The amount of alcohol being consumed is a measure of both the strength of the alcoholic drink and the amount or volume of the drink being consumed.

To calculate the alcohol unit intake for wines:

- wine at a specific percentage of alcohol by volume
- multiplied by the specified amount of wine in millilitres (ml)
- divided by 1000
- equals the units of alcohol in the specified amount.

For example, to find out how many units there are in a 75 cl bottle of wine at 12% alcohol by volume:

- The calculation is 12 x 750 ml ÷ 1000 = 9 units per bottle.
- Therefore this 75 cl bottle of wine will give 6 x 125 ml individual glasses of wine and each glass will contain 1.5 units of alcohol (9 units in the whole bottle divided by the 6 glasses).

Further examples for calculating the alcohol unit intake for other drinks are:

- Lager at 5% alcohol by volume x 50 cl measure = 5 x 500 ml ÷ 1000 = 2.5 units per half litre measure.
- Spirit at 40% alcohol by volume x 25 ml measure = 40 x 25 ml ÷ 1000 =1 unit per 25 ml measure.
- Sherry at 18% alcohol by volume x 50 ml measure = 18 x 50 ml ÷ 1000 = 0.9 unit per 50 ml measure.

Remember:

- The number of units required to reach the maximum permitted levels for driving a vehicle varies between individuals but it can be as little as two units.
- Some alcohol remains in the bloodstream for up to 18 hours after consumption. This should be considered in relation to the legal limits for alcohol in the blood when driving a vehicle.

Chapter 6

The service sequence (table service)

6.1 Taking bookings

Bookings may be taken by post, by email, via the internet, by telephone and in person. Booking a table is often the first contact that a potential customer has with the establishment and it is therefore important to give the right impression.

Procedure for taking bookings

When taking a booking by telephone the procedure shown below might be used.

- When the telephone rings, lift the receiver and say: 'Good morning (state the name of the establishment). May I help you?'
- If the customer is making the booking in person then say 'Good morning Sir/Madam, how may I help you?'
- When taking a booking the essential information required is as follows:
  - the customer's name
  - the day and date the booking is required
  - the number of covers
  - the time the booking is required.
  - any special requests.
- When you have received this information from the prospective customer it is advisable to repeat all of the details back to them as a means of confirmation.
- If a cancellation is being received then again confirm the cancellation with the customer by repeating his/her request over the telephone and then ask if you can take a booking for any other occasion in place of the cancellation.
- At the end of a telephone call for a booking you should say: 'Thank you for your booking, we shall look forward to seeing you.'

The procedures for taking a booking in person are similar to those for taking a booking via the telephone. When taking bookings by mail the information required is the same as that identified above. Confirmation is normally sent back to the customer by the same method as the booking was received, for example, by email or post. (See also Section 11.3, p.357.)

The booking sheet

Most establishments use some form of booking sheet, either manual or electronic. An example of the information that might be required on a booking sheet is given in Figure 6.1. This booking sheet shows the maximum number of covers to be booked for a service period and enables a running total of pre-booked covers to be kept. The booking sheet also has space for the customer's telephone number. This is required in case of emergency.

Depending on the policy of the establishment, written confirmation of bookings may be required or credit card details taken. Other information that might be sought includes whether the occasion of the meal is for a special event, customer preferences about the size, shape and location of a table, a guest arriving in a wheelchair or any vegetarians in the party.

If party bookings require special menus, the booking should be referred to the supervisor. Procedures similar to event booking will then be adopted (see Section 11.3, p.357).

Restaurant...........	Day...........		Date...........		Maximum covers...........		
Name	Tel. No.	Covers	Arrival time	Running total	Special requirements	Signature	

Figure 6.1 Example of a booking sheet

6.2 Preparation for service

The term 'mise-en-place' (literally 'put in place' but also meaning preparation for service) is the traditional term used for all the duties that must be carried out in order to ready the room for service. A duty rota showing the tasks and duties to be completed before service and the member of staff responsible is drawn up (see Figure 12.1, p.431).

Order of working

The duties should proceed in a certain order so that they may be carried out effectively and efficiently. For example, dusting should be done before the tables are laid and vacuuming should be completed before the tables and chairs are put in place. A suggested order of work might be as follows:

1 Dusting
2 Stacking chairs on tables
3 Vacuuming
4 Polishing
5 Arrange tables and chairs according to the table plan
6 Linen
7 Accompaniments
8 Hotplate
9 Stillroom
10 Sideboards/workstations
11 Silver cleaning
12 Other duties such as preparing trolleys

Some of these duties will be carried out at the same time and the supervisor must ensure they are all completed efficiently. As the necessary preparatory work is completed the staff should report back to the supervisor, who will check that the work has been carried out in a satisfactory manner and then re-allocate the member of staff to other work involved in the setting up of the service areas.

Using white gloves

In some establishments members of staff wear white cotton gloves when carrying out preparation tasks such as:

● handling linen and paper
● clothing up tables
● making napkin folds
● handling clean crockery, cutlery and glassware
● laying tables.

The gloves help to prevent soiling of clean service items and finger marks appearing on already cleaned and polished service equipment. For each separate task carried out clean gloves should be used. They should not be re-used for further tasks as this may present a hygiene risk.

Preparation duties

The duties to be carried out before the service commences are many and varied according to the particular food and beverage service area concerned. A list of the possible tasks and duties is shown below, but not all of these are applicable to every situation and there may be some tasks not listed which are specific to a particular establishment.

Supervisor

Duties might include:

- checking the booking diary for reservations
- making out the seating plan for the day and allocate customers accordingly
- making out a plan of the various stations and show where the staff will be working
- going over the menu with staff immediately before service is due to commence
- checking that all duties on the duty rota are covered and that a full team of staff is present.

Housekeeping duties

Housekeeping duties include the reception area and may involve the following:

- Every day:
  - vacuum the carpet and brush surrounds
  - clean and polish doors and glass
  - empty waste bins and ashtrays
- Perform one of the following daily tasks, as appropriate:
  - **Monday**: brush and dust tables and chairs
  - **Tuesday**: polish all sideboards, window ledges and cash desk
  - **Wednesday**: polish all brasses
  - **Thursday**: clean and polish the reception area
  - **Friday**: commence again as Monday.
- Each day, on completion of all duties, line up tables and chairs for laying up.

Linen/paper

This applies not only to table, buffet and slip cloths and glass and waiter's cloths, but also to paper slip cloths and napkins plus dish papers and doilies. Duties might include:

- collecting the clean linen from the linen store, checking items against list, distributing them to the various service points, laying tablecloths and folding napkins. Spare linen should be folded neatly into the linen basket
- ensuring that stocks are sufficient to meet needs
- ensuring that glass cloths and waiter's cloths are available
- providing dish papers and doilies as required
- the preparation of the linen basket for return to the linen store.

Crockery

Duties might include:

- checking and polishing side plates ready for lay-up
- preparation of service plates for sideboards/workstations
- preparation of stocks of crockery for sideboards/workstations, such as:
  - fish plates
  - side plates
  - coffee and tea saucers.

Hotplate (pass)

Duties might include:

- switching on the hotplate
- checking and polishing crockery for the hotplate according to the menu offered, and the service requirements. For example:
  - soup plates
  - consommé cups
  - fish plates
  - joint plates
  - sweet plates
  - teacups
  - demi-tasse
- ensuring all doors are closed
- stocking up the hotplate after each service with clean and polished crockery in readiness for the next meal service.

Cutlery

Duties might include:

- collection of cutlery from the storage area (sometimes called a silver room) and polishing and sorting onto trays the following items in quantities agreed with the supervisor:
  - service spoons
  - joint/service forks
  - soup spoons
  - fish knives
  - fish forks
  - joint knives
  - side knives
  - sweet spoons
  - sweet forks
  - tea/coffee spoons
  - specialist service equipment as required for the menu
- identifying broken items or those in need of replacing.

Glassware

Duties might include:

- collection of the required glassware from the glass pantry (store)
- checking and polishing glassware needed for the general lay-up
- checking and polishing glassware needed for any special events
- checking and polishing glassware required:
  - for the liqueur trolley, such as liqueur, port and brandy glasses
  - for any special menu dishes, for example goblets for prawn cocktails, tulip glasses for sorbets
- stacking the cleaned and polished glassware onto trays or placing into glass racks in readiness for setting up.

Cruets, table numbers and butter dishes

Duties might include:

- collection of cruets, table numbers and butter dishes from the silver room
- checking, filling and polishing the cruets
- laying on tables of cruets, table numbers and butter dishes with butter knives, according to the head waiter's instructions.

Stillroom

Duties might include:

- ordering of stores requirements (including bar and accompaniment requirements)
- preparation of:
  ○ beverage service items
  ○ butter scrolls/butter pats and alternatives
  ○ bread items
- polishing and refilling oil and vinegar stands, sugar basins and dredgers, peppermills and cayenne pepper pots
- preparing all accompaniments such as tomato ketchup, French and English mustard, ground ginger, horseradish sauce, mint sauce, Worcestershire sauce and Parmesan cheese
- distributing the accompaniments to the sideboards
- checking with the head waiter the variety of accompaniments and the number of sets of cruets to prepare for the number of sideboards/workstations and tables that will be in use during the service period.

Sideboards/workstations

After ensuring that the sideboard/workstation is clean and polished it can be stocked up. Figure 6.2 gives an example of a sideboard lay-up including:

1 water jug
2 butter dish
3 check pad on service plate
4 assorted condiments
5 hotplate
6 side knives
7 joint knives
8 fish knives and forks
9 soup spoons, tea and coffee spoons
10 sweet spoons and forks
11 service spoons and forks
12 bread basket
13 service salver/plate
14 underflats
15 coffee saucers
16 side plates
17 sweet/fish plates
18 joint plates
19 trays.

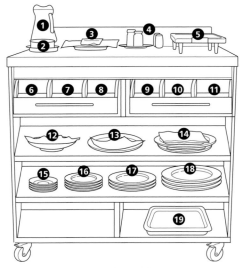

Figure 6.2 Example of a sideboard lay-up

Figure 6.3 Laid sideboard

Other items might include:

- specialist cutlery according to the menu, for example soup and sauce ladles
- various crockery according to the menu, such as saucers for consommé cups.

Guéridons may also have to be laid up in conjunction with the sideboards, according to the type of service offered (for information on service trolleys see Section 6.5, p.228 and for the guéridon see Section 10.1, p.295).

Display buffet

Duties may include:

- the preparation of the buffet table to the supervisor's instructions
- the display of:
  - butter dishes and butter knives
  - accompaniments
  - food items
  - special cutlery and tableware as required (e.g. grapefruit spoons)
  - underplates for large butter dishes
  - service spoons and forks
  - sauce and soup ladles, draining spoons, etc.
  - side plates with doilies or dish papers if necessary
  - water jugs and joint knives for pâtés or mousses
  - cold fish plates
  - carving knife, fork, steel and stand
  - spare joint plates to place used service gear on.

Trolleys

Carving trolley

- Check the trolley for cleanliness.
- Check and refill burners.
- Fill the water reservoir with boiling water from the still.
- Ensure the sauce and gravy reservoirs are in place (beside the plate platform).
- Lay-up for the bottom shelf service plate, to include:
  - service spoons and forks
  - sauce ladles
  - service plate with carving knife, fork and steel.

For a photograph of a carving trolley, see Figure 10.2 (p.328).

Sweet trolley

- Check trolley for cleanliness and ensure it is polished.
- Place doilies or cloths on top tiers.
- Place the following items on the bottom shelf on a folded slip cloth:
  - sweet plates/bowls
  - gâteau slice, pastry tongs (in the drawer or on a service plate)
  - service spoons and forks
  - joint knives
  - sauce ladles (in a folded napkin)
  - joint plate for dirty service items.

Cheese trolley
- Check the trolley for cleanliness.
- The top and bottom shelves may be laid up as follows:
  - Top shelf:
    - various cheeses on a cheese board
    - knives and forks for cheese service
    - salt and pepper
    - caster sugar
    - flat or dish with assorted biscuits or breads
    - celery glass on underplate.
  - Bottom shelf:
    - side plates
    - side knives.

See Figure 6.37 (p.232) for an example of a cheese trolley and Figure 6.38 (p.232) for examples of a sweet trolley.

Additional service equipment

Duties might include:
- Daily cleaning and checking level of fuel where appropriate:
  - spirit and electric heaters
  - flare lamps, spirit and gas.

Clothing-up

Nothing is more attractive in the room than tables clothed-up with clean, crisp and well starched linen tablecloths and napkins. The tablecloth and napkins should be handled as little as possible, which will be ensured by laying the tablecloth quickly and properly first time.

Laying the tablecloth

Before laying the tablecloth the table and chairs should be in their correct position. The tabletop should be clean and the table level, with care being taken to ensure that it does not wobble. If the table wobbles slightly, a disc sliced from a cork can be used to correct the problem.

Next, the correct size of tablecloth for the table to be laid should be collected. Most tablecloths are folded in what is known as a screen fold.

The waiter should stand between the legs of the table while the tablecloth is being laid, to ensure that the corners of the cloth cover the legs of the table once the clothing-up has been completed.

The screen fold should be opened out across the table in front of the waiter with the inverted and two single folds facing him, ensuring that the inverted fold is on top.

The cloth should then be laid in the following manner:

1 Place the thumb on top of the inverted fold with the index and third fingers either side of the middle fold (see Figure 6.4(a)).
2 Spread out your arms as close to the width of the table as is possible and lift the cloth so that the bottom fold falls free.
3 This should be positioned over the edge of the opposite side of the table from where you are standing (see Figure 6.4(b)).
4 Now let go of the middle fold and open the cloth out, shaking it slightly as you draw it towards you, until the table is covered with the cloth.
5 Check that the fall of the cloth is even on all sides (see Figure 6.4(c)).
6 Any adjustments should be made by pulling from the edge of the cloth (see Figure 6.4(d)).

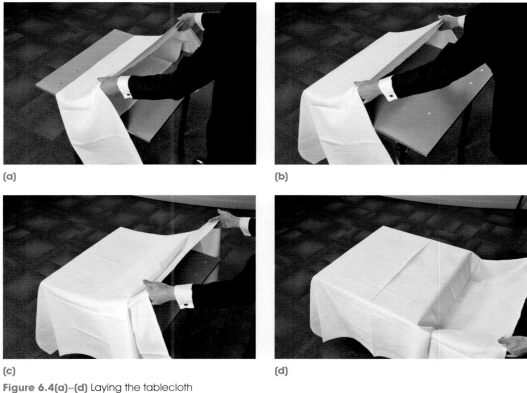

(a) (b)

(c) (d)

Figure 6.4(a)–(d) Laying the tablecloth

If the tablecloth is laid correctly the following should be apparent:
● the corners of the tablecloth should be over the legs of the table
● the overlap should be even all round the table: 30–45 cm (12–18 in)
● the creases of the tablecloth should all run the same way in the room.

If two tablecloths are necessary to cover a table for a larger party, then the overlap of the two tablecloths should face away from the entrance to the room. This is for presentation purposes of both the room and the table.

Napkin folds

There are many forms of napkin (or serviette) fold in use in the food and beverage service area. Some are intricate in their detail while others are simpler. The simpler folds are used in everyday service and some of the more complex and difficult folds may only be used on special occasions, such as luncheons, dinners and weddings.

There are three main reasons why the simple folds are better than the more complex ones.
1   The napkin, if folded correctly, can look good and add to the general appearance of the room, whether it is a simple or complex fold.
2   A simpler fold is perhaps more hygienic as the more complex fold involves greater handling to complete. In addition, its appearance, when unfolded to spread over the customer's lap, is poor as it often has many creases.
3   The complex fold takes much more time to complete properly than a very simple fold.

Many of the napkin folds have special names, for example:
● Cone
● Bishop's mitre
● Rose
● Cockscomb
● Triple wave
● Fan
● Candle.

The seven napkin folds shown in Figure 6.5 are, in the main, those used every day in the food and beverage service area and for special occasions. These are simpler folds that may be completed more quickly, requiring less handling by the operator and are therefore more hygienic.

The rose fold of a napkin is one in which rolls and breads or fruit are presented in a bowl or basket. It is not generally acceptable for a place setting. The triple wave is an attractive fold that may also be used to hold the menu and a name card.

  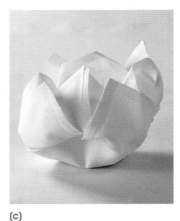

(a)   (b)   (c)

Figure 6.5(a) Cone; **(b)** Bishop's mitre; **(c)** Rose

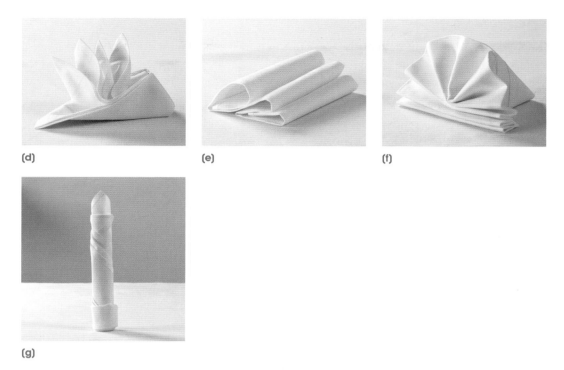

(d)   **(e)**   **(f)**

(g)

Figure 6.5(d) Cockscomb; **(e)** Triple wave; **(f)** Fan and **(g)** Candle

Napkin folding

Shown below are the methods for folding the seven napkin folds identified in Figure 6.5. These are: Cone; Bishop's mitre; Rose; Cockscomb; Triple wave; Fan and Candle. Once you become competent at these, you should learn the art of folding others to extend your repertoire.

> **Note**: The napkins must be clean and well starched. Run the back of your hand over every fold to make the creases firm and sharp.

Cone

1   Open the napkin out lengthways in front of you (see Figure 6.6(a)).
2   Take the top left corner and fold it diagonally on to the right end of the centre line (see Figure 6.6(b)).
3   Fold the bottom square on to the top triangle (see Figure 6.6(c)).
4   Take the two points at the top right corner, by placing your hand inside the napkin and fold them back towards you as far as possible (see Figure 6.6(d)).
5   Pull the base out so that it is circular and place it in the centre of the cover (see Figure 6.6(e)).

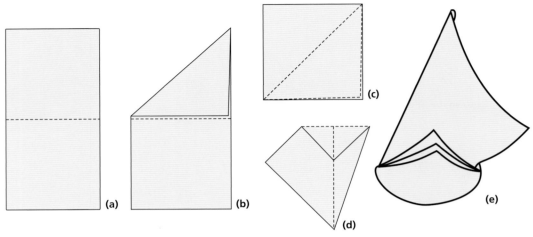

Figure 6.6 Cone

Bishop's mitre

1. Lay the napkin out flat in front of you (see Figure 6.7(a)).
2. Fold it in half, straight side to straight side (see Figure 6.7(b)).
3. Take the top right corner and fold it down to the centre of the bottom line (see Figure 6.7(c)).
4. Take the bottom left corner and fold it up to meet the centre of the top line (see Figure 6.7(d)).
5. Turn the napkin over so that the folds are now facing down (see Figure 6.7(e)).
6. Take the top line (edge) and fold it down to meet the base line (bottom edge), leaving the two peaks pointing away from you (see Figure 6.7(f)).
7. Take the bottom right-hand side and fold it under the flap on the left side. Make sure it tucks right under the flap for a snug fit (see Figure 6.7(g)).
8. Turn it completely over (see Figure 6.7(h)).
9. Again take the bottom right-hand side and fold it under the flap on the left side. Now stand the napkin up by pulling the sides of the base out until it is circular in shape (see Figure 6.7(i)).

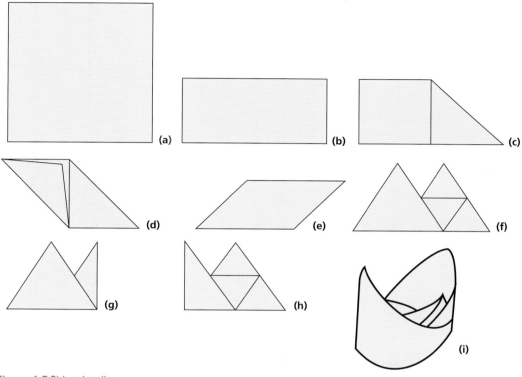

Figure 6.7 Bishop's mitre

Rose

1 Unfold the napkin and lay it out in a square (see Figure 6.8(a)).
2 Fold the corners into the centre of the napkin (see Figure 6.8(b)).
3 Fold the corners into the centre of the napkin for a second time (see Figure 6.8(c)).
4 Turn the whole napkin over so that all the corners folded into the centre are underneath (see Figure 6.8(d)).
5 Fold the corners into the centre once more (see Figure 6.8(e)).
6 Hold the four centre points down by means of an upturned wine goblet (see Figure 6.8(f)).
7 Holding the Paris goblet steady, place your hand under each corner and pull up a folded corner of the napkin (petal) onto the bowl of the glass. You now have four petals showing. Now place your hand under the napkin, but between each of the petals, and raise a further four petals (see Figure 6.8(g). Place on an underplate).

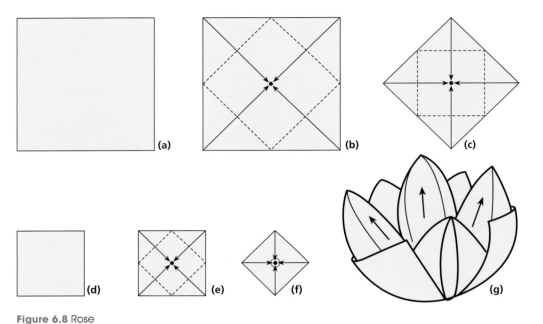

Figure 6.8 Rose

Cockscomb

1   Open the napkin into a square shape (see Figure 6.9(a)).
2   Fold it in half (see Figure 6.9(b)).
3   Fold it in half again to make a square (see Figure 6.9(c)).
4   Rotate the square so that it now forms a diamond shape in front of you. Make sure the four single folds are at the bottom of the diamond (see Figure 6.9(d)).
5   Fold the bottom corner of the diamond to the top corner. You will then have a triangular shape in front of you, with the four single folds on top (see Figure 6.9(e)).
6   Take the right side of the triangle and fold it over on to the centre line (see Figure 6.9(f)).
7   Do the same with the left-hand side (see Figure 6.9(g)).
8   Tuck the two lower triangles (A and B) under the main triangle (see Figure 6.9(h)).
9   Fold the two triangles (C and D) down from the centre line and hold it together. The four single folds should now be on top and at the peak of this fold (see Figure 6.9(i)).
10 Hold this narrow fold firmly, ensuring the four single folds are away from you. In turn, pull each single fold up and towards you (see Figure 6.9(j)).

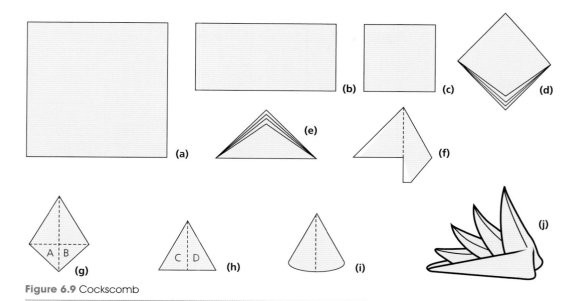

Figure 6.9 Cockscomb

Triple wave (French fold)

1 Unfold the napkin and lay it out in a square.
2 Fold the napkin in three along the dotted lines to form a rectangle as in Figure 6.10(a). NB. For napkins that are already folded in three and then three again, just open the napkin out so that it is in the rectangle as in Figure 6.10(b)).
3 Turn the napkin so that the narrow side is towards you
4 Fold each end of the napkin 'A' and 'B' inwards, along the dotted lines as indicated in Figure 6.10(b).
5 Fold 'B' over once more (Figure 6.10(c)).
6 Turn edge 'A' over so that it meets the edge of the top fold 'B' (Figure 6.10(d)).
7 Turn edge 'C' under so that 'A' is now the top.
8 The final form for this napkin is shown in Figure 6.10(e).
9 The fold is laid with the steps of the folds away from the customer. A name card or menu may be placed in between the steps of the fold.

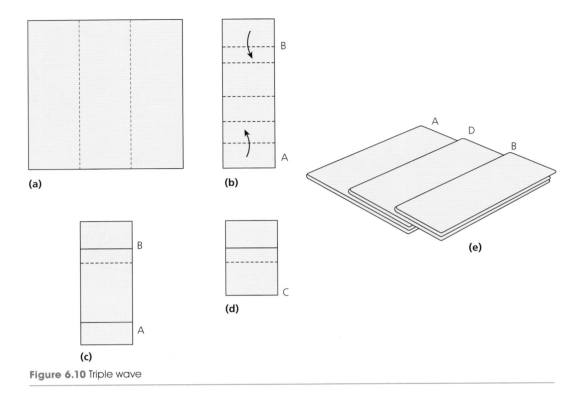

(a)   **(b)**   **(c)**   **(d)**   **(e)**

Figure 6.10 Triple wave

Fan

1 Unfold the napkin and lay out as a square (see Figure 6.11 (a)).
2 Fold the square in three as indicated in Figure 6.11(a). You now have a rectangle shape.
3 Fold the top of the rectangle A down to line B. This should be approximately 6 inches (15 cm) to line B (see Figure 6.11 (b)).
4 Now pleat evenly from line C to line B leaving section A on top of the pleated folds (see Figure 6.11(c)).
5 Fold in half by raising both sides up towards you (see front view in Figure 6.11(d)).
6 Fold triangle (A) down over the dotted line as indicated in the side view (see Figure 6.11(e)). Any excess from triangle A fold under the fan support.
7 Open out and evenly spread the pleated fan (see Figure 6.11(f)).

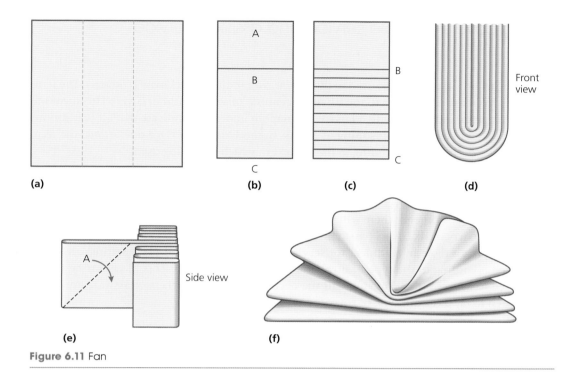

Figure 6.11 Fan

Candle

1   Open out the napkin and set on the table forming a diamond shape (see Figure 6.12 (a)).
2   Fold in half from bottom to top to form a triangle and fold along the dotted line (see Figure 6.12 (b)).
3   Turn over so the fold lies underneath (see Figure 6.12(c)).
4   Now roll the napkin evenly from right to left (see Figure 6.12(d)).
5   When almost completed tuck in the end to hold the napkin fold together.
6   Turn down the peaks at the tip of the candle except the top one (see Figure 6.12(e)).

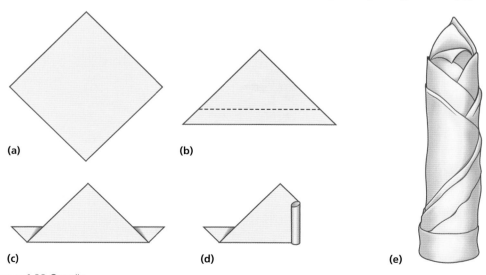

Figure 6.12 Candle

Laying covers for table service and assisted service

Cover

One of the technical terms often used in the foodservice industry is a 'cover' (couvert). The term originates from the custom, up to the fifteenth century, of serving 'under cover'. This meant to cover the courses and dishes with a large white napkin in order to indicate that all precautions had been taken to avoid the poisoning of guests. In modern foodservice operations, the term cover has two definitions, according to the context in which it is being used:

1   When discussing how many customers a restaurant or dining room will seat, or how many customers will be attending a cocktail party, we refer to the total number of customers concerned as so many covers. For example, a restaurant or dining room will seat a maximum of 85 covers (customers); there will be 250 covers (customers) at a cocktail party; this table will seat a party of six covers (customers).

2   When laying a table in readiness for service there are a variety of place settings that may be used according to the type of meal and service being offered. This place setting is also referred to as a cover and includes all the necessary cutlery, crockery, glassware and linen required to lay a certain type of cover for a specific meal or dish.

When deciding on the laying of covers there are two basic service considerations. The first is when cutlery for the meal is to be laid before each course is served. The second is when the cutlery for the meal is to be laid prior to the start of that meal and for all the courses that are to be served. The first approach is known as the à la carte cover, and the second is known as the table d'hôte cover.

À la carte cover

The à la carte cover follows the principle that the cutlery for each course will be laid just before each course is served. The traditional cover given below (and shown in Figure 6.13) therefore represents the cover for hors d'oeuvre, which is the first course in a classic menu sequence (see Section 4.2 Classic menu sequence, p.90).

- Fish plate (centre of cover)
- Fish knife
- Fish fork
- Side plate
- Side knife
- Napkin
- Water glass
- Wine glass.

Figure 6.13 À la carte cover

Where an à la carte cover has been laid, the cutlery required by the customer for the dishes he or she has chosen will be laid course by course. In other words, there should not, at any time during the meal, be more cutlery on the table than is required by the customer at that time.

Classic or basic lay-up

There is now a variety of approaches to what is laid for the à la carte form of service. This can include using large decorative cover plates and a side plate and knife only, or replacing the fish knife and fork with a joint knife and fork. This is sometimes known as a classic or basic lay-up. An example of this type of lay-up is shown in Figure 6.14.

Figure 6.14 Classic or basic cover

Note: If decorative cover plates are used for an à la carte cover it is common for the first course plates to be placed on this plate. The first course and the cover plate are then removed when the first course is cleared.

Table d'hôte cover

The table d'hôte cover follows the principle that the cutlery for the whole meal will be laid before the first course is served. The traditional cover is as follows.

- Joint knife
- Fish knife
- Soup spoon
- Joint fork
- Fish fork
- Sweet fork
- Sweet spoon
- Side plate
- Side knife
- Napkin
- Water glass
- Wine glass.

Again, there are some possible variations to this approach. The sweet spoon and fork may be omitted, for example, or the fish knife and fork replaced with a side knife and small/sweet fork.

Figure 6.15 Table d'hôte cover

Where a table d'hôte cover has been laid the waiter should remove, after the order has been taken, any unnecessary cutlery and relay any extra items that may be required. This means that before the customer commences the meal he or she should have the entire cutlery required for the dishes chosen, set out as their place setting or cover.

Figure 6.16 Traditional restaurant ready for service (image courtesy of Le Columbier Restaurant, London)

Laying the table

Once the table is clothed-up it should be laid in readiness for service. Cutlery must be laid consistently. This is often at 1.25 cm (½ in) from the edge of the table. An alternative to this is to line up the tops of all cutleries.

Crockery that has a badge or crest is laid so that the badge is at the head or top of the cover. After polishing the glasses should be placed at the top right-hand corner of the cover. Once the covers have been laid the table accompaniments should be placed on the table according to the custom of the establishment.

Cutlery should be laid from a service salver or service plate. When handling cutlery it is most often held between the thumb and forefinger in the centre at the sides to reduce the risk of finger marks. An alternative to this is to use a service cloth and to hold the items being laid in the service cloth, giving a final polish before setting the items on the table. In some establishments the service staff wear white gloves when laying cleaned and pre-polished tableware onto the tables in order to avoid finger marks.

When laying a cover, the cutlery should be laid from the inside to the outside of the cover. This ensures even spacing of the cover and reduces the need to handle items laid more than is necessary.

If an à la carte cover is being laid then the first item set on the table should be the fish plate in the centre of each cover.

If a table d'hôte cover is being laid then the first item to be set on the table should be the napkin or side plate in the centre of each cover. If the side plate is laid in the centre of each cover it will be moved to the left-hand side of the cover once all the cutlery has been laid. The purpose of initially placing something in the centre of the cover is to ensure that the covers are exactly opposite one another and that the cutlery of each cover is the same distance apart.

The order of laying these covers is as follows:

À la carte
1 Fish plate at the centre of the cover
2 Fish knife
3 Fish fork
4 Side plate
5 Side knife
6 Napkin – set on the fish plate
7 Water glass
8 Wine glass.

Table d'hôte
1 Side plate at centre of cover
2 Joint knife
3 Fish knife
4 Soup spoon
5 Joint fork
6 Fish fork
7 Sweet fork
8 Sweet spoon
9 Move side plate to left of cover
10 Side knife
11 Napkin – set in centre of the cover
12 Water glass
13 Wine glass.

In some operations a trolley is used for storing cutlery. When laying-up, without customers in the restaurant, this trolley is pushed around the tables and the cutlery items are laid after a final polish with the waiter's cloth.

Table accompaniments
The table accompaniments required to complete the table lay-up are the same whether an à la carte or table d'hôte cover has been laid:
- cruet: salt, pepper, mustard and mustard spoon
- table number
- floral table centre piece.

These are the basic items usually required to complete the table lay-up. In some establishments certain extra items will be placed on the table immediately prior to the service to complete its lay-up. These may include:
- roll basket
- gristicks
- peppermill
- butter and alternatives – after the customers are seated.

Figure 6.17 Formal restaurant ready for service (image courtesy of FCSI UK)

Polishing glassware

The following equipment is required to carry out this technique:
- a container of near-boiling water
- a clean, dry tea cloth
- the required glassware.

1 Using the base of the glass to be cleaned, hold the wine goblet over the steam from the boiling water so that the steam enters the bowl of the glass (see Figure 6.18(a)).

2 Rotate the wine goblet to allow the steam to circulate fully within the bowl of the glass and then hold the base of the glass over the steam.

3 Now hold the base of the wine goblet in the clean, dry tea cloth.

4 Place the other hand underneath the tea cloth in readiness to polish the bowl of the glass.

5 Place the thumb of the polishing hand inside the bowl of the glass and the fingers on the outside, holding the bowl of the wine goblet gently but firmly. Rotate the wine goblet with the hand holding the base of the glass (see Figure 6.18(b)).

6 When fully polished, hold the wine goblet up to the light to check that it is clean.

7 Ensure that the base of the glass is also clean.

Figure 6.18(a) Polishing glasses – allowing steam to enter the bowl of the glass

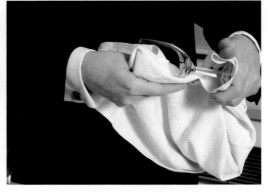

Figure 6.18(b) Polishing while rotating the glass

The process described here is for single glasses. Larger quantities of glassware may be polished by first placing a glass rack full of inverted glasses over a sink of very hot water in order to steam the glasses. A number of people would then work together to polish the glassware.

Preparing a simple floral table decoration

A simple centre table display can be made in a small shallow bowl using oasis – a green-coloured sponge-like material that holds moisture and is soft enough for greenery and flower stems to be pushed into it and to hold them secure.

Preparation

1 Using a sharp knife cut the oasis to size (unless it comes already cut and shaped as a round posy oasis). The oasis must be at least 5 cm higher than the rim of the bowl. This will allow enough room to fill it with greenery and flowers both on the top and round the side.
2 Soak the oasis (or foam) in water by placing it on the water and allowing it to sink of its own accord. Never push the oasis under, as this will leave air pockets in it and it will not fill with water properly. The oasis will be ready when bubbles stop forming and it has sunk to the bottom of the container.
3 Secure the moistened oasis into the posy bowl with oasis tape (green coloured, waterproof sticky tape) – if the bowl and secured oasis can be turned upside down without it moving then it is done correctly.

Foliage/greenery

4 'Greening up' the posy will help to make sure there are no gaps or holes in the arrangement (see (Figure 6.19(a)).
5 The greenery used is often leather leaf, a type of fern, or sometimes Cupresses, known commonly as conifer. When using leather leaf it usually needs to be cut in half, making sure that the top half is left with a stem that can be inserted into the oasis.
6 Use the top sections of the greenery to create a skirt around the bowl, making sure the foliage is facing up to show the correct side. Leave at least a couple of centimetres for the stem (which needs to be free and clean) to create a good anchor so that the greenery does not come free. Make sure that the foliage is angled down to cover the bowl and continue to fill with the remainder of the foliage.
7 Allow room for the flowers (see Figures 6.19(a)–(c)). When dressing the arrangement remember to keep turning the arrangement as this will help to keep its shape round.

Flowers

8 The first step in using flowers is to grade them. This means choosing flowers that will form the focal point of the arrangement (normally the largest in size or the most expensive). Examples are roses, large carnations, irises and lilies.
9 Prepare all flowers by stripping excess leaves to create clean stems, throwing away any marked or damaged flowers, and placing them in a size order, starting with the largest. Keeping the work area clear from cut stems and general mess will allow the full effect and shape of the arrangement to be seen as work progresses.
10 Decide which of the flowers will be used as a focal point from any of the flowers above, then use four of them. Place one in the posy as the central flower, with a height of usually two-thirds the width of the bowl, including the height of the oasis. Add on at least 5 cm and cut. Now push this into the centre of the arrangement.

11 With the three focal flowers that are left, angle these out at around 45 º and at half the height of the top central flower.

12 Remember to leave a couple of centimetres for anchorage and cut the three focal flowers to the same height. Place them at equal distances around the top flower.

13 Once the focal flowers are in place, the hard work is done and all that is needed is to neatly fill the gaps.

14 Depending on the flower choice, proceed by using, for example, spray carnations around and through the arrangement. Always use buds for the outskirts and open, larger flowers further in and closer to the oasis.

15 Again, gauge one spray carnation from the oasis to the tip of the foliage, then cut a few to the same length (don't forget to leave some excess stem for anchorage). Place these at equal points around the base of the arrangement. Always work in odd numbers, otherwise the posy will look square (see Figure 6.19b)).

16 Continue to fill. There may be a few buds poking between the focal flowers but never have these any higher than the top central flower. It is also useful to place a few open spray carnations, for instance, close to the oasis around the top section.

17 Repeat this process with the other flowers. Whether using, for example, chrysanthemums, alstromeria or other flowers, the same principle of using buds towards the outside and larger open flowers towards the top central section applies. Always remember to keep within the round dome shape (see Figure 6.19(c)).

18 Consider using filler flowers such as yellow Solidaster, blue or white September flower, gypsophilla, statice or limonium. These are very small flowers that don't have one head, but have branch-like stems. These can be used to fill gaps all over a posy, making sure that they are displayed the right side up and that the stems are clean. Leave enough to anchor into the oasis and stay within the intended shape. Again, gauge one against the arrangement and cut more to the same length as this will help to keep the arrangement within the shape.

> **Note:** The oasis should be kept moist to maximise the life of the flowers. Moisture content can be checked by lightly pressing the oasis – it should feel wet. The flowers can also be kept moist by lightly spraying them from time to time with a water gun.

19 As an alternative to the posy arrangement (see Figure 6.19(c)), many establishments purchase blooms, often single stem, on a daily basis or as required. These are presented in a single stem vase on the table. This approach is cheaper, less time consuming and equally effective in providing floral decor for tables.

Figure 6.19(a) Greening up the posy

Figure 6.19(b) Flowers to make a focal point and produce shape

Figure 6.19(c) The completed posy

6.3 Taking customer food and beverage orders

Methods of order taking

Essentially there are four methods of taking food and beverage orders from customers. These are summarised in Table 6.1.

Table 6.1 Main methods of taking food and beverage orders

Method	Description
Triplicate	Order is taken; top copy goes to the supply point; second copy is sent to the cashier for billing; third copy is retained by the server as a means of reference during service
Duplicate	Order is taken; top copy goes to the supply point; second copy is retained for service and billing purposes
Service with order	Order is taken; customer is served and payment received according to that order, for example, bar service or takeaway methods
Pre-ordered	a) Individually, for example, room service breakfast (see Section 9.2, p.306/309) b) Hospital tray system (see Section 9.4, p.316) c) Events (see Chapter 11, p.386)

All order taking methods are based upon these four basic concepts. Even the most sophisticated electronic system is based upon either the triplicate or duplicate method. Checks can be written on check pads or keyed in on handheld terminals.

Customers can also hand write orders (as in some bar operations) or use electronic systems such as iPads. There are also systems where the menu is projected onto tabletops enabling the seated customers to select their order from these interactive displays. The order is then communicated by hand or electronically to visual display units (VDUs) or printout terminals in the food production or beverage provision areas.

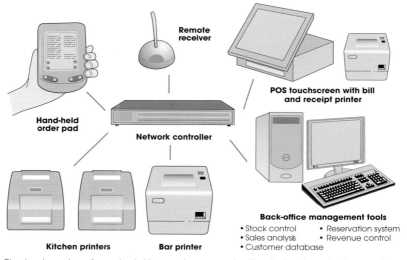

Figure 6.20 Electronic system for order taking and communication to food production and bar areas

Triplicate checking method

This is an order taking method used in the majority of medium and large first class establishments. As the name implies, the food check consists of three copies. To ensure efficient control the server must fill in the following information in the four corners of the check:

- table number
- number of covers
- date
- signature of server taking the order.

Writing the order

- On taking the food order it is written from top to bottom of the food check.
- Usually customers will initially only order their first and main courses.
- A second new food check is written out for the sweet course, this order being taken after the main course is finished.
- A third new check will then be completed if any beverages such as coffee, tea or tisanes are required.

All checks should be legible. Abbreviations may be used when taking the order as long as everyone understands them and they are not misinterpreted by the kitchen, as the wrong order may then be prepared.

When taking orders the use of positive selling techniques can encourage upselling of food and beverage items (for further information on personal selling see Section 12.2, p.383).

With all orders a note should be taken of who is having what order. This ensures that specific orders are identified and that they are served to the correct customer. A system for ensuring that the right customer receives the correct food is to identify on the order which customer is having which dish. A check pad design that might be used for this is shown in Figure 6.21. An electronic handheld order-taking system is show in Figure 6.22.

Figure 6.21 Check pad design enabling the waiter to identify specific orders (image courtesy of National Checking Co)

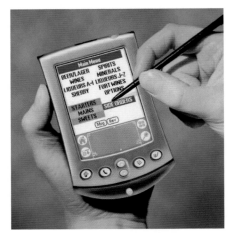

Figure 6.22 Handheld electronic pad for order taking (image courtesy of Uniwell Systems (UK) Ltd/ Palm TEQ UK)

The triplicate food check

- The top copy of the food order goes to the kitchen and is handed to the aboyeur at the hotplate (pass).
- The duplicate goes to the cashier who makes out the customer's bill.
- The flimsy, or third copy, is retained by the waiter at his or her workstation for reference.
- Any checks or bills that have to be cancelled should have the signature of either the head waiter or supervisor on them, as should checks and bills which have alterations made on them.

Duplicate checking method

This is a control system that is more likely to be found in the smaller hotel, popular price restaurant and cafés and department store catering. It is generally used where a table d'hôte menu is in operation and sometimes a very limited à la carte menu.

As the name implies, there are two copies of each of these food checks, each set being serial numbered. A check pad, or bill pad as it is sometimes termed, usually contains a set of 50 or 100 food checks. The top copy of the food check is usually carbon-backed but if not a sheet of carbon must be placed between the top and duplicate copy every time a fresh order is taken.

For control purposes the top copy may have printed on it a server's number or letter. This should be the number or letter given to a waiter on joining the staff. The control and accounts department should be informed of the person to whom the number applies, and he or she retains it throughout their employment.

Perforated checks

Sometimes the top copy of the food and drink checks is made up of a number of perforated slips, usually 4–5 in number. There is a section at the bottom of the food and drink check for the table number to be entered. The top copy sometimes has a cash column for entering the price of a meal or the dishes ordered, but if this is not the case, the waiter must enter the prices independently on both the top and duplicate copy (bill) and against the particular dishes ordered.

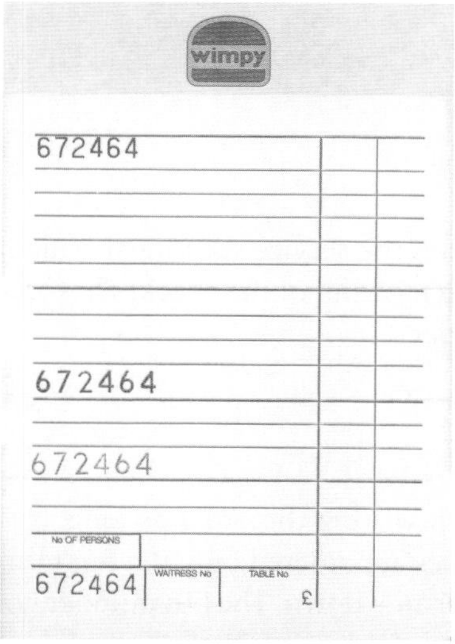

Figure 6.23 Example of a duplicated order pad with perforated sections

When writing out a customer's order a different perforated slip should be used for each course or beverage. The server must remember to write out the number of covers and the order on each slip. Before sending each slip to the hotplate, check that the details are entered correctly on the duplicate copy.

As soon as the first course is served and allowing time for this course to be consumed, the second perforated slip showing the next course or beverage order is taken to the hotplate or bar area by the waiter. Similar procedures as with the first course are followed and this dish will then be collected when required. This same procedure is carried on throughout the meal. When there are insufficient perforated slips, a supplementary check pad is used.

Beverage orders

For beverage orders an efficient system must operate here to ensure that:

- the correct wine and other drinks are served at the right table
- the service rendered is charged to the correct bill
- a record is kept of all wine and other drinks issued from the bar
- management is able to assess sales over a financial period and make comparisons.

The various order taking processes are similar to those for foods. Sometimes a duplicate check pad is used. The colour of the wine check pad may be pink or white, but is generally pink or some other colour to distinguish it from a food check (see Figure 6.24).

Figure 6.24 Wine check

Taking the beverage order

When the beverage order is taken the service staff must remember to fill in the four items of information required, one in each corner of the check. These are as follows:

- table number or room number
- number of covers
- date
- signature.

Abbreviations are allowed when writing the order as long as they are understood by the bar staff and the cashier. When wines are ordered only the bin number, together with the number of bottles required, should be written down. The bin number is an aid to the bar staff and cellar staff in finding the wine quickly. Each wine in the wine list will have a bin number printed against it.

On taking the order staff should hand both copies to the bar staff, who retain the top copy, put up the order and leave the duplicate copy with the order. This enables the staff to see which their order is when they come to collect their wines and drinks. After serving the wines and drinks the duplicate copy is handed to the cashier.

Special checks

In certain instances, when the triplicate checking system is in operation, it may be necessary to write out special checks, as described below.

To follow/suivant

Sometimes it is necessary to write out more than one food check for a meal, for instance where a sweet check is written out after the first and main course has been cleared. At the head of this check should be written the word 'suivant' which means 'follow on' and shows that one check has already been written out for that particular table (see Figure 6.25).

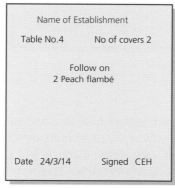

Figure 6.25 Food check: suivant/follow on

Supplement

When an extra portion of food is required because insufficient has been sent from the kitchen, a special check must be written out headed 'supplement' (see Figure 6.26). This means the food is a supplement to what has already been previously sent and should be signed by the head waiter or supervisor. Normally there is no charge (n/c), but this depends on the policy of the establishment concerned.

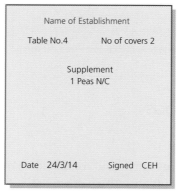

Figure 6.26 Food check: supplement

Return and in its place/retour and en place

Where a wrong dish has been ordered and has to be sent back to the kitchen and replaced, a special check must again be made out (see Figure 6.27). If the service being carried out is from an à la carte menu then the prices of the two dishes concerned must be shown. Two main headings are used on this special check, 'retour' (or 'return') and the name of the dish going back to the kitchen, and 'en place' (or 'in its place') and the name of the new dish to be served.

Name of Establishment

Table No.4   No of covers 2

Return
1 Roast chicken

In place
1 Poached Chicken

Date   2/2/10   Signed   CEH

Figure 6.27 Food check: return/in its place

Accident

It occasionally happens that the server may have an accident in the room and perhaps some vegetables are dropped. These must be replaced without any extra charge to the customer. Here a check must be headed 'accident' (see Figure 6.28). It will show the number of portions of vegetables required and should be signed by the head waiter or supervisor in charge. No charge (n/c) is stated on the check to ensure that no charge is made to the customer.

Name of Establishment

Table No.4   No of covers 2

Accident
2 vegetables N/C

Date   2/2/10   Signed   CEH

Figure 6.28 Food check: accident

Other checking methods

Menu order and customer bill

This shows the menu order and customer's bill combined on one sheet and is allocated to each party. Each customer's requirements are written down in the column next to the price column. Thus, if a party of two customers requested two cream soups, one mushroom omelette and chips and one fried cod and chips, it would be noted as shown in Figure 6.29.

Soup		
Cream soup	2.60	2
Hot dishes		
Omelette served with chips and salad		
Plain		
Cheese		
Ham		
Mushroom	4.50	1
Tomato		
Fried cod and chips	4.75	1

Figure 6.29 Quick service menu order and customer bill

Single order sheet

A further simple form of checking is the single order sheet which is used in cafés, quick turnover restaurants and department stores. It is a simple form of ordering which may be used in various forms of operation.

The menu is normally very limited. The server takes the order and marks down the customer's requirements, calls for the order verbally over the hotplate and, when the customer requests the bill, prices the order sheet and hands it to him/her. The customer then hands it to the cashier on leaving and pays the required amount. There is only one copy of this order and bill combined, and the cashier retains this for control purposes, after the customer has made the necessary payment. Should the customer require a receipt it would be hand written/printed out by the cashier.

Customer self-complete order

A more modern trend is to ask customers to take their own food and drink order. This method is often found in bar operations and it allows staff to concentrate on the service of food (plate service) and beverages, and to accept payments. The customer order form may take the format shown in Figure 6.30.

Please note down your table number and choice of meals on this slip. Take it with you and place your order and pay at the food till

TABLE NUMBER

Main meals

Starters

Children's meals

Side orders

Drinks

Desserts, coffees and teas may be ordered at the food till at the end of your meal

Figure 6.30 Example of customer self-complete order sheet

The order for the food and drink requirements, once complete, is taken by the customer to the food till and sent electronically by a member of staff to the kitchen where a printed copy is processed for the kitchen staff to produce the dishes required.

After submitting the initial food and beverage order at the food till, an account will be opened for the table number and by processing the customer's credit card. This is so any additional items such as sweets, coffee or alcoholic beverages may be added to the bill. The customer may then pay the total bill at the conclusion of their meal. Additional items required may be ordered at the food till or at the customer's table.

Taking children's orders

Staff should pay special attention when taking orders for children. Staff need to be aware of:

- the availability and choice of children's meals
- what the children's meals consist of
- portion size, for example, the number of sausages
- the cost per head
- the need to make a special note of any specific requests, such as no baked beans
- the need to serve young/small children first as they often become agitated when everyone else has been served and their meal is still to come
- the importance of not overfilling cups, bowls or glasses
- the need to always ensure children's plates are warm rather than hot to avoid mishaps
- providing children with the establishment 'give aways' in order to keep them occupied, for example, a place mat to be coloured in. This can also encourage sales.

Customers with additional needs

Customers with additional needs may require particular attention. These are customers who may be hearing impaired, blind or partially sighted or with language difficulties (see Section 2.5, p.47). In these instances consider the following:

- Where applicable, when taking the order, face the customer so they see you full face.
- Speak normally but distinctly.
- Keep descriptions to a minimum.
- Indicate precisely any modifiers that are available with a specific dish, for example, a choice of dips available with a starter, or the degrees of cooking available for a grilled steak.
- Read back the order given for confirmation.

Other additional needs may relate to vegetarians, those with particular religious or cultural restrictions and those with special dietary needs (see Section 4.4, p.97).

6.4 The order of service

Pre-service tasks

Food and beverage service staff should be on duty with sufficient time before the service is due to commence to:

- check the sideboards/workstations have all the equipment necessary for service
- check that tables are laid correctly
- check the menu and have a full understanding of the dishes, methods of cooking, garnishes, the correct covers, accompaniments and mode of service
- ascertain the allocation of stations/work areas and other duties, if these are not already known
- allow the head waiter/supervisor to check that all staff are dressed correctly in a clean and well-presented uniform of the establishment.

Order of service of a meal

In the example for the order of service given below, customers are having a starter, main course and sweet, to be accompanied by apéritifs (pre-meal drink, e.g. a gin and tonic), wine with the meal and liqueurs.

1   Greet customers and check to see if they have a reservation.
2   Assist with customers' coats as required.
3   Offer an apéritif in the lounge or reception area, or if preferred to have one at their table.
4   If they are to have the apéritif at their table lead the customers to their table.
5   Assist customers with their seats and place their napkin over their lap (see Figure 6.31(a)).
6   The order for any apéritifs is taken and the order is then served.
7   Present open menus to each customer, host last (see Figure 6.31(b)). Bread is offered, butter and alternatives are placed on the table and any chilled water ordered is poured.

Figure 6.31(a) Laid table with napkin being placed onto customer's laps

Figure 6.31(b) Menus being presented

Note: At this point all the customers at the table will have something to read, drink and eat, so they can be left for a while to allow them time to make their selection.

8   If required explain the menu items and take the food order, usually from the host but each guest may be asked separately. Confirm all the items ordered together with degrees of cooking and sauces ordered.
9   Immediately after the food order has been taken check with the host to see if wine is required to accompany the meal. Adjust the glassware for the wine to be served.
10 Adjust the cover for the first course. In more casual establishments the covers are laid for the first and main course at the beginning of the meal.
11 The wine ordered will be presented to the host to confirm that the correct bottle of wine is about to be opened.
12 The wine or other beverages are always served before the food. Offer the host (or whoever ordered the wine) to taste the wine to assess the quality of the contents and that the serving temperature is correct. The person tasting the wine always has their glass topped up last.
13 Serve the plated first course(s) now, cold before hot, and the accompaniments are then offered (see Figure 6.31(c)). Once all plates are on the table, explanations of the dishes are given to the customers.

Figure 6.31(c) Plated first course being served from the right

14 The server will now check the table to ensure everything is satisfactory and the customers have all they require.

15 Wine and water glasses will be topped up as necessary (see Figure 6.31(d)). Remove used or empty glasses.

Figure 6.31(d) Wine glasses being topped up

16 When all the customers have finished their first courses, clear the first course plates (see Figure 6.31(e)) using the correct stacking techniques and remove any accompaniments (for more detailed information on clearing during service see Section 6.8, p.248).

Figure 6.31(e) Plated first course being removed

17 If necessary the covers should be laid or adjusted for the main course.

18 If a different wine is to be served with the main course, the correct glasses should be placed on the table and the wine then served before the food in the same way as the previous wine. If a bottle of the same wine is to be served then this is normally offered with a clean glass for tasting the new wine.

19 The plated main course(s) are served from the right-hand side of the customer, cold before hot, and accompaniments offered (see Figure 6.31(f)). When all plates are on the table, explain the dishes to the customers.

Figure 6.31(f) Plated main course being served from the right

20 The server will now check to ensure everything is satisfactory and the customers have all they require.

21 Wine and water glasses will be topped up as necessary.

22 When customers have finished eating their main courses, clear the main course plates and cutlery, side plates and knives, all accompaniments, butter dish and the cruet set using the correct clearing techniques (see Figure 6.31(g) and Figure 6.31(h)). (For further information on clearing during service see Section 6.8, p.248.)

Figure 6.31(g) Plated main course being cleared

Figure 6.31(h) Side plates being cleared

23 The table is then crumbed down (see Figure 6.31(i)). (For further explanation of this process, see Section 6.8, p.248.)

Figure 6.31(i) Crumbing down with a 'crumber']

24 Present the sweet menu. Advise customers on the dishes as necessary. Take the order and confirm the order back to check it is correct.

25 Covers for the sweet course are laid (see Figure 6.31(j)).

Figure 6.31(j) Sweet cutlery being put into position

26 Empty or used wine glasses and bottles are cleared away.

27 If wine is to be served with the sweet course, the correct glasses should be placed on the table and then served before the food.

28 The plated sweet course(s) will now be served from the right-hand side of the customer, cold before hot, and accompaniments offered (see Figure 6.31(k)). Once all plates are on the table, explain the dishes to the customers.

Figure 6.31(k) Plated sweet course being served from the right

29 Offer any appropriate accompaniments such as caster sugar, custard or cream with the sweet course.

30 Clear the sweet course and remove accompaniments.

31 The server will now take the hot beverage order for tea, coffee or other beverages if not taken with the sweet order.

32 While the hot beverages are being prepared a drink order for digestives, such as liqueurs, brandy or port, will be taken.

33 Tea and coffee or other beverages will be served (see Figure 6.31(l)). (For further information on the service of tea, coffee and other hot beverages, see Section 6.7, p.244.)

Figure 6.31(l) Service of coffee

34 If petits fours/friandises are to be served then these are offered to the customers or placed on the table.

35 When required the bill will be presented to the host. The server will receive payment from the host. (For billing see Section 12.6, p.403.)

36 The server will see the customers out, assisting with their coats if required.

37 The table is cleared down and then re-laid if required.

Removal of spare covers

In many instances the number of customers in a party is fewer than the table is laid for. The waiter must then remove the spare cover(s) laid on the table. Judgement must be used as to which cover is removed – this may depend on the actual position of the table. General considerations are that customers, where possible, should face into the room. The cover should be removed using a service plate or a service salver. When this has been done the position of the other covers should be adjusted if necessary and the table accompaniments re-positioned. The spare chair should also be removed.

Where there is an uneven number of customers each side of a table, the covers should be positioned so that the full length of the table is used for both sides, by spacing the covers out on each side. This ensures that one customer is not left facing a space on the other side of the table.

Re-laying of tables

It is very often the case in a busy restaurant or dining room that a number of tables have to be re-laid in order to cope with the inflow of customers. Where this is the case the table should first be completely cleared of all items of equipment and then crumbed down. At this stage, if the tablecloth is a little soiled or grubby a slip cloth should be placed over it, or if necessary the tablecloth may be changed. The table may then be re-laid.

6.5 Silver service and service enhancements

Silver service is a higher technical level of service which is not as widely used as it once was but is still used in a wide variety of establishments. Expertise in this technique can only be achieved with practice.

The order of service for silver service is similar to that given in Section 6.4. The key difference is in the way the food is served at the table.

First courses

For silver service of the first course the plates will be laid in front of each customer, the dishes to be served will be presented to the table and an explanation of the dishes given. The first course(s) will then be silver served to the customers from their left-hand side and any accompaniments will be offered. Plated foods will be offered from the right-hand side.

Service of soup

Soup may be served pre-plated, silver served from an individual tureen as shown in Figure 6.32 or served from a multi-portion tureen at the sideboard or on the guéridon (see Figure 6.33). The waiter ensures that the soup is poured away from the customer to avoid splashes onto the customer's clothing. The underflat acts as a drip plate to prevent any spillage from going onto the tablecloth.

Figure 6.32 Individual tureen of soup being served

Figure 6.33 Service of soup from a multi-portion tureen

Consommé is traditionally served in a consommé cup on a consommé saucer with a fish plate underneath. It is traditional for this type of soup to be eaten with a sweet spoon. This is because consommé was originally taken after a function, before going home, as a warming beverage. It was originally drunk from this large cup. The garnish was eaten with the sweet spoon. The tradition of the sweet spoon has continued, but a soup spoon is also acceptable.

Silver service of main courses

The main course(s) will be silver served to the customer from their left-hand side and accompaniments will also be offered from the left.

- The correct cover is laid prior to the food item ordered being served.
- Dishes to be served will be presented to the table and explanations given.
- The service cloth is folded neatly and placed on the palm of the hand as a protection against heat from the serving dish.
- The fold of the cloth should be on the tips of the fingers.
- The dish is presented to the customer so they may see the complete dish as it has come from the kitchen. This is to show off the chef's artistry in presentation.
- The serving dish should be held a little above the hot joint plate with the front edge slightly overlapping the rim of the hot joint plate.
- The portion of food is placed in the 6 o'clock position (i.e. nearest to the customer) on the hot joint plate.
- When moving to serve the second portion, the flat should be rotated on the service cloth so the next meat portion to be served will be nearest the hot main course plate.
- Note that the portion of food served, on the plate nearest to the customer, allows ample room on the plate to serve and present the potatoes and other vegetables attractively.
- If vegetables are being served onto separate plates, then the main food item (meat or fish) is placed in the middle of the hot main course plate.

Figure 6.34 Silver service of main course

Silver service of potatoes and vegetables

- The general rule is for potatoes to be served before vegetables.
- When serving either potatoes or vegetables, the vegetable dish itself should always be placed on an underflat with a napkin on it. This is for presentation purposes.
- The purpose of the napkin is also to prevent the vegetable dish slipping about on the underflat while the service is being carried out.
- A separate service spoon and fork should be used for each different type of potato and vegetable dish to be served.
- Note again the use of the service cloth as protection against heat and to allow the easier rotation of the vegetable dish on its underflat. This ensures the items to be served are nearest the hot main course plate.
- With the serving dish in its correct position the potato dish nearest the hot joint plate should be served.
- The potato dish served is placed on the hot joint plate on the far side in the 2 o'clock position, allowing the server to work towards themself as they serves the remaining food items ordered and making it easier to present the food attractively (Figure 6.35(a)).
- The vegetables to be served are therefore placed on the hot joint plate nearer to the server and in the 10 o'clock position (Figure 6.35(b)).
- Creamed potato is served by placing the service fork into the service spoon and then taking a scoop of the creamed potato from the vegetable dish. This is then carried to the hot main course plate and the fork moved slightly. The potato should then fall off onto the plate.

Figure 6.35(a) Silver service of potato

Figure 6.35(b) Silver service of vegetables

Figures 6.35(a) and (b) show the use of an underflat under the potato and vegetable dishes. They also indicate:

● how a variety of potatoes and vegetables can be served at one time by using a large underflat
● the use of a service cloth for protection from heat and to prevent the underflat from slipping
● the correct handling of the service spoon and fork
● the separate service spoon and fork for each different potato and vegetable dish to be served.
● service from the left-hand side of the customer.

Service of accompanying sauces

● The sauce should be presented in a sauceboat on an underplate, with a sauce ladle.
● A ladleful of sauce should be lifted clear of the sauceboat.
● The underside of the sauce ladle should then be run over the edge of the sauceboat to avoid any drips falling on the tablecloth or over the edge of the customer's plate.
● The sauce should be napped over the portion of meat already served or at the side of the meat depending on the customer's preference.

Figure 6.36 Silver service of accompanying sauce

Sweet and cheese trolleys

Sweet and cheese trolleys should be attractively presented from the customer's point of view and well laid out from behind for the server. Plates for dirty service equipment should therefore be to the back of the trolley. Staff should explain food items to customers, either from behind the trolley, to the side of the trolley or standing by the table, but not in front of the trolley.

When the customer makes a selection, a plate should be positioned near the item to be served. Then, with a service spoon in one hand and a service fork in the other (or a gâteau slice, etc.) food should be portioned and transferred neatly to the plate. The plate should then be placed in front of the customer from the right. For larger parties, two people will be required – one to take the orders and place the plate with food in front of the customer, the other to stand at the trolley and portion and plate the foods.

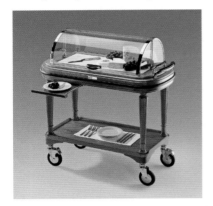

Figure 6.37 Cheese trolley (image courtesy of Steelite International)

Figure 6.38 Modern chilled sweet trolley with cover (image courtesy of Euroservice UK)]

Figure 6.39 Placing the plated sweet course – a cake showing the point towards the customer

Some sweet trolleys have a plate holding ring within their design. In this instance the dish holding the food item ordered must be placed next to this holding ring. Thus when the food item is portioned it may be transferred easily and safely onto the customer's sweet plate, there being minimum distance between the dish holding the food item ordered and the customer's sweet plate.

For temperature control purposes many sweet trolleys now come with ice pack compartments which should be replenished before each service. For further notes on the service of cheese and sweets see Section 4.13 (p.119) and Section 4.14 (p.123) respectively.

6.6 Service of alcoholic beverages

The bar areas may be said to be the shop window of an establishment as they are often a meeting point for customers prior to business and social events. The first impressions given here are therefore of prime importance in gaining further sales. The presentation of bar personnel, together with a well-stocked, organised and efficiently run bar, are essential for good customer service. Bar personnel must have good technical skills, product knowledge and social skills and be able to work as part of a team, in order to meet the needs of customers.

Service of apéritifs

The term apéritif covers a wide range of drinks that may be served before a meal. Apéritifs may be offered at the table once customers have been seated or may be offered in the lounge/reception area.

An indication of the glassware for a variety of beverages is given in Section 3.11, p.79. The service of examples of popular bar drinks is shown in Table 6.2.

Table 6.2 Examples of popular bar drinks and their service

Drink	Service
Baileys	Either chilled or with crushed ice as frappé
Brandy	No additions to good brandies. Popular mixers for lesser brandies are lemonade or peppermint, together with ice
Campari	Soda water or lemonade together with ice and a slice of orange
Dark rum	Lemonade or cola with ice and slice of lemon/lime or with blackcurrant and no ice
Sherries	Served chilled
Fruit juices	Served chilled or served with lemonade, tonic water or sparkling mineral water. Also served with ice and a slice of lemon, orange or other fruit
Gin	Angostura bitters and ice (Pink Gin) or with tonic water or bitter lemon together with ice and a slice of lemon/lime
Liqueurs	May be served naturally or on crushed ice as frappé
Mineral water	Properly served chilled only, but can be with ice and lemon/lime at the request of the guest. Sometimes served with cordials or fruit juices
Aerated waters (e.g. cola)	Served chilled or with ice and a slice of lemon/lime or orange. Sometimes served with cordials
Pernod	Chilled water and sometimes with cordials or lemonade
Pimm's	Lemonade, ice and slice of lemon, cucumber, apple, orange and a sprig of mint. Sometimes also topped up with ginger ale, soda or tonic water
Port (white)	Serve chilled, sometimes with ice and a slice of lemon/lime
Port (ruby)	Good port served naturally. Lesser port either by itself or with lemonade and ice
Sambucca	Coffee bean and set alight (for safety reasons this should be done at the table and the flame extinguished as soon as the oil from the bean is released into the drink)
Vermouths	With ice and a slice of lemon/lime or sometimes with lemonade. Dry vermouths may alternatively be served with an olive; sweeter vermouths with a cocktail cherry

Drink	Service
Vodka	Tonic water or lemonade, ice and a slice of lemon/lime; orange cordial, ice and a slice of orange; lime cordial, ice and a slice of lemon/lime; tomato juice, ice, a slice of lemon and Worcestershire sauce, sometimes with salt offered and also celery sticks
Whisk(e)y	Natural or with water (often still mineral water), with ice offered or with dry ginger or Canada Dry or soda water and with ice offered
Wine	By the glass and sometimes, for white wine, with soda water or sparkling mineral water or lemonade, as spritzer
White rum	Natural with ice or with cola, ice and a slice of lemon/lime

Many establishments now serve bar drinks onto a glass coaster (often paper) at the point of sale.

Service of cocktails

There are four main methods of making cocktails:

1 Shaken, for example a Whiskey Sour.
2 Stirred, for example a Dry Martini.
3 Built (sometimes referred to as 'muddled'), for example a Mojito.
4 Layered (sometimes referred to as 'poured'), for example a B52.

Figure 6.40 Various cocktails: (from left to right) Whiskey Sour, Dry Martini, Mojito, B52

Cocktails should always be served well chilled in an appropriately sized glass with the correct garnish, straw and umbrella, according to the policy of the establishment. Many cocktails are served in the traditional V-shaped cocktail glass but, if the cocktail is a long drink, then a larger glass such as a Highball will be better suited.

● Examples of bar equipment are shown in Section 3.6, p.62.
● Examples of glassware for the service of cocktails are shown in Section 3.11, Figure 3.12 (p.80).
● Additional notes on cocktails are given in Section 5.8, p.155.
● A list of cocktail recipes and methods is given in Annex B, p.427.

In all cases the presentation of the cocktail is paramount:

● The presentation should match the description of the cocktail. This is especially important if it is one of the classic and internationally known cocktails.
● The customer needs to feel that the cocktail has been specially made for them individually.

Points to note in making cocktails

- Ice should always be clear and clean.
- Use cube ice in a shaker as crushed ice can block the strainer.
- Do not overfill the cocktail shaker.
- Effervescent drinks should never be shaken.
- To avoid spillage, do not fill glasses to brim.
- When egg white or yolk is an ingredient, first break the egg into separate containers before use.
- Serve cocktails in chilled glasses.
- To shake, use short and snappy actions.
- Always place ice in the shaker or mixing glass first, followed by non-alcoholic and then alcoholic beverages.
- To stir, stir briskly until blend is cold.
- As a general rule the mixing glass is used for those cocktails based on liqueurs or wines (clear liquids).
- Shakers are used for cocktails that might include fruit juices, cream, sugar and similar ingredients.
- When egg white or yolk is an ingredient then the Boston shaker should normally be used.
- Always add the garnish after the cocktail has been made and to the glass in which the cocktail is to be served.
- Always measure out ingredients; inaccurate amounts spoil the balance of the blend and taste.
- Never use the same ice twice.

> **Note**: The same methods and skills that are used for alcoholic cocktails are also used for non-alcoholic cocktails. More often non-alcoholic cocktails are now referred to as 'mocktails'.

Service of wines

The sommelier or wine waiter should be able to advise and suggest wines to the host as required. This means that the wine waiter must have a good knowledge of the wines contained within the wine list and be able to identify examples of wines that will pair well with the menu dishes. Immediately the food order has been taken the wine list should be presented to the host so that he or she may order wine to accompany the meals that the guests have ordered.

The wine ordered is presented to the host to confirm that the correct bottle of wine is about to be opened. The wine is opened, decanted if necessary and the host (or whoever ordered the wine) is asked to taste the wine to assess its quality and determine that the serving temperature is correct. Although the host (or whoever ordered the wine) may taste the wine, they can if they so wish designate another of their guests to taste the wine ordered. In either case the person tasting the wine always has their glass topped up last.

If a different second wine is to be served, the correct glasses should be placed on the table and the wine then served before the food in the same way as the previous wine. If a bottle of the same wine is to be served then this is normally presented to the host with a clean glass for tasting the new wine.

Key principles of wine service

There are seven key principles to be taken into account when serving wines.

1 The wine waiter must be able to describe the wines and their characteristics honestly – bluffing should be avoided.
2 Always serve the wine before the food. Avoid any delay in serving the food once the wine has been served.
3 Serve wine at the correct temperature – it is better to tell the customer that the wine is not at the right temperature for service, rather than resorting to quick heating or cooling methods as these can damage the wine.
4 Treat wine with respect and demonstrate a high level of technical skill, supported by the use of high quality service equipment. As the customer is paying for the wine and the service they have the right to expect their chosen wine to be treated with care.
5 When pouring wine, the neck of the bottle should be over the glass but not resting on the rim in case of an accident. Care should be taken to avoid splashing the wine and when pouring is complete, the bottle should be twisted and raised as it is taken away. This prevents drops of wine falling on the tablecloth or on a customer's clothes. Any drops on the rim of the bottle should be wiped away with a clean service cloth or napkin.
6 Do not overfill glasses. Fill glasses to the right level, usually to the widest part of the bowl or to two-thirds full, whichever is the lesser. Sparkling wine served in a flûte is usually filled to about two-thirds to three-quarters of the glass. Doing so helps the wine to be better appreciated and looks better too.
7 Avoid unnecessary topping up – it does not sell more wine and it often irritates customers. Another reason for being cautious about topping up wine glasses is that the customer may be driving. If wine is constantly topped up the customer may not notice how much they are consuming. In general, it is preferable to ask the customer before topping up their wine.

Serving temperatures for wines

● **Red wines**: 15.5–18 °C (60–65 °F). Some young red wines may also be drunk cool at about 12.5–15.5 °C (55–60 °F).
● **White wines**: 10–12.5 °C (50–55 °F).
● **Dessert wines, Champagne and other sparkling white wines**: 4.5–10 °C (40–50 °F).

Wine glasses

Wines may be served in the types of glasses indicated below:
● **Champagne and other sparkling wines**: flûtes or tulip-shaped glass.
● **German and Alsace wines**: traditionally long-stemmed German wine glass but nowadays a medium-size wine glass.
● **White wines**: medium-size wine glass.
● **Rosé wines**: flûtes or medium-size wine glass.
● **Red wines**: large wine glass.

For examples of glassware and bottle types see Section 3.11, p.79.

Service of white wines

1 Obtain the wine from the bar or storage area. Check that the order is correct and that the wine is clear and at the correct service temperature.
2 Take to the table in an ice bucket and place the ice bucket in a stand.
3 Present the bottle to the host with the label showing – this allows him or her to check that the correct wine is to be served (see Figure 6.41(a)).

4   Ensure the correct glasses are placed on the table for the wine to be served.

5   Make sure a clean napkin is tied to the handle of the ice bucket – this is used to wipe away condensation and water from the outside of the bottle before pouring the wine.

6   Using a wine knife, cut the foil all the way round, below or above the bottle rim at the top of the bottle (some bottles have small caps rather than foils). The top of the foil only is then removed and the top of the cork is wiped with the napkin (see Figure 6.41(b)).

7   Remove the cork using a wine knife (see Figure 6.41(c)). Smell the cork in case the wine is 'corked'.

8   Place the cork in the ice bucket. If the wine is a high quality vintage wine then the cork would generally be placed on a side plate at the head of the host's cover. This cork should have the name and year of the wine printed on it.

9   Wipe the inside of the neck of the bottle with the napkin.

10 Wipe the bottle dry.

11 Hold the bottle for pouring so that the label may be seen. Use the waiter's cloth in the other hand, folded, to catch any drips from the neck of the bottle (see Figure 6.41(d)).

12 Give a taste of the wine to the host, pouring from the right-hand side. He or she should acknowledge that the wine is suitable, i.e. that it has the correct taste, bouquet and temperature.

13 Serve ladies first, then gentlemen and the host last, always commencing from the host's right. However, nowadays service often follows from one customer to the next, anti-clockwise.

14 Fill each glass two-thirds full or to the widest part of the bowl – whichever is the lower. This leaves room for an appreciation of the bouquet.

15 Replace the remaining wine in the wine bucket and refill the glasses when necessary.

16 If a fresh bottle is required, then fresh glasses should be placed upon the table, and the host asked to taste the new wine before it is served.

17 On finishing pouring a glass of wine, twist the neck of the bottle and raise it at the same time to prevents drops of the wine from falling on the tablecloth.

(a)   (b)

Figure 6.41(a) Service of white wine – presenting the bottle; **(b)** Removing the foil

(c)

(d)

Figure 6.41(c) Removing the cork; **(d)** Pouring the wine

Note: For bottles with screw caps, the opening procedure is to hold the whole length of the seal in the opening hand and to hold the base of the bottle in the other hand. The closure is held firmly in the opening hand with more pressure, from the thumb and first finger, around the cap itself. The bottle is then sharply twisted using the hand holding the base. There will be a click and then the upper part of the screw top can be removed.

Service of red wine

The basic procedure for the opening and serving of red wines is the same as for white wines described above. If the red wine to be opened is young the bottle may stand on an underplate or coaster on the table and be opened from this position. This adds to the overall presentation of the bottle and may prevent drips of red wine from staining the tablecloth. Although there is no technical reason why red wine should be served with the bottle in a wine basket or wine cradle, these are used in a number of establishments for display/presentation purposes. They also assist in retaining the sediment, found in some older red wines, in the base of the bottle.

The cork should be removed from the bottle of red wine as early as possible so that the wine may attain room temperature naturally. If the wine is of age and/or is likely to have heavy sediment, then it should be decanted. It should be placed in a wine basket and first presented to the customer. Placing the bottle in a wine basket helps to keep the bottle as horizontal as possible, comparable to its storage position in the cellar, in order to prevent the sediment from being shaken up. The wine should then be decanted. Alternatively, if the wine is ordered in advance it can be left standing for a few days before being opened for service (see Figure 6.42(a)).

There is a trend nowadays to decant younger red wines and also some white wines simply because exposure to air improves the bouquet and softens and mellows the wine. Decanting also enhances the appearance of the wine, especially when presented in a fine wine decanter. However, the permission of the host should always be sought before decanting a wine in the restaurant.

Decanting is the movement of wine from its original container to a fresh glass receptacle, leaving the sediment behind.

1. Extract the cork carefully. The cork may disintegrate because of long contact with alcohol, so be careful.
2. Place a single point light behind the shoulder of the bottle, a candle if you are decanting in front of customers, but a torch, light bulb or any light source will do (see Figure 6.42(b)).
3. Carefully pour the wine into an absolutely clean decanter. The light will reveal the first sign of sediment entering the neck of the bottle (see Figure 6.42(c)).
4. As soon as sediment is seen, stop pouring into the decanter but continue pouring into a glass (see Figure 6.42(d)). The latter wine, when it settles, can be used as a taster or for sauces in the kitchen.
5. The wine should always be checked to make sure that it is clear before being presented at the table for service.
6. If the wine is not clear after decanting then it should be decanted again into a fresh decanter, but this time using a wine funnel which has a piece of fine muslin in the mouth of the funnel. If the wine is still not clear it should not be served and a new bottle of the wine selected. It is more common now for a wine funnel to be used as part of the decanting process generally, as shown in Figure 6.42.

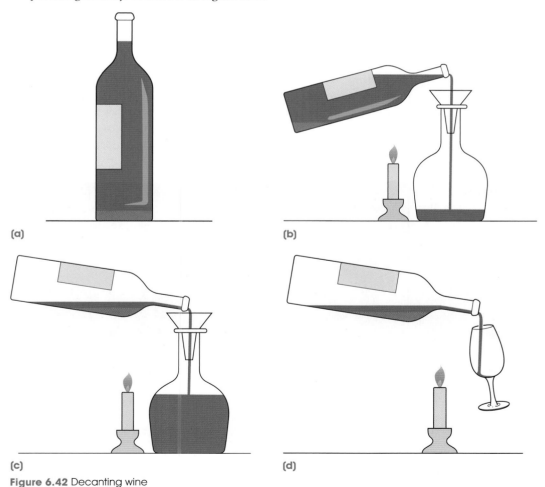

(a)

(b)

(c)

(d)

Figure 6.42 Decanting wine

Very old red wine can break up with too much exposure to air. Such wines can be left to stand for a few days to allow the sediment to settle in the bottom of the bottle. The bottle is then opened before the meal is served and the wine is poured very carefully straight into the glass, with the bottle held in the pouring position as each glass is approached. This prevents the wine slopping back to disturb the sediment. Sufficient glasses should be available to finish the bottle, thereby ensuring that the wine does not re-mingle with its sediment during the pouring process.

Service of Champagne and sparkling wine

The same method is used for opening all sparkling wines. The wine should be served well chilled in order to obtain the full effect of the secondary fermentation in the bottle, namely, effervescence and bouquet. The pressure in a Champagne bottle, due to its maturing and secondary fermentation, will be about 5 kg per cm^2 (about 70 lb per sq in). Great care must therefore be taken not to shake the bottle otherwise the pressure will build up and could cause an accident.

1   After presenting the bottle to the host, for agreement of the wine chosen, the wine is ready for opening.
2   The neck of the bottle should be kept pointed towards a safe area in the restaurant during the opening process. This is to avoid any accidents to customers should the cork be released suddenly.
3   The thumb should be held over the cork with the remainder of the hand holding the neck of the bottle.
4   The foil around the top of the cork is separated from the foil around the neck of the bottle (see Figure 6.43(a)) by pulling on the tab on the foil. Alternatively a wine knife may be used to cut the foil. The foil is not removed.
5   The wire cage is untwisted and is carefully loosened, but not removed (see Figure 6.43(b)).
6   Then, holding the cork and the cage in one hand, with the thumb still over the top of the cork, the bottom of the bottle should be twisted with the other hand to slowly release the cork (see Figure 6.43(c)).

(a)   (b)

Figure 6.43 Opening sparkling wine: **(a)** Bottle is held firmly with thumb on top; **(b)** Foil is separated

(c) **(d)**

Figure 6.43 Opening sparkling wine: **(c)** Wine cage is untwisted and loosened but not removed; **(d)** Cork and cage are held as bottom of the bottle is twisted

Sparkling wine should be served in flûtes or tulip-shaped glasses, from the right hand side of each customer. It is also worth considering lifting the glass from the table so as to pour the wine more easily and quickly, and to reduce the frothing of the wine.

Service of wine by the glass

Many establishments offer a range of wines for sale by the glass. Wines are mostly offered in 125 ml or 175 ml measures. With the exception of sparkling wines, it is often better to serve the wine in a glass larger than the measure. This allows the aroma to develop in the glass and the wine to be better appreciated. Many establishments now also pour a measure of wine into a small carafe for the service of wine by the glass. This then allows the customer to pour the wine into their glass as required.

Storage of open wine

Once a bottle is opened the wine can deteriorate quite quickly as it reacts with the air and oxidises. There are various methods of keeping wines once they have been opened. Some work by creating a vacuum within the bottle and then sealing the bottle with a removable closure, either manually or mechanically. Another system involves putting a layer of carbon dioxide gas (CO_2) on the surface of the wine, thus preventing air getting to it.

Service of beer

Beers should be served at a temperature of 12.5–15.5 °C (55–60 °F), with lagers generally cooler than other beers at 8.0–10.5 °C (48–51 °F). Many different varieties of bottled beers are also served chilled. Draught beer, on its route from the keg/cask to the pump, often passes through a chilling unit.

Types of beer glasses

All glasses used should be spotlessly clean with no finger marks, grease or lipstick on them. Pouring beer into a dirty glass will cause it to go flat very quickly.

The main types of beer glass are:
- half pint/pint tankards for draught beer
- pint tumblers for draught beer
- tumblers for any bottled beer
- short-stemmed 34.08 cl (12 fl oz) beer glass for Bass/Worthington/Guinness
- lager glass for lager
- Paris goblets in various sizes including 22.72, 28.40, 34.08 cl (8, 10, 12 fl oz) for brown/pale/strong ales.

Increasing sales of beers to be consumed with restaurant meals has encouraged changes in styles of glassware used. Generally these beer glasses, although often based on the listing above, are more elegant in style, made of higher quality glass and may also be branded to match the product.

Pouring beers

Draught or bottled beer should be poured slowly down the inside of the glass, with the glass held at a slight angle (see Figure 6.44). This is especially important where a beer may produce a large head if it is not poured slowly and carefully, for example, Guinness or stouts.

Draught beers should have a small head on them and the bar person should ensure that he or she serves the correct quantity of beer with a small head, and not a large head to make up the quantity required. A beer in a good condition will have the head, or froth of the beer, clinging to the inside of the glass as the beer is drunk. This is sometimes called lace on the glass. Some establishments will also train staff to create a pattern in the froth to tie in the brand, such as a shamrock for Guinness.

Figure 6.44 Service of draught beer

For bottled beers, the bottle and the glass are held at an angle to each other (Figure 6.45(a)). The neck of the bottle should not be placed in the beer when pouring, especially where two bottles are being held and poured from the same hand. The beer is poured slowly so as not to form too much of a head (Figure 6.45(b)). As the bottle becomes empty the glass should then be upright in the hand (Figure 6.45(c)). If a bottled beer has sediment, a little beer must be left in the base of the bottle to ensure that the sediment does not go into the poured beer.

(a)   (b)   (c)

Figure 6.45 Service of bottled beer

Service of liqueurs

Liqueurs (sweetened and flavoured spirits) may be served by the glass or in a restaurant they may be offered from a liqueur trolley at the table (see Figure 6.46). The wine butler should present the trolley immediately the sweet course is finished to ensure that any liqueurs required will be on the table by the time the coffee/tea is served. Again, the wine butler must have a good knowledge of liqueurs, their bases and flavours, and their correct mode of service. Traditionally all liqueurs were served in an Elgin-shaped liqueur glass but many alternatives are now used.

If a customer asks for a liqueur to be served frappé, for example Crème de Menthe frappé, it is served on crushed ice and a larger glass will be needed. The glass should be two-thirds filled with crushed ice and then the measure of liqueur poured over the ice. Two short drinking straws should be placed into the glass before the liqueur is served.

If a liqueur is requested with cream, for example Tia Maria with cream, then the cream is slowly poured over the back of a teaspoon to settle on the top of the selected liqueur.

Basic equipment required on the liqueur trolley:

- assorted liqueurs
- assorted glasses – liqueur/brandy/port
- draining stand
- 25 and 50 ml measures
- service salver
- jug of double cream (for topping drinks such as Tia Maria)
- teaspoons
- ice
- drinking straws (short stemmed)
- cigars – according to local legal requirements
- matches
- cigar cutter
- wine list and check pad.

Other items served from the liqueur trolley include brandies and fortified (liqueur) wines such as Port or Madeira.

Figure 6.46 Bar trolley for the service of liqueurs (image courtesy of Euroservice UK)

6.7 Service of non-alcoholic beverages

Service of bar beverages (non-alcoholic)

Non-alcoholic bar beverages are categorised into five main groups:

1 Aerated waters
2 Natural spring water or mineral waters
3 Squashes
4 Juices
5 Syrups.

Their correct service is essential in order that the customer may enjoy the beverage to the full. This is where experienced bar personnel come into their own, ensuring that the drink ordered has the correct garnish, is served at the correct temperature and in the correct glass.

Aerated waters

Aerated waters may be served on their own, chilled, in Slim Jim tumblers, Paris goblets, Highball glasses or 34.08 cl (12 fl oz) short-stemmed beer glasses, depending on the requirements of the customer and the policy of the establishment. They may also accompany other drinks as mixers, for example:

● whisky and dry ginger
● gin and tonic
● vodka and bitter lemon
● rum and cola.

Figure 6.47 Aerated waters (clockwise from left: soda water, bitter lemon, dry ginger, tonic water)

Natural spring waters/mineral waters

Natural spring or mineral waters are normally drunk on their own for medicinal purposes. However, as previously mentioned, some mineral waters may be mixed with alcoholic beverages to form an appetising drink. In all cases they should be drunk well chilled, at approximately 7–10 °C (42–48 °F). If drunk on their own, they should be served in an 18.93 cl (6⅔ fl oz) Paris goblet or a Slim Jim tumbler. Examples include Apollinaris, Buxton, Malvern, Perrier, Saint Galmier and Aix-la-Chapelle.

Squashes

A squash may be served on its own diluted by water or lemonade. Squashes are also used as mixers for spirits and in cocktails, or used as the base for drinks such as fruit cups.

- **Service from the bar**: A measure of squash should be poured into a tumbler or 34.08 cl (12 fl oz) short-stemmed beer glass containing ice. This is topped up with iced water or the soda syphon. The edge of the glass should be decorated with a slice of fruit where applicable and drinking straws added.
- **Service from the lounge**: The wine butler or lounge waiter must take all the items required to give efficient service on a service salver to the customer. Such items will include:
  - a measure of squash in a tumbler or 34.08 cl (12 fl oz) short-stemmed beer glass
  - straws
  - jug of iced water (on an underplate to prevent the condensation running onto the table)
  - small ice bucket and tongs (on an underplate because of condensation)
  - soda syphon
  - a coaster on which to place the glass in the lounge.
- The coaster should be placed on the side table in the lounge and the glass containing the measure of squash placed on the coaster. The waiter should then add the ice and enquire whether the customer wishes iced water or soda to be added. The drinking straws should be placed in the glass at the last moment if required. It may be necessary to leave the iced water and ice bucket on the side table for the customer. If this is the case they should be left on underplates.

Juices

Juices are held in stock in the bar as either bottled/canned/carton or freshly squeezed.

All juices should be served chilled in a 14.20 cl (5 fl oz) goblet or alternative glass.

- **Tomato juice:** Should be served chilled in a 14.20 cl (5 fl oz) goblet or other glass, on a doily on an underplate with a teaspoon. The Worcestershire sauce should be shaken, the top removed, placed on an underplate and offered as an accompaniment. The goblet may have a slice of lemon placed over the edge as additional presentation.
- **Fresh fruit juice:** If fresh fruit juice is to be served in the lounge, then the service should be similar to the service of squash described above, except that a small bowl of caster sugar on an underplate with a teaspoon should be taken to the table.

Syrups

Syrups are never served as drinks in their own right. They are concentrated, sweet, fruit flavourings used as a base for cocktails, fruit cups, long drinks and milk shakes. They may be mixed with soda water as a long drink. Further information on non-alcoholic bar beverages may be found in Section 5.6, p.146.

Coffee and tea

Tray service

The following equipment is required for the tray service of coffee or tea:

Coffee tray:

- tray or salver
- tray cloth/napkin
- teacup and saucer
- sugar basin and tongs or a teaspoon according to the type of sugar offered
- coffee pot
- jug of cream or hot milk
- stands for the coffee pot and hot milk jug
- teaspoon.

Tea tray:

- tray or salver
- tray cloth/napkin
- teapot
- hot water jug
- slop basin
- tea strainer
- stands for teapot and hot water jug
- teacup and saucer
- teaspoon.
- jug of cold milk
- sugar basin and tongs

Figure 6.48 Tea tray

Variations of this basic equipment will depend on the type of coffee or tea that is being served. General points to note in laying up a coffee or tea tray are given below.

● Position the items to ensure an evenly balanced tray for carrying.
● Position the items for the convenience of the customer: beverage on the right with spouts facing inwards and handles outwards and towards the customer for ease of access.
● Ensure the beverage is placed on the tray at the last moment so that it is served hot.

Service of tea and coffee for table and assisted service

Tea is not usually served but the teapot is placed on the table, on a stand, and to the right-hand side of the person who ordered. The customers will now help themselves. The cold milk and sugars (and alternatives) are also placed on the table.

Coffee may be silver served at the table from a service salver. This traditional method of serving coffee is less common today and generally other speedier methods are used, such as placing the cafètiere on the table together with milk and sugars (and alternatives) for customers to help themselves.

Other methods of serving tea and coffee are as follows:

● Service from a pot of tea or a pot of hot black coffee held on the sideboard on a hotplate. Cold milk, hot milk or cream and sugars are placed on the table.
● Service of both cold milk and hot milk or cream together with the tea and coffee from pots, one held in each of the waiter's hands. Sugars are placed on the table for customers to help themselves.
● In event catering where larger numbers often have to be served, the cold milk, hot milk or cream and sugars are often placed on the table for customers to help themselves. The tea and coffee is then served from a one litre plus capacity vacuum flask, which may be kept on the waiters' sideboard in readiness for replenishment should customers require it. This method of holding and serving tea and coffee ensures that it remains hot at all times. (For examples of vacuum jugs for tea or coffee see Figure 5.6, p.146.)

> **Note:** When serving tea and coffee from multi-portion pots/urns it is usual to remove the tea leaves, coffee grounds or tea/coffee bags once the beverage has brewed, so that the tea and coffee does not become stewed. See Section 5.1, p.135, for the various types of tea and their service. Also see Section 5.2, Table 5.2 (p.148) for a list of modern by-the-cup coffee styles.

Placement of tea and coffee cups

● Figure 6.49(a) shows the beverage equipment required, positioned on the service salver, and assuming a table of four customers is to be served. Using this method the server only has to make one journey from the sideboard/workstation to the restaurant or lounge table.
● Note the beverage service for each customer is made up of a teacup on its saucer, with a teaspoon resting in the saucer and at right angles under the handle of the cup.
● The beverage service is placed on the table from the customer's right-hand side, as the beverage ordered will be served from the right.
● The beverage service is positioned on the right-hand side of the customer with the handle to the right and the teaspoon set at right angles under the handle of the cup.

- While moving to the right-hand side of the second customer, the server will place a teacup upon the tea saucer and the teaspoon in the saucer and at right angles under the handle of the cup. This beverage service is then ready to be placed on the right-hand side of the second customer (see Figure 6.49(b)).
- This procedure is then repeated until all the beverage services have been placed on the table for those customers requiring tea or coffee.

Figure 6.49(a) Service salver prepared in readiness for placement of each beverage service

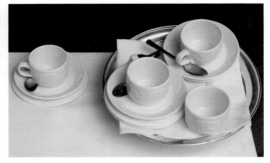

Figure 6.49(b) Service salver by the time the second customer is reached

> **Note**: When coffee is served after lunch or dinner, teacups are more commonly used. The use of small coffee cups (demi-tasse) has declined for conventional coffee service although they are still sometimes used in event catering. These cups are also used for espresso.

6.8 Clearing during service

Developing good clearing techniques helps to:
- enhance speed and efficiency
- avoid the possibility of accidents
- create minimum inconvenience to customers
- allow more to be cleared, in less time and in fewer journeys
- provide the opportunity for plates, cutlery, glassware and linen paper and food waste items to be separated according to the needs of the establishment
- allow for dirties to be collected and stacked neatly and correctly on the sideboard/workstations or trolleys.

The main method of clearing in a plated and table service operation, and with customers in the room, is described below.

Clearing tables

Clearing techniques
All clearing techniques stem from the two main hand positions shown in Section 2.4, Figure 2.2(a) and Figure 2.2(b) on p.39. Then, depending on what is being cleared, the technique is built up from there. Remember, expertise comes with regular practice.
- Dirties should always be cleared from the right-hand side of the customer.
- The waiter should position himself, taking up a sideways stance at the table.

Clearing soup plates

- The waiter having positioned himself correctly will then pick up the first dirty soup plate on its underplate. This stance allows the waiter to pass the dirty soup service from the clearing hand to the holding hand.
- Using this procedure ensures the dirty plates are held away from the table and customers, reducing the likelihood of accidents.
- Figure 6.50(a) shows one of the two main hand positions previously mentioned, and the first dirty soup plate cleared.
- This dirty soup plate should be held firmly on its underplate with the latter pushed up firmly between the thumb and the first and second fingers.
- It is important that this first dirty soup plate is held firmly as succeeding dirties are built up on this one, meaning there is a considerable weight to be held.
- Figure 6.50(b) shows the second dirty soup plate on its underplate cleared and positioned on the holding hand.
- Figure 6.50(c) shows the position of the second dirty soup plate on the holding hand. The soup spoon is taken from the lower soup plate to be placed in the upper soup plate.
- Figure 6.50(d) shows the upper soup plate with its two soup spoons now placed in the lower soup plate, leaving the upper underplate behind.
- The third dirty soup plate with its underplate is now cleared from the right and placed on the upper underplate on the holding hand. The above procedure is then repeated each time a dirty soup plate on its underplate is cleared.

Figure 6.50 Clearing soup plates: **(a)** First soup plate is cleared

Figure 6.50(b) First stage of clearing the second soup plate

Figure 6.50(c) Second stage of clearing the second soup plate

Figure 6.50(d) Second soup plate is cleared in preparation for the next dirty soup plate

Clearing joint plates

- Figure 6.51(a) shows one of the two main hand positions previously shown in Section 2.4, p.38/39, and the first dirty joint plate cleared.
- The dirty joint plate should be held firmly pushed up to the joint between the thumb and the first and second finger.
- Note the position of the cutlery: the fork held firmly with the thumb over the end of its handle and the blade of the joint knife placed under the arch in the handle of the fork.
- Any debris or crumbs will be pushed into the triangle formed by the handles of the joint knife and joint fork and the rim of the plate. This is nearest the holding hand.
- Figure 6.51(b) shows the second dirty joint plate cleared and positioned on the holding hand.
- Figure 6.51(c) shows the second dirty joint knife positioned correctly and debris being cleared from the upper joint plate onto the lower joint plate using the second dirty joint fork cleared. This procedure is carried out as the waiter moves on to his next position in readiness to clear the third dirty joint plate.
- Figure 6.51(d) shows the holding hand with the already cleared items held correctly and ready to receive the next dirty joint plate to be cleared.

Figure 6.51 Clearing joint plates **(a)** First joint plate is cleared

Figure 6.51(b) Second joint plate is cleared

Figure 6.51(c) Clearing debris from the upper plate

Figure 6.51(d) Preparing to clear the next dirty plate

Clearing joint plates and side plates together

- Figure 6.52 shows the dirty joint plates and cutlery correctly stacked, and with the side plates and side knives also being cleared in one journey to the table. This is an alternative to clearing the joint plates and then the side plates in two phases.

Figure 6.52 Clearing joint and side plates in one journey

Clearing side plates

- Side plates are cleared using a service salver or service plate. The reason for this is to allow a larger working surface on which to clear the dirty side knives and any debris remaining.
- Figure 6.53(a) illustrates the method of clearing debris from the upper dirty side plate and onto the service salver/plate.
- Figure 6.53(b) shows the holding hand having cleared four place settings with the dirty items and debris stacked correctly and safely.
- This method generally allows the waiter to clear more dirty side plates and side knives in one journey between sideboard/workstation and table and is especially useful when working in a banqueting situation.

Figure 6.53 Clearing side plates: **(a)** Clearing debris from the side plate to the service plate

Figure 6.53 (b) Hand position having cleared four side plates and side knives

Crumbing down

The process of crumbing down usually takes place after the main course has been cleared and before the sweet order is taken and served. The purpose is to remove any crumbs or debris left on the tablecloth at this stage of the meal and to freshen up the appearance of a table after the main course has been consumed and all the dirty items of equipment cleared from the table. The waiter brushes any crumbs and other debris lying on the tablecloth onto the service plate, with the aid of either the folded service cloth or a small brush designed for the purpose. There are also metal crumbers that can be used.

The items of equipment used to crumb down are:
- a service plate (a joint plate with a napkin on it)
- the waiter's cloth or service cloth.

Alternatively a small pan and brush or metal crumber may be used.

On the assumption that a table d'hôte cover has previously been laid, the sweet spoon and fork, prior to crumbing down, should normally be positioned at the head of the cover. However, if an à la carte cover has initially been laid, then, after the main course has been cleared, there should be no tableware on the table prior to crumbing down.

Crumbing down the customer's place settings:

1 Crumbing down commences from the left-hand side of the first customer. The service plate is placed just beneath the lip (edge) of the table. Crumbs are brushed towards the plate using a folded napkin, a specialist crumber brush or a metal crumber.

Figure 6.54 Crumbing down with a 'crumber' **Figure 6.55** Crumbing down (with a neatly folded napkin)

2 This having been completed, the sweet fork is moved from the head of the place setting to the left hand side of the cover.
3 The waiter now moves to the right-hand side of the same customer and completes the crumbing down of this place setting.
4 The sweet spoon is then moved from the head of the place setting to the right-hand side of the cover.
5 While the sweet spoon and sweet fork are being moved to their correct positions, the service cloth is held under the service plate by the fingers of the holding hand.
6 Having completed the crumbing down procedure for one place setting the waiter is now correctly positioned to commence again the crumbing down of the next place setting, i.e. to the left of the next customer.

Figure 6.56 Sweet cutlery in place after crumbing down

This method of crumbing down ensures that the waiter does not, at any time, stretch across the front of a customer to complete a place setting in readiness for the sweet course, and does not interrupt any conversation between guests.

6.9 Clearing following service

At the end of service a range of duties need to be completed, as shown below. These duties are carried out without customers in the service areas.

- Clear the cold buffet to the larder. Collect and wash all carving knives and assist generally in clearing the restaurant.
- Collect all linen, both clean and dirty, and check that the correct quantities of each item of linen are returned. Used napkins should be tied in bundles of ten. All linen should be placed in the linen basket and returned with the linen list to the linen room or according to the establishment policy.
- Switch off the hotplate. Clear away any service silver or other service dishes remaining and restock the hotplate with clean crockery.
- Return cutlery, hollow-ware, flatware and trolleys to their appropriate storage areas.
- Collect all cruets and accompaniments and return them to their correct storage place. Where appropriate, return sauces, etc., to their original containers.
- Check all the sideboards/workstations are completely empty. Hotplates should be switched off and the dirty linen compartment emptied.
- Empty the liqueur trolley. Return stock and glassware to the bar.
- Restock the bar from the cellar.
- Clear down the bar top, put all the equipment away and wash and polish used glasses. These should be put away in their correct storage place. Remove all empty bottles, etc. Complete consumption and stock sheets. Bar shutters and doors should be made secure.
- Empty all beverage service equipment, wash and put away. All perishable materials should be put away in their correct storage places. Still-sets and milk urns should be emptied, washed out and then left standing with cold water in them.
- Empty and clean all trolleys and return them to their storage places. Any unused food items from the trolleys should be returned to the appropriate department. Any service equipment used on the trolleys should be cleaned and returned to storage areas.
- Reset duties should be completed in readiness for the next service period. This might include both table lay-ups and sideboard/workstation lay-ups. In many contemporary establishments this process is ongoing.
- At all times consideration should be given to environmental issues, including the recycling of used items, the management of waste and the control of energy.

Specific after service duties

At the completion of service certain after service duties will need to be carried out by different members of the food and beverage service staff. The allocation of specific responsibilities helps to ensure that all areas are left safe, clean and replenished in readiness for the next service. Examples of what might be involved for specific members of staff are shown in the checklists below.

Head waiter/supervisor

1 Ensure gas and electrical appliances are switched off and plugs removed from sockets.
2 Return any special equipment to the appropriate work/storage area.
3 Secure all windows and check fire exits.
4 Check that all tasks are completed in a satisfactory manner prior to staff completing their shift.

Station waiter/server

1 Replace all equipment in the sideboard according to the sideboard checklist.
2 Wipe down the sideboard and trolleys, clearing all dirty equipment to the wash-up area.
3 Clear down tables and crumb down. Re-lay tablecloths and slip cloths as appropriate.
4 Reset tables and sideboards/workstation if required.
5 Switch off and clean sideboard hotplates.
6 Return special equipment to work/storage areas.
7 Return to store cupboards any surplus crockery and silver.
8 Remove plugs, having switched off all electrical sockets.
9 Return food/drink check pads and menus to the drawer in the head waiter's desk.
10 Check area of responsibility with the head waiter/supervisor.

Bar person

1 All working surfaces to be wiped down.
2 Ensure that all equipment is washed, dried and put away in its correct place for future use.
3 Make sure all glassware is washed, rinsed, dried and then stored correctly.
4 Empty the bottle trolley and waste bin. Replace the bin liner in the waste bin.
5 Place surplus orange/lemon slices onto plates and cover with cling film. Store in the chilling unit or fridge.
6 Sweep and mop the floor.
7 Return the liqueur trolley to the bar.
8 Drain the glass-washing machine.
9 Turn off the chiller lights.
10 Complete the control system.
11 Replenish bar stock.
12 Make the bar secure.
13 Check area of responsibility with head waiter/supervisor.

Stillroom staff

1 Ensure the correct storage of such food items as bread, butter, milk, teabags and ground coffee.
2 Wipe down all working surfaces.
3 Clean and tidy the stillroom fridge and check its working temperature.
4 Check that all equipment is left clean and stored in its correct place.
5 Leftover foods to be placed into clean containers and stored correctly.
6 All surplus accompaniments to be stored correctly in proprietary jars and their lids to be wiped down.
7 Switch off applicable electrical appliances.
8 Make sure all carrying trays are wiped down and stacked correctly.
9 All surplus teapots/coffee pots, etc., to be stored in the appropriate storage area.
10 All beverage making equipment is cleaned according to the maker's instructions.
11 Check area of responsibility with the head waiter/supervisor, or the person taking over the area, prior to leaving.

Chapter 7

The service sequence (self-service, assisted service and single point service)

7.1 Service methods

The three groups of service methods discussed in this chapter are:

1 **Self-service**: where customers are required to help themselves from a counter or buffet.
2 **Assisted service**: where customers are served part of the meal at a table and are required to obtain part through self-service from some form of display or buffet.
3 **Single point service**: where customers order and receive food and beverages at one point.

For these three groups of service methods, the customer comes to the area where the food and beverage service is offered. This type of service is provided in areas primarily designed for that purpose and to meet the needs of the customer. In these service methods, customers can:

- view the menu and beverages on offer
- make a selection
- be served with the food and beverage items selected/ordered
- pay for the items chosen
- collect ancillary items (e.g. cutlery, seasonings, sauces, napkins) as required
- select a table where their food and beverage order may be consumed or leave the establishment if the order is for takeaway
- dispose of dirties as appropriate.

The customer processes for these three groups of service methods are summarised (together with the other two groups of service methods) in Section 1.6, Table 1.9 (p.15). (For a full description of the five groups of service methods, see Section 1.6, p.15.)

Self-service

The main form of self-service is found in cafeterias. In this form of service customers collect a tray from the beginning of the service counter, move along the counter to select their meal, pay and then collect the required cutlery for their meal, together with any ancillary items. Some 'call order' (cooked to order) food production may be included in cafeterias.

Menus should be prominently displayed at the entrance to the cafeteria or foodservice area so that customers may decide as far as possible what meal they will purchase before arriving at the service points. This saves time and ensures that the customer turnover is as quick as possible.

The menu offered may show a wide range of dishes from simple hot and cold snacks and beverages to full meals. The menu is likely to take account of the nature of the clientele, customer preferences, regional preferences, nutritional values, ethnic requirements, local produce available, vegetarian choice and cost factors to ensure profitability on the dishes offered.

Cafeterias often have a *straight-line counter* where customers queue in line formation past a service counter and choose their menu requirements in stages before loading them onto a tray and then proceeding to a payment point at the end of the counter. The layout/design of the counter may include a carousel (a revolving stacked counter) to enhance display and save space.

Where customer turnover is particularly high within a very narrow period of time, and when space is limited, then variations on the cafeteria straight-line counter type service may operate. Examples of these are:

- **Free-flow**: selection as in the straight-line counter type service, but customers may move at will to random service points. These customers will then exit the service area via a payment point.

- **Echelon**: series of service counters at angles to the customer flow within a free-flow area, thus saving space and time. Each of these service counters may offer a different main course dish, together with the potatoes, vegetable dishes, sauces and accompaniments as appropriate. Other service points offer hot and cold sweets, beverages, sandwiches, pastries, confectionery items and miscellaneous foods. On entering the foodservice area, the customer can check the menu to see what they require and then go immediately to the appropriate service point. The advantage of this system is those selecting a full meal do not hold up customers who require just a sandwich and a hot drink.
- **Supermarket/shopping mall**: island service points within a free-flow area.

Assisted service

The main form of assisted service is found in carvery-type operations. The customer is served part of the meal at a table and is required to obtain part through self-service from some form of display or buffet. Customers are able to help themselves from carved joints and other dishes, usually with the assistance of a carver or server at the buffet. This form of service is also used for breakfast service (see Section 8.1 (p.273) and for Events (see Section 11.4, p.360).

Single point service

The main forms of single point service are found in:

- **takeaways**: the customer orders and is served from a single point at a counter, hatch or snack stand; the customer consumes off the premises although some takeaway establishments provide dining areas. This category includes drive-thrus where the customer drives their vehicle past the order, payment and collection points
- **food courts**: series of independent, self-contained counters where customers may order and eat, or takeaway, or buy from a number of counters and eat in a separate eating area
- **kiosks**: outstation used to provide service for peak demand or in a specific location. It may be open for customers to order and be served, or used for dispensing to staff only
- **vending**: provision of food service and beverage service by means of automatic retailing
- **bars**: order, service and payment point and consumption area in licensed premises.

7.2 Preparation for service

The success of all types of service is determined by the detailed preparation that goes into setting up the service areas prior to the start of service. Successful preparation enables staff to provide efficient service and to create an atmosphere that is attractive and pleasant for customers.

Cafeteria/counter service

Layout

Within the seating area an allowance of about 0.5–1 m² (3–10 sq ft) per person is sufficient to take account of table space, gangways and access to counters. A tray stand is placed at the beginning of the service counter or at the entrance to the service area, so that each customer can collect a tray before proceeding along the counter. The layout of the dishes on the counter generally follows the order in which they appear on the menu. This could be as follows: starters, cold meats and salads, bread items, soups, hot fish dishes, hot meat dishes, hot vegetables, hot sweets, cold sweets, ice-cream, assorted sandwiches, cakes and pastries, beverages and cold drinks.

The length of the counter will generally be determined by the size of the menu offered, but should not be too long as this will restrict the speed of service. Payment points are sited at the end of the counter or at the service area exit so that customers may pay for their meal before they pass to the seating area.

Cutlery stands should be placed after the cashiers, together with any ancillary items that may be required, such as napkins and accompaniments. This helps to ensure that the throughput of customers along the service counter remains continuous. Cutlery stands are also placed here to allow customers to choose the items they need after making their food and beverage choices. Another advantage of placing the cutlery stands and ancillary items here is that the customer can return to collect these items, should they initially forget to do so, without interrupting the main queue of customers.

Service considerations

With this form of service, portion control equipment is used to ensure standardisation of the portion size served. Such equipment includes scoops, ladles, bowls, milk dispensers and cold beverage dispensers. Pre-portioned foods such as butter, sugars, jams, cream, cheese and biscuits may also be used.

The meal may either be completely pre-plated or the main meat/fish dish may be plated with the potatoes, vegetables, sauces and other accompaniments added according to the customer's choice. Pre-plating can ensure a quicker service and customer turnover through the service points and requires less service counter top space.

Serving onto plates to order reduces service speed and the turnover of customers is slower. More counter top space is also required for vegetable and potato dishes, sauces and accompaniments to be kept hot in readiness for service. This also increases the staffing level required.

Figure 7.1 Free-flow cafeteria area (image courtesy of FCSI UK)]

Carvery-type operations

On the carvery point itself the servers and carvers must ensure sufficient crockery (main course plates) are kept in the hot cupboard or plate lowerators for the service and as back up stock. Small paper napkins should be at hand for customers to be able to hold hot main course plates.

To avoid delays and congestion around the carvery point, it is important to ensure there is sufficient back up of both equipment and food. The carvers should have available suitable carving equipment for the joints to be carved together with service equipment such as slices, ladles, scoops and draining spoons, all in readiness for the food items to be served.

After cooking, the joints and other main dishes are normally put into a hot cupboard (or closet) where they can be held until required for presentation on the counter. On the carvery counter itself the hot meats, fish and other food dishes are maintained at a constant temperature, often by the use of overhead infrared heat lamps. These lamps are generally mounted on telescopic stands so various sized joints may be accommodated and carving may be carried out safely. Cold meats, fish and other food dishes are held on chilled counters. For holding temperatures see Section 7.3, p.266.

Buffet preparation

The various types of buffet are knife and fork, fork, and finger buffets. The requirements of a particular occasion and the host's wishes will determine the exact format in setting up the room. Whatever the nature of the occasion the principles described below should be followed.

- The buffet should be set up in a prominent position in the room – the buffet may be one complete display or split into several separate displays around the room, for example starters and main courses, desserts, hot beverages and bar service.
- There should be ample space on the buffet for display and presentation.
- The buffet should be within easy access of the stillroom and wash-up so that replenishment of the buffet and the clearing of 'dirties' may be carried out without disturbing the customers.
- There must be ample space for customer circulation – buffets can be positioned and set up so that customers can access one or both sides of the buffet.
- Provision should be made for sufficient occasional tables and chairs within the room.
- The total presentation of the room should be attractive and promote a good atmosphere that is appropriate for the occasion.

Setting up the buffet

The exact equipment required when setting up the room will be determined by the occasion (see Section 11.4, p.360).

The buffet tables will be covered with suitable sized buffet cloths, making sure that the drop of the cloth is within 1.25 cm (approx ½ in) of the ground, all the way around the front and sides of the buffet. If more than one cloth is used, the creases should be lined up, and where the cloths overlap the overlap should be facing away from the entrance to the room. The ends of the buffet should be box pleated, thereby giving a good overall presentation of the buffet.

To achieve a neat, crisp finish, the above procedure needs to be carried out with as little handling of the buffet cloths as possible. This may be achieved by taking the following steps:

1 Open the screen folded buffet cloth along the length of the buffet table (see Figure 7.2(a)).
2 With a person at either end unfold the buffet cloth and follow the procedure for laying the tablecloth as described in Section 6.2 (p.193), so that the front and sides of the buffet table are covered and the buffet cloth is no more than 1.25 cm from the ground.
3 Stand at the end of, and in front of, the buffet table and from this position place your thumb on the front corner to assist in holding the buffet cloth in position. Following the line along the front edge of the buffet table pick up the end of the buffet cloth, lift and bring it back towards you in a semi-circle motion (see Figure 7.2(b)). This will bring the side of the buffet cloth to a position which is horizontal with the ground.

4   The fold on top of the table will now resemble a triangle (see Figure 7.2(c)). This should be folded back towards the side of the table, ensuring that the folded edge is in line with the side/edge of the table (see Figure 7.2(d)).

5   Use the back of your hand to flatten the fold.

6   Repeat the procedure at the other end of the table.

Should more than one buffet cloth be used to cloth up the length of the buffet the clothing up procedure should be repeated. All creases should be in line, the overlap of the two buffet cloths should face away from the room entrance and slip cloths (white or coloured) may be used to enhance and finish the top of the buffet table.

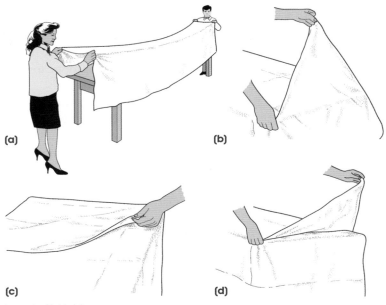

(a)   **(b)**   **(c)**   **(d)**

Figure 7.2 Boxing a buffet table

Buffet displays may be further enhanced by the introduction of a box that has been box-clothed. This can be placed on the buffet table to give extra height and to provide display space for special features.

Table skirting

Alternative methods of dressing a buffet table may include the use of table skirting (see Figure 7.3(b)). Although the initial outlay for such skirting may be high, the ease and simplicity of use makes it very popular for buffet and table decoration. One other feature of skirting is that it is made up of separate panels so that it is comfortable when customers are seated at a table.

A tablecloth is laid on top of the table and then the skirting is attached to the edge of the table by a plastic clip (see Figure 7.3(a)), which is fitted to the top of the skirting. The skirting is attached to the table by sliding the clip into place over the lip of the table. The plastic clips are removable to allow the fabric to be cleaned.

Figure 7.3(a) Attaching table skirting to a table edge

Figure 7.3(b) A buffet table with table skirting attached (images courtesy of Snap-Drape Europe Limited)

Alternative methods of covering buffet tables are 'stretch covers' (Figure 7.4) and custom measured 'fitted covers' (Figure 7.5).

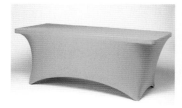

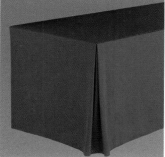

Figure 7.4 Example of contour stretch cover for buffet table (image courtesy of Snap-Drape Europe Limited)

Figure 7.5 Examples of custom made buffet table covers (image courtesy of Snap-Drape Europe Limited)

Buffet napkin fold

For buffets, a commonly used napkin fold is the buffet napkin fold (see Figure 7.6(a)). This can be made with paper or linen napkins (see Figure 7.6(b)). It is especially useful as it can be used to hold cutlery so that customers can either help themselves to this at the buffet or it can be given out by staff as customers collect their food from the buffet.

Steps to follow in making the buffet napkin fold:
1 Open out the napkin and fold into four, ensuring the four loose edges are at A.
2 Fold down top flap as indicated.
3 Fold the top flap again along dotted line.
4 Fold down second flap.
5 Fold second flap again along dotted line.
6 Tuck second fold under first fold.
7 Fold napkin along dotted line putting the folded part underneath.
8 Fold napkin along dotted line.
9 Finished fold.

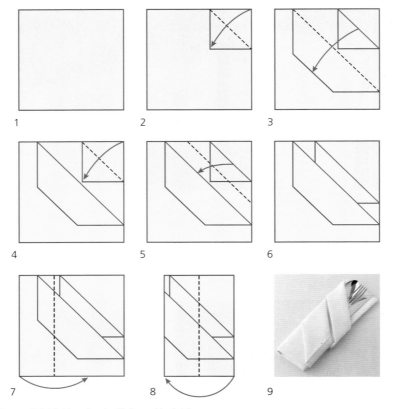

Figure 7.6 Making the buffet napkin fold

Checklists

Typical checklists for the preparation of a hot food counter, salad bar, dining area, takeaway service, buffet display and bar are described below.

Hot food (counter preparation)

1 Turn on hot counter, allowing enough time for it to heat up to the correct temperature.
2 Ensure that an adequate number of plates for the day's service are available on the hot food service counter or in plate lowerators and in an accessible place near the hot food counter as back-up stock.
3 Transfer regenerated hot food from the oven to the hot food counter. Use oven cloths when handling hot food and a tray when transferring hot food to avoid accidents and spillages.
4 Check hot food menu items for the day and ensure that before service begins there is one dish of each menu item available on the hot food counter. Check also the availability of 'back-up' menu dishes.
5 Ensure that all hot food is properly covered to prevent any heat loss and deterioration in quality.
6 Have cleaning materials available to wipe any spills.

7   Ensure that for each dish on the hot food counter there is an appropriate service implement. The implements will depend on the dish but are likely to include:
  O large spoons for dishes such as lasagne
  O perforated large spoons for dishes such as boiled vegetables (to drain off excess water)
  O ladles for dishes such as seafood mornay and aloo brinjal bhajee
  O food tongs for dishes such as fried plantain and Caribbean chicken
  O fish slices for dishes such as pizza.

8   When service implements are not in use, remember to return each one to its designated position on the hot food service counter. This prevents any confusion during a busy service period, which may otherwise arise if service implements have been misplaced.

Figure 7.7 Food counter ready for service

Salad bar (counter preparation)

1   Turn on the salad bar, allowing enough time for it to chill to the correct temperature.
2   Ensure an adequate number of the required salad bowls and plates are available for the day's service of salads, pâtés, cold meats, cold quiches and flans, cold pies, cheeses and items such as taramasalata, humous and tsatsiki. At any one time there should be enough salad bowls and plates on the cold counter for customer service, plus a back-up stock beneath the salad bar.
3   Ensure that service utensils are ready and situated in their designated places for service, including:
  O salad tongs for dry salads such as freshly prepared green salad
  O large spoons for wet salads such as champignons à la grecque
  O fish slices for pâté, cold meats, cold quiches or flans and cold pies
  O large spoons for taramasalata, humous and tsatsiki
  O tongs for sliced French sticks and granary rolls.
4   Transfer prepared salad items from the kitchen to the chilled salad bar.
5   Cover all food prior to service.
6   Have cleaning materials ready to maintain appearance and cleanliness.

Dining area for cafeteria/counter service (preparation)

1   Arrange tables and chairs, making sure they are all clean.
2   Wipe each table.
3   Ensure sufficient clean cutlery provisions for the day's service are in place.

4   Ensure trays are clean and there is an adequate supply in the tray stack, ready for use.

5   Ensure all salt and pepper cruets are filled and that there is one pair on each table. If using sachets of salt and pepper ensure that there are two bowls, containing salt and pepper respectively, at the counter near the payment point. Other sauces should be immediately available, for example sachets of tomato sauce, brown sauce, mayonnaise and tartare sauce. White and brown sugars and alternatives must also be on hand to accompany hot beverages.

6   Fill drinking water jugs and place them in their designated place or make sure the water dispenser is in working order.

7   Ensure the napkin dispenser is filled up.

8   Ensure the clearing up trolley and lined bins for different kinds of waste are in position.

9   Have cleaning materials ready to wipe clean tables and used trays during service.

Takeaway service (preparation)

1   Ensure all equipment is functioning correctly and switched on.

2   Check all temperature-controlled equipment is at the correct temperature.

3   Make sure adequate supplies of packaging, napkins and plates are available.

4   Ensure that the takeaway menu and prices are clearly displayed.

5   Ensure that sufficient supplies of ready-prepared food items and beverages are to hand to ensure minimum delay on receipt of orders.

6   Prepare foods to ensure the quality of the product at all times.

7   Ensure that the necessary uniforms, such as hats, overalls and aprons, are worn in all preparation areas.

8   For safety reasons, have available such items as oven cloths, tea towels and trays.

9   Have sales literature available to assist in projecting the image of the establishment.

10 Make sure all serving utensils are available and to hand.

11 Ensure that everything is in its place and therefore easily found as required. This will assist in an efficient work method.

12 Check that waste bins for the different types of waste are available with clean plastic sacks.

13 Ensure that all working/serving surfaces are clean and have been wiped down prior to service with the appropriate cleaning materials.

14 Have cleaning materials available for wiping down and in case of spillages.

> **Note**: In a takeaway service, care must be taken to ensure the quality of the product, hygiene, packaging and labelling, and temperature control.

Buffet (preparation)

Duties may include:

- the preparation of the buffet table to the supervisor's instructions.
- the display of:
  - accompaniments
  - food items
  - underplates for large dishes
  - service spoons and forks and other serving utensils, including carving knifes if required
  - water jugs and joint knives for pâtés or mousses
  - crockery, glassware and cutlery.

Figure 7.8 Chafing dishes used for buffets (image courtesy of Steelite International)

Bar preparation

Generally bar areas are on show to customers and therefore their overall presentation helps add to the ambiance of an area. Three key factors which help to ensure success here are safety, hygiene and attention to detail in the preparation of the bar. These will determine the efficient and successful service from the bar.

Duties may include:
- opening the bar
- bar silver requiring cleaning to be taken to the silver person
- clearing any debris left from the previous day
- wiping down bar tops
- cleaning shelves and swabbing the bar floor
- checking optics
- restocking the bar with beverage items as required
- preparing ice buckets, wine coolers, service trays and water jugs
- organising check pads and wine lists
- cleaning and polishing apéritif and wine glasses
- preparing and checking the liqueur trolley for glasses, stock and bottle presentation
- preparing the bar service top according to the standards of the establishment. This may include some or all of the following items:
  - cutting board
  - fruit knife
  - fruit: lemons, oranges, apples
  - cucumber
  - fresh eggs (for cocktails)
  - mixing glass and bar mixing spoon
  - Hawthorn strainer
  - wine funnel
  - olives, cocktail cherries
  - cocktail shaker/strainer
  - nuts and crisps
  - coloured sugar
  - Angostura bitters
  - peach bitters
  - Worcestershire sauce
  - cocktail sticks
  - cherries in glass
  - straws in sherry glass
  - tea strainer
  - wine coasters
  - spirit measures
  - soda siphon
  - ice bucket and tongs.

For further information on the bar and bar equipment see Section 3.6, p.62.

7.3 The order of service

Members of staff must be on duty before service begins to allow sufficient time to:

● check that all work areas have the required equipment in readiness for the service to commence
● check that the dining area is set up correctly
● ensure that they have a complete knowledge of all beverages and which wines complement the food dishes being offered. They should know the ingredients that make up the menu dishes, accompaniments that should be offered, vegetarian dishes and those dishes not suitable for allergy sufferers
● determine the availability of back-up food and in what quantities
● determine the amount of back-up crockery on hand, should it be required
● check all temperature-controlled equipment is functioning at the required temperatures
● ensure that they themselves are presented correctly, with the recognised uniforms and service cloths for use with the hot equipment and crockery.

Cafeteria/counter service

The following list describes a customer's progress from their entry into the eating area (counter service) until the conclusion of their meal.

1   Enters the eating area.
2   Views the menus and dishes available.
3   Collects a tray from the tray stack, which may be sited at the entrance to the service area or at the beginning of the service counter, or at each separate service point.
4   Proceeds to the service counter (straight line) or single service point (echelon) or island service point (shopping mall) to view the display of food and drink available and to make their choices and place them on the tray.
5   At the end of the counter complete the payment required.
6   Proceed to the cutlery stand and select their requirements.
7   Select napkins, seasonings and sauces.
8   Choose table and consume meal.
9   At the conclusion of the meal take the tray of 'dirties' to the nearest tray stand and deposit. Disposable items placed in the correct waste bins provided (according to the type of waste for recycling).
10 Table cleaners/clearers clear anything remaining and wipe down tabletops in readiness for the next customers.

Carvery service

This assisted service involves the customer in two methods of food service, namely table service and self-service. Here the server is usually responsible for the service of both food (starters, desserts and hot beverages) and alcoholic beverages on their allocated tables. They will be assisted by chefs/carvers at the carvery point for the service of the main course.

The order of service for a meal in a carvery-type operation will proceed in almost exactly the same way as for table service (see Section 6.4, p.222). The difference here is that the main course is not served at the table. Instead the customer approaches the carvery point to select and receive their choice of main course – this is the self-service part of the carvery service. Customers may also, should they wish, return to the carvery point to replenish their plates.

Service of food at the carvery display

All food items served onto plates should be attractively presented and arranged. If food has not already been pre-plated, it should be served onto plates using a service spoon in one hand and a service fork in the other, and should be placed neatly on to the customer's plate. Alternative service equipment might be used and this will be determined by the nature of the dishes displayed at the carvery, for example scoops, sauce ladles, soup ladles, slices, serving spoons and knives. Care must be taken to ensure there is adequate back-up stock immediately to hand of the crockery used at the carvery point to avoid delays and congestion. Food items should be re-ordered before they run out and not left until the last portion has been served.

> **Note**: For food safety reasons prepared foods must be held at specific temperatures.
> - Chilled foods must be kept at or below 8 °C (26.4 °F).
> - Foods being kept hot should remain at or above 63 °C (145.4 °F).
>
> Food may be left at room temperature for limited periods during service or when on display. However, these flexibilities can be used only *once* for each batch of food.
> - The temperature of chilled foods can only exceed 8 °C for a maximum of four hours.
> - The temperature of hot foods can only fall below 63 °C for a maximum of two hours.

Checklists

Typical checklists for staff to follow to achieve the appropriate service standards for a hot buffet or counter, salad bar and dining areas are given below.

Hot food

- The hot food service counter should not be left unattended once service begins, as this will cause congestion in the flow of service.
- Staff should arrange for someone to take their place if they have to leave the service area.
- Spillages should be wiped up immediately. Spillages left on a hot counter for too long will harden and create problems later with cleaning.
- When serving, it is important to adhere to portion control specifications.
- When a dish of hot food is only one-third full the kitchen should be informed that more will be needed. Food items must not be allowed to run out during service. If the end of service time is approaching, a member of staff should check with the supervisor before requesting more.
- Plates must be kept well stocked. If running low on plates on the service counter, staff should replenish immediately from back-up stock.
- Hot food items left too long in the hot food service counter, prior to service, may deteriorate. The time factor here is important. Minimum time should be allowed between placing food in/on the hot food service counter and serving. This will help to ensure that when requested, the food item is served in prime condition.
- Staff should ensure the correct holding temperatures are set for the hot counter as this will mean that all hot foods are served at their correct temperature and will retain their quality as a menu item.

Salad bar

- A constant check should be kept on food levels in the salad bar.
- Bowls and plates should never be replenished at the counter. They should be taken to the kitchen and filled or replenished there.
- Service spoons and slices, etc., should be replaced to their respective bowls, dishes and plates, if misplaced by customers.
- Spillages should be wiped up immediately.
- The salad bar should be tidy, well arranged and well presented at all times.
- A regular check on the supply of bowls and plates for salad counter service should be made.
- Staff should not wait for the supply of salad bowls and plates to run out before replenishing from the back-up supply (beneath the cold counter). During a busy service period this would inevitably hinder the flow of service.

Dining areas

- Staff should ensure the clearing station is ready and that the following items are available:
  o lined bins
  o bin liners
  o clearing trolley
  o wiping cloth
  o recommended cleaning materials.
- A constant check on tables should be made to ensure they are clean and tidy at all times. Table covers should be changed regularly, as and when required, as an untidy and messy table is unpleasant for the customer.
- The dining area service may be self-clearing, i.e. customers are requested to return their trays containing used plates and cutlery to the clearing station. Should they fail to do this, staff should promptly clear tables of any dirty items and trays and wipe down table surfaces.
- At the clearing station staff should:
  o empty the tray of used plates and cutlery, etc. and stack ready for the dishwasher
  o empty disposable contents of a tray into a lined standing bin
  o wipe the tray clean with recommended cleaning materials.
- Staff should return the stack of cleaned trays to the tray stack, lining each tray with a paper liner (if used) before putting into place.
- A check should be made to ensure there is always enough water in the drinking water jugs and sufficient napkins in the napkin dispenser.
- Cutlery containers should be checked to ensure they are adequately stocked.

> **Note**: During service always ensure that at any one time there is an adequate supply of trays in the tray rack, ready for the customers' use.

Bar service

Food and beverages in bars may be served to customers at the bar or seated at tables. If customers are to be served at tables then the procedures for this are based on table service as described in Section 6.4. Customers at the bar will have their order taken and served at the bar, with payment usually taken at the same time.

For information on bar preparation refer to Section 3.6 (p.62) and Section 6.2 (p.193). For information on the service of alcoholic drinks, refer to Section 6.6 (p.233) and for non-alcoholic drinks see Section 6.7 (p.244).

Figure 7.9 Bar and seating area (image courtesy of Gleneagles Hotel, Scotland)

7.4 Clearing during service

The main methods for clearing in foodservice operations are summarised in Table 7.1.

Table 7.1 Clearing methods (source: Croner's Catering)

System	Description
Manual	Collection and sorting to trolleys by operators for transportation to the dish wash area
Semi-self-clear	Placing of soiled ware by customers on strategically placed trolleys within the dining area for removal by operators
Self-clear	Placing of soiled ware by customers on a conveyor or conveyor belt tray collecting system for mechanical transportation to the dish wash area
Self-clear and strip	Placing of soiled ware into conveyor belt dish wash baskets by customers for direct entry of the baskets through the dishwashing machines

In all cases food waste and disposable items are usually put directly into the waste bins provided, which are often separated into different recyclable types such as food, paper, plastics and cans.

Clearing tables in the dining areas

As tables are vacated and with customers in the room the procedures described below should be followed.

Clearing plates and glassware

The basic clearing techniques described in Section 2.4 (p.33) and Section 6.8 (p.248) may be employed if appropriate.

Points to note:
- Debris (food wastage) should be scraped from plates into a plastic bowl. These bowls of food waste are cleared on a regular basis from the workstations for hygiene reasons and to avoid smells affecting the dining area.
- Used cutlery is often initially placed into a plastic bowl containing hot water and a liquid soap detergent. This loosens grease and oil from the cutlery prior to it being placed into the dishwasher for washing, rinsing and sterilisation.
- Alternatively, dirty cutlery may be placed into cutlery stands at the workstation or on the clearing trolley in readiness for transportation to the wash-up area, where they would be placed in the dishwasher.
- The same sized plates should be stacked together on a tray (sizes should never be mixed as this can cause a safety hazard resulting in accidents to staff or customers). The weight load on a tray should be evenly spread to make it easier to carry the tray. Further information on carrying trays may be found in Section 2.4, Figure 2.7 (p.38).
- Glassware is usually cleared onto separate trays from crockery and cutlery. In this way it is less likely that accidents will occur. The dirty glassware on the tray will be taken to the workstation and often put into glass racks for transportation to the wash-up area.
- Immediately customers vacate their tables the dining area staff should clear any remaining equipment from the table onto trays and return it to the workstation. The tables should be wiped down with anti-bacterial cleaning agents and any table accompaniments normally set on the table as part of the lay-up should be replenished.

7.5 Clearing following service

At the end of service a range of duties need to be completed. These duties are carried out with or without customers in the service/dining areas. Depending on the type of establishment these duties may be carried out at the conclusion of a meal period, towards the end of the working day or be ongoing throughout the working day. For details of regular clearing tasks to be carried out, see Section 6.9 (p.253).

Specific after service clearing tasks

At the completion of a meal service period certain after service tasks will need to be carried out by different members of the dining area staff. The allocation of specific responsibilities helps to ensure that all areas are left safe, clean and replenished in readiness for the next service. Examples of what is involved for specific members of staff are shown in the checklists given in Section 6.9 (p.253). Additional tasks relevant to the forms of service discussed in this chapter are given below.

The server/dining area attendant

1 Replace all equipment in the workstations according to the workstation checklist.
2 Wipe down the workstation and trolleys, clearing all dirty equipment to the wash-up area.
3 Clear down tables. Wipe table tops and re-cloth as appropriate.
4 Reset tables and workstations if required.
5 Switch off and clean workstation hotplates.
6 Return special equipment to work areas.
7 Return to store cupboards any surplus crockery and cutlery.
8 Remove plugs, having switched off all electrical sockets.
9 Return food/drink check pads and menus to the hostess/supervisor
10 Sweep and mop floors.
11 Check area of responsibility with the supervisor.

Buffet or counter staff

1 Turn off the electricity supply to the hot food and cold food counters.
2 Clear the hot food counter and cold food counter and return all leftover food to the kitchen.
3 Turn off the power supply to the oven at the wall.
4 Clear the oven of any remaining food.
5 Clean all service utensils such as serving spoons, ladles, fish slices, knives and trays that have been used during the course of the day in hot food preparation and service. Wipe them dry.
6 Return all cleaned and dried service utensils to their appropriate storage places ready for the next day's use.
7 Check the stock of plates needed for the next day's service of food.
8 Check area of responsibility with supervisor.

> **Note**: It is important to write down on the day sheet the number of portions of each type of regenerated meal that is left over as waste. This exercise is essential for portion control monitoring and gives an indication of the popularity or otherwise of any one particular dish. Hand in the daily sheet to the supervisor who will then prepare a consumption sheet (see Section 12.6, p.451) to show what was taken out and what is now left. The result will then be entered into the sales analysis book.

Chapter 8

The service of breakfast and afternoon tea

8.1 Breakfast service

Many hotels now offer room-only rates or only serve a continental breakfast inclusive in the room rate, with a full breakfast available at an extra charge.

Breakfast in hotels may be served in the hotel restaurant or dining room, in a breakfast room set aside for this meal, or in the hotel guest's bedroom or suite. The service of breakfast in rooms or suites is dealt with in Section 9.2 (p.282).

Types of breakfast

A variety of terms indicate the form in which breakfast may be offered and these describe what the customer might expect to receive for their breakfast meal.

Café complet

The term 'café complet' is widely used in continental Europe and means a continental breakfast with coffee as the beverage. The term 'thé complet' is also used, with tea as the beverage.

Café simple or thé simple

Café simple or thé simple is just a beverage (coffee or tea) with nothing to eat.

Continental breakfast

The traditional continental breakfast consisted of hot croissant, brioche or toast, butter and preserves and coffee as the beverage. The current trend in the continental breakfast menu is to offer a wider variety of choice, including cereals, fruit, juices, yogurt, ham, cheese, assorted bread items and a wide selection of beverages.

Full breakfast

A full breakfast menu may consist of from two to eight courses and usually includes a cooked main course. Traditionally this was a very substantial meal and included such items as chops, liver, game, steak, kippers and porridge as the main part of the meal. This type of breakfast was traditionally known as an English Breakfast, but is now also known as Scottish, Irish, Welsh or more simply British Breakfast. The term 'full breakfast' is also becoming more common.

Modern full breakfast menus have changed to include a much more varied choice of items. Today customers expect to see such items as fresh fruit juices, fresh fruit, yogurt, muesli, continental pastries, preserves, margarines, decaffeinated coffee and mineral waters on the full breakfast menu. Examples of full breakfast menu items are given in Table 8.1.

Table 8.1 Examples of breakfast menu items

Menu	Examples of food items
Juices	Orange, pineapple, grapefruit, tomato, prune, carrot, apple
Fresh and stewed fruit	Melon, strawberries, grapefruit (half or segments), pineapple, apricots, peaches, mango, paw paw, lychees, figs, prunes (fresh and stewed)
Cereals	Cornflakes, Weetabix, Special K, muesli, bran flakes, Rice Krispies, porridge
Yogurt	Natural and fruit, regular and low fat

Menu	Examples of food items
Fish	Fried or grilled kippers, poached smoked haddock (sometimes with poached eggs), grilled herring, fried or grilled plaice, fried or grilled sole, kedgeree, smoked fish (sometimes including dishes like smoked salmon with scrambled eggs), marinated fish such as gravadlax
Eggs	Fried, poached, scrambled, boiled, plain or savoury filled omelette, eggs Benedict
Meats	Bacon in various styles, various sausages, kidney, steak, gammon
Potatoes and vegetables	Hash browns, sauté potatoes, home fries, mushrooms, baked beans, fresh or grilled tomato
Pancakes and waffles	Regular pancakes or waffles, with maple syrup or other toppings, blueberry pancakes, wholemeal pancakes, griddle cakes
Cold buffet	Hams, tongue, chicken, smoked cold meats, salamis, cheeses (often accompanied by fresh salad items)
Bread items	Toast, rolls, croissants, brioches, crisp breads, plain sliced white or brown bread, rye and gluten-free bread, Danish pastries, American muffins, English muffins, spiced scones, tea cakes, doughnuts
Preserves	Jams (strawberry and blackcurrant), marmalade, honey
Beverages	Tea, coffee (including decaffeinated), chocolate, tisanes, proprietary beverages, milk, soy/rice milk, mineral waters

Breakfast covers

The breakfast cover may be divided into two types: a continental breakfast cover and a full breakfast cover.

Cover for a continental breakfast

For a continental breakfast consisting of hot croissant/brioches or hot toast, butter, preserves and coffee or tea, the cover would be as follows:

- napkin
- side plate with side knife
- table number.
- sugar basin and tongs or individual sugar packets (and alternatives) in a bowl
- tea or breakfast cup and saucer and a teaspoon
- stands or underplate for coffee/tea pots and hot milk/hot water jug

If the beverage is tea and loose leaves are used then a slop basin and a tea srainer will be needed.

Figure 8.1 Example of a continental breakfast (image courtesy of Six Continents Hotels)

Cover for a full breakfast

The full breakfast consists of a number of courses, usually three or four, with a choice of dishes within each course, as shown in Table 8.1. The cover will therefore include some or all of the following:

- napkin
- side plate and side knife
- fish knife and fork
- joint knife and fork
- sweet spoon and fork
- tea or breakfast cup, saucer and teaspoon
- sugar basin and tongs or individual sugar packets (and alternatives) in a bowl
- slop basin
- tea strainer
- stands or underplates for teapot/coffee pot and hot water jug/hot milk jug
- salt and pepper
- caster sugar in shaker
- table number.

The majority of the items listed above for the two types of breakfast cover are often placed on the table as part of the mise-en-place, before the customer is seated. A number of items are then placed on the table once the customer has been seated:

- butter dish, butter knife, with butter and alternatives
- preserve dish with preserve and preserve spoon
- jug of cold milk
- toast rack with warm toast and/or bread basket with hot rolls
- teapot, jug of cold milk and hot water jug or pot of hot coffee and a jug of hot milk or cream
- other items according to the customer's choice.

Figure 8.2 Example of a full breakfast cover

Breakfast served in the restaurant (table service)

The basic mise-en-place for the service of breakfast is normally carried out the evening before, after the service of dinners has been completed. To ensure protection against dust until the breakfast staff arrive for duty, the corners of the table cloths may be lifted up and over the basic mise-en-place that has been set on the table. This basic mise-en-place will be completed the following morning before the service of breakfast begins. This will include turning breakfast cups the right way up and laying the breakfast buffet with items usually served for the first course, such as chilled fruit juices, cereals and fruit compôte, together with all the necessary glasses, plates and tableware required for the service.

The breakfast buffet should also contain preserves and butter with alternatives. Jugs of chilled/iced water and glasses should be ready on the buffet throughout the meal. Preserves are usually now served in individual pots.

Summary of the order of service for breakfasts (table service)

- Greet the customer and escort them to a particular table to be seated. The breakfast menu should then be presented and the customer given time to make their choice.
- Take the customer's order. The food order is written on one check and sent to the kitchen and the beverage on another check, which is sent to the stillroom.
- Ensure the cover is adjusted as per the customer's order. While the orders are being attended to in the various departments, the waiter must remember to remove any unwanted cutlery from the cover and, where appropriate, to lay fresh cutlery together with any accompaniments that may be required. For example, Worcestershire sauce if the first course is tomato juice.
- Serve the first course plus accompaniments.
- After the first course is cleared serve the following:
  - **beverage**: the teapot and hot water jug or the coffee pot and hot milk jug should be placed on the stands or underplates to the right of the lady (or the elder if more than one) in the party or, in the case of an all-male party, by the senior gentleman present. The handles of the pots should be placed in the most convenient position for pouring
  - **croissant, brioche, rolls, and toast**: hot fresh toast and/or hot rolls should then be placed on the table together with preserves and butter before serving the main course.
- Serve the main course (plated) plus accompaniments. The main course at full breakfast is usually plated and all necessary accompaniments should be on the table before it is served.
- Check any other requirements.
- On clearing the main course the waiter should move the side plate and side knife in front of the customer (centre of the cover) and then enquire if more toast, butter, preserves or beverage is required.

Buffet or American breakfast

Many hotels have in recent years introduced a self-service breakfast buffet, which provides a fast breakfast service. The change towards buffet style of service for breakfast has also increased the range of foods on offer. The buffet can be used for any type of breakfast, with the most extensive often called American buffet breakfast. Examples of the full range of menu items that may be found are given in Table 8.1 on p.273.

Figure 8.3 Breakfast buffet system (image courtesy of Dunk Ink UK)

Buffet breakfast menus are often priced and offered at three levels:
1 **Continental**: includes juices, bread items and beverages.
2 **Cold buffet**: includes those items of continental breakfast plus a selection of cold items from the buffet.
3 **Full breakfast**: full selection from the buffet including hot cooked items.

With the buffet breakfast, all items are self-served from the buffet, with perhaps the exception of egg dishes or other cooked-to-order items and the beverages required.

8.2 Afternoon tea service

The old English tradition of taking afternoon tea has had a resurgence in recent years. Once the domain of hotels and tea shops, afternoon tea service is now offered in a wide range of catering establishments. With the advent of all-day dining menus, the traditional division of mealtimes is also changing.

Types of afternoon teas

Afternoon tea is served in many establishments and can be classified into three main types:
1 **Cream tea**: served in first class hotels, popular price restaurants, department (high street) stores, food courts, mezzanines or cafés.
2 **Full afternoon tea**: served in first class hotels and restaurants.
3 **High tea**: served in popular price restaurants, department stores and cafés.

Cream tea

A cream tea consists of scones (fruit or plain), which may be served warm. Clotted cream, but sometimes whipped cream, is offered to accompany the warm scones. Strawberry jam is the usual preserve offered with this style of tea service. Due to the richness of the clotted cream in a cream tea, butter is only offered upon request.

Cover for cream tea

The cover for a cream tea may include:
- side plate
- side knife
- pastry fork
- napkin
- teacup, saucer and teaspoon
- teapot and hot water jug stands
- slop basin and tea strainer
- sugar basin and tongs and alternatives
- floral table centre.

> **Note:** The jug of cold milk, preserve dish, and beverage (tea) are brought to the table when the guests have been seated and the order taken, and are not part of the mise-en-place.

Afternoon tea

The menu for an afternoon tea usually consists of some or all of the items listed in Figure 8.4. These are generally served in the order in which they are listed. Beverages are served first. An afternoon tea pastry stand is often used as part of the service of full afternoon tea.

Afternoon Tea Menu

Variety of teas, tisanes and coffees

Assorted Afternoon Tea Sandwiches:

Smoked Salmon, Cucumber, Tomato, Sardine,
Egg, Gentleman's Relish

Brown and White Bread and Butter

Fruit Bread and Butter

Hot Buttered Toast or Toasted Teacake or Crumpets

Warmed Scones (with butter or whipped or clotted cream)

Raspberry or Strawberry Jams

Gâteaux and Pastries

Figure 8.4 Afternoon tea menu

Cover for afternoon tea

The following cover will normally be laid for a full afternoon tea:

- napkin
- side plate with side or tea knife
- pastry fork
- teacup and saucer and a teaspoon
- jug of cold milk and/or side plate with lemon slices (depending on the type of tea served)
- teapot and hot water jug stands or underplates
- sugar basin and tongs or individual packets of sugar (and alternatives)
- slop basin and tea strainer
- butter dish and butter knife with butter and alternatives
- preserve dish on an underplate with a preserve spoon or side plate with a variety of small individual preserve (jam) pots
- table number.

> **Note**: The beverage, jug of cold milk, preserve dish and butter dish are only brought to the table when the customers are seated, and are not part of the mise-en-place.

Figure 8.5 Cover for afternoon tea after the order has been taken

Figure 8.6 Afternoon tea stand

High tea

A high tea may be available in addition to the full afternoon tea. It is usually in a modified à la carte form and the menu will offer, in addition to the normal full afternoon tea menu, such items as grills, toasted snacks, fish and meat dishes, salads, cold sweets and ices. The meat dishes normally consist of pies and pastries, whereas the fish dishes are usually fried or grilled.

The following accompaniments (proprietary sauces) may be offered with high tea:

- tomato ketchup
- brown sauce (e.g. 'HP')
- Worcestershire sauce
- vinegar
- mustards.

Cover for high tea

The cover for high tea may include the following items:

- napkin
- joint knife and fork
- side plate and side knife
- cruet: salt, pepper, mustard and a mustard spoon
- teacup, saucer and teaspoon
- jug of cold milk and/or side plate with lemon slices (depending on the type of tea served)
- teapot and hot water jug stands or underplates
- slop basin and tea strainer
- sugar basin and tongs or individual packets of sugar
- butter dish and butter knife with butter and alternatives
- preserve dish on an underplate with a preserve spoon or side plate with a variety of small individual preserve (jam) pots
- table number.

> **Note**: As for the full afternoon tea cover, the jug of cold milk, butter dish and the preserve dish are not part of the mise-en-place and should only be brought to the table when the customers are seated. Any other items of tableware that may be required are brought to the table as for the à la carte service.

Figure 8.7 Cover for high tea

Order of service for afternoon tea and high tea (table service)

The general order of service for afternoon tea and high tea is:

1 beverages
2 hot snacks – bread and butter
    (sometimes salads)*
3 assorted sandwiches
4 assorted bread items, with butter and alternatives, and preserves
5 hot toasted items
6 scones, with butter, preserves and double cream
7 cakes and pastries.

*High tea only

Service of high tea and afternoon tea

1 The beverage should be served first, followed by the hot snack ordered, which is often accompanied by bread and butter. When this has been consumed and cleared, the service then follows that of a full afternoon tea.
2 Order taking is usually carried out using the duplicate checking method.
3 The sandwiches may be dressed on silver flats and are set out on the buffet prior to service. Alternatively, sandwiches are pre-plated with a predetermined selection and then served to the customer at the table as for family service.
4 Toast, teacakes and crumpets are often served in a soup plate or welled dish with a silver cover on an underplate. An alternative to this is the use of a muffin dish, which is a covered silver dish with an inner lining and hot water in the base of the container. When serving hot buttered toast for afternoon tea, the crusts from three sides only are removed and the toast is then cut into fingers with part of the crust remaining attached to each finger – this makes it easier for the customer to hold the toast when eating it.
5 The scones and assorted buttered breads are often dressed on dish papers on flats and are also set out on the buffet or brought from the stillroom as required and served as for family service.
6 Preserves are served either in individual pots or in preserve dishes, both of which may be served on a doily on an underplate with a preserve spoon.
7 Gâteaux and pastries may be presented on cake boards, which are placed on plates or on round silver flats or service salvers. An alternative to this is the use of a pastry trolley or the afternoon tea pastry stand.
8 Ice creams and other sweet dishes are becoming more popular and are usually served last.

> **Note:** Afternoon tea may also be served in the lounge (see Section 9.3, p.288).

Chapter 9

Specialised forms of service

9.1 Service in situ

Specialised forms of service are those where the food and beverages are taken to where the customer is. In other words, the customer is served *in situ* and the service takes place in areas not conventionally designed for food and beverage service. It includes tray service methods found in hospitals and aircraft, as well as lounge service, room service, service on trains and home delivery. It also includes off-premises catering, which is covered in Section 11.6 (p.378).

The customer processes for this service method group, together with the other four service method groups, are summarised in Section 1.6, Table 1.9 (p.17). For a full description of the five groups of service methods, see Section 1.6 (p.15).

9.2 Floor/room service

Floor or room service varies from basic tea and coffee making facilities in the room and possibly a mini bar, to vending machines on floors or the service of a variety of meals in rooms. The extent of service in hotel guest rooms will depend on the nature of the establishment. In five star hotels 24-hour room service is expected, whereas in two and three star hotels service may be limited to tea and coffee making facilities in the room and only continental breakfast will be available to be served in the room.

Figure 9.1 Room service (image courtesy of Six Continents Hotels)

Full and partial room service

An example of a room service menu is shown in Figure 9.2. In this establishment full room service is offered and the room service staff provide 24-hour service.

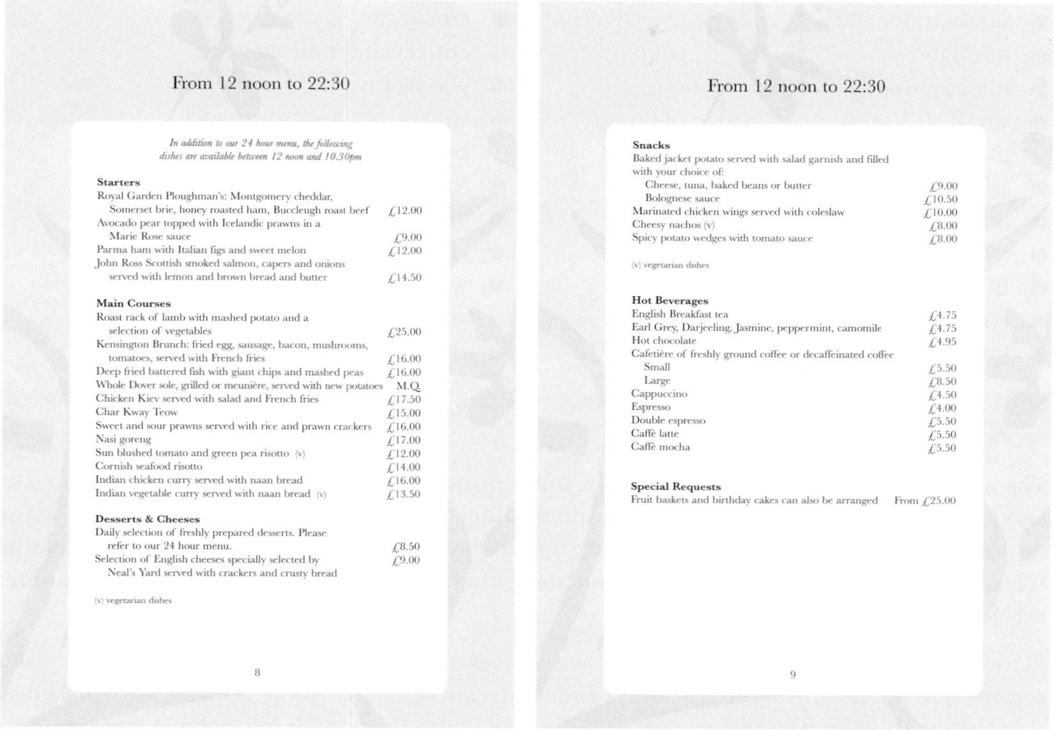

From 12 noon to 22:30

In addition to our 24 hour menu, the following dishes are available between 12 noon and 10.30pm

Starters

Royal Garden Ploughman's: Montgomery cheddar, Somerset brie, honey roasted ham, Buccleugh roast beef	£12.00
Avocado pear topped with Icelandic prawns in a Marie Rose sauce	£9.00
Parma ham with Italian figs and sweet melon	£12.00
John Ross Scottish smoked salmon, capers and onions served with lemon and brown bread and butter	£14.50

Main Courses

Roast rack of lamb with mashed potato and a selection of vegetables	£25.00
Kensington Brunch: fried egg, sausage, bacon, mushrooms, tomatoes, served with French fries	£16.00
Deep fried battered fish with giant chips and mashed peas	£16.00
Whole Dover sole, grilled or meunière, served with new potatoes	M.Q.
Chicken Kiev served with salad and French fries	£17.50
Char Kway Teow	£15.00
Sweet and sour prawns served with rice and prawn crackers	£16.00
Nasi goreng	£17.00
Sun blushed tomato and green pea risotto (v)	£12.00
Cornish seafood risotto	£14.00
Indian chicken curry served with naan bread	£16.00
Indian vegetable curry served with naan bread (v)	£13.50

Desserts & Cheeses

Daily selection of freshly prepared desserts. Please refer to our 24 hour menu.	£8.50
Selection of English cheeses specially selected by Neal's Yard served with crackers and crusty bread	£9.00

(v) vegetarian dishes

8

From 12 noon to 22:30

Snacks

Baked jacket potato served with salad garnish and filled with your choice of:

Cheese, tuna, baked beans or butter	£9.00
Bolognese sauce	£10.50
Marinated chicken wings served with coleslaw	£10.00
Cheesy nachos (v)	£8.00
Spicy potato wedges with tomato sauce	£8.00

(v) vegetarian dishes

Hot Beverages

English Breakfast tea	£4.75
Earl Grey, Darjeeling, Jasmine, peppermint, camomile	£4.75
Hot chocolate	£4.95
Cafetière of freshly ground coffee or decaffeinated coffee	
Small	£5.50
Large	£8.50
Cappuccino	£4.50
Espresso	£4.00
Double espresso	£5.50
Caffè latte	£5.50
Caffè mocha	£5.50

Special Requests

Fruit baskets and birthday cakes can also be arranged   From £25.00

9

Figure 9.2 Part of a room service menu (courtesy of The Royal Garden Hotel, London)

Service may be operated from a floor pantry – there may be one on each floor of an establishment or one sited to service two or three floors. An alternative system is where all food and beverages come from a central kitchen and are sent to the different floors by lift, before being taken to the rooms, possibly in a heated trolley.

Floor service staff must have considerable experience as they have to deal with the service of all types of meals and beverages. The floor service staff tend to work on a shift system, in order to provide 24-hour service.

The hotel guest may call direct to the floor pantry or telephone their request to reception or the restaurant or dining room. Orders are taken and recorded. When the order is delivered to the room it is important that a signature is obtained in case of any query when the bill is presented to a hotel guest on leaving the establishment. All orders, once processed and signed for by the hotel guest, should be passed immediately to reception or control so that the services rendered may be charged to the guest's account.

The pantry from which the floor service staff operate may be likened to a mini stillroom and holds the equipment required for the preparation and service of any meal. This equipment can include:

- gas or electric rings
- salamander
- hotplate
- hot cupboard
- small still-set or other coffee making machine
- sink unit
- refrigerator
- ice making machine
- lift to central kitchen
- cutting boards
- knives
- storage shelves and cupboards
- crockery
- cutlery and hollow-ware
- glassware
- sugars, cruets, proprietary sauces and other accompaniments
- linen
- guéridon/service trolley
- chafing lamps and Suzette pans
- wine service equipment, wine buckets, stands, baskets, etc.
- trays.

Sufficient equipment must be available to maintain a high standard and to enable efficient service to be given.

The service staff carry out all their own pre-service preparation (mise-en-place) before the service of meals. This includes checking and refilling cruets and other accompaniments, laying up breakfast trays, changing linen, laying up tables, washing and polishing glasses, cleaning trays and so on. Some establishments provide a different style and design of crockery for room service of meals.

Floor service staff must also co-operate with other staff within the establishment. The floor service staff should ensure that all trays and debris are cleared as soon as meals are finished so that the meals are not in the way when rooms are being cleaned, or left in bedroom corridors outside guest doors, as this constitutes a trip hazard and looks unsightly.

Breakfast only service

In some hotels only breakfast service is available, which is often provided by the housekeeping staff. An example of a breakfast menu is shown in Figure 9.3. This menu also acts as an order which, when completed, is hung on the outside of the hotel guest's bedroom door. The bottom portion of the card is detached and sent to the billing office for charging to the guest's account. The remaining portion goes to the floor service pantry or to the central kitchen. A tray is then made up and delivered to the room at the appropriate time.

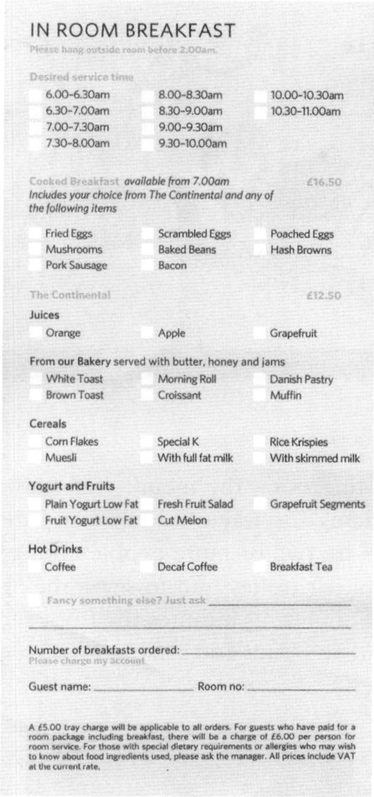

IN ROOM BREAKFAST

Please hang outside room before 2.00am.

Desired service time

6.00-6.30am	8.00-8.30am	10.00-10.30am
6.30-7.00am	8.30-9.00am	10.30-11.00am
7.00-7.30am	9.00-9.30am	
7.30-8.00am	9.30-10.00am	

Cooked Breakfast *available from 7.00am* £16.50

Includes your choice from The Continental and any of the following items

Fried Eggs	Scrambled Eggs	Poached Eggs
Mushrooms	Baked Beans	Hash Browns
Pork Sausage	Bacon	

The Continental £12.50

Juices

Orange	Apple	Grapefruit

From our Bakery served with butter, honey and jams

White Toast	Morning Roll	Danish Pastry
Brown Toast	Croissant	Muffin

Cereals

Corn Flakes	Special K	Rice Krispies
Muesli	With full fat milk	With skimmed milk

Yogurt and Fruits

Plain Yogurt Low Fat	Fresh Fruit Salad	Grapefruit Segments
Fruit Yogurt Low Fat	Cut Melon	

Hot Drinks

Coffee	Decaf Coffee	Breakfast Tea

Fancy something else? Just ask ______________

Number of breakfasts ordered: ______________

Please charge my account

Guest name: ______________ Room no: ______________

A £5.00 tray charge will be applicable to all orders. For guests who have paid for a room package including breakfast, there will be a charge of £6.00 per person for room service. For those with special dietary requirements or allergies who may wish to know about food ingredients used, please ask the manager. All prices include VAT at the current rate.

Figure 9.3 Room service breakfast menu and order card (image courtesy of Hilton Hotels and Resorts)

Laying up a breakfast tray involves the same procedure (with a few exceptions) as laying up a table for a full or continental breakfast in the restaurant. As most orders for the service of breakfast in the room are known in advance the tray may be laid according to the order. The main differences between laying a tray and a table for the service of breakfast are as follows:

- a tray cloth replaces the tablecloth
- underplates are usually left out because of lack of space and to reduce the weight of the tray.

With standard orders for breakfast in the rooms, trays are often laid up the night before, placed in the pantry and covered with a clean cloth. The beverage, toast, rolls, etc., cereals and juices, together with preserves and other accompaniments that may be required according to the order given will normally be prepared by the floor service staff in the service or floor pantry. The main course is sent up already plated from the kitchen in the service lift. Before taking the tray to the room it is important to check that nothing is missing and that the hot food is hot.

The positioning of items on the tray is important:

- Items should be placed so that everything is to hand for the guest. For example, the beverage and breakfast cup, saucer and teaspoon should be placed to the top centre-right of the tray, as this is in the correct position for pouring and helps balance the tray.
- Any bottled proprietary sauce required should be laid flat to avoid accidents when carrying the tray.
- The spouts of hot beverage pots or jugs should face inwards, to avoid spillages, which may cause scalding to the server or slippages on wet floors.

Figure 9.4 Breakfast tray laid for a continental breakfast

● On arriving at the door of the room, the member of staff should knock loudly, wait for a reply, and then enter, placing the tray on a table and then adjusting the items on the tray as appropriate. If there are two or more people taking breakfast in the room, it may be necessary to lay up a table or trolley and to serve the breakfast in the same way as in the restaurant. After approximately 45 minutes the floor service staff should return to the room, knock and wait for a reply, enter and ask if it is convenient to clear the breakfast tray away.

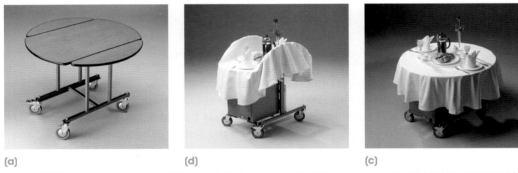

(a)   (d)   (c)

Figure 9.5 Room service tables **(a)** Opened; **(b)** Laid and folded for transportation; **(c)** Laid and opened for service, with hot cupboard fitted (images courtesy of Burgess Furniture Ltd, London, UK)

When breakfast service is finished all equipment must be washed up in the floor service pantry and foodstuffs such as milk, cream, butter, rolls and preserves should be returned to the refrigerator or store cupboard. The pantry is then cleaned and the mise-en-place carried out for the day.

In-room facilities

Mini bar

An example of a mini bar menu is shown in Figure 9.6. This card also acts as a hotel guest self-completion bill; many modern mini bars now have automatic sensors, which charge to the guest's room bill when items are lifted from the fridge. This reduces theft and increases control. Mini bars are usually audited and restocked each day with the consumption recorded and the billing office advised.

PRICE LIST

BEERS	SIZE	ABV	PRICE
Peroni	330ml	5.0%	£4.50
Heineken	330ml	5.0%	£4.50

SPIRITS			
Beefeater Gin	50ml	37.5%	£6.50
Havana Club Añejo Especial Rum	50ml	37.5%	£6.50
Absolut Vodka	50ml	40%	£6.50
Chivas Regal Whisky	50ml	40%	£6.50
Jack Daniel's Whiskey	50ml	40%	£6.50
Martell VS Brandy	50ml	40%	£6.50

WINES & CHAMPAGNE		SIZE	PRICE
Pommery Pop		20cl	£20.00

SOFT DRINKS			
Coca-Cola		330ml	£2.70
Diet Coke		330ml	£2.70
Fanta		330ml	£2.70
Sprite		330ml	£2.70
Red Bull Energy Drink		250ml	£4.50
Tonic Water		200ml	£2.20
Mineral Water Still or Sparkling		330ml	£2.00

SNACKS			
Salted Mix Nuts			£3.95
Jelly Beans			£3.95
Toblerone			£3.95

Automatic Mini-bar System, every item moved will be charged. Please do not store any food items inside the mini-bar.
If you require a refrigerator, please contact Concierge.

AMERICAS · EUROPE · MIDDLE EAST · AFRICA · ASIA · AUSTRALASIA

Figure 9.6 Mini bar menu (image courtesy of Hilton Hotels and Resorts)

Tea and coffee making facilities

The standard stock for these (usually complimentary) facilities includes a teacup and saucer, a teaspoon (one per person), tea/coffee pot (or both), kettle (self-switching) and a selection of tea, coffee, sugar, chocolate, creamer, non-sugar sweetener and, possibly, biscuits. The courtesy tray stock should be a standard stock, replaced and checked for freshness each day by the room attendants.

Figure 9.7 Courtesy tray

9.3 Lounge service

Lounge service may include service of continental breakfast, morning coffee, luncheon snacks, afternoon tea, dinner or late evening snacks as well as alcoholic beverages. Although mainly associated with hotels, lounge service is also found in public houses, wine bars and on ships. An example of a lounge service menu is given in Figure 9.8.

Figure 9.8 Part of a lounge and bar menu (image courtesy of the Westbury Hotel, London)

Organisation of lounge service

The lounge is very often the 'front window' of the establishment, so the standards of service should be high. This responsibility rests with the lounge staff and they must therefore be of smart appearance, efficient and attentive to the guests and other customers. They should have a good knowledge of food and beverage service, especially licensing laws. Throughout the day the lounge staff must ensure that the areas are presentable at all times. Before luncheon and dinner, cocktail snacks may be placed on the coffee tables and, after lunch, the tables must be prepared for the service of afternoon tea.

In a first class establishment lounge service staff may operate from their own service pantry. However, in many instances the lounge staff work and liaise with the stillroom or one of the dispense bars for the service of all types of beverages required, both alcoholic and non-alcoholic. Lounge staff may have access to a dedicated storage area that holds a basic stock of items they may need in case of emergency.

These items may include:

- small stock of linen
- salvers
- ashtrays (depending on smoking policy)
- assorted glasses
- cups, saucers and teaspoons for the service of hot beverages
- dry goods: coffees, teas and sugars
- check pads, bill pads and stock sheets for alcoholic drinks

- basic alcoholic drink stock (for use when hotel guests must be served in the lounge because the bars are closed) to include spirits, brandies, mineral waters, aperitifs, liqueurs, soft drinks and wines
- cocktail snacks – cocktail onions, salted peanuts, gherkins, cocktail cherries, olives, cheese sticks, etc.
- other beverages – Horlicks, Bovril, cocoa, Ovaltine, tisanes and chocolate.

The lounge staff must be prepared for the following types of service in the lounge:

- various breakfast foods
- morning coffee
- apéritifs and cocktails before luncheon
- coffee, liqueurs and brandy after luncheon and dinner services
- afternoon tea
- apéritifs and cocktails before dinner
- service of late night beverages, both alcoholic and non-alcoholic
- other snacks throughout the day, depending on the type of establishment.

The triplicate checking method is normally used for lounge service (or the electronic equivalent), with the top copy going to the supplying department – the stillroom or dispense bar. The second copy should either stay with the lounge staff if they have to make out a bill for a casual customer or go to reception or control so the resident's account can be charged accordingly. The flimsy or third copy remains with the lounge staff as a means of reference.

Casual customers usually pay for the service at the time. Resident hotel guests may not wish to pay in the lounge and staff must then ensure that they sign the check to confirm the services received as well as checking the key card to confirm the guest's room number. The amount should then be charged to the guest's hotel account.

Stocktaking should be held at regular intervals with the occasional spot check on certain items. Stock sheets should be completed daily and are often in the form of a daily consumption sheet (see Section 12.6, p.403) showing the daily sales and the cash received, which may be compared with the checks showing the orders taken.

Buffets and trolleys

For some types of lounge service such as afternoon tea, a buffet may be set up to display the range of foods on offer. Alternatively, a guéridon (trolley) may be used to offer a selection of foods to customers seated within the lounge areas.

9.4 Hospital tray service

Hospital catering services have major foodservice goals, as all meals should reach the patient quickly, look attractive and be of specific nutritional value. Patients in hospital often have special dietary needs (for examples of these see Section 4.4, p.97).

Meal times in hospitals

The timing of patients' meals generally follows a similar pattern, for example:

Breakfast:	07.30–08.00
Lunch:	12 noon
Tea:	15.00–15.30
Supper:	18.00–18.30
Later hot drink:	Anytime between 20.00 and 22.00

Order taking

Menu order forms are used to take orders from patients in the main wards of hospitals. The menu contains a choice for breakfast, lunch and dinner and is given to each patient the day before. The patient marks off their requirements for each meal for the following day. They may also indicate on the card whether they require a large or small portion. The menus are then collected and sent to the foodservice department.

When the order cards have been collected, menu reader terminals are often used to scan the hand marked menu cards. The menu reader terminals are used to transmit food and beverage requirements to production areas, print records and control the individual meal assembly for the hospital conveyor systems. The menu reader terminals can also be interfaced with computer systems for dietary and recipe analysis.

Tray systems

There are a number of commercially available tray service methods used in hospital foodservice. Individual patient trays are made up on a conveyor system according to the patients' pre-ordered requirements. Various methods are used to keep the food hot or cold, ranging from the heated or chilled pellet method to specially insulated trays. Trays, once completed, are transported to the wards in ambient cabinets. At service time, depending on the type of dish, extra portions are available if required. Beverages may be added at ward sites before presentation to the patient.

The advantages of this system are:
- the patient is able to select the meal items required from a menu
- over the period of a week or a fortnight, the patient has a wide and varied selection of dishes
- patients receive their meal presented appetisingly on the plate and at the correct temperature
- labour and administration costs can be reduced
- time originally spent in the ward plating up meals may now be used for other duties.

Microwave ovens are also used in hospitals to provide quick re-heating facilities for food at certain periods of the day and night. All forms of dishes required can be prepared the day before during off peak hours in a central kitchen using cook-chill or cook-freeze methods. When required the following day, the dishes can quickly be regenerated for service.

> **Note**: Private patients' choice of food and beverages is usually larger and more varied than in the main wards, and here the service is similar to hotel room service.

9.5 Home delivery

Home delivery services range from Indian and Chinese takeaway deliveries, to restaurants providing full meals (hot, or cold for customers to re-heat). One chain of pizza restaurants was specifically designed to be primarily a home delivery operation and was based upon an American concept. There are also social foodservice deliveries for the infirm or elderly.

Methods of delivery vary, but all endeavour to preserve the product in heat retention presentation packages. The most simple, but nevertheless effective, is the pizza home delivery system, which utilises thick cardboard with internal corrugations to provide a form of insulation to keep the pizza hot. The time required for heat retention is limited by the extent of the delivery area. Indeed, the companies who operate these services endeavour to deliver the pizza within 30 minutes.

9.6 Airline tray service

Most airlines now operate using a catering commissary. A commissary is a term used to cover the catering, cabin requirements, bonded stores, cleaning and other passenger requirements. It is now accepted that on many short-haul routes, only snack-type meals or sandwiches and beverages are offered. For some operators the provision of food and beverages is provided for an additional charge to the customer. On long-haul flights, airlines provide a more extensive service of food and beverages. The airline will provide dishes to meet its passengers' particular needs, for example, meals that meet a range of dietary requirements.

Service on airlines is often a combination of the trolley service used for the service of beverages and a service involving trays distributed from the trolley in which they are stacked. Great use is also made of pre-portioned foods, such as salt, pepper, mustards, sugars, cream, cheeses, dry biscuits and preserves.

For economy and tourist flights all meals tend to be of the same size, with identical portions. The meals are arranged in individual portion containers, sealed, chilled and then stored until required. The economy or tourist class meal is often served on a plastic or melamine tray and uses disposable place mats, cutlery, tableware and napkins, together with disposable glasses for any drinks required.

Business and first class passengers will often receive a food and beverage service equivalent to that of a first class hotel or restaurant (see Figure 9.9). The first class service may offer joints of meat that are carved from a carving trolley as it moves up the central aisle, served with the appropriate garnish and vegetables. This, combined with the use of fine bone china, glassware and silver-plated tableware, creates an atmosphere of quality while the meal is being served.

The foodservice organisation includes foods being held in hot cupboards and kept hot until transported to the plane, or chilled and stored in the foodservice unit until being re-heated on board the aircraft. High-speed ovens can heat meals in 20 minutes. The tray containing the meal is then taken to the passenger. On long flights, tea, coffee, cold drinks, biscuits, cakes and other snacks are often served between meals. All alcoholic beverages and cigarettes are drawn from the bonded stores on the foodservice premises under the supervision of a representative of HM Revenue & Customs.

Each airline will supply its own equipment such as tableware, crockery and glassware. In order to achieve greater fuel economy some airlines have stopped providing metal cutlery, depending on the food supplied, as the combined weight of unnecessary cutlery uses extra fuel.

When the aircraft is in the air cabin crew provide the food and beverage service to passengers. Their job can be very difficult, especially if the flight is of a short duration, as this can leave little time for a meal to be served. Many budget flights under two hours now only serve hot and cold beverages.

9.7 Rail service

Foodservice on trains is provided on the move and away from the home base and suppliers. The logistics of providing on-train foodservice are therefore similar in organisation to off-premises catering.

Food and beverage operations on trains generally fall into one of four categories:

1 conventional restaurant (including having kitchen facilities on board)
2 kiosk (takeaway)
3 trolley service operations
4 limited type of room service for sleeper trains.

Rail foodservice has also seen the introduction of tray service systems, similar to airlines. The food and drink is served on trays to passengers at their seat (see Figure 9.10), rather than in a restaurant car where tables are laid as in a restaurant.

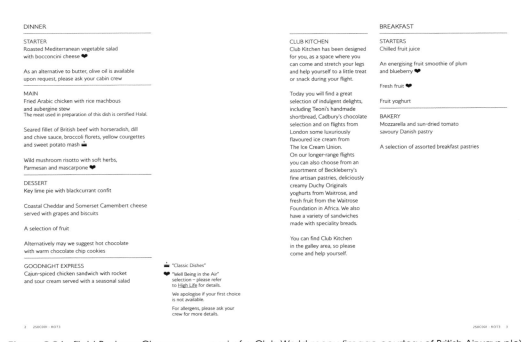

Figure 9.9 In-flight Business Class menu – part of a Club World menu (image courtesy of British Airways plc)

Welcome to East Coast First Class

Our staff are here to make you feel at home.

As part of your journey, sit back and enjoy our all-day menu served at your seat with our compliments.

If you are only making a short journey with us today, you can look forward to a selection of complimentary drinks and snacks.

A member of our on-board team will be along shortly to take your order.

All-Day

Please choose from the following

Sliced beechwood smoked ham and a tangy Mull of Kintyre cheddar with a sweet pickle onion chutney sandwich on soft white bread or A creamy egg mayonnaise topped with sliced egg and a hint of tarragon sandwich on soft grain bread (v) served with hand cooked crisps
Or
Traditional deep filled steak and red wine pie served with salad garnish
Or
Jacket potato served with vegetable tagine accompanied with salad dressing (v)

~~~

Date and cherry loaf cake (v)

~~~

A selection of fruit (v)

Figure 9.10 Part of the on-train first class at seat service menu (image courtesy of East Coast)

Chapter 10

Enhanced service techniques

10.1 Guéridon service

The definition of the term guéridon is 'a movable service table or trolley from which food may be served'. In effect, the guéridon is a movable sideboard or service station carrying sufficient equipment for the service requirements, together with any spare equipment that may be necessary.

Guéridon service usually indicates serving foods onto the customers' plates at the guéridon, but may also refer to other enhanced service techniques such as service using a drinks trolley, carving trolley, cheese trolley or a sweet trolley. These trolleys also act as selling aids as they display the items on offer to the customer.

Guéridon service is an enhanced form of table service but is more costly as it requires:
- a higher level of technical service skills
- the use of more expensive and elaborate equipment
- larger service areas to allow for the movement of trolleys.

Further enhancements to guéridon service include:
- preparing and serving foods in the service area such as salads and dressings
- carving, jointing or filleting foods in a service area
- flambage (the preparation and finishing or cooking of foods in the restaurant, which are also flambéed).

Approaches to guéridon service

For guéridon service, taking food orders is similar to that described in Section 6.3 (p.216). With guéridon service all dishes must be presented to the customers at the table before the actual service of the food and especially before any portioning, filleting, jointing, carving. This is so that the customers can see the dishes, as the kitchen has presented them, and before the dishes are to be served. Customers can also confirm that the orders are correct.

Mise-en-place for guéridon service

In many establishments where guéridon service is carried out, the basic layout is standardised. This is to ensure that the required standards of service are met and that safety is a prime consideration of all the service staff. There are many designs of guéridon available on the market today, but an example of a basic format for the lay-up for the top of the guéridon is shown in Figure 10.1.

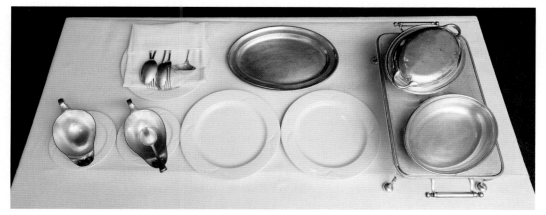

Figure 10.1 A basic guéridon lay-up

Depending on the design of the guéridon and its general appearance the top and under shelf of the guéridon will be covered with a folded slip cloth. For convenience, the cutlery layout should be similar to that of a sideboard as this saves time in the preparation of the guéridon and speeds up the service. Cutlery may include:

- service spoons and forks (joint)
- sweet spoons and forks
- soup, tea and coffee spoons
- special equipment (e.g. a soup and sauce ladle)
- joint and side knives.
- fish knives and forks

If hotplates or food warmers are used then these are placed on the left-hand side on the top of the guéridon. These heaters may be gas, electric or methylated spirit.

Underneath may be placed a service plate and service salver, side plates and some joint plates on which to place dirty cutlery and service gear as the service is being carried out. There should also be some underflats of assorted sizes for the service of vegetables and sauces. A selection of doilies or dish papers may be useful for the presentation of sauces and other accompaniments. Any other mise-en-place required, such as coffee saucers, accompaniments and check pads will normally be on the waiter's sideboard or workstation, together with a surplus of all the guéridon equipment in case of emergency.

Procedure for guéridon service

- Guéridon service is essentially a chef and commis service. There must therefore be complete liaison and teamwork between them and the other members of the team.
- Always push the guéridon, never pull it. This helps to control and steer the guéridon in the right direction and avoid accidents.
- The guéridon should be kept in one position for the service of a complete course and not moved from customer to customer.
- Unlike silver service, where the spoon and fork are used together in one hand, guéridon service requires that the spoon and fork are used one in each hand. This gives more control and makes the service quicker.
- The dish is first presented to the customer and the name of the dish is stated for example, 'Your Dover sole, madam'. The dish is then returned to the guéridon.
- Hot joint plates are placed along the front edge of the trolley (nearest to the customer), with the dish containing the food to be served placed onto the hotplate at the back edge of the trolley, near the waiter.
- The food dishes are then served onto the customers' plates. This may also include portioning, carving, jointing or filleting if necessary.
- When transferring foods and liquids from the service flats and sauce boats to the hot joint plate always run the fork along the underside of the spoon to avoid drips.
- The waiter may then serve the potatoes and vegetables onto the hot joint plate while they are still on the guéridon. The waiter also serves the sauces onto the hot joint plates. The plates are then placed in front of the customers.
- Alternatively, where more than two covers are being served from the guéridon, only the main dish of each customer would be served from the guéridon, with potatoes and vegetables, sauces and accompaniments being silver served to the customer once the main food items have been served onto the customers' hot joint plates and placed in front of them.
- The commis must always keep the guéridon clear of 'dirties'.
- When the service is finished at one table, wipe and clear down the guéridon, and move it on to the next table immediately. It will then be ready for service at the next table to be served and the commis coming from the kitchen with a loaded tray.

> **Note**: Never carve on silver or stainless steel flats or dishes as a knife can ruin them. Use either a carving board or a hot joint plate.

Guidance on how different foods might be served in guéridon service are shown in Table 10.1.

Table 10.1 Service considerations for different foods

Foods	Considerations
Hors d'oeuvres or other appetisers	Served in the usual way except for speciality dishes (see also Section 4.6, p.112)
Soups	Always served from the guéridon, whether in individual soup tureens or in larger soup tureens requiring a ladle
Egg dishes	Unless there is any special treatment required these are served straight to the table
Pasta and rice dishes	Served onto the customers' plates at the guéridon. The pasta is served by lifting the pasta high from the serving dish using a service spoon and fork and then moving this over to the customer's plate and lowering the pasta onto the plate. Accompaniments are offered at the table
Fish dishes	Served from the presentation dishes or flats onto the customers' plates. Some fish dishes may be presented for filleting or carving at the guéridon. The food item being served is then presented attractively onto the customer's plate at the guéridon
Meats	Served from the presentation dishes or flats onto the customers' plates. Some meat dishes may be presented for carving or jointing at the guéridon and this is then carried out but always on a carving board. The dish concerned is then served directly onto the customer's plate at the guéridon. Presentation is all important here
Potatoes and vegetables	Either served onto the customers' plates at the guéridon or served as in silver service, after the main courses have been put onto the customers' plates and placed in front of them. Sauces and accompaniments are then served at the table
Cheese	May be served plated or often served from a cheese trolley, but may also be served from a cheese presentation (such as a cheese board) which is presented on the guéridon
Sweet	Unless pre-plated or served from a cold sweet trolley, sweet dishes are served from the presentation dishes or flats onto the customers' plates at the guéridon. Some sweet dishes may be presented for portioning at the guéridon and this is carried out and then served directly onto the customer's plate at the guéridon
Savoury	Unless pre-plated these are served onto the customer's plate at the guéridon
Coffee and tea	Usual service is at the table unless speciality coffees are required

10.2 Introduction to carving, jointing and filleting

Carving techniques are craft skills of real value to the foodservice trade. They will be required in those restaurants using a carving trolley, in carvery-type operations, for serving at a buffet and for special occasions. In some establishments these tasks are carried out by the service staff as part of their usual service duties, especially in guéridon service. In other establishments there may be a specialist carver (trancheur). Carving, filleting and jointing skills are also necessary for counter or buffet assistants.

All customers have their likes and dislikes – the meat to be medium or well done, some with fat or very little fat, a portion carved from the end of the joint, sliced thinly or thickly, white meat only, a mix of white and brown meat and so on. Service staff must acknowledge all of these requests while remaining organised and efficient. They must have all the correct equipment to hand for the foods to be served together with the appropriate accompaniments and sauces.

Carving, jointing and filleting skills

Carving, jointing and filleting are skilled arts only perfected by continual practice. General considerations are given below.

- Always use a very sharp knife, making sure it is sharpened beforehand and not in front of the customer. Remember you are going to carve a joint, not cut it to pieces.
- Carving is best achieved by pulling the knife back towards you, not pushing it forwards.
- Use the whole length of the knife's blade so as to let the knife cut the food properly.
- Cut economically and correctly to maximise the portions obtained and to keep wastage to a minimum.
- Work quickly and efficiently to avoid hold ups in the room.
- Meat is carved across the grain, with the exception of saddle of mutton or lamb, which is sometimes cut at right angles to the ribs.
- The carving fork must hold the joint firmly to prevent accidents. For smaller joints use the fork with the prongs pointed down to hold the food. For larger joints use the fork to pierce the meat to hold it steady while carving.
- Practise as much as possible to acquire expertise in the art of carving and to develop confidence in front of the customer.

Selection of tools

- For most joints a knife with a blade 25–30 cm (10–12 in) long and 2.5 cm (1 in) wide is required.
- For poultry or game a knife with a blade 20 cm (8 in) long is more suitable.
- For ham a carving knife with a long flexible blade is preferred. This is often referred to as a ham knife.
- Serrated knives do not always cut better than the plain bladed knife, with the latter giving a cleaner cut.
- A carving fork is needed to hold the joint firmly in position when carving.
- Carve on a board, either wooden or plastic. Avoid carving on china plates or metal. Apart from the damage this can cause (especially with silver) small splinters of metal can become attached to the meat slices.

Cleanliness and hygiene

The standard of cleanliness of the carver and their equipment during the practical application of the craft are of the utmost importance. Good service practices are described below.

- Always wear clean protective clothing. Remember, customers are watching a demonstration of the craft.
- Ensure that personal cleanliness is given priority as you are working in the vicinity of your customers as well as handling food.
- Always pre-check work areas and equipment to ensure good hygiene practices.
- Do not move meat, poultry or game excessively when on a board for carving or jointing.
- Carve as required and do not pre-carve too much or too early.

● Keep all meat, poultry or game under cover, be it hot or cold, and at the correct temperature.
● Be vigilant for any sign of deterioration in the food being offered.
● At the conclusion of each service ensure equipment is thoroughly cleaned and well rinsed.

Methods of carving, jointing and filleting

Carving hot food must be performed quickly so that there is minimum heat loss. General guidance on carving, jointing and filleting is given in Table 10.2. More detailed information is given in the various sections in the remainder of this chapter.

Table 10.2 General guidance on carving, filleting and jointing

Beef and ham	Always cut very thinly
Rib of beef	May either be carved on the bone or by being first removed from the bone and then sliced
Steaks	Chateaubriand or entrecôte double are sliced at angles, either in half or into more slices, depending on the customer's preference
Lamb, mutton, pork, tongue and veal	Carved at double the thickness of beef and ham
Saddle of lamb	Carved along the loin in long, fairly thick slices
Shoulder of lamb	This has an awkward bone formation. Starting from the top, cut down to the bone, then work from top to bottom, then turn the piece over and work gradually round
Lamb best ends	These are sliced into individual culets by carving between the cutlet bones. Best ends can also be double cut by cutting close to each side of the bone
Boiled beef and pressed meats	Generally carved slightly thicker than roast meats and each portion will include some fat. Boiled beef should be carved with the grain to avoid the meat shredding
Cold ham	Carved onto the bone from top to bottom in very thin slices
Whole chicken	A medium-sized bird is often dissected into eight pieces, making up four portions
Poussin and small feathered game	May be offered whole or split into two portions
Duckling	May be carved into four/six portions, two legs, two wings and the breast cut into long strips
Turkey and other large birds	Often portioned into legs, wings and breast and then carved into slices separately. Make up portions with white meat from the wings or breast together with a slice of brown meat off the leg and a share of the stuffing. Alternatively, the bird may be left whole with the joints separated from the main carcass so as to allow for carving without jointing first
Poached salmon	This is first skinned whether it is hot or cold. It is then served in fillets, one from each side of the bone. Cut slices up to 10 cm (4 in) long and 2.5 cm (1 in) thick
Lobster and crayfish	Hold firmly. Pierce vertically with a strong knife and cut with a levering motion towards tail and head. Hold shell down with a spoon on a dish, slowly lifting out the meat with a fork. Slice the meat diagonally
Sole	First remove the bones along either edge (side). Then draw the fillets apart with the aid of two large forks. Serve a top and bottom fillet per portion

Carving trolley

The carving trolley is a very expensive item of equipment. Because of this, great care must always be taken with the maintenance and use of the carving trolley to ensure that it functions correctly.

Purpose

The purpose of the carving trolley is to act as an aid to selling. During service the staff must be salespeople and be able to sell the dishes on the menu by brief and accurate description. The carving trolley supplements this by being a visual aid to selling and should be at the table as the waiter takes orders so that they may suggest and show particular items to the customer.

Figure 10.2 Carving trolley (image courtesy of Euroservice UK)

> **Note**: Always remember to push trolleys and not pull them. This enables a trolley to be controlled when moved from one table to another and allows the server to see where they are going so ensuring the trolley is moved safely to avoid accidents.

Maintenance

The carving trolley should be cleaned at regular intervals with the aid of plate powder, always ensuring that all the powder is finally polished off so that none comes into contact with any foodstuffs. A toothbrush may be used for cleaning any intricate design work.

Safety factors

There are certain safety factors to observe in the handling of the carving trolley and these must be carefully adhered to.

- The container on which the carving board rests contains hot water. Ensure the base is filled with hot water before the burners are lit.
- Make sure the safety valve on the base is put on correctly and screwed down tight. There is a small hole set in the top of the safety valve that allows surplus steam to escape. This valve must be positioned so it is on the opposite side of the trolley from where the carver will be positioned and working. This is in order to avoid the hands being scalded by escaping steam. The safety valve must never be blocked or covered over. If it is, pressure will build up within the base, which can buckle the trolley and may cause an accident.

- Two methylated spirit or flammable gel lamps heat the carving trolley. Ensure the lamps are functioning properly, with trimmed wicks and the spirit holders filled with methylated spirit or the gel holders filled. There must be sufficient fuel to last throughout the service period.
- The lower shelf should be used for carrying the service plate, spare service cutlery and a clean joint plate.
- Handle the carving implements correctly and safely, especially when using a steel for sharpening the carving knifes.

Mise-en-place

For its satisfactory operation in the restaurant, the correct equipment must be placed on the carving trolley before service. This includes:

- carving board
- carving knives/forks
- sauce ladles
- service spoons and forks
- joint plates for dirty cutlery
- extra service plate
- spare napkin and service cloth.

Preparation of joints

The correct preparation of joints before cooking is very important and any bones which may make carving difficult should be removed prior to cooking. At the same time, the person carving must have knowledge of the bone structure of a joint in order to carve correctly, acquire the maximum number of portions and ultimately the maximum profit from the product purchased. Therefore, the carver must be able to:

- recognise the joint, poultry or game to be carved
- be aware of the bone structure and muscle fibre of the product being carved
- select the correct carving implements required.

Presentation of the trolley

- The carver must always ensure that the carving trolley is correctly laid up before it is taken to a table.
- The plate rest for the hot joint plates should be extended and the two containers for gravy and sauces should already be filled. These two containers should always be placed at that end of the carving trolley nearest the plate rest. This is for ease of service and also provides the shortest distance between the containers and the plates.
- When being used the carving trolley should be positioned next to the customer's table and in between the customer and the carver. This ensures that the customer can see every operation performed by the carver and appreciate the skills involved.
- The trolley should also be positioned to ensure that the safety valve is on that side of the carving trolley away from the trancheur (carver) while he is carving. This is to ensure that the carver will not be scalded when using the trolley.
- The trolley should be positioned in such a way that the lid is drawn back from the trolley towards the carver so as to reveal the foods items on offer to the customer.

10.3 Flambé lamps, Suzette pans and hotplates

Crêpes Suzette is claimed to be the first flambé dish, which was supposedly invented by Henri Charpentier when working as a commis at the Café de Paris in Monte Carlo in 1894.

The Japanese art of cooking at the table, known as Tepanyaki, is another more modern and specialist approach, with great visual appeal for the customer. It involves the service of teriyaki, a Japanese dish of meat or fish that is grilled or broiled after being soaked in a seasoned soy sauce marinade. It is prepared on a tepan or hibachi table, where the Japanese chef prepares teriyaki meat together with shrimp, rice and vegetables immediately in front of the customers. This creates a dining experience that combines cooking, dining and entertainment in one.

Flare lamps

These are an essential item of equipment for guéridon service and are used in cooking and flambéing dishes. The maintenance of the flare lamp is very important to maximise the life of the lamp and to minimise the possibility of accidents.

The main types of lamp used today are fuelled in one of three ways:

1 **Methylated spirits**: these have a good flame (heat) but care must be taken to trim the wick, which will help to avoid fumes. All components must fit together well as any leakage of the spirit can cause a serious fire hazard. The use of these lamps is on the decline.
2 **Flammable gel**: this is very clean and safe to refill as the gel either comes in individual lamp size containers, which fit directly into the lamp, or in a large container with a dispenser. However, the flame can be fairly weak.
3 **Calor gas**: these lamps are very popular and replacement canisters can be obtained that fit directly into the lamp. The gas is odourless and excellent control of the flame can be achieved. These lamps are often used in purpose- built trolleys where the lamp is incorporated into the structure, thus giving the same working height all along the trolley top. This is much safer and there is less chance of accidents.

The top of the trolley is stainless steel, which allows for easy cleaning. The guéridon will normally also have a control switch for the gas lamp, a drawer for surplus service equipment, a cutting board for use when cooking dishes at the table, a bracket on the lower shelf used for holding bottles of spirit and liqueurs and an indentation in the top to hold accompaniments.

In recent years, portable gas stoves, which were first produced as camping stoves, have begun to be used for cooking purposes on the guéridon trolley. These are lightweight, self-contained, portable stoves with their own carry case. They have an automatic push button ignition and built-in safety features. The stove will operate for up to two hours on a Sunngas P220 cartridge. In addition, these stoves are considerably less expensive than the average flare lamp.

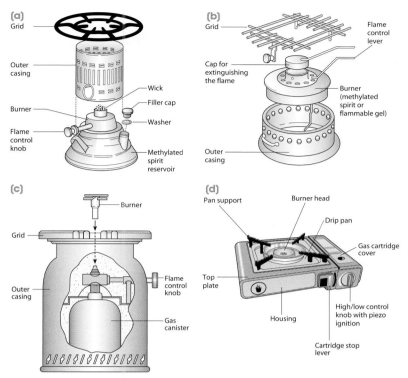

Figure 10.3 Four types of guéridon lamp: **(a)** Traditional methylated spirit lamp; **(b)** Modern methylated spirit gel lamp; **(c)** Gas lamp; **(d)** Gas stove

Chafing dish or Suzette pans

The true chafing dish is deep, has a lid and is designed to fit onto its own individual heating unit. Larger versions of these are now found on buffets (for a picture of a chafing dish used for buffets, see Section 7.2, Figure 7.8, p.265). The shallower pans which are used for lamp cookery are called Suzette pans. They resemble frying pans in shape and size and have a diameter of 23–30 cm (9–12 in), with or without a lip. The lip is usually found on the left-hand side. The pans are generally made of silver-plated copper as this gives an even distribution of heat.

Hotplates

The main function of a hotplate is to keep food hot before it is served to the customer. They are usually positioned on the sideboard, but may be found on both the sideboard and the guéridon. They come in a vast range of sizes and may be heated by gas, electricity, methylated spirits or flammable gel. Infrared hotplates are also available.

Liquors used in lamp cookery and flambé work

There are many different types of liquors used for lamp cookery and flambé work (flambage). Examples are shows in Table 10.3.

Table 10.3 Examples of liquors used in lamp cookery and flambé work

Types	Purposes
Spirits and liqueurs	
Fortified (liqueur) wines	
Sparkling wines	To flambé, sweeten, colour, and balance flavours
Still (light) wines	To remove excessive fat/grease
Beer	To achieve the correct flavours and consistency for sauces
Cider	
Syrups	

Care and maintenance of equipment

It is the visual display of preparing food at the table that is attractive to many customers. All actions must therefore meet the highest hygiene and safety standards and good planning and organisation can achieve this. The hygiene and safety factors relating to guéridon service are given below.

- Hygiene and appearance of staff should be of the highest standard (see Section 2.2, p.27).
- All equipment should be spotlessly clean and polished daily.
- Food should not be handled with bare hands.
- Trolleys should be wiped down between each use.
- The hotplate or lamp should never be placed outside of the trolley legs.
- The trolley should not be positioned for use close to curtains or soft furnishings.
- Spirits should never be left near heated trolleys or naked flames.
- Spirits should be handled carefully when flaming dishes.
- The trolley should not be moved around the restaurant with food or equipment on it.
- Lamps should be checked on a daily basis to ensure they are in good working order.

A daily safety inspection and cleaning programme should be enforced through the use of a cleaning rota or schedule. The food service personnel should carry out this work as part of the normal mise-en-place period and under the supervision of a senior member of the team.

All large equipment such as flambé lamps, Suzette pans, hotplates and trolleys should be hand-cleaned with the correct cleaners on a daily basis. Remember always to use non-abrasive cleaners otherwise the surface of the equipment will become scratched. For copper-based items a mixture of salt, lemon and a little vinegar is generally sufficient.

Specific maintenance of certain parts of the equipment is essential. This might include the lubrication of castors on trolleys and any moving parts of equipment, such as hinges and drawer runners using a product such as three-in-one oil or WD40.

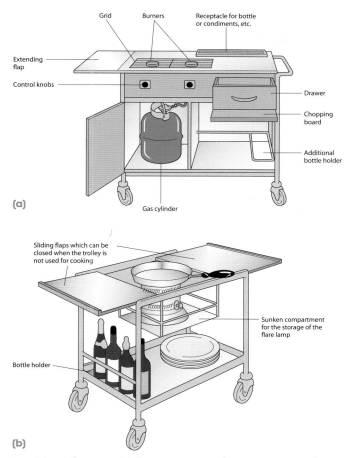

Figure 10.4 Examples of flambé trolleys: (a) Gas-gulled flambé trolley; (b) Flambé trolley with flare lamp

Checklists

To ensure efficiency and safety in the care and maintenance of equipment a checklist should be drawn up for staff to follow. An example is given below.

Gas lamps
- Check that all moving parts move freely.
- Ensure both the jet and burners are free from soot and dirt.
- Clean by the correct methods, using Silvo or Goddard's plate powder for example. Remember never to immerse in water.

Gas bottles
When changing a gas bottle the following factors should be considered:
- Ensure at all times there is no heated equipment or naked flames near the lamp.
- Follow the manufacturer's instructions and use the correct spanner.
- Check all taps are in the 'off' position.
- All gas bottles should be kept cool during storage.

Spirit lamps

- Check the amount of methylated spirit and refill if necessary.
- Ensure the air hole is free.
- Trim the wick and check it for length.
- Clean off any excessive dirt and spent matches.
- Ensure all moving parts move freely.
- Clean by the appropriate method. Remember not to immerse in water.
- Any elaborate decoration on equipment should be checked carefully and, if necessary, cleaned with a toothbrush.

10.4 Hors d'oeuvres and other starters

For the service of traditional hors d'oeuvres see Section 4.6 (p.112).

Smoked eel (anguille fumée)

Ingredients	
trimmed whole smoked eel or large section of the fish	

Equipment

- carving board
- small sharp knife
- joint fork
- spare debris plate for skin and bone
- plate for used service gear
- service spoon and fork.

Accompaniments

- creamed horseradish sauce
- cayenne pepper
- peppermill
- segment of lemon
- traditionally brown bread and butter.

Cover

- fish knife and fork
- cold fish plate.

Method

1 Ensure all ingredients and equipment are organised before commencing.
2 Start at the tail end.
3 Cut a section about 10 cm (4 in) long.
4 Insert the knife between skin and flesh on one side and loosen the skin.
5 Insert the skin between the prongs of the fork and roll up on the fork towards the backbone.
6 Cut round the backbone.
7 Roll the skin off the other side and cut free with the knife
8 Fillet each side removing the backbone.
9 Place on to a cold fish plate, together with the lemon segment and serve.
10 Offer horseradish sauce separately.

> **Note**: Eel is very often carved at the buffet rather than on the guéridon because of the great length of the whole eel and the space required to lay it out on a flat surface for carving.

Smoked trout (truite fumée)

Ingredients

smoked trout dressed on a silver flat

Equipment

- service spoons and forks on a service plate
- plate for used service gear
- cold joint plate.

Accompaniments

- creamed horseradish sauce
- cayenne pepper
- peppermill
- segment of lemon
- traditionally brown bread and butter.

Cover

- fish knife and fork
- cold fish plate.

Method

1. Ensure all ingredients and equipment are organised before commencing.
2. Present the dish to the customer then return to the guéridon.
3. Place a few crisp lettuce leaves and tomato on the fish plate.
4. Place the smoked trout onto a cold joint plate
5. Holding the trout with the flat of the fork, make an incision with the point of a small knife along the backbone of the trout from head to tail and similarly along the belly.
6. Secure the trout with the prongs of the fork gently behind the shoulder bone at the head and inside the fish (so as not to pierce the flesh).
7. Detach the skin by sliding the spoon between the skin and flesh. Then turn the fish over and repeat for the underside.
8. With the aid of a service spoon and fork, remove both the head and tail.
9. Set the smoked trout neatly onto the cold fish plate and serve.
10. Offer horseradish sauce separately.

Smoked salmon (saumon fumé)

Ingredients

side of smoked salmon on a board

Equipment

- carving knife (usually a ham knife or long thin flat knife)
- joint fork
- service spoon and fork
- plate for used service gear.

Accompaniments

- cayenne pepper
- peppermill
- half of lemon wrapped in muslin or segment of lemon
- traditionally brown bread and butter
- sometimes chopped shallots and capers are offered together with soured cream.

Cover

- fish knife and fork
- cold fish plate.

Note: Because of the size of a side of smoked salmon it is often carved on the buffet or on a dedicated service trolley.

Method

1 Ensure all ingredients and equipment are organised before commencing.
2 Present the salmon on the board to the customer, or the trolley with the salmon and board on it.
3 Ensure that the side of smoked salmon has been prepared for service with the skin being trimmed and any small bones removed using a small pair of fish pliers.
4 Carve from the head towards the tail and start about halfway down so that slices will not be too long when laid onto the fish plate for service.
5 Remove the black line in the middle of each slice by making a small V-shaped incision at the centre of the side of smoked salmon before carving each slice.
6 Carve each slice wafer thin, giving 2–3 slices per portion.
7 As each slice is made, use a joint fork to slide the edge of the slice of smoked salmon between the prongs of the joint fork and roll up. Lift over to the cold fish plate and unroll neatly onto the fish plate. Repeat for each slice.
8 Serve and offer accompaniments.

Caviar (Caviare – roe of the sturgeon)

Ingredients	
caviar pot(s) in a dish of crushed ice on an underflat	

Equipment

- sweet spoon or two teaspoons for service
- plate for used service gear.

Accompaniments

- blinis (buckwheat pancakes) or hot breakfast toast
- butter
- segments of lemon
- sieved hard-boiled white and yolk of egg
- chopped shallots
- sometimes soured cream.

Cover

- caviar knife on the right-hand side of the cover
- cold fish plate.

Method

1 Ensure all ingredients and equipment are organised before commencing.
2 Present the guéridon at the table.
3 If a sweet spoon is used then generally one spoonful weighing approximately 30 g is a portion.
4 If two teaspoons are used, the caviar is moulded in the two spoons (quenelle), 3–4 teaspoonful per portion.
5 When served direct from the pot(s), the caviar is usually weighed before and after service and then the amount used is charged according to the amount served.

Note: Caviar may also be served in small glass bowls set on crushed ice. These are usually placed on the table at the top of the cold fish plate and the accompaniments are then offered at the table. Caviar may also be served already pre-plated, from the kitchen/larder.

If a caviar knife is not available then a side knife can be used.

Whole melon (melon frappé)

Ingredients	
whole melon set in a small container of crushed ice	1
cocktail cherries, or a range of fresh berries in a small silver or glass dish	handful

Equipment

- cutting board
- sharp knife
- clean napkin
- plate for debris from the melon
- plate for used service gear
- service spoons and forks on a service plate
- cocktail sticks in a holder.

Accompaniments

- ground ginger
- caster sugar.

Cover

- sweet spoon and fork or a small (side) knife and fork (especially if the melon is a little unripe)
- cold fish plate.

Method

1 Ensure all ingredients and equipment are organised before commencing.
2 The melon should be set in a small container of crushed ice.
3 Present the melon to the customer then return to the guéridon.
4 Lift the melon with the aid of a clean napkin onto a carving board.
5 Trim both ends.
6 Stand the melon on end and cut out the required portion or portions. Use your judgement as to the size of a portion but, as a guide, there should be approximately four to six portions to one whole melon.
7 Place the cut portion on a clean napkin and hold it firmly in the left hand. Scoop out any pips with the aid of a service spoon into the remainder of the whole melon. If there is less than half the melon left then scoop the pips straight onto a debris plate.
8 Trim the base of each portion so it stands squarely on the cold fish plate and will not roll or slide about.
9 If required the waiter may cut (separate) the flesh of the melon from the rind and slice.
10 Decorate with a cocktail cherry on a stick and serve.
11 Offer the caster sugar and ground ginger at the table.

> **Note**: Charentais melon, which is usually served half to a portion, is often served in a bowl on crushed ice. A sweet spoon (or teaspoon) is placed on the underplate or on the right-hand side of the cover.

Pâté and terrines

A wide range of flavoured pâtés are now offered, sometimes known as pâté maison (pâté of the house or establishment) where each recipe may vary. There are also a range of meat, fish and vegetable terrines.

Ingredients	
pot of foie gras or terrine of pâté, or terrine presented in a terrine	

Equipment

- two teaspoons or a joint knife
- silver jug of very hot water
- if pâté maison or a terrine is being offered, then a side knife will be required
- service spoons and forks on a service plate
- plate for used service gear.

Accompaniments

- hot breakfast toast, with crusts removed, cut into triangles and served in a napkin on a side plate
- alternatives are various breads, often warmed, including brioche.

Cover

- small side knife and a sweet fork
- cold fish plate.

Note: The word terrine refers to both the cookware, usually an earthenware oblong dish (but may also be metal) for cooking a terrine, and also to the terrine itself, which is either a forcemeat similar to a pâté, or a layered combination of various foods.

Method

1 Ensure all ingredients and equipment are organised before commencing.
2 Present the dish to the customer then return to the guéridon.
3 If foie gras is being offered, place the two teaspoons in the silver jug of very hot water.
4 Using each in turn, draw the teaspoon across the surface of the foie gras so that curls of the foie gras may be formed.
5 Give four or five curls per portion and, as they are formed, place them on the cold fish plate.
6 Decorate with a few crisp lettuce leaves and some segments of tomato. Serve.
7 If pâté or other form of terrine is being offered, the waiter uses the joint knife, frequently dipped in very hot water, to cut two or three slices per portion. Decorate as above and serve.

Note: In some instances the pâté may come already sliced from the larder and dressed on a flat. In this case serve as for silver service or guéridon service.

Shellfish cocktail (cocktail de crevettes)

Ingredients	
shellfish	1 portion
shredded lettuce	15 g
tomato concassé	15 g
sieved hard-boiled white and yolk of egg	1 egg
mayonnaise	60 ml
tomato ketchup	1 tsp
Worcestershire sauce	dash
lemon juice	30 ml
chopped parsley	½ tsp
slice of lemon	1

Equipment

- small glass dishes, with teaspoons, to hold the ingredients, all placed on a silver salver
- soup plate for mixing the sauce
- service spoons and forks on a service plate
- plate for used service gear.

Accompaniments

- lemon wedge
- traditionally brown bread and butter.

Cover

- teaspoon
- sweet (small) fork or oyster fork
- shellfish cocktail holder on a dish paper on a side plate.

Note: A shellfish cocktail holder has an insert which is placed into the holder that contains crushed ice. An alternative would be to use a small glass bowl set on a soup plate of crushed ice. Shellfish cocktails are also served in various types of glassware. The fork and teaspoon may be placed to the right and left of the cover or on the doily on the side plate on either side of the shellfish cocktail holder.

Method

1 Ensure all ingredients and equipment are organised before commencing.
2 Present the guéridon at the table.
3 Ensure there is some crushed ice around the base of the shellfish cocktail holder and that it is well chilled.
4 Place the tomato concassé into the base of the shellfish cocktail holder.
5 On top of this place some shredded lettuce followed by the shellfish, which may be prawns or shrimps. Keep one or two shellfish by for decorating the finished dish.
6 Make up the sauce by mixing together the mayonnaise, tomato ketchup, Worcestershire sauce and a little lemon juice in the soup plate.
7 Coat the shellfish with the tomato flavoured mayonnaise. Be careful not to have been excessive when coating the shellfish as too much of the sauce may overpower the rest of the ingredients.
8 Now decorate the top with the sieved hard-boiled yolk and white of egg and chopped parsley.
9 Place the remaining shellfish and slice of lemon over the edge of the holder and serve.

10.5 Salads and dressings

Salads may be served:
- as part of a selection of hors d'oeuvres (see also Section 4.6, p.112)
- as a starter course (see Section 4.6, p.112 for examples of salad appetisers)
- to accompany a roast or other main course
- as a separate course usually after the main course (see Section 4.12 p.123 for the general service of salads).

General points in salad making

When mixing salads either at the guéridon or within the stillroom or kitchen, always ensure that:
- hands and utensils are scrupulously clean
- ingredients are fresh, crisp, cool and moisture free to avoid impairing the dressing by dilution
- there is a contrast of colour and flavour even for plain, green salads
- the mixing bowl is large enough – do not attempt to overload it with salad leaves. To mix well, salad must lie loosely and be capable of free movement within the bowl.

Salad dressings

The standard equipment required on the guéridon when preparing a salad dressing is:
- soup plate or shallow bowl in which to mix the dressing
- service cloth
- service spoons and forks on a service plate
- teaspoons in a small jug of water (for tasting the dressing as it is being made)
- plate for used (dirty) service gear.

The ingredients will depend upon the type of dressing required. Examples of seven different dressings are given below.

French dressing

Ingredients	
French or Dijon mustard	1 tsp
seasonings of salt, pepper, cayenne pepper (sometimes caster sugar)	pinch
four to six parts olive oil to one part vinegar	teaspoons

Method

Place the mustard and seasonings in a soup plate which is resting on the folded service cloth at an angle, thus retaining the mixture in one part of the soup plate to make mixing easier.

1 Blend the seasonings together with a service fork.
2 Add the measure of vinegar to the seasonings and mix well to form a smooth mixture.
3 Now add the oil slowly blending together with the service fork.
4 Taste and adjust seasonings if required.

English dressing

As for French dressing (except that English mustard powder replaces the French mustard), the proportions of oil to vinegar are one to two, and one teaspoon of caster sugar is sometimes added to the seasonings.

Sauce vinaigrette

Ingredients	
French, Dijon or English mustard	1 tsp
seasoning of salt and peppermill	pinch
vinegar	1 tbs
oil	2 tbs

Method

1 Place the mustard, seasoning and vinegar in a soup plate and mix together using a fork.
2 Add the oil slowly, mixing steadily.
3 The proportions of vinegar and oil used are according to individual taste.

Roquefort dressing

Ingredients	
Roquefort cheese	60 g
wine vinegar (see Method A)	1 tbs
olive oil (see Method A)	1 tbs
sauce Mayonnaise (see Method B)	3 tbs
seasoning (salt)	pinch
jug of single cream	small jug
lemon juice	small jug

Method A

1 Break down the Roquefort cheese into small lumps or cream it right down by mixing in a soup plate with a little wine vinegar or lemon juice.
2 Add the olive oil and season with salt. This will help to bring out the full flavour of the cheese. A little single cream may be added.

Method B

1 Break down the Roquefort cheese into small pieces in a soup plate.
2 With the aid of a large fork, fold the pieces of Roquefort cheese into some sauce mayonnaise.
3 Season with salt to help bring out the flavour. Taste and adjust seasonings as necessary.

Acidulated cream dressing

This form of dressing is mainly offered with salads containing fruit, such as orange salad (*salade d'orange*).

Ingredients	
lemon juice	1 sweet spoon
seasoning (salt)	pinch
jug of single cream	small jug
paprika	pinch

Method

1 Mix the lemon juice with the seasoning.
2 Add the single cream.
3 Check the taste.

> **Note:** For the preparation of a fresh orange for orange salad, see Fresh fruit, p.351.

313

Mustard cream

Ingredients	
single cream	⅓ litre (½ pint)
mustard	1 tbs
juice of a lemon	1 lemon
seasonings (salt)	pinch

Method

1 Place the dry ingredients into the soup plate and blend together using a service fork.
2 Mix the single cream in slowly and thoroughly to avoid lumps.
3 Add juice of the lemon to taste.
4 Adjust seasoning if necessary.

Lemon dressing

Ingredients	
oil	2 tbs
fresh lemon juice to taste	small jug
Seasonings (salt)	pinch

Method

1 Blend the oil and seasonings well together in a soup plate using a service fork.
2 Add the fresh lemon juice sparingly.
3 Taste as the dressing is made. The dressing should produce a 'bite' at the back of the throat.

Making and serving salads

The following equipment is required for making and serving salads:

- salad bowl
- fresh, clean, dry salad ingredients in the bowl or on a separate plate ready for moving to the bowl when the salad is to be put together.
- soup plate for mixing dressing
- the dressing ingredients
- salad servers (metal or wood) for use after dressing the salad (mixing the salad ingredients with the freshly made dressing) and serving onto salad crescents (saladiers – quarter-moon shaped dishes), plates or bowls
- salad crescents, plates or bowls for the number of covers to be served
- garlic press (if required)
- teaspoons for tasting
- joint plate for dirty cutlery.

General method

1 Ensure all ingredients and equipment are organised before commencing.
2 Present the guéridon at the table.
3 Place salad ingredients into the salad bowl.
4 Use a service spoon and fork or salad servers (one in each hand) to break the leaves if required.
5 Make dressing (see pp.341–343 for a selection of dressings).

6 Pour the dressing over the salad in the bowl.

7 Use salad servers or a service spoon and fork to thoroughly blend the salad with the dressing by turning over the leaves from top to bottom.

> **Note**: Dressings are usually blended together before being added to the salad. However, if ingredients are to be added separately to the salad, then these stages are followed:
> 1 oil first until all leaves glisten softly with a film of oil
> 2 followed by vinegar or lemon juice (sparingly)
> 3 then seasoning (salt and peppermill).

Service of salad

1 Place the dressed salad onto the salad crescents.

2 Place the salad crescent at the top left-hand corner of the customer's cover.

3 Place a sweet fork with the prongs facing down on the left-hand edge of the salad crescent with the fork handle at an angle of 45 ° to the cover for service.

4 Now serve the course that the salad is to accompany (for example, hot roast poultry, game) as quickly as possible.

> **Note**: If salad is to be served alone the cover is a small knife and fork, with the salad served onto a cold plate (rather than a salad crescent) or into a bowl or a soup plate.

Caesar salad

Ingredients	
fresh clean, dry cos (or Romaine) salad leaves on separate joint plate	
croûtons	30 g
grated or shaved Parmesan cheese	30 g
Ingredients (dressing)	
olive oil	2 tbs
white wine vinegar	2 sweet spoon
Dijon mustard	1 tsp
raw egg yolk*	1 egg
Worcestershire sauce	to taste
salt and pepper mill	to taste
peeled garlic cloves or pre-crushed garlic	to taste
chopped anchovy fillets	30 g

*Some establishments may substitute pasteurised egg for fresh egg yolk.

Equipment
- salad bowl
- service spoons and forks
- plates or bowls for numbers of covers to be served
- garlic press if not using pre-crushed garlic.

Accompaniments
- none.

Cover
- small knife and fork
- cold plates or bowls with underplates.

Method

1 Ensure all ingredients and equipment are organised before commencing.

2 Present the guéridon at the table.

3 Mix the ingredients for the dressing in the salad mixing bowl using a service fork.

These include crushed garlic (depending on the customer's requirements), mustard, dash of Worcestershire sauce, vinegar and raw egg yolk.

4 Drip in the oil from a small jug (as for making mayonnaise) and blend this in using a service fork. Two forks may be used as a whisk, in order to make a sauce of creamy consistency.

5 Add chopped anchovies.

6 Add seasonings to taste (according to the customer's requirements) and stir.

7 Put the whole lettuce leaves into the mixing bowl and break into smaller pieces (largish fragments) using a spoon and fork (one in each hand).

8 Add the croûtons and fold in.

9 Move the salad in the bowl with the service spoon and fork to ensure that it is fully covered by the dressing.

10 Present the salad onto the cold plates for service.

11 Sprinkle with grated (or shaved) Parmesan.

12 Serve.

There are many variations to this salad. One specific variation replaces the egg that is incorporated into the dressing with a one-minute boiled egg broken over the salad just before serving.

Other variants include making the dressing by incorporating two or three chopped anchovy fillets into basic vinaigrette that has been seasoned with garlic and some horseradish cream.

Some recipes substitute English mustard for Dijon. Garlic is usually used but some variants involve rubbing this over the wooden bowl before making the salad, while others use chapons (garlic croûtons). Other ingredients that might be used include Roquefort cheese and seasonings such as Tabasco.

Some recipes keep the anchovy fillets separate and then decorate the salad with them rather than incorporating them, chopped, into the dressing. As well as finishing with the sprinkling of grated Parmesan, some variations also include sprinkling with ground pepper and lemon juice.

10.6 Soups

General guéridon service of soup

Ingredients	
Portions of soup in a soup tureen	

Equipment

- lamp
- soup ladle.

Accompaniments

- depends on the soup being served – see examples of soups in Section 4.7, p.109.

Cover

- soup spoon (or sweet spoon which is traditional when eating consommé – see Section 4.7, p.109)
- soup plate or bowl on an underplate or hot consommé cup with saucer and underplate.

Method

1 Ensure the mise-en-place is complete before beginning.
2 Present the guéridon at the table
3 Service from the guéridon – the tureen of soup may be kept hot on a lamp or hotplate.
4 Ladle into the soup bowl or consommé cup already on an underplate or on a consommé saucer and underplate as appropriate. When ladling, once one ladleful is lifted touch bottom of the ladle back down onto the surface of the soup. This will prevent the ladle dripping as it is moved over to the soup bowl.
5 Serve immediately.
6 Offer accompaniments as appropriate.

For an image of the service of soup at a guéridon see Figure 6.33, p.229.

Clear soup with sherry (consommé aux xérés)

Ingredients	
portion of soup in a soup tureen	
measure of warm sherry (or Madeira) added by the waiter at the guéridon	60 g

Equipment

- lamp
- sauce ladle (but more often a soup ladle as this has more visual appeal) to assist in warming the sherry.

Accompaniments

- segments of lemon in a lemon press, placed on a side plate at the head of the cover
- cheese straws are offered and traditionally brown bread and butter.

Cover

- sweet spoon (this is traditional when eating consommé – see Section 4.7, p.109)
- hot consommé cup on a consommé saucer on an underplate.

Method

1 Ensure the mise-en-place is complete before commencing.
2 Present the consommé to the table from the guéridon and serve from the guéridon.
3 Keep the soup hot on a lamp or hotplate and then ladle/pour into the warm consommé cups which will be sitting on the consommé saucer on an underplate.
4 The measure of sherry may be warmed and added to the soup at the last moment in the kitchen, or it may be heated in a sauce (or soup) ladle over the lamp, flambéed, and then poured over the soup.
5 Serve immediately.

10.7 Hot fish dishes

Grilled, poached or shallow fried sole (sole grille, pochée ou meunière)

Ingredients	
silver flat with the sole together with lemon wedges	

Equipment

- lamp
- service spoons and forks on a service plate
- hot joint plate for filleting
- plate for used service gear
- plate for fish debris.

Accompaniments

- lemon wedge.

Cover

- fish knife and fork
- hot joint plate.

Method A

1 Ensure the mise-en-place is complete before commencing.
2 Present the dish to the customer then return to the hot plate or lamp on the guéridon.
3 Remove the fish from the silver flat onto the hot joint plate.
4 With the aid of a service spoon and fork remove the side bones (see Figure 10.5(a)).
5 Run the tip of the spoon down the backbone.
6 Place two large forks back to back at the head of the fish and on the backbone. Press the forks down so that the tips of the forks pierce the flesh on either side of the backbone (see Figure 10.5(b)). Now ease the fillets slowly away from the backbone.
7 Continue to do this working the forks gradually down the backbone towards the tail.
8 Lift out the bone.
9 Place the fillets back together in their original shape on the silver flat.
10 Coat with beurre fondue or other sauce as provided, replace garnish and serve.

(a)

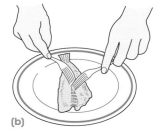

(b)

Figure 10.5 Preparation of a Dover sole

Method B

1 Steps 1–5 as in Method A above.
2 Start at the head of the fish and, with the aid of a service spoon and fork, loosen the two top fillets.
3 Hold the fish firmly with the spoon and run the fork down from head to tail between the two top fillets and the backbone.
4 Repeat this with the other two fillets, placing the fork between the bottom fillets and the backbone.
5 Lift out the backbone.
6 Proceed as in steps 9 and 10 in Method A above.

Poached or grilled salmon cutlet (darne de saumon poché ou grillé)

Ingredients	
poached or grilled salmon in an earthenware dish plus garnishes	

Equipment

- lamp
- service spoons and forks on a service plate
- plate for debris
- plate for used service gear.

Accompaniments

- according to the garnish, for example, Hollandaise, Doria.

Cover

- fish knife and fork
- hot fish plate or hot joint plate if to be served as a main course.

Method

1 Ensure all the mise-en-place is complete before commencing.
2 Present the dish to the customer then return to the lamp or hotplate on the guéridon.
3 Hold the salmon firmly in place with the service fork.
4 Insert the point of the spoon curved side outwards, between the outer black skin and the flesh of the salmon and run gently around the edge of the darne removing the outer black skin.
5 As an alternative to this method of removing the outer black skin a joint fork may be used, inserting the skin between the prongs of the fork. Twist the fork around the outer edge of the darne rolling up the skin on the fork as you proceed.
6 Insert the point of the spoon between the flesh and the centre bone and push the fillets of salmon away from the bone.
7 Remove the bone.
8 Lift the two fillets of salmon onto the hot fish plate or joint plate, being careful not to break the flesh, and add the garnish. Serve.

Note: This type of dish is generally served in an earthenware dish and therefore it is not necessary to remove it to a hot joint plate for the skinning and filleting of the darne (thick slice across the bone).

Whole sea bass cooked in a crust of Brittany rock salt (Le bar cuit en croûte de sel du Bretagne)

Ingredients	
serving flat with the sea bass	

Equipment

- lamp or hotplate
- service spoons and forks on a service plate
- joint knife
- large fish serving knife (or palate knife)
- depending on the size of the fish, a hot joint plate or, for larger fish, a board for filleting (the filleting can be done on the serving dish but be careful not to cut down onto the silver)
- plate for used service gear
- plate for fish debris
- gourmet spoons.

Accompaniments

- none.

Cover

- fish knife and fork
- hot joint plate.

Method

1 Ensure all the mise-en-place is complete before commencing.
2 Present the fish to the customer then return to the guéridon and place on the hotplate.
3 Using a joint knife and fork gently break away the salt, being very careful not to touch the skin of the fish. The fork is for leverage and the heel of the knife is used to repeatedly tap the salt hard, in a straight line along the backbone and belly of the fish. This helps to remove the salt in one single piece.

4 Neatly scrape the salt away making sure that there is clear access to the backbone and belly.
5 Place a service spoon at the top of the sea bass between the head and the body and place the service fork with the prongs inverted under the head (or in the mouth of the fish). Bring the fork upward and the spoon down through the neck to remove the head. Do not discard the head – see below.
6 Using a joint knife, make an incision along the back of the fish from head to tail above the bones and then repeat this around the gut. Trap the tail between the prongs of the fork; flip it upward so that it separates from the body, and then discard.
7 Remove the skin by placing the spoon under the top incision, holding the fork on top of the spoon and lifting the skin back towards the belly. Alternatively, use the tip of the knife to loosen the skin from the tail and slightly forward under the rear of the belly, then trap the tail skin between the prongs of the fork, roll to the side and the skin will peel off.
8 Run the serving knives down the line of the fish above the bones to separate the top side and belly fillets, then push the serving knife slightly forwards and the fillet should loosen itself from the main bone – it is then easy to slide the serving knife under to lift.
9 Cut across the fillet at an angle to the size of the portion required.
10 A service spoon and fork may then be used to lift the flesh from the bones.
11 Repeat this process until all the flesh has been removed from the top side and belly fillets.

12 When all the top and belly fillets have been removed, use the joint knife to gently scrape away any gut stuffing and any loose bones, and then use a service spoon and fork to completely remove the bone away from the bottom fillets. To ensure a clean removal of the bone, run the knife along the bone first.

13 Using a service spoon and fork remove any bones that may be left lying on the bottom fillets.

14 Run a knife down the centre of the fish to separate the bottom side and belly fillets.

15 Portion the bottom fillets following the same process as for the top fillets.

16 Arrange the fish portions on hot joint plates and serve.

17 An additional touch is to remove and serve the cheek meat to the customer. Taking the head, and using the fork for leverage, flip open the gill and remove the cheek meat and place on a gourmet spoon. Then repeat with the other side of the head. Coat the cheek meat with just a touch of the sauce and offer the tasting spoons to the customers.

> **Note**: Although this example is for sea bass, the same method can be applied to all large round fish served whole. In the case of cold whole salmon, points 5 to 16 may be followed, although it is normal practice to present cold salmon, or other round fish served whole, with the skin removed, in which case points 8 to 16 should be followed. Although cold salmon and other round cold fish may be presented on their belly, rather than on their side, the process for filleting and portioning the fish is similar.
>
> Sometimes excess bones can be difficult to see. Resting the blade of the joint knife on the fillet and gently dragging it along the surface can check for this, as the knife will detect any bones.

Flambéed scampi with a cream sauce (scampi à la crème flambée)

Ingredients	
portion of floured scampi	200 g
sliced mushrooms and chopped onions	30 g each
glass of sherry, white wine, vermouth or spirit, e.g. brandy, Pernod or whisky, depending on the specific dish	
butter	60 g
oil	1 tbs
seasonings: salt, peppermill, cayenne pepper and Tabasco sauce on a service plate	
sauce boat of single cream	1

Equipment

- lamp
- pan on an underplate
- service plate with service spoons and forks
- plate for used service gear.

Accompaniments

- peppermill.

Cover

- fish knife and fork
- hot fish plate or hot joint plate if to be served as a main course.

Method

1 Ensure all ingredients and equipment are organised before commencing.
2 Present the guéridon at the table.
3 Place the pan on a slow heat to melt the butter, then add a little oil.
4 Sauté the onions lightly and add the mushrooms.
5 Add the scampi and cover. After a short while add the flavouring liquor.
6 Season with salt, peppermill, Tabasco and cayenne.
7 When the scampi are cooked, quickly flambé and then douse with acidulated cream.
8 Reduce the cream and thicken the sauce.
9 Serve onto a hot fish plate or hot joint plate and offer to the customer.
10 Often the scampi is served on a nest of rice pilaff.

> **Note**: This dish can have many variations through the use of different flavouring liquors and flambé spirits. It can also include fresh fruits such as fresh black grapes, pineapple chunks and peaches.

10.8 Steaks and meat dishes

Double Entrecôte steak (Entrecôte double)

Comes from the boned out sirloin.

Ingredients	
silver flat with the double Entrecôte steak on it	

Accompaniments

● English and French mustard or alternatively sauce béarnaise.

Cover

● steak knife and joint fork
● hot joint plate.

Equipment

● lamp or hotplate
● pan
● board for portioning the Entrecôte steak
● sharp knife for carving
● service spoons and forks on a service plate
● two side plates for pressing the trimmed ends to extract all the juices
● plate for used service gear.

Method

1 Ensure the entire mise-en-place is complete before commencing.
2 Present the dish to the customer then return to the guéridon.
3 Lift the double Entrecôte steak from the silver flat onto the board.
4 Trim the ends.
5 Cut on the slant into two portions. Place back onto the silver flat on the lamp.
6 Press the trimmed ends between two hot side plates, allowing juices extracted to fall over the two portions of steak.
7 Place the portions of steak onto the hot joint plates and add the garnish. Set out attractively.
8 Serve.
9 Offer accompaniments.

> **Note**: This dish is normally offered for two customers. When taking the order the waiter should ask how the customers wish the steak to be cooked. If one customer wants their steak to be rare and the other customer medium, then the steak will come in from the kitchen rare and, once carved, one portion may be cooked a little longer in a pan on the lamp at the table.

Double fillet steak (Chateaubriand)

Method

The cover, accompaniments, equipment required for the guéridon and the method are as for Entrecôte double. However, each portion of the Chateaubriand is cut at an angle into approximately two or three slices, each 13 mm (½ in) thick, rather than being left in one whole piece per portion, as is the case with an Entrecôte double.

> **Note**: Although the Chateaubriand is commonly termed a double fillet steak, it may be large enough to serve a party of two, three, four or five customers as required.

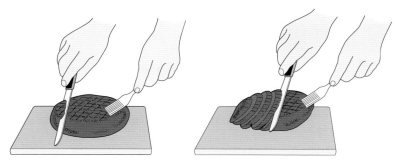

Figure 10.6 Carving of Chateaubriand

'T' bone steak/Porterhouse steak

This is a steak made up of part sirloin and part fillet, the whole being held together by the backbone, with a rib separating the sirloin from the fillet.

Ingredients	
silver flat containing the Porterhouse steak	

Equipment

- lamp
- board for carving
- sharp knife
- plate for debris
- service spoons and forks on a service plate
- plate for used service gear.

Accompaniments

- English and French mustard.

Cover

- steak knife and joint fork
- hot joint plate.

Method

1 Ensure the entire mise-en-place is complete before commencing.
2 Present the dish to the customer then return to the guéridon.
3 Remove from the silver flat onto the carving board.
4 Cut out the 'T' bone to give two separate pieces of meat: one of sirloin and one of fillet.
5 Return the two pieces of meat to the silver flat and place on the lamp to keep hot.
6 Dress attractively on the hot joint plate with the garnish.
7 Serve.
8 Offer accompaniments.

> **Note**: If the Porterhouse steak is for more than one person then carve the fillets as for a Chateaubriand and the sirloin as for the double entrecôte.

Steak tartare

Ingredients	
chopped raw fillet steak, moulded into a cake shape and presented on a round silver flat	200 g
one egg yolk	1 egg
salt and peppermill	to taste
chopped gherkins, capers, parsley and shallots	30 g each
oil and vinegar	2 tbs/1 tbs
French mustard	1 tsp
Worcestershire sauce	dash
cayenne pepper	to taste

Equipment

- soup plate
- service spoons and forks on a service plate
- plate for debris
- plate for used service gear
- containers for the various ingredients.

Accompaniments

- peppermill.

Cover

- joint knife and fork
- cold joint plate.

> **Note**: The portion of raw fillet steak is usually welled in the centre to hold a half eggshell with the egg yolk inside. (Some establishments may substitute pasteurised egg for fresh egg yolk.) The quantity of ingredients are all according to the customer's taste.

Method

1 Ensure the guéridon has all the necessary mise-en-place before proceeding.
2 Present the guéridon at the table.
3 Begin by making the sauce in the soup plate in which the dish is to be completed.
4 Put the seasoning of salt, pepper and French mustard in the soup plate. Mix well.
5 Place the yolk in the soup plate and beat the yolk and seasoning together using a service fork.
6 Add a small amount of vinegar and mix in
7 Drip in the oil from a small jug as if for making mayonnaise.
8 Be careful of the quantity of sauce being made as the finished product should be moist but not runny or too liquid.
9 Add the chopped gherkins, capers, parsley and shallots and bind together well.
10 Now place in the raw chopped fillet steak together with a dash of Worcestershire sauce. Incorporate these ingredients with the sauce you have already made and blend well together.
11 Taste and adjust seasoning as appropriate.
12 Shape into a round flat cake and place on the cold joint plate.
13 Serve.

Steak Diane

Ingredients	
sirloin steak batted out thinly	
olive oil	1 tbs
butter	60 g
French mustard	1 tbs
Worcestershire sauce	dash
salt and pepper	pinch
chopped shallots	30 g
sliced mushrooms	30 g
chopped parsley	1 tsp
small jug of double cream	50 ml
one measure of brandy	50 ml

Equipment

- lamp
- pan on an underplate
- service spoons and forks in a napkin on a service plate
- teaspoon for the parsley
- plate for placing used service gear on.

Accompaniments

- usually none.

Cover

- joint knife/steak knife and fork
- hot joint plate.

Method

1 Ensure the guéridon is correctly laid up with all the mise-en-place.
2 Present the guéridon at the table.
3 Ask the customer how they would like their steak cooked.
4 Heat about one table spoon of olive oil in a pan.
5 Add 50 g of butter and melt, blending with the heated olive oil (Figure 10.7(a)).
6 Add the shallots and mushrooms and cook gently on a low heat (Figure 10.7(b)).
7 Season the steak and smear both sides with French mustard (Figure 10.7(c)).
8 Cook shallots and mushrooms until part done.
9 Move the shallots and mushrooms to the side of the pan.
10 Raise the heat and add the steak to the pan, sealing and cooking on both sides (Figure 10.7(d)).
11 Flame the dish with the brandy (Figure 10.7(e)).
12 Now season the steak with a dash of Worcestershire sauce.
13 Add double cream to enhance the sauce and mix in well (Figure 10.7(f)).
14 Taste the sauce and adjust seasoning if required.
15 Serve from the pan onto a hot joint plate and use a teaspoon to sprinkle the chopped parsley on the steak (Figure 10.7(g).

Figure 10.7(a) Blending in the butter with the heated oil

Figure 10.7(b) Add the shallots and mushrooms

Figure 10.7(c) Smear both sides of the steak with French mustard

Figure 10.7(d) Adding the steak to the pan

Figure 10.7(e) Flambé the dish with brandy

Figure 10.7(f) Add double cream to enhance the sauce

> **Note**: There are many variations in the making of Steak Diane, each done to an establishment's traditional recipe or being a speciality of the waiter who is making the dish.

Figure 10.7(g) Serve the steak and sprinkle with chopped parsley

Monkey Gland Steak

The preparation and service of a Monkey Gland Steak follows a similar method to Steak Dianne. The differences are that a batted out fillet steak replaces the sirloin steak and Dijon mustard is used instead of French mustard.

Flaming is with brandy or whisky and the dish is traditionally served with a green salad, and often also with Pommes Pont Neuf.

Peppered minute steak (steak au poivre)

Ingredients	
flattened sirloin steak coated with crushed black pepper on a plate	
chopped parsley	1 tsp
jug of double cream	small jug
measure of cognac	60 ml
whole green peppercorns	30 g
olive oil	60 ml (2 fl oz)
butter	60 g
consommé or meat stock	60 ml (2 fl oz)
dry white wine	75 ml (2½ fl oz)

Equipment

- lamp
- pan on an underplate
- service spoon and forks on a service plate
- plate for dirty cutlery
- teaspoons
- ramekins or small bowls for ingredients on a large salver.

Accompaniments

- green salad, and often served with sauté or fried potatoes.

Cover

- joint knife and fork

- hot joint plate.

Method

1 Ensure the mise-en-place is complete before commencing.
2 Present the guéridon at the table.
3 Explain the dish to the customer.
4 Ensure the minute steak is adequately coated with crushed pepper and then season with a little salt.
5 Heat the oil and then add butter and combine.
6 Raise the heat slightly and lay into the pan the seasoned steak.
7 Allow the steak to cook quickly and brown well on both sides.
8 Remove steak to a warm platter to keep hot, using a warm plate to cover it.
9 Deglaze the pan with white wine and a little consommé over a high flame and reduce to half.
10 Add the green peppercorns and flambé with the cognac.
11 Add the double cream to make a rich sauce.
12 Taste the sauce and adjust seasoning if required.
13 Serve the steak onto a hot joint plate and coat with the sauce.
14 Place in front of the customer.

Beef stroganoff (filet de boeuf stroganoff)

Ingredients	
fillet steak cut into baton shapes	
chopped shallots	30 g
chopped parsley	1 tsp
sliced button mushrooms	30 g
chopped chutney (mango)	1 sweet spoon
jug of double cream	small jug
cayenne pepper	to taste
salt and peppermill	to taste
olive oil	1 tbs
butter	60 g
Worcestershire sauce	dash
measure of brandy	60 ml
garlic (optional)	1 clove
fried rice	100 g

Equipment

- lamp
- pan on an underplate
- service spoons and forks on a service plate
- plate for dirty cutlery
- teaspoons
- timbales for ingredients on a large silver flat.

Accompaniments

- none.

Cover

- joint knife and fork
- hot joint plate.

Method

1 Ensure the mise-en-place is complete before commencing.
2 Present the guéridon at the table.
3 Explain the seasonings to the customer.
4 Melt the butter in a pan with a little oil.
5 Season the steak.
6 Sauté the shallots to the 'pearl' stage (without colouring). Add garlic if required and the mushrooms and partially cook.
7 Now add the batons of filet steak and sauté.
8 Season with Worcestershire sauce.
9 Add mango chutney to the desired taste.
10 Flambé with brandy.
11 Finish with double cream and chopped parsley.
12 Serve onto a hot joint plate and place in front of the customer.
13 If fried or savoury rice is to be served then make a nest of rice and place the stroganoff in the centre.

Veal escalope suédoise (escalope de veau suédoise)

Ingredients	
escalope of veal on a plate	
chopped shallots	30 g
chopped parsley	1 tsp
French mustard	1 tsp
half measure of orange curaçao	30 ml
Worcestershire sauce	dash
butter	60 g
olive oil	60 ml
salt and pepper	to taste
cayenne pepper	to taste
sliced mushrooms	30 g
measure of brandy	60 ml
double cream	small jug

Equipment

- lamp
- pan on an underplate
- service spoons and forks on a service plate
- plate for dirty cutlery.

Accompaniments

- none.

Cover

- joint knife and fork
- hot joint plate.

Method

1 Ensure the mise-en-place is complete before commencing.
2 Present the guéridon at the table.
3 Melt the butter and add a little oil.
4 Season the escalope.
5 Sauté the shallots without colouring, then add the mushrooms and partially cook.
6 Add the escalope of veal and cook, colouring both sides.
7 Season with salt, pepper, cayenne pepper and Worcestershire sauce.
8 Add the half measure of curaçao without flambéing. This assists in flavouring the sauce.
9 Ensure the escalope is cooked and then flame with spirit (brandy).
10 Add double cream and adjust the consistency.
11 Taste and adjust seasoning if required.
12 Serve onto a hot joint plate, coat with the sauce and finish with a little chopped parsley.

10.9 Meat joints

All the descriptions for joints are for carving from a carving trolley. Before beginning carving the trolley must be checked to ensure all the mise-en-place has been completed. The trolley is then presented at the table.

For all the joints listed the cover is a joint knife and fork and a hot joint plate.

Boned sirloin of beef (contrefilet de boeuf)

Accompaniments

- roast gravy (from the carving trolley)
- Yorkshire pudding (from the carving trolley)
- English and French mustard and horseradish sauce, placed on the table by the waiter or offered to the customer and served as required.

Note: The beef is normally cooked to be a little underdone. Beef is carved in thin slices giving mainly lean meat and a little fat per portion.

Sirloin of beef on the bone (aloyau de boeuf)

The accompaniments offered are as for a boned sirloin of beef. The sirloin is comprised of two parts:

1 The undercut, which can be removed from the sirloin and may be served separately, either as fillets or tournedos, or larded and roasted. If it is to be carved then this should be done across the joint and not parallel to the side with the grain. A piece of fat should be served with each portion.

2 The uppercut, where the portions should be carved in thin slices down towards the ribs. On reaching a rib bone the waiter must release the meat attached to the bone by running the knife along and between the bone and the sirloin. This then allows the slices of meat carved to fall free.

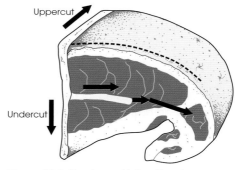

Figure 10.8 Carving a sirloin of beef

Note:
- Boiled beef is carved with the grain as this prevents shredding. A little cooking liquor should accompany each portion.
- Ribs of beef are carved in a similar fashion to the uppercut of the sirloin.

Best end of lamb (carré d'agneau)

Accompaniments

- roast gravy
- mint sauce
- redcurrant jelly.

> **Note**: Carve two/three cutlets per portion.

Method A

1 Hold the best end firmly on the board by inserting a service fork into the base at one end.

2 Turn the best end upright.
3 Carve into cutlets using the exposed end of the ribs as a guide to the correct amount per portion.

Method B

1 Lay the best end flat on the board with the exposed end of the ribs pointing downwards.
2 Holding the best end firmly with a service fork and using the exposed ends of the ribs as a guide, carve into cutlets.

Saddle of lamb (selle d'agneau)

> **Note**:
> - The loin may be roasted, or boned, stuffed, rolled and roasted or may be cut into chops.
> - The two loins undivided make up a saddle.

Accompaniments

- roast gravy
- mint sauce
- redcurrant jelly.

> **Note**: There are *two* alternative methods of carving the saddle.
>
> With Method A, each customer is given a portion of some lean meat and a little fat.
>
> With Method B, if the waiter is not careful it is possible for one customer to have a portion of all lean meat and another to receive nearly all fat and very little lean meat.

Method A

1 Remove the whole side loin from the saddle.
2 Carve into slices parallel with the ribs and approximately 6 mm (½ in) thick.
3 Serve some lean meat and some fat per portion.

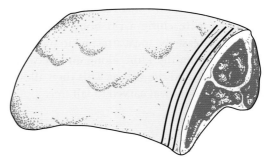

Figure 10.9 Carving a saddle of lamb (Method A)

Method B

1 Cut down one side of the backbone reaching approximately halfway along the length of the saddle.
2 Cut right down the side of the backbone to the short ribs.
3 At the point where cutting finishes, halfway along the backbone, turn the knife at right angles and cut down through the meat and fat.
4 Cut out lengths of meat from the saddle, commencing at the backbone, parallel to the backbone where the initial incision was made.

5 Work outwards to the edge of the saddle.
6 Each wedge of meat should then be carved into thin slices lengthwise.

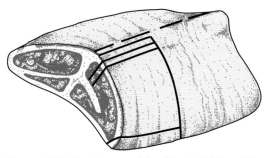

Figure 10.10 Carving a saddle of lamb (Method B)

Leg of lamb (gigot d'agneau)

Accompaniments

● roast gravy
● mint sauce
● redcurrant jelly.

Method

1 The carver (trancheur) must remember that initially he should carve onto the bone.
2 Take out a small V-shaped portion of meat just above the knuckle.
3 Proceed to carve the portions of meat by carving on to the bone from the V-shaped cut. This part of the joint is known as the 'nut' and is the choicest part.
4 After the initial portions have been carved from the nut of meat, the succeeding portions should be carved – a slice from the nut and a slice from the underside.

Note: When carving a leg of lamb, the waiter should hold the knuckle in a clean napkin to keep it steady on the board. The flesh of lamb should be cooked evenly and be rosé (pink) in colour. Always cut generously.

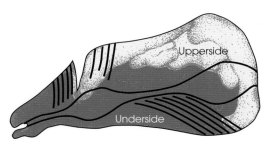

Figure 10.11 Carving a leg of lamb

Leg of pork (cuissot de porc)

Accompaniments

- roast gravy
- apple sauce
- sage and onion stuffing.

Method

1 Carved in a similar fashion to a leg of lamb, but the slices carved should be thin.

Ham (jambon)

There are two methods of carving hams:

1 French: the ham is cut into very thin slices down the length of the ham.
2 English: the ham is carved at the thick end where the meat is at its most tender.

> **Note**: If the ham is boned and rolled it will then be carved in slices across the fibre of the meat.

10.10 Poultry and game

Roast chicken (poulet rôti)

Ingredients	
roast chicken on a silver flat	

Equipment

- lamp
- carving board
- sharp carving knife (a filleting knife can also be used)
- service spoons and forks on a service plate
- plate for used service gear
- plate for debris.

Accompaniments

- bread sauce
- roast gravy
- parsley and thyme stuffing
- bacon rolls
- game chips
- watercress.

Cover

- joint knife and fork
- hot joint plate.

Method

1 Ensure all the mise-en-place is complete before commencing.
2 Present the whole chicken to the host at the table, and then return to the lamp or hotplate on the guéridon.
3 With the service spoon and fork lift the chicken from the silver flat onto the carving board, draining off any liquid that may be inside the chicken.
4 Lay the chicken on its side on the board from right to left in front of you, with a leg uppermost.
5 Holding the bird firmly on the board with the flat of the knife, insert the service fork beneath the leg joint and raise the leg until the skin surrounding it is taut.
6 Cut round the taut skin surrounding the leg with the tip of the knife, at the same time pulling the leg away from the joint and cutting through the flesh where necessary.
7 Cut the leg into two pieces through the joint, also removing the claw end.
8 Place the two pieces of leg onto the silver flat.
9 Proceed in the same manner with the other leg.
10 Turn the chicken onto its back. Insert the joint fork into the base of the carcass to hold it firmly.
11 Carve part of the breast and down through the wing joint, giving one piece made up of the wing and a little breast.
12 If necessary turn the chicken on its side and, with the aid of the service fork, lever the wing away from the carcass, at the same time holding the chicken firmly with the flat of the knife.
13 Proceed in the same manner with the other wing.

14 Position the bird on its back. Cut down one side of the breastbone and lever off half the breast.

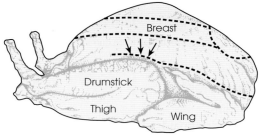

Figure 10.12 Carving a roast chicken

15 Proceed in the same manner with the other side of the breast.
16 An alternative method of removing the breast is by turning the chicken on its side and cutting through the wishbone joints.
17 Turn the chicken onto its breast, holding it firmly in place with the service fork.
18 Insert the knife between the flesh and the wishbone. Holding the whole breast on the board with the knife, lever the carcass away with the aid of the service fork.
19 Cut the whole breast into two portions lengthways.
20 Replace the carved chicken on the lamp. If necessary, while the carving operation is being carried out add a little liquid (gravy) to the silver flat to prevent the carved portions of chicken from burning.
21 Serve the chicken, giving some brown and some white meat per portion. Remember to add some game chips, bacon rolls and watercress if these make up the garnish.

> **Note:** Having completed the carving of the chicken, the carcass should be turned over. The 'oyster' piece is found on the underside of the carcass and is a small brown portion of meat found on either side of the back.

Poussin (young (baby) chicken, six weeks old)

Ingredients	
poussin on a silver flat with the garnish	

Equipment

- lamp
- carving board
- jointing knife
- plate for debris
- service spoons and forks on a service plate
- plate for dirty cutlery.

Accompaniments

- as per the menu garnish.

Cover

- joint knife and fork
- hot joint plate.

Method

1 Ensure all the mise-en-place is complete.
2 Present the dish to the customer then return to the guéridon.
3 Lift the poussin from the silver flat onto the carving board with the aid of the service spoon and fork.
4 Insert the service fork into the base of the carcass and hold firmly on the board with the breast uppermost.
5 Using the length of the blade cut through the hip joint, and using the breastbone as a guide, cut around the carcass keeping the whole side of the poussin intact.
6 Repeat this process on the opposite side.
7 You now have two portions each made up of the breast, leg and wing all intact.
7 If necessary place the two portions of poussin on the silver flat and re-heat.
9 Present on a hot joint plate, adding and arranging the garnish.
10 Serve accompanying gravy/sauces.

Flambéed chicken breast (suprême de volaille flambée)

Ingredients	
prepared suprêmes on a silver flat the suprêmes may be marinated beforehand)	
red or white wine	1 glass
Drambuie	60 ml
double cream in a sauceboat	120 ml
butter	60 g
olive oil	60 ml
tomato concassé	30 g
sliced mushrooms	30 g
finely chopped onions	30 g
salt, pepper, cayenne pepper	to taste

Equipment

- lamp
- pan on an underplate
- service spoons and forks on a service plate
- plate for used service gear
- butter knife and sauce ladle.

Accompaniments

- none or possibly a side salad.

Cover

- joint knife and fork
- hot joint plate.

Method

1 Ensure the entire mise-en-place is complete before commencing.
2 Present the guéridon at the table.
3 Place the pan on a low heat to melt the butter and add a little oil.
4 Season the sûpremes.
5 Sauté the onions to the pearl stage without colouring and add the mushrooms.
6 Add the sûpremes and cook, on a raised heat, as quickly as possible but without browning too much.
7 Add the wine and reduce the liquor.
8 Flambé with Drambuie and add the double cream.
9 Taste and adjust seasoning if required

10 Reduce the cream as quickly as possible and finish by combining the tomato concassé with the cream sauce.
11 Serve onto the hot joint plate and place in front of the customer.

> **Note:**
> ● During the cooking time a salad dressing could be prepared, ready to add to the salad once the main course is served.
> ● There are many variations to this dish, for example, ingredients such as curry powder and other seasonings may be added, and alternative wines and flambé spirit may be used.

Roast duck (canard rôti)

Ingredients	
roast duck on a silver flat	

Equipment
● lamp
● carving board
● sharp carving knife
● service spoons and forks on a service plate
● plate for used service gear
● plate for debris.

Accompaniments
● apple sauce
● sage and onion stuffing
● roast gravy.

Cover
● joint knife and fork
● hot joint plate.

> **Note:** Before beginning to carve a duck, remember that the joints are much tighter and more compact than those of a chicken and are therefore more difficult to find and cut through when carving. Also, the wing joints are a little further under the base of the carcass than those on a chicken.
>
> The initial stages in carving a duck are the same as for a chicken until the legs and wings have been removed.

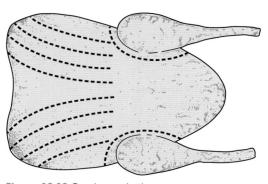

Figure 10.13 Carving a duck

Method

1 Ensure all the mise-en-place is complete before commencing.
2 Present the dish to the customer then return to the guéridon.
3 Transfer the duck to the carving board using a service spoon and fork.
4 Hold the duck firmly on the carving board with the aid of a joint fork in the base of the carcass.
5 The breastbone on a duck is wide and flat in comparison with that of the chicken. It is therefore easier to remove the complete half breast from the breastbone.
6 Now cut into long thin slices (aiguillettes) on the carving board.
7 Repeat with the other half breast.
8 Dress back onto the silver flat. Re-heat if necessary. Serve with the appropriate accompaniments.

Note:
- In the case of a duckling, very often the wing and breast are carved all in one portion.
- When carving the breast, a cut on an angle should be made with the carving knife along the length of the breast. This is because the meat is shallow and to carve straight down onto the flat breastbone would take the edge off the carving knife. This method allows aiguillettes to be carved with the breast still on the carcass.
- The carving of wild duck (canard sauvage) is similar to the above, but the accompaniments are orange salad with acidulated cream dressing.

Roast turkey (dindonneau rôti)

Ingredients	
roast turkey on a silver flat	

Equipment

- lamp
- carving board
- sharp carving knife
- service spoons and forks on a service plate
- plate for used service gear
- plate for debris.

Cover

- joint knife and fork
- hot joint plate.

Accompaniments

- cranberry sauce
- bread sauce
- chestnut stuffing
- chipolatas
- gravy
- game chips
- watercress.

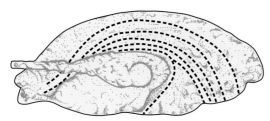

Figure 10.14 Carving a turkey

Method

1 Ensure the entire mise-en-place is complete before commencing.
2 Larger birds are normally served from a carving trolley. The trolley is presented at the table before carving. For smaller birds, which are served on a flat, present the whole turkey to the host at the table then return to the lamp or hotplate on the guéridon. Using the service spoon and fork lift the turkey from the silver flat onto the carving board, draining off any liquid that may be inside.
3 The legs and wings should be separated but not entirely removed from the carcass (i.e. pulled to one side). This is to allow the trancheur to carve thin slices of breast the full length of the body on either side.
4 If possible, carve and serve the stuffing with the slices.
5 As with roast chicken, the dark (brown) meat from the legs should be carved and a portion made up of both white and dark meat.
6 Serve with accompaniments.

Grouse (grouse)

The grouse season is from 12 August to 12 December. Grouse is regarded as a particularly choice dish and, if small, it is generally served whole. Otherwise it should be split into two portions by carving down through the middle of the breastbone.

> **Note:**
> ● A larger bird may be carved into three portions as indicated – from both sides of the bird remove a leg and wing in one piece. This gives two portions. The third portion is made up of the remainder of the breast separated from the carcass.
> ● Partridge may be carved in the same fashion (see below).

Partridge (perdeau)

The partridge season is from 1 September to 1 February. Depending on its size the partridge may be carved into two or three portions. If large, the three portions would consist of:

1 leg and one wing with a little of the breast attached
2 as above
3 the breast left on the bone.

If small the partridge should be split into two portions by carving down through the breastbone.

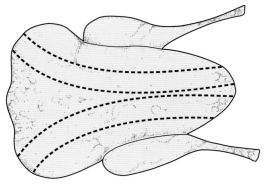

Figure 10.15 Carving a partridge or grouse

Woodcock (bécasse)

The woodcock season is from 1 August to 1 March. The woodcock is carved into two portions as for grouse or partridge. Generally woodcock is served on a croûte spread with a pâté made from the giblets of the woodcock.

Snipe (bécassine)

The snipe season is from 1 August to 1 March. Snipe are served whole as they are too small for carving into portions.

Pheasant (faisan)

The pheasant season is from 1 October to 1 February. The flesh of the pheasant is very dry and the carver should use a very sharp knife. Remove the legs as for chicken or duck. These are not normally served. Carve in thin slices on either side of the breast down to the wing joint. The wing is not normally removed as a separate portion.

Wood pigeon (pigeon)

The wood pigeon season is from 1 August to 15 March. Wood pigeon is carved in half through the breast to give two portions.

Saddle of hare (selle de lièvre)

The season is from 1 August to 28 February. Saddle of hare is carved in slices lengthwise as in a saddle of lamb. The flesh is dark in colour.

10.11 Sweet dishes

Peach flambé (pêche flambée)

Ingredients	
one measure of brandy	60 ml
caster sugar	25 g
portions of warmed peaches in peach syrup in a timbale	1 portion

Equipment

- lamp
- pan on an underplate
- matches
- plate for used service gear
- service spoons and forks on a service plate.

Accompaniments

- caster sugar.

Cover

- sweet spoon and fork
- hot sweet plate.

Method

1 Ensure the entire mise-en-place is complete before commencing.
2 Present the guéridon at the table.
3 Place a little of the peach syrup into the pan on a low heat.
4 Add the portion of peaches. If half peaches place the rounded side down.
5 Pierce the peaches with a fork to allow the heat to penetrate more quickly.
6 Baste the peaches occasionally and turn over. Should your peach syrup reduce too quickly turn the heat down and add a little more to prevent the peaches from burning.
7 Allow the peach syrup to reduce right down until it is almost caramelised.
8 At this stage sprinkle with caster sugar. This speeds up the caramelising effect and aids flambéing.
9 Pour over the brandy and flambé.
10 Serve onto hot sweet plates at the guéridon trolley or serve from the pan onto hot sweet plates at the table.

Pear flambé (poire flambée)

- As for peach flambé but using pears and pear syrup.

Banana flambé (banane flambée)

Ingredients	
banana	1
measure of dark rum (or Pernod depending on the specific dish)	60 ml
butter	60 g
caster sugar (sometimes Demerara sugar may be used)	30 g
fresh orange juice (optional)	1 small jug

Equipment

- lamp
- pan on an underplate
- service spoons and forks on a service plate
- plate for used service gear
- carving board
- small carving knife (12.5 cm/5 in).

Accompaniments

- caster sugar.

Cover

- sweet spoon and fork
- hot sweet plate.

Method

1 Ensure the entire mise-en-place is complete before commencing.
2 Present the guéridon at the table.
3 Prepare the banana at the guéridon, as explained on p.351.
4 Place the pan on a low heat and sprinkling the base with caster sugar, melt until light golden in colour.
5 Place the butter in the pan and allow to melt.
6 Blend the melted sugar and butter together using the back of the service fork (Figure 10.17(a)).
7 Pierce the banana carefully with the prongs of the service fork, this will allow the heat to penetrate when in the pan. If care is not taken here the banana may break.
8 Carefully place the banana rounded side down in the pan and heat (Figure 10.16(b)).
9 Baste with the butter and sugar mixture. Colour slightly and then turn the banana over.
10 Be careful not to overheat the banana or to cook for too long, as it will become too soft.
11 When the sauce is golden brown add a little fresh orange juice and blend well. This produces the sauce and removes the surplus fat from within the sauce.
12 When heated sufficiently, flambé with the rum (Figure 10.16(c)).
13 Serve onto a hot sweet plate at the flambé trolley or serve at the table from the pan onto the hot sweet plate (Figure 10.16(d)).

Note: Sometimes vanilla ice cream is served with Banana flambé.

Figure 10.16(a) Blend melted sugar and butter together

Figure 10.16(b) Place the banana rounded side down in the pan

Figure 10.16(c) Flambé with rum

Figure 10.16(d) Service of banana

Cherries flambé with Kirsch (cerises flambées au Kirsch)

Ingredients	
cherries in syrup in a timbale	1 portion
Kirsch	60 ml
caster sugar	25 g

Accompaniments
- caster sugar.

Equipment
- lamp
- pan on an underplate
- service spoons and forks on a service plate
- plate for used service gear.

Cover
- sweet spoon and fork
- hot sweet plate.

Method

1 Ensure the entire mise-en-place is complete before commencing.
2 Present the guéridon at the table.
3 Place the cherries and cherry syrup into the pan on a low heat.
4 Reduce the cherry syrup to a minimum.
5 Sprinkle with caster sugar to help caramelise any of the remaining syrup and as an aid to flambéing.

6 Add the Kirsch and flambé.
7 Serve onto a hot sweet plate at the flambé trolley or serve at the table from the pan onto a hot sweet plate.

> **Note:** With this dish it is also common for vanilla ice cream to be served onto the plate immediately before the cherries.

Cherries jubilées (cerises jubilées)

Ingredients	
cherries in syrup in a timbale	1 portion
brandy	60 ml
caster sugar	25 g

Equipment

● lamp
● pan on an underplate
● service spoons and forks on a service plate
● plate for used service gear.

Accompaniments

● caster sugar.

Cover

● sweet spoon and fork
● hot sweet plate.

Method

1 Ensure that the guéridon trolley has the correct mise-en-place before commencing.
2 Present the guéridon at the table.
3 Place the portion of cherries with a little of the syrup in the pan and heat up to simmering point.
4 Allow the syrup to reduce quickly until almost caramelised.
5 When the syrup is reduced to a minimum, sprinkle with caster sugar. This is an aid to flambéing and speeds up caramelisation.
6 The measure of brandy is now added and the cherries are flambéed.
7 Serve immediately from the pan onto a hot sweet plate, either at the guéridon or at the table.

Strawberries Romanoff (fraises Romanoff)

Ingredients	
portion of strawberries	250 g for two portions
Curaçao (or Cointreau or Grand Marnier)	60 ml
caster sugar	30 g
lemon (or orange)	1 half
double cream (or Chantilly cream)	200 ml

Equipment

- two large glass bowls
- service spoons and forks on a service plate
- plate for used service gear.

Accompaniments

- caster sugar.

Cover

- sweet spoon and fork
- glass bowl on an underplate or cold sweet plate.

Method A

1 Rinse the strawberries and pat dry with kitchen paper or clean tea cloth.
2 Taste a strawberry to see how sweet it is – this will help in determining how much lemon juice to add.
3 Reserve two whole strawberries.
4 Halve and hull the remainder of the strawberries.
5 Put the cut strawberries into a bowl and sprinkle with the liqueur, a little fresh lemon juice and 30 g of caster sugar, then set aside to chill and macerate.
6 Whip the double cream in a glass bowl (with vanilla essence and caster sugar for Chantilly cream) to firm peaks.

At the guéridon

1 Ensure all the mise-en-place is complete before commencing.
2 Present the guéridon at the table.
3 At the guéridon, stir the strawberries in the bowl to make sure they are fully coated in the marinade.
4 Spoon the strawberries into two small glass bowls (cooled) and top with whipped cream and a decorative strawberry.

Method B

1 As for Method A stages 1 to 4.

At the guéridon

1 Ensure all the mise-en-place is complete before commencing.
2 Present the guéridon at the table.
3 In a glass bowl, pour the liqueur to be used together with the lemon juice (depending on the sweetness of the strawberries) over the strawberries and allow to macerate for a few minutes.
4 Whisk the double cream in a glass bowl with two forks until it thickens.
5 Remove two-thirds of the strawberries plus the liquid into a glass bowl.
6 Add the thickened double cream a little at a time until the mixture is firm.
7 Set on to a cold sweet plate and decorate the top with the remaining strawberries. Sprinkle with a little caster sugar and serve.

> **Note**: Alternatives are:
> - Eton Mess – flavoured with Curaçao and lemon juice, strawberries are cut into smaller pieces and folded into the whipped cream.
> - Fraises royale – flavoured with Van der Hum, Kirsch and orange juice.
> - Pêches à la royale – strawberries and peaches combined with brandy and cream.

Pineapple flambé (ananas rafraîchi au Kirsch flambé)

Ingredients	
whole pineapple or tinned pineapple slices	1 pineapple
cocktail cherries for garnish	
Kirsch	60 ml
butter	60 g
caster sugar	30 g

Equipment

- lamp
- pan on an underplate
- service spoons and forks on a service plate
- plate for used service gear
- carving board
- carving knife (at least 20 cm/8 in).

Accompaniments

- caster sugar.

Cover

- hot fruit plate or sweet plate
- fruit knife and fork or a sweet spoon and fork.

Method

1. Ensure the entire mise-en-place is complete before commencing.
2. Present the guéridon at the table.
3. If the pineapple is fresh, prepare the pineapple as per instructions on p.384.
4. Sprinkle the caster sugar into the pan on a low heat and allow to melt and become golden brown in colour.
5. Put the butter into the pan and allow to melt. Blend with the sugar
6. Pierce the pineapple with a fork to allow the heat to penetrate more quickly.
7. Place the portion of prepared pineapple into the pan and baste.
8. Allow to heat quickly, reducing the liquid to the stage where it is almost caramelised.
9. Flambé with Kirsch.
10. Serve onto the hot fruit or sweet plate from the pan, at the guéridon or at the table.

Crêpes Suzette

Ingredients

Ingredients	
caster sugar	60 g (2 oz)
butter	60 g (2 oz)
Orange Curaçao or Grand Marnier	50 ml
fresh lemon juice	60 ml (2 fl oz)
brandy	50 ml
fresh orange juice	150 ml (5 fl oz)
zest of two oranges (sometimes included)	2 oranges
four thin pancakes on an oval flat	4 pancakes

Accompaniments

● none.

Cover

● sweet spoon and fork
● hot sweet plate.

Equipment

● lamp
● pan on an underplate
● service spoons and forks on a service plate
● two teaspoons in a jug of warm water for tasting purposes
● sauceboat on an underflat for the fresh orange juice
● brandy and liqueur glass on an underplate
● one bottle of Orange Curaçao or Grand Marnier
● one bottle of brandy
● two hot sweet plates
● sauceboat on an underflat for the zest of orange
● sauceboat on an underflat for the fresh lemon juice.

Method

1 Ensure the mise-en-place is complete before beginning.
2 Present the guéridon at the table.
3 Pour out the required measure of the liqueur and the spirit.
4 Melt the caster sugar and add the butter and combine together (Figure 10.17(a)).
5 Add orange zest if required.
6 Add fresh orange and fresh lemon juice and blend well.
7 Taste and adjust flavouring as required.
8 Add one measure of Orange Curaçao, or Grand Marnier (Figure 10.17(b)).
9 Mix well, stirring with a service fork, then taste and adjust flavour if required.
10 Add the first pancake and coat the topside of the pancake with the sauce (Figure 10.18(c)).
11 Heat well, then fold into four and place to the side of the pan to allow room for the next pancake to be put into the pan (Figure 10.17(d)).
12 Repeat the process for the other three pancakes (Figure 10.17(e)).
13 Work quickly as during this process the sauce should be reducing all the time and thickening. Take care it does not burn.
14 When the sauce is reduced sufficiently, add the measure of brandy and flambé.
15 Serve onto the hot sweet plates from the pan, at the guéridon trolley or at the table (Figure 10.17(f)).

Note: Sometimes vanilla ice cream is served with Crêpe Suzette.

Figure 10.17(a) Blend melted sugar and butter together

Figure 10.17(b) Add measure of Orange Curaçao or Grand Marnier

Figure 10.17(c) Coat the top side of the pancake with sauce

Figure 10.17(d) Fold pancake into four

Figure 10.17(e) Repeat process for remaining pancakes

Figure 10.17(f) Serve onto hot sweet plates

10.12 Fresh fruit

General service notes

Fruit may be prepared on the guéridon at the table. (For the preparation and service of fresh melon see p.338.)

Fresh fruit

Ingredients (examples shown below)	
fresh dessert apples or pears on a plate	4
fresh ripe but firm bananas on a plate	4
oranges on a plate	2
fresh pineapple on a plate	1

Equipment

- small very sharp knife
- sweet fork
- fruit plate
- plate for used service gear
- small glass dish
- cutting board
- service spoons and forks on a service plate
- plate for debris
- spare napkin
- apple corer.

Accompaniments

- caster sugar
- one measure of dark rum, Kirsch or other spirits or liqueurs as requested by the customer and to accompany the dish ordered.

Cover

- fruit knife and fork or sweet spoon and fork or small (sweet) fork depending on how and when to be served
- fruit plate
- finger bowl on a doily on a side plate and filled with lukewarm water and a slice of lemon
- spare napkin.

> **Note**: The equipment, ingredients and accompaniments listed above, together with the cover, may vary slightly depending on the specific requirements of the customer.

Apple or pear (pomme ou poire)

Method

1 Before commencing ensure that the mise-en-place is complete.
2 Present the guéridon at the table.
3 Present the fruit to the customer at the table then return to the guéridon.
4 Cut a cone from the top of the apple or pear around the stalk approximately 2.5 cm in diameter and put aside for later use (see Figure 10.18(a)).
5 Cut the base of the apple or pear so it will sit squarely on the plate.

6 Place a fork into the top of the apple or pear where the stalk cone was removed from.
7 Peel the apple in strips from top to bottom or in a spiral from top to bottom (see Figure 10.18(b) or (c)).
8 Cut the apple into two (see Figure 10.18(d)).
9 Then into quarters removing the core from each quarter (see Figure 10.18(e)).
10 Decorate on the plate using the stalk cone to garnish (see Figure 10.18(f)).
11 Dress with spirit or liqueur should the customer request it.

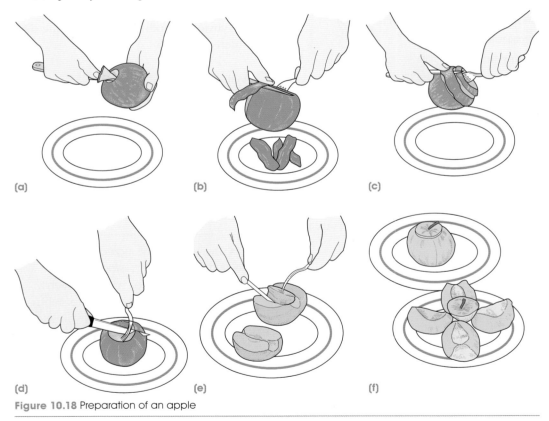

(a)   (b)   (c)

(d)   (e)   (f)

Figure 10.18 Preparation of an apple

Banana (banane)

Method

1 Before commencing ensure that the mise-en-place is complete.
2 Present the guéridon at the table.
3 Present the fruit to the customer at the table then return to the guéridon.
4 Remove the end of the banana (see Figure 10.20(a)).
5 Slice through the banana and through the stalk lengthways, using the fork to steady the banana, to give two even slices (see Figure 10.19(b)).

6 Insert the end of the banana skin between the prongs of a joint fork and carefully roll back away from the flesh, using your knife on the outside of the skin to keep the half banana firmly held on the board (see Figure 10.19(c)). Care should be taken here to ensure the flesh of the banana does not become broken.
7 Dress with dark rum if requested. Present neatly on the cold fruit plate.

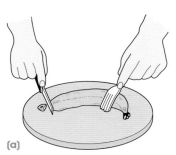
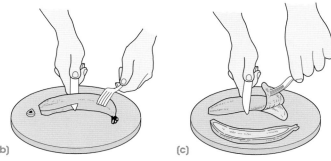

(a) (b) (c)

Figure 10.19 Preparation of a banana

Orange (orange)

Method

1 Before commencing ensure that the mise-en-place is complete.
2 Present the guéridon at the table.
3 Present the fruit to the customer at the table then return to the guéridon.
4 Cut a slice from one end of the orange with the aid of a sharp knife.

5 Pierce the cut slice with the fork to act as a guard when sectioning the whole orange.
6 Now pierce the whole orange with the fork from the uncut end, so that it is firmly held on the fork.
7 Make an incision around the uncut end of the whole orange through the skin to the flesh (through the rind and pith).

8 Remove the peel and pith by cutting strips from the cut end to the incision made around the orange (see Figures 10.21(a) and (b)).

9 At this stage you should have a whole orange on the fork with the peel and pith removed.

10 Holding the orange over the glass bowl, cut out each segment of the orange leaving the pith on the fork. Let the segments of orange fall into the glass bowl (see Figure 10.21(c)).

11 With the aid of a second fork, squeeze the pith over the glass bowl to remove all the juice.

12 Sprinkle with caster sugar.

13 Dress onto the fruit plate and serve (see Figure 10.20(d)).

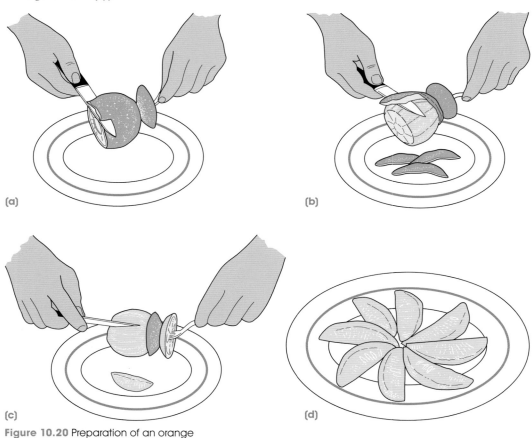

(a)

(b)

(c)

(d)

Figure 10.20 Preparation of an orange

Pineapple (ananas)

Method

1 Before commencing ensure that the mise-en-place is complete.
2 Present the guéridon at the table.
3 Present the fruit to the customer at the table then return to the guéridon.
4 Hold the pineapple by the stem with a clean napkin and remove the base of the pineapple.
5 Peel the pineapple in strips from top to bottom (see Figure 10.21(a)) or cut the pineapple peel in a spiral from bottom to top (see Figure 10.21(b)).

6 Remove the eyes by cutting a V-shaped channel. Note that each channel should go from left to right as this will give a less complex spiral that does not all run into one (see Figure 10.21(c)).
7 Remove the core before slicing the pineapple using the point of a pairing knife (see Figure 10.22(d)).
8 Alternatively slice the pineapple and then remove the core (see Figures 10.22(e) and (f)).
9 Dress with Kirsch if requested. Present neatly onto the cold fruit plate.

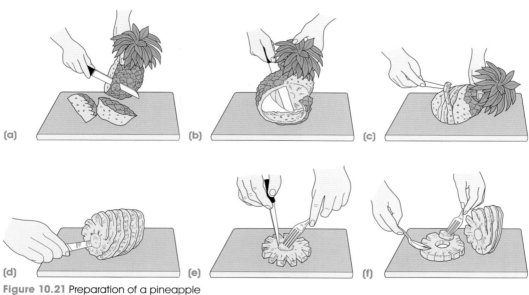

(a)   (b)   (c)

(d)   (e)   (f)

Figure 10.21 Preparation of a pineapple

Events

11.1 Types of events

Event catering is the term used for the service of special events for specific groups of people at pre-set times, with the food and beverages provided being pre-determined. It includes occasions such as luncheon parties, conferences, cocktail parties, weddings and dinner dances. In larger establishments all functions take place within the banqueting suites and are under the administrative control of the banqueting/event manager. In a smaller operation these events normally take place in rooms set aside for the purpose and come under the jurisdiction of the manager or assistant manager. There are also specialist banqueting conference centres. Most of the staff available for events are employed on a casual basis. At busy periods there may be a number of events running at the same time.

Figure 11.1 Example of a room laid for a function (Palm Court at the Waldorf Hilton Hotel, London, image courtesy of FCSI, UK)

Events are as popular as ever but the purpose and style of events are changing. Theme evenings, for example, are becoming increasingly popular. There is also a trend towards less formality. Guests have higher expectations of the overall standard of decor, lighting effects and tableware used, as well as higher standards of food, beverages and comfort, while still seeking value for money as budgets are more fixed and scrutinised by booking organisations and budget holders.

There are two main types of events:
- Formal meals (sometimes called banquets):
  o luncheons
  o dinners
  o wedding breakfasts.
- Buffet receptions:
  o wedding receptions

- o cocktail parties
  o buffet teas
  o dances
  o anniversary parties
  o conferences.

A further breakdown of the types of events may be as follows:
- Social:
  o dinners
  o luncheons
  o receptions
  o cocktail parties
  o charity dinners.
- Public relations:
  o press party to launch a new product
  o fashion parade

- o exhibition
  o seminars.
- Conferences:
  o political
  o trade union
  o training seminars
  o national and international
  o sales conferences
  o academic conferences.

11.2 Event service staff roles

In larger establishments there is generally a small number of permanent staff dealing solely with events. This often includes a sales manager, banqueting/events manager, assistant managers, banqueting/events head waiters, service staff, technical staff and porters together with an administration office. In smaller establishments, where there are fewer events, the manager, assistant manager and food and beverage service staff undertake the administrative and organisational work as part of their regular duties.

Sales manager

The main role of the sales manager is to promote the event facilities of an establishment and, where necessary, to make the initial approaches and contacts. The sales manager must have an extensive knowledge of room specifications, size, light switches, electric points and output, IT capabilities, height and width of doorways, maximum floor loads and so on. This enables them to respond quickly to any queries at the initial meeting with a client. Most establishments offer various forms of banqueting and/or meetings and conference sales packages (see p.389) and these provide a range of information about the facilities available and the charges for them.

Banqueting/conference manager

The banqueting/conference manager is responsible for all administration, including meeting prospective clients and discussing the arrangements for the menu, table plans, costs, wines, band, and toastmaster. They must communicate to all the departments concerned the date of an event, numbers expected and any other details that might be required by a particular department, usually by the means of an 'event sheet' and a daily/weekly meeting.

Administration office staff

The administration staff work with the managers and are responsible for handling all incoming and outgoing mail, ensuring that information about an event is passed to the relevant internal departments and for record keeping. Administrative staff handle enquiries and may take provisional bookings for events, ensuring the details are entered on the events booking form (see p.389) which in turn becomes the details for the events sheet.

Banqueting/events head waiter

The banqueting/events head waiter is in charge of the events rooms plus the organisation required to prepare the rooms for various events. They may also be responsible for booking staff on a casual basis to cover the various duties at an event.

Dispense bar staff

The dispense bar staff are responsible for the allocation of bar stock for the various events, setting up the bars, organisation of the bar staff, control of stock and cash during service and stocktaking after an event has taken place. They are also responsible for restocking the event bars.

Banqueting/events head wine waiter

The banqueting/events head wine waiter may work in conjunction with dispense bar staff and is often responsible for organising and employing (if on a casual basis) the banqueting/events wine waiters. They will allocate the wine waiters' stations, give them cash floats if there are cash wines and discuss the service with them.

Permanent service staff

The permanent service staff are usually experienced staff that can turn their hand to any job concerning events and banqueting. They generally do most of the mise-en-place before the event, for example laying the tables.

Casual staff

Casual staff are hired on a part-time basis to work at the events as needed. These can be from a bank of staff the establishment run themselves or an agency specialising in waiting staff.

Porters

There are generally a number of porters on the permanent events staff. They are essential members of staff as there is often a great deal of work involved in preparing room layouts before and after events.

11.3 Event administration

Event sales

In order to promote the sale of events (meetings/conferences/banquets, etc.) most establishments now have banqueting/events and/or meetings and conference sales packs. These range from the very simple to the elaborate and complex, depending on the nature of the establishment. Examples of the content often included in these types of packs are:

- location and contact details of the establishment and the staff involved
- examples and descriptions of the type of events that can be accommodated
- information on how to get to the venue, local attractions and car parking availability
- examples and costs of set packages; for example, for conference delegates this might be day rates, overnight rates and meal rates
- room plans indicating size, possible layouts, availability of services (such as electric sockets, telephone and IT points), air-conditioning, access points and the maximum weight the floor will take, etc.
- provision for disabled visitors
- room hire charges
- list and description of styles of tables and chairs and other equipment available (e.g. meeting tables, conference chairs, lounge areas, technical equipment such as public address systems, multimedia players and TV monitors, flip chart stands and paper, lecterns, data projectors, computers, interactive white boards, blackout curtains, double glazing and sound proofing)
- charges for additional equipment such as projectors, etc.
- availability of room decoration, flowers and lighting systems
- availability of disco, resident bands, presenters, Masters of Ceremony, Toast Masters, etc.
- examples of meal packages (such as a set menus, snack menus and conference lunches) and details of the service methods available (such as formal table service, buffet and in-room service)
- other services such as car rental, limousine and private bus services, catwalks, business services and other services of the establishment such as restaurants and fitness and leisure facilities
- standard terms and conditions of bookings.

Booking and administrative procedures

When the client is ready to make a booking a file is opened; this can be hand-written or computerised depending on the establishment. The file will contain the client's details and will be used to hold all the requirements for the particular event, as well as all correspondence sent and received. At the meeting when the booking is confirmed an event booking form will be completed. The basic information that is recorded is shown below.

- Date and time of event (including access and clear down times)
- Client details
- Type of event
- Location of event within the establishment
- Food and beverage requirements
- Service methods (including wines and drinks being inclusive or cash)
- Expected number of people attending (and confirmation of final deadline for actual numbers attending)
- Table plan
- Price being charged (e.g. inclusive or per head)
- Inclusive or cash bar and wines
- Provision for guests with special needs
- Additional charges for equipment hire, etc.
- Contractual requirements (deposit payments, payment in advance, etc.).

The requirements for a function will depend upon the nature of the event and it is useful to have a checklist of these. In addition to the information listed above, the following might also be considered:

- overnight accommodation
- list of toasts
- date for final inspection visit by client
- floral decor for the tables, rooms, reception area and button holes
- colour of linen if able to offer a choice
- telephones
- security
- lectern
- marketing
- secretarial facilities
- toastmaster
- audio-visual equipment
- syndicate/breakout/interview rooms
- band, cabaret, dancing (and meal requirements)
- photographer
- place cards
- seating plan
- special liquor licence
- music, dancing or entertainment licences
- sign-posting
- car parking
- private bar facilities
- cloakrooms
- cancellation policies
- weddings – time of service, arrival time at venue, who is providing the wedding cake and stand and cake knife (client or venue).

An example of a summary of the administrative procedures for events is given in Figure 11.2.

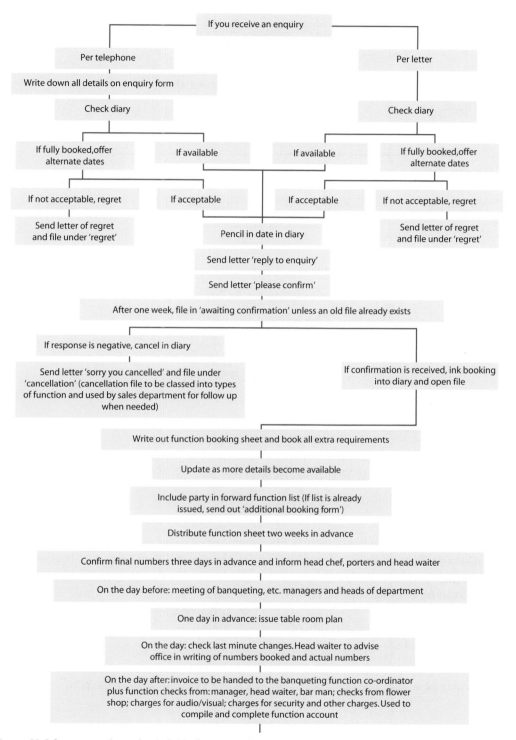

Figure 11.2 Summary of event administrative procedures (continues on following page)

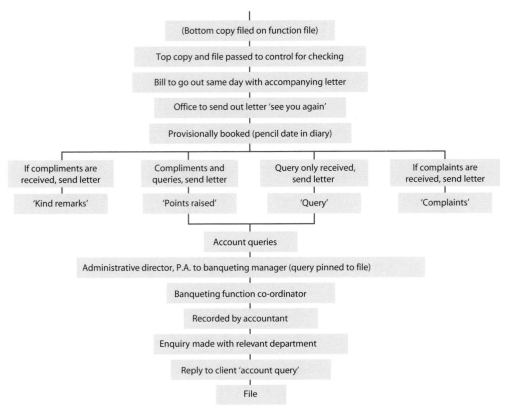

Figure 11.2 continued

11.4 Event organisation

Event menus

There should be a varied choice of menu within a wide price range, with special menus available for occasions such as weddings, twenty-first birthday parties and New Year's Eve. The number of courses at a banquet is normally four, plus beverages, but can be many more, and often includes:

- hors d'oeuvres or other appetisers
- soup or fish
- meat /vegetarian – with a selection of seasonal vegetables
- sweet
- coffee or tea – with a selection of petits fours.

This approach is generally popular, but extra or alternative courses such as entrées, cheese or savouries may be added. The sequence of courses is described in Section 4.2, p.90.

Wines

The banqueting/event wine list is often smaller than the main wine list of an establishment but usually contains a selection of good wines from the main wine list. Wines may be inclusive with the meal or on a cash basis, the money being payable to the sommeliers who may work on a float system. Very often the apéritif served before an event is also inclusive with the meal but if not, there may be a cash bar set up in the reception area.

Service methods in event catering

For events the service method may take any of the following forms (see Section 1.6, p.17 for definitions of service methods):

- silver
- plate
- self-service
- family
- assisted service.

The type of service method chosen is usually determined by the:

- host's wishes
- equipment available
- type of function
- food and beverages to be served
- time available for the function
- skills of the service staff available.

Formal seating arrangements

Of the total number of people attending an event, the number to be seated on the top table and the number on the sprigs, round or oblong tables that make up the full table plan will need to be known. The banqueting staff will also need to know whether the number on the top table includes the ends of the table, and in the UK care is normally taken to avoid seating 13 people on this table. (Other cultures may observe different numbers as being unlucky.)

All tables, with the exception of the top table, are numbered. Letters of the alphabet may also be used for the table designation rather than numbers. The table numbers themselves are usually on stands of such a height that they may be seen from the entrance of the banqueting room, the approximate height of the stands being 75 cm (30 in). After the guests are seated, and before the service commences, these stands are usually removed. However, if they are left on the table then they can provide an aid to the sommeliers when checking for cash wines.

Table seating plans

It is common now for table seating plans to be produced in two main ways:

1 An alphabetical list of the people attending, giving an indication of the table, or location on a sprig, where the person has been seated.
2 A listing of the people attending by table, showing all the people seated on a particular table or section of a sprig.

Before the event a copy of each of the two types of table seating plans are made. These go to:

- **the organiser**: before the event so that they may check all necessary arrangements.

Finalised plans are then prepared for:

- **the guests**: the table seating plans should be placed in a prominent position at the entrance of the banqueting suite so that all guests may see where they have been seated, the position of their table in the room, and who else is sitting at the same table or section of a sprig
- **the banqueting/events manager**: for reference purposes.

Table layout

The type of table layout used for a particular function will depend upon a number of factors, including the:

- organiser's wishes
- nature of the event
- size and shape of the room where the event is to be held
- number of covers attending.

For the smaller type of event a U- or T-shaped table may be used. Where the luncheon or dinner party is more formal there may be a top table and separate tables (round or rectangular) for the various parties of guests.

When an event is booked, careful consideration should be given to the type of table plan used, as the widths of covers, gangways and size of chairs will affect the space available. It is important to allow a reasonably comfortable seating space for each guest and, at the same time, to give waiting staff sufficient room for the service of the meal. The gangway space must be sufficient for two waiters to pass one another during the service without fear of any accident occurring.

The general considerations for table spacing are described below.

- Minimum space between sprigs should be 2 m (6 ft). This is made up of two chair widths (from the edge of the table to the back of the chair (46 cm or 18 in)) plus a gangway of 1 m (3 ft), allowing each waiter sufficient passing space: total of 2 m (6 ft).
- Table widths are approximately 75 cm (2 ft 6 in).
- The length along the table per cover should be 50–60 cm (20–24 in).
- The space from the wall to the edge of the table should be a minimum of 1.4 m (4 ft 6 in). This is made up of a 1 m (3 ft) gangway, plus one chair of width 46 cm (18 in).
- The height of the chair from the ground will vary according to the style and design, but is approximately 46–50 cm (18–20 in).
- The length of the table used is generally 2 m (6 ft) but 1.2 and 1.5 m lengths (4 and 5 ft) may be used to make up a sprig.
- Round tables are 1.0, 1.5 or 2 m (3, 5 or 6 ft) in diameter with the appropriate extensions.
- Suggested area allowance for sit-down functions per person is approximately 1.0–1.4 m² (12–15 sq ft); for buffets the allowance is 0.9–1.0 m² (10–12 sq ft).

Examples of banquet/event layouts

Top table and sprigs

- Event for 110 covers: 15 guests on top table; 3 sprigs required.
- Dimension of room = 18 m (60 ft) long by 11 m (36 ft) wide.

Method of working

1   Length of table required for top table:
    15 guests x 60 cm (2 ft) cover width   = 9 m (30 ft) or 5 x 2 m (6 ft) tables.
2   Number of covers on each sprig:
    110 covers – 15 covers on top table   = 95 covers
    95 covers ÷ 3 sprigs   = sprigs of 32, 32 and 31 covers
    Therefore, each side of a sprig will have 16 covers, except one, which will have 15 covers.
3   Length of sprig:
    16 covers x 60 cm (2 ft) cover width   = 9.7 m (32 ft) or 5 x 2 m (6 ft) tables.
4   To check if three sprigs may be fitted on top table:
    sprigs x 75 cm (2 ft 6 in) (width)   = 2.25 m (7 ft 6 in)
    2 gangways x 1 m (3 ft) (width)   = 2 m (6 ft)
    4 chair depths 46 cm (18 in)   = 2 m (6 ft)
    Total   = 6.25 m (19 ft 6 in)
    Thus, there is plenty of room (see Figure 11.3).

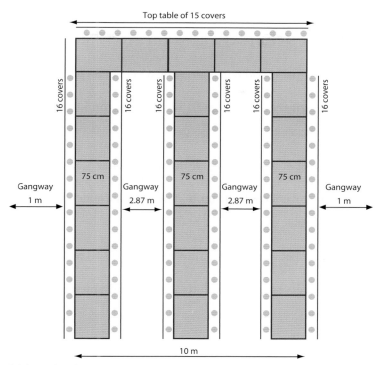

Figure 11.3 Top table and sprigs

This layout also allows for five extra covers in case of emergency. These are located:

1 either end of the top table	= 2
1 either end of the sprigs	= 3
Total	= 5

A similar plan could be developed to make the layout more compact, for use in a slightly smaller room. It would it be possible to get four sprigs on a 9 m (30 ft) long top table.

4 sprigs x 75 cm (2 ft 6 in) width	= 3 m (10 ft)
3 gangways x 1 m (3 ft) width	= 3 m (9 ft)
6 chair depths = 46 cm (1 ft 6 in)	= 3 m (9 ft)
Total	= 9 m (28 ft)

Four sprigs would give a more compact layout and bring everyone closer to the speakers on the top table. This alternative plan allows for 12 covers on each side of the four sprigs and additional seating at the top table ends and sprig ends if required.

Top table and round tables

Event for 110 covers: 15 guests on top table, 95 covers on round tables.
Dimension of room = 18 m (60 ft) long by 12 m (36 ft) wide.

> **Note**: When using round tables it is first necessary to calculate the number of covers that could be seated at round tables of different diameters. In all cases it is necessary first to calculate the circumference of the round table. This is done by multiplying the diameter measurement of the table by pi (π) (where $\pi = 22 \div 7$). Therefore, circumference is the diameter of the table x 22 ÷ 7. A cover would normally require 60 cm (2 ft) width on the circumference of a round table.

The calculations for 1 m, 1.5 m and 2 m diameter tables are as follows:

Circumference of a round table 1 m (3 ft) in diameter:

   1 m x 22 ÷ 7 = 3.1 m

Number of covers available per round table (allowing 60 cm (2 ft) per person):

   3m ÷ 0.6m = 5.0 m

Therefore the number of covers will be 5 per 1 m diameter round table.

Circumference of a round table of diameter 1.5 m (5 ft):

   1.5 m x 22÷7 = 4.7 m

Number of covers available per round table (allowing 60 cm (2 ft) per person):

4.7 m ÷ 0.6 m = 7.9 m

Therefore the number of covers could be up to 8 per 1.5 m diameter round table.

Circumference of a round table of diameter 2 m (7 ft):

   2 m x 22 ÷ 7 = 6.3 m

Number of covers available per round table (allowing 60 cm (2 ft) per person):

6.3 m ÷ 0.6 m = 10.5 m

Therefore the number of covers could be up to 11 per 2 m diameter round table.

Method of working

1   Length of table required for top:

    15 guests x 60 cm (2 ft) cover width   = 9 m (30 ft) or 5 x 2 m (6 ft) tables.

2   Number of round tables required:

    110 covers – 15 top table covers   = 95 covers to be laid on round tables.

    Assuming using tables all same diameter (1.5 m/5 ft), i.e. 8 covers per table.

    Number of tables required is

    95 covers ÷ 8 covers per table   = 11.875 tables.

    Therefore 12 tables will be required (11 x 8 covers and 1 x 7 covers).

3   To check if the tables will fit in the length of the room, i.e. 18 m (60 ft), as per the table plan:

    For top table:

    Gangway behind top table to wall   = 1 m (3 ft)

    Top table chair depth   = 0.46 m (1 ft 6 in)

    Top table width   = 0.75 m (2 ft 6 in)

    Gangway below top table   = 1 m (3 ft)

    Total for top table   = 3 m approx (10 ft)

    For round tables:

    Round table diameter   = 1.5 m (5 ft) diameter

    Chairs depth x 2 per table   = 1 m (3 ft)

    Gangways (allow below each table)   = 1 m (3 ft)

    Total   = 3.5 m (11 ft)

    Total for round tables x 4   = 14 m (44 ft)

    Total length required = 3 m (10 ft) for top table

    plus 14 m (44 ft) for four round tables   = 17 m (54 ft).

    The length of the room is 18 m (60 ft) so the proposed table plan fits.

4 To check if the tables, as per the table plan, will fit in the 12 m width of the room:

3 round tables each 1.5 m (5 ft) diameter	= 4.5 m (15 ft)
6 chair widths each 0.46 m (1 ft 6 in)	= 3 m (9 ft)
4 gangways each at 1 m (3 ft)	= 4 m (12 ft)
Total	=11.5 m (36 ft)

Thus the table plan will fit within the 12 m width of the room (see Figure 11.4).

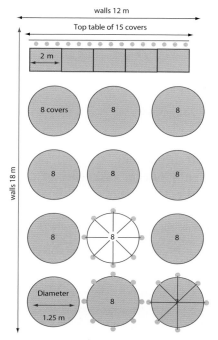

Figure 11.4 Top table and round tables

Clothing up

The minimum size of banqueting cloths is 2 m (6 ft) in width by 4 m (12 ft) in length. They are available in longer lengths, for example, 5.5 m or 18 ft. These cloths are used on top tables and sprigs, thus often avoiding the necessity of overlapping of the cloths that will occur when smaller-sized tablecloths are used. The front edge of a top tablecloth should always touch the floor and the ends should be 'boxed' to facilitate the modesty of the top table guests and neatness of the table's appearance.

When laid, the centre crease should run straight down the centre of the table, with the overlap the same all around the table. All cloths should be in the same fold and have the same pattern. Any overlap of cloths should face away from the main entrance so that the join is not visible to the guests as they look down the room on arrival. When laying the cloth it may require three or four waiters to manipulate it (depending on size), to ensure it is laid correctly, with the minimum of handling, and without creasing or becoming dirty.

For round tables square cloths are often used. The cloth will normally be 1.4 m larger diagonally than the diameter of the table. This is to ensure a maximum drop of 70 cm where the cloth hangs lowest (at the four corners of the cloth) and a minimum drop of 20 cm where the cloth hangs highest (at the centres of the four edges of the cloth).

The calculation for this is as follows:

Diameter of table plus the maximum drop each side of the table = diagonal measurement of tablecloth, corner to corner.

For example, a 200 cm diameter table plus 2 x 70 cm maximum drop = 340 cm.

Therefore the diagonal measurement of the tablecloth corner to corner = 340 cm.

To find the size of the square cloth then the formulae is:

Length of edge = $\sqrt{(\text{diameter}^2 \div 2)}$

For example:

(340 cm diameter x 340 diameter cm) ÷ 2 = 57,800 cm

The square root of 57,800 cm = 240 cm

Therefore the cloth will be 240 cm by 240 cm.

A cloth of 240 cm by 240 cm will ensure that:
- the longest drop will be 70 cm ((340 cm – 200 cm) ÷ 2) at each of the four corners of the cloth (so that the corners of the cloth do not touch the floor)
- the shortest drop will be 20 cm ((240 cm – 200 cm) ÷ 2) at the centre of each of the four sides of the cloth (so that the table will be covered where the cloth has the shortest drop).

Using this approach for tables of 1 m, 1.5 m and 2 m the tablecloth will be as shown in Table 11.1.

Table 11.1 Tablecloth sizes

Table diameter	Cloth size	Longest drop at the four corners of the cloth	Shortest drop at the centre of the four sides of the cloth
1 m	170 x 170 cm	70 cm	35 cm
1.5 m	205 x 205 cm	70 cm	27 cm
2 m	240 x 240 cm	70 cm	20 cm

Lay-up

For table service of banquets and formal meals the preparatory tasks will be similar to those identified in Section 6.2, p.193. With pre-ordered menus it is normal to lay the table for the whole meal. The key factors to take into account are:
- lay-ups are normally based on the table d'hôte lay-up (see Section 6.2, p.193)
- customers use the cutlery from the outside of the cover inwards
- glassware is normally laid at the top right of the cover and in order of use, usually with the lowest glass to the highest at the back
- some establishments will not lay for the whole meal – the sweet cutlery being laid at the time the course is to be served or the glassware being brought out onto the table before the later wines are served
- often the tableware for beverage service of tea and coffee will be laid when these are to be served.

Service organisation

Traditional

For formal events it is normal practice that the top table service staff always begin to serve/clear first. Therefore, the banqueting/events head waiter will organise his staff so that, at a given signal, the top table service staff can begin to serve, immediately followed by all the other service staff. The banqueting/events head waiter will not give a signal to clear a course until all guests have finished eating.

All staff should leave and enter the room led by the top table staff and followed by the other service staff in a pre-determined order. This pre-determined order generally means that those staff with stations furthest from the service doors should be nearer the top table service staff in the line-up (see Allocating stations, p.402). Theoretically this means that, when entering the room, all service staff reach their stations at more or less the same time. Each member of staff then serves their own table using the pre-determined service method – either full silver service or a combination of plated and silver service. When deciding on the pre-determined order, another factor that should influence the final decision is that of safety. As far as it is possible, any cross-flow of staff and bottlenecks in their movement to and from the room should be avoided.

Wave service

Wave service can be used mainly when meals are plated, although some establishments also use this style of service organisation for silver service and other forms of service. It is a way of saving on staffing for conventional service and/or speeding up service for plated systems. The term wave comes from the approach where tables are not served altogether but are served over a period of time, with individual guests on some tables being served quickly at one time before the service on other tables is started. There are two basic approaches to this:

1   For both plated service and traditional silver service the staff from two tables next to each other will work together as a team. This happens throughout the room. The pair work together to serve one of the tables completely and then will assist each other to completely serve the other table.

2   The alternative is for a larger group of staff to work as a team, serving one table completely at a time before going on to the next. This is especially useful when plated service is being used for the food.

The resulting effect of adopting these approaches is that tables are served throughout the room, over a period, but with each individual table's service being completed quickly.

Wave service may also be used for events where guests are seated on a top table and sprigs. In this case, sections of the banquet tables are served before moving to another section of the table layout.

For plated service, one of the difficulties is ensuring that the food is hot when being served. For table service the speed of the transfer of the plate from the kitchen can ensure that the food is hot when reaching the table, assuming of course that the food has always been first presented onto hot plates.

Buffets

There are three types of buffet:

1 **Finger buffet**: the guests select and consume the food with their fingers. The food and beverages may be available at a buffet or on trays that are carried by the waiters. Usually napkins are also available on the passed trays. The room is organised to ensure there is ample space for the guests to circulate and that a number of occasional tables and chairs are placed round the room. These occasional tables may be covered with linen cloths and may have a small vase of flowers placed on them. Any dirties are then removed from these tables by clearing staff as required.

2 **Fork buffet**: the guests select foods that are transferred onto a plate and they then eat the food using only a fork. In this case, the food should be of such a shape and size that this is easily accomplished. Glass holders are usually available which clip to the side of the plate in which a wine glass may be secured. Napkins are also available on the buffet. The room organisation is similar to that used for finger buffets.

3 **Display buffet**: the guests select their food and then eat at a table. Here the guests approach the buffet at its various service points to select their requirements course by course. Ancillary items such as rolls, butter, sauces, napkins and tableware may also be collected at the buffet. Guests then return to their tables to consume the meal. The table layouts are similar to the standard banquet layouts. Clearing tables takes place in the same way as for formal banquets.

Staff organisation

General considerations for service staff for events are given below.

- A waiter at a banquet is generally expected to serve between 10 and 12 covers on a station but this may be up to 20 depending on the service organisation (see above).

- A wine waiter will serve approximately 25 covers, but this depends on the type of event, the number of wines on offer and whether any wine is inclusive in the price of the menu or if cash drinks are being served. The wine waiters will also often assist the food waiters with the service of vegetables and sauces for the main course.

- The wine waiters may also be required to serve apéritifs at a reception before a meal. If so, they will be required to do the necessary mise-en-place to ensure the reception area is ready, for example, ashtrays (where allowed), cocktail snacks, setting up of a portable bar and polishing glasses.

- When cash wine and drinks are served the wine waiters are normally given a float with which they may pay the cashier or bar person as drinks are ordered and collected from the bar. The responsibility then rests with the wine waiter to collect the payments for any drinks served.

Using white gloves

In some establishments members of staff wear white cotton gloves when carrying out various preparation tasks. The gloves help to prevent soiling of clean service items and also avoid putting finger marks on cleaned and polished service equipment.

White gloves may also be used during service, instead of service cloths, when serving plated foods that are presented on hot plates. If white gloves are to be used then there must be a clean edge on the plate so that the food or sauces on the plates do not easily soil the gloves.

Allocating stations

When all the necessary mise-en-place has been completed and all the staff are assembled together, the stations are allocated to the waiters and wine waiters. More experienced and proficient members of staff are usually allocated to the top table.

The waiters (brigade) should queue up in an orderly fashion at the hotplate for each course, with the waiter for the top table at the head of the queue. The waiters or 'teams' then queue in order according to the distance of their station from the service hotplate. This order must be maintained throughout the service.

After the service of each course the brigade should remain outside the banqueting room in readiness to clear and serve the next course.

An example of allocating stations, the staff required and the order at the hotplate for a dinner of 84 covers (silver service) is given below.
- 12 covers on the top table and 24 covers on each sprig (12 on each side).
- Table requirements (see plan in Figure 11.5):
- Top: 4 x 2 m (6 ft) tables = 8 m allowing for 60 cm (24 in) table width per cover.
- Sprigs: 4 x 2 m (6 ft) tables = 8 m allowing for 60 cm (24 in) table width per cover. This will mean a total of 3 sprigs in all: 12 covers on each side.
- Stations will be:
  ○ top table: 12 cover = 12 covers
  ○ sprigs: 6 x 12 cover = 72 covers
- There will be 7 stations of 12 covers = total 84 covers. For the plan given in Figure 11.5, the order of staff at the hotplate, by station number, will be: 1, 2, 3, 4, 5, 6, and 7.
- The staff for stations 2, 4 and 6 will enter the room through the service doors and proceed down the room to their right. The staff for stations 3, 5 and 7 will enter through the service doors and proceed down the room to their left (see the plan in Figure 11.5).

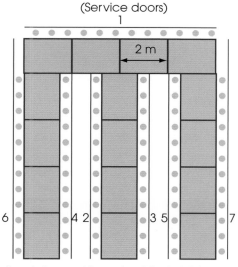

Figure 11.5 Example of allocating stations and the order at the hotplate

Staff instruction/event sheets

Staff instruction/event sheets are provided for each event. These sheets give detailed instructions for all staff working at the event. Their purpose is to ensure that all the required duties are covered, that a particular event is laid up correctly and everything is in order in the shortest possible time. They also provide guidance to casual staff.

Forms of address

For all events, formal and informal, etiquette is very important and great care should be taken to ensure the correct forms of address are used to suit the occasion. At very formal events, royalty or other dignitaries may be attending as guests. Etiquette therefore demands a certain order of precedence when proposing and replying to toasts, and the correct mode of address should be adhered to.

Table 11.2 gives some examples of the correct modes of introduction, address and place cards for both formal and social occasions.

> **Note**: Formality is always followed on occasions involving members of the Royal Family. Table 11.2 below gives the social forms of address for Peers, Baronets and Knights. For details related to more formal events, *Debrett's Peerage and Baronetage* or *Debrett's Correct Form* should be consulted.
>
> The Royalty listed in Table 11.2 are shown in order of precedence.

Table 11.2 Precedents and forms of address

Title	Introduction	Verbal address	Place cards
Royalty			
Monarch	'His/Her Majesty the King/Queen'	'Your Majesty' and subsequently 'Sir/Ma'am'	
Royal Prince	'His Royal Highness, Prince …'	'Your Royal Highness' and subsequently 'Sir'	His Royal Highness, The Prince of …
Royal Princess	'Her Royal Highness, The Princess …'	'Your Royal Highness' and subsequently 'Ma'am'	Her Royal Highness, The Princess …
Royal Duke	'His Royal Highness, The Duke of …'	'Your Royal Highness' and subsequently 'Sir'	His Royal Highness, The Duke of …
Royal Duchess	'Her Royal Highness, The Duchess of …'	'Your Royal Highness' and subsequently 'Ma'am'	Her Royal Highness, The Duchess of …
Peers, Baronets and Knights			
Duke	'The Duke of …'	'Duke'	The Duke of …
Duchess	'The Duchess of …'	'Duchess'	The Duchess of …
Earl	'Lord …'	'Lord …'	Lord …
Countess	'Lady …'	'Lady …'	Lady …
Viscount	'Lord …'	'Lord …'	Lord …
Viscountess	'Lady …'	'Lady …'	Lady …

Government members			
The Prime Minister	By appointment or by name	'Prime Minister' or by name	The Prime Minister
Chancellor of the Exchequer	By appointment or by name	'Chancellor' or by name	Chancellor of the Exchequer
Ministers	By name	'Minister' or 'Mr …'	Mr …
The clergy			
Archbishops	'The Archbishop of …'	'Archbishop' (socially)	His Grace, The Archbishop of …
Bishop	'The Bishop of …'	'Bishop' (socially)	The Bishop of …
Local government			
Lord/Lady Mayor	By appointment or appointment and name	'My Lord/Lady Mayor' or 'Lord/Lady Mayor'	The Lord/Lady Mayor
Mayor	By appointment or appointment and name	'Mr/Madam Mayor'	The Mayor of …
Mayor's Consort	By appointment or appointment and name	'Mayoress' or if a man Mayor's Consort or by name	The Mayoress of … or if a man Mayor's Consort or by name

The Loyal Toast

At any formal event it is common for the Loyal Toast to be made. The toastmaster generally announces this toast as soon as the sweet course has been cleared, but before the coffee/tea is to be served. Staff should ensure before this time that all glasses have been charged (topped up) in readiness for the coming toasts.

The Loyal Toast should be announced by the toastmaster and is then normally proposed by the host for the evening, for example, the Chairman or President of an Association. The Loyal Toast is a toast to the head of state, which may be a president or reigning monarch: the King/Queen.

Example of an order of service for a formal event (table service)

1 The toastmaster announces the luncheon or dinner.
2 Guests proceed to their places in the room.
3 Grace or some other prayer is sometimes said.
4 Guests are seated. Chairs pulled out by waiters.
5 The waiters place napkins across the guests' laps.
6 Water and first wine is served.
7 If first course is not already on the table, proceed to hotplate to collect first course.
8 Line up according to the conventional system (see p.400), top table first.
9 Serve first course – top table waiter to commence service first.
10 All food waiters to leave room after each course is served.
11 Take in fish course plates.

12 Clear first course.

13 Second wine is served.

14 Lay fish plates.

15 Take out dirties and collect fish course.

16 Serve fish course. Leave room taking dirty silver.

17 Take in meat plates.

18 Third wine is served.

19 Clear fish course.

20 Lay meat plates.

21 Take out dirties and collect potato and other vegetable dishes.

22 Place on a hotplate on a sideboard or side table.

23 Return to hotplate and collect main meat dish.

24 Present on each table and serve together with sauces if appropriate.

25 Serve accompanying potatoes and vegetables.

26 Leave room taking dirty silver.

27 Continue with a similar process for the remaining courses of the meal through to the beverages.

> **Note**: The head waiter will control all the food waiters at the hotplate although variations on this service may be adopted according to the situation. The head waiter also controls the exit from the hotplate into the banqueting room.

The order of service on the top table at functions, especially very formal occasions, is the one time when the host might be served first or at exactly the same time as the Guest of Honour, should they be seated on different stations.

At formal events there may be speeches and toasts. These often take place at the end of a meal. However, it has become more common for these to take place at different times during the meal.

Ordering drinks and wines

If required, a bar must be set up in the reception area away from the main entrance so as to avoid overcrowding in one area as the guests are arriving and being announced by the toastmaster. The bar should be clothed up as a buffet, with the cloth within 1.3 cm (½ in) from the ground in the front, and with both ends boxed in (see Section 7.2, p.280). Keep the rear of the bar open so it may be used for storing extra supplies of drink, glasses and any necessary equipment such as glass jugs, soda syphons, extra ice and so on. Always allow ample working space behind the bar. The back of the bar is generally higher from the ground than the average table and, if no shelves are available for storage purposes, then sometimes smaller tables may be incorporated under the bar to be used for storage.

There should always be a good stock of drink, which is generally brought from the cellar approximately 45 minutes before the reception is due to commence. Once the drink stock is at the bar there should always be one barman on duty at all times. Depending on the event, drinks may be served either 'cash' or 'inclusive'. Whichever may be the case, stocktaking should be undertaken when the service is completed. Where necessary, do not forget to have on hand price lists, till, floats, notices regarding size of measures and liquor licence (if required).

When the drinks are to be served on a cash basis, this can very often be a lengthy process. To speed this up there should be wine waiters on duty near the table plan in the reception area together with commis. They should have:

- menus
- wine lists
- check pads
- table plan
- list of stations
- wine waiters' names.

> **Note**: The objective here is to get as many orders as possible for wine to accompany the meal, prior to the meal service commencing.

The order should be written in duplicate with the guest's name at the top of the check to assist in identifying customers' orders at the tables. One copy should go to the cellar or dispense bar and the duplicate to the correct wine waiter. The order should be prepared by the dispense barman or cellarman and when the wine waiter shows the duplicate he should be given the required order. Do not open the wine until the guests arrive at the table – this avoids wastage if the wrong wine is presented. Red wine should be at room temperature and white wine should be chilled. At a cash reception the wine waiters very often act as lounge waiters and therefore are always to hand to receive any orders in readiness for the service.

As for food service, the top table must always be served first with drink. The toasts very often commence immediately the coffee is served. By this stage the wine waiters should have taken all the liqueur orders, served them and collected all the cash outstanding in the case of cash drinks. While the speeches are going on all the food waiters should be out of the room. The wine waiters may circulate if necessary.

On completion of the event, and when the food and wine waiters have cleared their stations and the latter returned any floats, they should be paid off or signed out, after returning service cloths, jackets and other equipment provided for the service.

11.5 Weddings

There are two main types of wedding celebration: wedding breakfast and wedding reception.

At the initial meeting between the client and the banqueting manager to arrange a wedding breakfast/reception, the approaches are similar to those detailed in Section 11.3 (see p.389).

The requirements of the client will depend on the type of wedding breakfast/reception, the number of guests attending and the cost per head to be paid. The type of wedding (civil or religious) will also affect the arrangements and have implications for the specific requirements for the wedding breakfast/reception. Other considerations are requirements concerning a wedding cake, stand and knife, whether a room should be available for the bride and bridegroom to change prior to leaving the breakfast/reception to go on their honeymoon, whether the wedding presents will be displayed and, if so, how much space will be needed and whether the services of a photographer will be required.

The menu may be printed by the venue using various publishing packages now available, together with the names of the couple and the date. As the menus are often kept as souvenirs, this should be carefully discussed with the couple prior to the day to ensure they are happy with the design. Alternatively the couple may have menus professionally printed but care must be taken to have the copy checked before it goes to printing.

For a wedding the content of the menu and beverages will be affected by cultural and religious dietary influences, as well as any special dietary needs (see Section 4.4, p.97).

Wedding breakfast (banquet)

When the wedding breakfast is to be a formal banquet then the details given in Section 11.4 will apply. This includes the same considerations for:

- seating arrangements
- table plans
- table layouts
- clothing up
- service organisation
- staff organisation
- order of service.

In addition, consideration needs to be given to:

- time and venue of wedding ceremony (may be on site)
- due arrival time at venue
- who is providing the wedding cake, stand and knife
- additional floral arrangements
- time for evening reception.

In addition to the customary toasts, the cutting of the wedding cake will need to be organised. This is usually at the end of the meal, after the tea/coffee has been served.

Wedding reception (buffet)

Where the reception is to be a buffet then the buffet itself should be placed in such a position that it is on view to all guests as they enter the room, but within access of the service doors for ease of clearing and restocking. The buffet should be clothed up so that the buffet cloth reaches within 1.3 cm (½ in) of the floor and both ends should be boxed neatly (see Section 7.2, p.257 and Section 11.4, p.360). The creases along the top and front of the buffet should be lined up. Adequate room should be left between the buffet and wall to allow two people to pass and for any extra supplies and equipment required.

If the breakfast/reception is being carried out in a marquee then the ground is normally boarded or covered with canvas or a form of corded matting. Behind the buffet and in the service areas duckboards may be used on canvas to avoid walking on wet ground or in mud and carrying it into the main part of the marquee.

The buffet itself may be split into three sections for ease of service, as described in Table 11.3.

Table 11.3 Service sections of a buffet

Section	Requirements
Service of food	Should be presented appetisingly and attractively on the buffet with the cutlery and crockery required placed in a decorative manner, conveniently near the service points. Food for replenishing the buffet should be close to hand. The centre of the buffet may be raised in order to show off the dishes to greater effect
Service of tea and coffee	This section should have all the necessary equipment close to hand. This will include teacups and saucers, teaspoons, sugar basins, cold milk jugs, tea and coffee urns and hotplates for the pots of hot milk. The service of beverages does not normally take place until after all the toasts have been completed. It is advisable to allow a little more in quantity than is actually required

Section	Requirements
Service of alcoholic and non-alcoholic drinks	This section of the buffet should have all the correct size glasses for the drinks to be served (spirits, soft drinks and mineral waters, cocktails, wines and Champagne), plus ice buckets for the white, sparkling and rosé wines to be chilled, service salvers, waiters' cloths and all the ancillary equipment required for mixing drinks and cocktails to give the correct form of service. A surplus of glasses should be kept under the buffet in their appropriate boxes. Diet, juices and non-alcoholic drinks should be on hand if required

As an alternative the buffet itself may be used entirely for displaying the food and separate service points may be set up for the service of beverages, both alcoholic and non-alcoholic. This depends upon the exact nature of the function, the room available, number of guests, requirements of the client and the type and amount of drinks to be served.

Floral arrangements

The floral arrangements are an important aspect of the decoration and help show off the room to best effect. A large floral arrangement should normally be placed near the entrance to be noted on arrival by all the guests. A further large centrepiece of flowers may be placed in the centre of the buffet and other smaller arrangements of flowers placed at intervals around the room on the occasional tables. The final floral arrangements will depend on the cost involved. The front of the buffet cloth may be decorated with some greenery of some sort, or some coloured velvet may be draped along in order to take away the plainness of the white buffet cloth. Purpose-made pleating can also be used to enhance the front and overall appearance of the buffet. This pleating may be purchased in a variety of colours.

The wedding cake

The wedding cake may be used as a separate focal point away from the buffet and should be placed upon its stand with a knife on a special table clothed-up for the purpose. This is a very important aspect of the dressing of the room, as the main formalities of the breakfast/reception take place, at a certain stage of the proceedings, around the wedding cake. The cake must therefore be in full view to everyone in the room. The bride's and bridesmaids' bouquets are often placed on the table around the base of the wedding cake, together with any telegrams of congratulations that are to be read out by the best man or toastmaster as part of the speeches.

Arrangement of the room

Occasional tables should be placed at regular intervals around the room and clothed up in a suitable manner. Groups of chairs should be placed around each table, ensuring there is still space for people to walk around and meet.

All the ancillary items required for the efficient service of the meal should be placed upon the occasional tables. Items might include butter, rolls/French bread, side plates, side knives, napkins, sugar basins and tongs, accompaniments for cold meats and salads and ashtrays (depending on the smoking policy of the establishment/country). Thus, the majority of the brigade on duty can be either serving drinks or clearing away items, and not be involved in the service of food which will be done from the buffet by other members of the brigade or one or two chefs if there is any carving involved.

Other requirements

The client may request that you arrange for a photographer to be present and this then is a further charge that has to be made; however, it is advisable to leave this booking to the clients to arrange personally. The photographer will usually take photographs of the bride and bridegroom on arrival at the reception, together with a group photo of those in the receiving line, one of the bride and bridegroom cutting the cake and maybe one or two of the buffet while it is complete.

Fully attended cloakrooms must be available for all guests on arrival.

Staffing

The number of staff required will depend on the nature and requirements of a particular event. As a guide, at a buffet-type reception, the following staffing would be required:

● Brigade:
   ○ 1 head waiter/banqueting head waiter
   ○ 1 waiter to every 25–30 covers
   ○ 1 wine waiter to every 40 covers
   ○ 1 barman to every 3 wine waiters
   ○ 1–2 commis for fetching, carrying and clearing
   ○ 1 chef to every 35–40 guests for service

Procedure at a wedding buffet reception

1. Any casual staff required should report approximately one hour beforehand to complete the necessary mise-en-place, to be allocated duties and to be briefed on the procedure to be carried out.
2. If a toastmaster is required, he should arrive approximately 30 minutes before the arrival of the bride and bridegroom to acquaint himself with the room where the buffet is being held and to enquire what his duties will be with regard to announcing the guests on arrival. He must liaise with the best man to discuss the timing of cutting the cake and the toasts and who is to give them. If there is to be a social evening afterwards then the toastmaster may act as master of ceremonies (MC) for the duration of the event.
3. The bride and bridegroom should arrive first. Some photographs may be taken at this stage and an apéritif offered or a glass of Champagne.
4. Immediately following the bride and bridegroom should be the parents of the bride and bridegroom and bridesmaids and/or pages. These people will generally make up the 'receiving line' to greet the guests as the toastmaster announces them.
5. All the guests should generally arrive together. Cloakrooms at this stage must be fully staffed. Guests announced by the toastmaster then pass down the receiving line and enter the room.
6. The wine waiters should be placed at strategic points in the reception area for the service of apéritifs or Champagne to the guests as they move on from the receiving line. These trays should be replenished with full, fresh glasses. The wine waiters at the initial briefing should be allocated different sections of the room for service after the reception to ensure efficient service for all guests in the room.

7 After the reception the buffet should be open for service. The turnover on the buffet should be quick and efficient to avoid any major delays that may cause congestion. The wine waiter should be going round serving drinks and topping up glasses. An important factor to note during the service of the food and drink is to ensure that there are always some members of staff circulating, keeping the tables clear of any dirty equipment.

8 At the agreed time the toastmaster should announce the cutting of the cake by the bride and bridegroom. Portions of the cake should then be passed around to all guests and Champagne taken round by the wine waiters. When this has been done the toastmaster will begin the toasts. All the principal people concerned should be in a group by the wedding cake or in a central position so they can be seen and heard by everyone present.

9 After the toasts any remaining cake and tiers must be packed, ready to be taken away by the host. The top tier is sometimes kept for a christening.

10 The bride and bridegroom may then change. If required, food and Champagne should be placed in the changing rooms. Here, liaison is required between floor service, housekeeping and banqueting staff to ensure that timing is correct as far as the movements of the bride and bridegroom are concerned.

11 When the bride and bridegroom have left the reception the flowers should be packed up for the host to take away.

Family line-up to greet guests at a wedding breakfast or wedding reception

There are two basic approaches for the family line-up:

Approach A
Toastmaster

Entrance
1 Bride's mother
2 Bride's father
3 Bridegroom's mother
4 Bridegroom's father
5 Bride
6 Bridegroom
7 Best man
8 Bridesmaid/Matron of honour

Approach B
Toastmaster

Entrance
1 Bride's mother
2 Bride's father
3 Bride
4 Bridegroom
5 Bridegroom's mother
6 Bridegroom's father
7 Bridesmaid/Matron of honour
8 Best man

Note: The best man is responsible for ensuring that everyone leaves the place where the wedding ceremony has taken place and that no one is left behind. He therefore does not always arrive in time for the beginning of the reception.

Table arrangement for the top table at a wedding

Below is a general arrangement for the seating for the top table.

Looking from the front of the table left to right:

Approach A

1   Best man
2   Groom's mother
3   Groom's father
4   Bride
5   Bridegroom
6   Bride's mother
7   Bride's father
8   Matron of Honour/Principal Bridesmaid

Approach B

1   Best man
2   Groom's mother
3   Bride's father
4   Bride
5   Bridegroom
6   Bride's mother
7   Groom's father
8   Matron of Honour/Principal Bridesmaid

Procedure for toasts at a wedding

Method A

1   Cutting of the cake.
2   While it is being cut the best man may read out telegrams.
3   Pass the cake and Champagne or alternative for toasts.
4   Toastmaster announces a toast to the bride and bridegroom, proposed by the bride's father or near relation.
5   Response of the bridegroom who also proposes a toast to the best man and bridesmaids.
6   Response of the best man who also replies on behalf of the bridesmaids.
7   Any other toasts: close relative of bride or bridegroom.

Method B

1   Pass the Champagne or alternative for toasts.
2   Toastmaster announces a toast to the bride and bridegroom, proposed by the bride's father or near relation.
3   Response by the bridegroom who also proposes a toast to the best man and bridesmaids.
4   Response by the best man who also replies on behalf of the bridesmaids.
5   Any other toasts: close relative of the bride or bridegroom.
6   Cutting of the cake: telegrams of congratulations read by the best man.
7   Pass cake and more Champagne.

11.6 Outdoor catering (off-premises catering)

The business of an outdoor catering firm should, as far as possible, continue throughout the year to ensure the plant (equipment provided for a particular event) and staff are used to the full. At each event carried out the organiser should aim to give a fully comprehensive sales service, covering not only meals and drinks but also such things as confectionery and snack kiosks. As in event catering the organisation must be planned to the last detail and an initial survey should be exact and thorough. The following points are usually included in the initial survey:

- type of event
- date of event
- any special liquor or other licences or permissions required and when needed to be applied for and received
- site and distance from depot/premises
- local transport
- local commodity purchase
- staff recruitment
- layout of site
- number of people expected to attend
- provision for people with special needs
- availability of water, gas, electricity, drainage and refrigeration
- spending power of people attending
- kiosk and stand details
- time allowed for setting up and dismantling catering units
- mobile units adaptable to hot and cold food
- lines of communication to ensure control of staff and continuous supplies
- photographers
- press
- changing room and toilets
- insurance against weather/fire
- first aid
- cost of overheads on a particular site
- type of service (the type most suited to each particular catering operation will need to be decided), for example:
  - buffet-style service may be preferred to restaurant service
  - provision of takeaway meal service in disposable containers
  - supply of some simple hot dishes – soup, fish and chips, etc.
  - flexibility of drink service: hot or cold – according to weather
- washing-up facilities
- containers supplied for litter and disposable items.

Each outdoor catering operation is different and so the main points to be noted during the initial survey will vary. From the basic list shown above it is clear that organisation beforehand is the key to success. The person in charge needs to be decisive, quick-thinking, able to command, adaptable to varying situations and circumstances and, above all, needs to have the respect of the staff working under them.

The majority of staff employed at outdoor catering events are taken on as casual staff. This involves a high administration load for the organisers and also the scrutiny checks of the staff must be very thorough to ensure the quality of the personnel.

The organisation of outdoor catering events must be very thorough too, because once on site it is often virtually impossible to rectify errors. Any items forgotten or not packed on the transport will have to be gone without. This can affect the success of the event and can also damage the reputation of the service provider.

Chapter 12

Supervisory aspects of food and beverage service

12.1 Legal considerations

There are a wide variety of legal requirements for foodservice operations. These include company law, liquor licensing regulations and employment law. A summary of the key responsibilities of the foodservice supervisor are given below.

Health, safety and security

There is a common law duty to care for all lawful visitors. In addition, establishments must not:
- sell (or keep for sale) food and beverages that are unfit for people to eat
- cause food or beverages to be dangerous to health
- sell food or beverages that are not what the customer expects, in terms of content or quality
- describe or present food in a way that is false or misleading.

It is important for a foodservice operator to be able to demonstrate that steps have been taken to ensure good food hygiene (this is called due diligence).

A supervisor's responsibilities include ensuring that:
- service standards comply with health, safety, environmental and food hygiene regulations
- there are arrangements to ensure the safety, security and well-being of staff and customers
- periodic risk assessments are carried out and recorded
- emergency exits are clearly marked and regular fire drills are carried out
- staff have been trained in fire procedures and how to use fire-fighting equipment
- staff are aware of evacuation procedures in the event of fires or security risks
- health and safety notices are displayed in working areas
- staff and customers are trained, as appropriate, on correct usage of equipment and facilities
- food handlers have all been trained in safe and hygienic working practices.

Staff responsibilities for health, safety and security are described in Section 2.6, p.48.

Liquor and other licensing

The sale of alcoholic liquor is subject to liquor licensing requirements, which have four key objectives:
1. the prevention of crime and disorder
2. public safety
3. the prevention of public nuisance
4. the protection of children from harm.

There are usually requirements for:
- the display of a summary of the licence, including the days and times of opening, name of the registered holder, licence number and valid date
- drinks price lists to be displayed
- restrictions on under-aged persons being served alcohol and employed to serve alcohol
- requirements for an authorised person to be on site at all times.

Other types of licences may include, for example, licences for music (live or pre-recorded), dancing, gambling, theatrical performance and television display. In all cases the supervisor and the staff should be aware of the provisions and limitations of the licences to ensure compliance.

Selling goods by weights and measures

All sales of goods by weight or measure should be in accordance with the legislative requirements:

- A display of prices and measures used for all spirits, wines, ales and any other alcohol served.
- Ensuring the food and beverage items for sale are of the quantity and quality demanded by the customer and can include, for example, spirits that have been inadvertently (or deliberately) watered down. This can occur through the use of speed pourers which effectively leave bottles open, leading to evaporation of the alcohol. Equally, if the pourers are washed and then replaced in the bottles when they are wet, the water can become introduced to the spirit and cause a reduction in the percentage of alcohol by volume (abv).

Contracts

A contract is made when one party agrees to the terms of an offer made by another party. In food and beverage service there are essentially two types of customer: those who pre-book and those who do not (often called chance or casual customers). All foodservice operations should be clear on how they will deal with these different types of customers including:

- circumstances where the restaurant may seek compensation from the customer if they do not turn up or pay for their meals or services
- taking care when making contracts with minors (i.e. persons under 18).

Selling goods by description

It is good practice for the foodservice supervisor to ensure:

- all food, beverages and services provided are fit for purpose and of satisfactory quality in relation to price and description
- food, beverages and other services are accurately described in terms of size, quality, composition, production, quantity and standard
- all statements of price, whether in an advertisement, brochure, leaflet or on a website, or those given by letter or orally in person or over the telephone are clear and accurate
- food, beverages and other services correspond to their description in promotional material
- times, dates, locations and nature of service promised are adhered to
- customer billing is fair, transparent and reflects the prices quoted either orally or in writing.

Care must therefore be taken when:

- wording menus and wine lists
- describing menu and beverage items to customers
- stating if prices include local and/or government taxes
- describing conditions such as cover charges, service charges or extras
- describing the service provision.

Avoiding discrimination

The foodservice supervisor should be aware of and take steps to ensure that the operation and the staff do not discriminate on grounds of ethnic origin, race, creed, sex or disability. There are potentially three ways in which discrimination can take place.

1 **Direct discrimination**: for example, refusing service to customers of particular ethnic origin, race, creed, sex or disability.
2 **Indirect discrimination**: for example, denying consumer services by imposing unjustifiable conditions or requirements that have ethnic origin, sex or disability implications.

3 **Discrimination through victimisation**: for example, by (a) refusal of provision, that is refusal of admission on the basis of ethnic origins, sex or disability; or (b) omission of provision, that is providing services to ethnic customers that are markedly inferior to those available to the public in general or which may only be available at a price premium.

It is the supervisor's responsibility to ensure that no such discrimination occurs.

Providing services

Generally a food and beverage operator is under no specific requirement to serve anyone. However, it is important that the supervisor and staff are aware of:
- circumstances where there may be a mandatory requirement to provide services
- valid reasons for refusal.

Customer property and customer debt

Good practice usually means that supervisors need to ensure:
- proper care is taken of customer's property to minimise potential loss or damage. Notices warning customers of 'no responsibility' may help in defence but do not guarantee exemption from liability for the food and beverage operator
- clear guidance is given on the procedures to follow if the customer is unable or unwilling to pay.

Data protection

Customers generally have a right to expect that data about them is kept secure and is only used for the published business purposes. The supervisor is generally required to ensure that:
- information on customers is kept up to date, fairly, lawfully and securely
- customer information is not passed on to third parties without prior consent from the customer
- staff are aware of the importance of the protection of customer information and the procedures to follow to ensure it is held securely.

12.2 Sales promotion

The range of foodservice operations within the hospitality industry was considered in Section 1.1 (p.3). Sectors were identified based on the nature of demand being met rather than the type of operation. Factors that affect the customer's enjoyment of a meal were identified in Section 1.3 (p.11) and customer service concepts within Section 1.4 (p.11). This section now considers the various aspects of sales promotion relevant to food and beverage operations.

Promoting features and benefits

To meet specific food and beverage needs customers tend to view an operation as providing benefits and solutions *not* products. In addition to the needs for food and beverage, customer may also be seeking benefits such as:
- security/peace of mind
- time savers
- money savers
- health and safety
- status
- convenience
- comfort
- flexibility
- enjoyment
- to comply with legislation.

In dealing with customers staff need to concentrate on the selling of features and benefits and should know how these compare with those of competitors. Members of staff can also adopt personal and positive selling techniques when taking food and beverage orders (see p.387).

Determining promotional channels

Determining promotional channels is important because it will identify how consumers will be reached and attracted to the product. Food and beverage operators should identify and monitor consumers in order to be informed as to which promotional channels are best for their product. When choosing promotional channels the target market segment variables are considered in relation to the product message and the medium through which it may be delivered. The message to be delivered should relate to the consumer's needs, wants and demands, and be delivered through a medium used by the target consumers, reflecting their life style and self-image. Table 12.1 shows possible messages and media for different food and beverage products.

Table 12.1 Possible message and media for food and beverage products

Product	Possible message	Media
Branded pizza restaurant	Meet friends and have fun	Television, local radio and press, mailshots
New Year's Eve dinner dance	Celebrate in style and spoil yourself	Local radio and press, in-house literature, direct selling to existing customer base
Local bistro	A touch of Continental style	Word of mouth, local press
Public house	Traditional British hospitality	Word of mouth, local press, food guides
Destination restaurant	Michelin starred, high end quality, personal attention	Food guides, online reviews, web presence

Choosing the message and the medium is a critical element in promoting the product. Large businesses spend millions of pounds promoting their product through national television, radio, press and billboards. Small operations may only spend hundreds of pounds but the criterion is the same; is it effective? Reviewing promotional activity and spending and how it relates to increased sales and profits will enable effective evaluation of the process to take place. Consumer responses to promotional activities should always be researched.

Approaches to sales promotion

Sales promotion involves activities designed to promote regular sales. It is also concerned with promoting temporary sales to encourage increased business at slack periods such as Mondays, early evenings and during January/February. Examples of such activities include:
- offering meal (deal) packages, for example free wine (or a 'buy one get a second free' deal), or offering a free soup or starter as part of the meal package
- developing customer loyalty schemes.

Special product sales may also be used to increase sales by promoting particular products, such as:
- festival promotions or links with local, regional or national celebrations
- wine and spirit or food promotions (possibly in association with suppliers)
- children's menus
- diabetic menus
- 'Taste of the Country' menus, etc.
- products to complement specific calendar dates, etc.

Four types of sales promotion are particularly useful for foodservice operations:

1 **Sales promotion through advertising**: concerned with contacting and informing the existing or potential market of a business, providing information on the products available and encouraging purchase.

2 **Sales promotion though internet and social media**: similar to using advertising with coverage potentially far wider than an intended market. Can provide the opportunity for more information to be available to customers on demand. Not so easy to target potential customers and control as the medium is also interactive and volatile.

3 **Sales promotion through merchandising**: related mainly to point-of-sale promotion. Its main role is to improve the average spend per head of the customer. However, it is also used to promote particular services or goods.

4 **Sales promotion through personal selling**: refers to the ability of the staff in a food and beverage operation to actively contribute to the promotion of sales.

Advertising

Advertising media includes:

- **broadcast**: radio, television
- **print**: newspapers – national daily, regional daily, national Sunday, regional Sunday, weekly regional and free distribution
- **consumer publications**: directories (Yellow Pages, Thompson's), guides, business publications, executive travel publications, technical and professional publications, journals and other magazines (including local free ones)
- **other media**: commercial transport, terminals and stations, posters, cinema
- **postal advertising**: direct mail, hand drops.

In addition to the above, it is worth considering the use of mailing lists to advise existing customers of special events, etc. Retaining existing customers is always less costly than finding new ones.

Internet presence and social media

Websites are now a common way to communicate a product to a wide audience. Nowadays the organisation's website is one of the first stops for consumers when deciding on a product. Therefore operators need to ensure that their website is attractive, easy to use, up to date and a true reflection of what is offered. Furthermore, the website is now a platform to receive reservations directly through built-in online booking systems, provide virtual menus and to stay in contact with customers through blogs and comments. Third-party booking sites (restaurant marketing portals) for example, Toptable.com are also a way to source bookings and to promote and monitor customer experiences.

In addition, when considering marketing activity, an emerging trend is the use of Web 2.0 applications within hospitality organisations. Web 2.0 applications are tools that are user generated content websites; these may include TripAdvisor, Facebook, twitter etc. These tools include applications that may include blogs, social networks, metaverse, podcast, wiki, tags and RSS (Rich Site Summary).

Currently these applications tend to be used more by large chain and luxury food and beverage operations rather than budget and small independent operators but this is changing fast. Table 12.2 describes some examples of these applications and their uses within hospitality and food and beverage operations.

Table 12.2 Examples of Web 2.0 applications and their potential uses within the hospitality industry

Examples	Potential uses
TripAdvisor, Toptable websites	Consumers regularly post comments and ratings of their experiences of hotels and restaurants on specialised websites. These opinions are for the most part neutral and unbiased and can have a powerful impact on consumer decision and overall image
Facebook and twitter	Operators can use social network sites as part of their customer relations management (CRM) system in order to have a better understanding of their customers and as a way to keep in contact. They are also a vast platform for advertising
YouTube	Media such as YouTube is becoming very powerful because it is convenient for customers to upload videos with recommendation and critiques of visits to restaurants and other hospitality organisations. Organisations can also upload videos of their own to promote and showcase their operations
Hotel websites	Some hotels encourage complete interactivity with their customers allowing them to upload comments and videos of their experiences
Podcasts	Some large corporations provide podcasts on their website informing potential customers of their facilities and what is taking place within their operations
Industry blogs	Operators should monitor and participate in industry blogs. There are various tools and resources available to inform operators when comments have been made about their business and brands
Applications (Apps)	Many large restaurant chains now use applications for iPhones and iPads to inform customers of product updates, events and promotions
Voucher sites	Some restaurants now use commercial voucher sites to inform consumers of discounted promotions

Some of the benefits of social media include:
- a way to distribute, promote, monitor and keep in touch with customers and potential customers
- a more cost effective media for many operators
- more of a level playing field for independent operators against larger competitors.

Some challenges include:
- no strategic plans or rules can govern what happens
- operators must constantly interact and engage with social media users and as a result it can be extremely time consuming
- for some consumers very little information is considered to be private, therefore anything is posted and they expect operators to do the same
- once information is posted it is permanent as it is often repeated on other sites
- operators may be unsure how to use this medium to their advantage, as it is very customer driven.

Merchandising

Merchandising relates mainly to point-of-sale promotion. Its main role is to improve the average spend per head of the customer. It is also used to promote particular services or goods.

Examples of food and beverage merchandising tend to be mainly visual, but may also be audio or audio-visual. Food and beverage merchandising stimuli can include:

- aromas
- bulletins/blackboards/floor stands
- directional signs
- display cards/brochures
- displays of food and drinks
- trolleys (sweet, liqueurs, etc.)
- other customers' food/drink.
- drink coasters and placemats
- facia boards and illuminated panels
- menus, drinks and wine lists
- posters
- tent cards
- buffets/salad bars, self-service counters, bar displays, flambé work, etc.

Written/printed merchandising materials should be effective. As well as considering using images, make sure the words used are descriptive and attractive, as shown in these examples:

- **Describing the freshness of the product**: freshly prepared, pure, natural, real, freshly squeezed, handpicked each day, fresh.
- **Describing the environment**: free range, corn fed, a specific location, source or a herd name, stating that foods are from a local market, home grown, or referring to 'happy animals'.
- **Describing the overall product**: local flavour, traditional, warming, inventive use of ingredients, house speciality, signature dish.

> **Note**: Care should be taken in using terms such as healthy – what may be part of a healthy diet for one person is not necessarily part of a healthy diet for another (see Section 4.4, p.103 for information on health influences on menus).

Personal selling

Merchandising materials must also be supported by good personal (or positive) selling techniques. Personal selling refers specifically to the ability of the staff in a food and beverage operation to contribute to the promotion of sales. This is especially important where there are specific promotions being undertaken. The promise of a particular type of menu or drink, a special deal or the availability of a particular service can often be devalued by the inability of the staff to fulfil the requirements as promised. It is therefore important to involve service staff in the formulation of particular offers and to ensure that briefing and training are given so that the customer can actually experience what has been promised.

Members of staff will feel more confident about selling if they have information about the products on offer. If staff can tell well they can sell well. Examples of the type of information staff will need to know include:

- a description of what the item is and an explanation of how it is served
- where the produce comes from
- what the local animals are fed on
- where the fish are caught
- where the local fruit and vegetables are grown
- how the produce is delivered
- where and how the local drinks are made
- what the specialities of the establishment are and their origin.

There are various ways of enhancing the product knowledge of staff, such as:
- arranging for staff visits to suppliers
- arranging visits to other establishments that use local produce
- seeking out supplier information
- allowing staff to taste products
- arranging for staff to visit local trade fairs
- organising training and briefing sessions for staff.

Within the context of personal selling, the service staff should be able to:
- describe the food, wines and drinks on offer in an informative and appealing way, that makes the product sound interesting and desirable
- use the opportunity to promote specific items or deals when seeking orders from the customer
- seek information from the customer in a way that promotes sales, for example, rather than asking *if* a sweet is required, ask *which* sweet is required
- use opportunities for the sales of additional items such as extra garnishes, special sauces or accompanying drinks, such as a dessert wine with a sweet course
- provide a competent service of the items for sale and seek customers' views on the acceptability of the food, drinks and the service.

Ability in personal selling is necessary for all aspects of successful food and beverage service. The contribution of service staff to the meal experience is vital. The service staff contribute to the customers' perception of value for money, hygiene and cleanliness, the level of service and the perception of atmosphere that the customer experiences.

Good food and beverage service staff therefore must have a detailed knowledge of the food and beverages on offer, be technically competent, have well developed interpersonal skills and be able to work as part of a team.

12.3 Customer relations

The importance of interpersonal skills for service staff was highlighted in Section 2.5, p.44 and included information on interpersonal skills associated with different tasks and duties in food and beverage service.

Customer relations are concerned with the conditions staff work under which may assist or prevent good standards of interpersonal skills being maintained. There are two aspects to this: first, the physical conditions experienced by staff and, second, the satisfaction or otherwise customers receive from the food and beverage service experience.

In order to develop and maintain good customer relations, the supervisor must be able to:
- recognise the symptoms of a deterioration in customer relations
- minimise the causes of customer relations problems.

Some of the symptoms that can indicate customer relations problems are:
- increasing complaints about products/staff
- increasing accidents
- mistakes by staff in orders, etc.
- customers arriving without prior bookings having been recorded
- arguments between staff
- poor staff morale
- breakages or shortages of equipment
- high turnover of staff.

Minimising customer relations problems

Below is a series of questions that the supervisor should consider in order to minimise customer relations problems.

- **Why is that member of staff not smiling or being courteous to customers?** If a waiter is not smiling her feet might be hurting and no amount of telling her to smile will change this. Her shoes might be the problem.
- **Why is that member of staff not speaking politely to customers?** In foodservice operations the use of 'sir', 'madam', 'please', 'excuse me' and 'thank you' is expected. If it is not being done, the supervisor needs to ask: Is the member of staff in the wrong job? If he or she is in the right job, then what is the problem?
- **What are the problems of each department in working with other departments?**
- **How do each department's problems affect other departments?**
- **What are the difficulties that a customer could experience?** For example, lack of information or direction signs.
- **Is the emphasis in the work areas put on the customer?** For example, a barman eating behind the bar takes the emphasis away from the customer.
- **What problems can be solved by physical changes?** For example, staff congregating round a central sideboard will face inwards and not outwards to observe customers.
- **What problems exist because information for customers is insufficient other than that which can be obtained from staff?**
- **Are members of staff given enough information about the establishment and locality?**
- **Are foreseen problems minimised?** For example, are large parties organised in advance?
- **Are members of staff informed of set procedures for foreseen problems?** For example, running out of food items?
- **Are complaints used as an opportunity to show care for customers?**
- **Are there set procedures for dealing with complaints?**
- **Are there set procedures for dealing with difficult customers?** For example, customers who are quarrelsome, drunk or non-compliant with establishment requirements such as smoking, dress codes or the use of mobile phones.
- **How can staff be encouraged to identify and propose solutions for their problems?**

Customer satisfaction

In Section 1.3 (p.11) the factors contributing to the meal experience were summarised. Customer service considerations were then outlined in Section 1.4 (p.13). The factors that might affect the customer's enjoyment of a specific meal experience in a particular operation include the following:

- welcome, decor and ambience of the establishment
- level of efficiency shown, for example, has the booking been taken properly, using the customer's name?
- location of the table
- presentation and cleanliness of the menu and drinks list
- order being taken – recognition of the host
- availability of dishes/items
- speed and efficiency of service
- quality of food and drink
- courteousness of staff
- obtrusiveness/attentiveness of staff
- ability to attract the attention of staff
- other customers' behaviour
- method in which complaints are handled
- method of presenting the bill and receiving payment
- attentiveness towards customers at their departure.

The supervisor is responsible for minimising potential customer relations problems. They should be as much concerned with the physical aspects of the service as with the way in which the service is operated and with the interpersonal interaction between customers and staff.

In food and beverage service operations interaction also takes place with people outside the service areas, such as kitchen staff, bill office staff, dispense bar staff and stillroom staff. It is important that the provision of food and beverages within an establishment is seen as a joint effort between all departments, with each department understanding the needs of the others in order to meet customer demands.

Monitoring customer satisfaction

A food and beverage operation must continually monitor its performance and levels of customer satisfaction so that it can take action as appropriate to maintain and improve the level of business.

Examples of various performance measures are outlined Section 12.8, p.460. In addition to considering financial performance measures, there are various other methods used for monitoring.

- **Informal approaches**: subjective and intuitive approaches, which include asking customers directly for feedback and monitoring the service periods for signs of issues with the service, can be very effective.
- **Monitoring financial data**: includes both financial performance and sales mix data which can indicate changes in customer trends for the business.
- **Customer satisfaction questionnaires**: these can be available, or given out within the operation or sent to customers afterwards. The forms usually ask for some rating of the experience with details ranging from factors such as warmth of greeting to value for money and also the likelihood of the customer recommending the operation to someone else.
- **Complaint monitoring**: monitoring complaints (and compliments) can be helpful in measuring levels of customer satisfaction. However, it is also possible that complaints might be unjustified or the result of some other dissatisfaction which is not in the control of the operation.
- **Monitoring media**: this includes printed media such as magazines, television, social media and customer rating websites such as TripAdvisor and OpenTable.
- **Staff focus group sessions**: staff focus groups can provide a valuable review process, especially when independent people lead the sessions. These sessions provide an opportunity to review the customer service specification against the experience of those members of staff who work within it.
- **Mystery shopper**: this means using an unidentified customer who tests the services of the organisation and then provides a report to the organisation. The individual will check that standards are maintained and will usually work to a brief and checklist. Mystery shoppers are not professionals; they need by necessity to remain customers, although the companies that employ them are professional.
- **Process reviewer**: the process reviewer differs from a mystery shopper in that the process review is undertaken to identify problems in how the operation works and also opportunities for improvement.

12.4 Staffing levels, staff organisation and training

Staff organisation in food and beverage service centres on having sufficient trained and competent staff on duty to match the expected level of customer demand.

Level of demand and customer throughput

The first step in staff organisation is to determine the expected level of customer demand. This can be done from sales records. As most operations have limitations in the number of customers that can be served at any particular time, it is also necessary to calculate the potential customer throughput.

There is a relationship between the volume of customers to be served and the length of time they stay on the premises. The time customers take in different types of operation varies. An indication of these times is given in Table 12.3.

Table 12.3 Seating/consumption times in various types of operation

Operation	Consumption time (minutes)
Restaurant	60–120
Carvery	45–90
Popular catering	30–60
Cafeteria	15–40
Wine bar	30–60
Pub (food)	30–60
Takeaway with seating	20–40
Fast food with seating	10–20

There is also a relationship between the volume of customers and the opening times of the operation. For example, in a full service restaurant the seating time of customers might average one and a half hours. If the restaurant is open for four hours, then it might be possible to fill the operation twice. If, however, the opening hours were only two and a half hours, then would not be possible.

Opening times are determined by:
- local competition
- proximity to local attractions, such as a theatre
- location of the premises, for example city centre/country/suburb
- transport systems
- staffing availability
- volume of business anticipated
- local tradition.

Customer throughput in table and assisted service operations

Customer throughput can be determined since all customers are usually seated for both table and assisted service methods. For new operations the throughput must be estimated as it is limited by the length of seating time and the opening hours of the operation. For existing operations sales records will provide a guide to potential throughput.

Staffing for each service period can then be estimated and staff allocated to specific jobs. Staffing will also need to be estimated for mise-en-place duties prior to the service period and for clearing following the service period. Thus, a restaurant that is open for two and a half hours at lunchtime may require staff to be on duty for up to five hours.

To calculate the total staffing required:
1 Estimate the number of staff required per service period in one week.
2 Multiply the number of staff per service period by the number of hours worked in each period.
3 Divide total staff hours by full-time working week hours. This will give the full-time equivalent of number of staff required.
4 Mix part-time and full-time staff hours to cover all service periods.
5 Draw up staff rota, which may be on a two- or three-week cycle to allow for days off, etc.

The example below is for a restaurant open six days per week for luncheon and dinner; maximum of 80 covers.

Volume of customers							
	Mon	Tues	Wed	Thurs	Fri	Sat	Sun
Luncheon	65	75	85	80	85	54	–
Dinner	85	90	120	140	135	160	–

Opening times		
Luncheon	12.30 p.m. to 2.30 p.m.	Last order 2.00 p.m.
Dinner	6.30 p.m. to midnight	Last order 11.30 p.m.

Staff time		
Luncheon	11.00 a.m. to 3.00 p.m.	4 hours
Dinner	6.00 p.m. to 1.00 a.m.	7 hours

The number of staff to each service period can now be calculated.

For this example the staffing and staff calculations might be estimated as shown below.

Service staffing	M	Tu	W	Th	F	Sa	Su	Total staffing	Total number of working hours
Lunch	3	4	4	4	4	3	–	22	88 (22 staff x 4 hours)
Dinner	4	5	6	7	7	8	–	37	259 (37 staff x 7 hours)
Total number of staff hours for the week									347 (88 + 259)
Number of full-time equivalent staff (at 35 hours per week)									10 (347 hours ÷ 35 hours)

As the numbers of staff for each service period have been calculated, a working time rota can be drawn up. In this example the full-time equivalent staffing is 10. Mixing full- and part-time staffing could mean that this operation might employ, for example, five full-time staff working 175 hours (5 staff x 35 hours) with the rest of the required 172 working hours (347 hours – 175 hours) being covered by overtime and/or part-time staffing.

Similar approaches for estimating staffing requirements exist for the other service method groups although the calculation of throughput differs, as indicated below.

Customer throughput in cafeteria operations

There are five factors that influence potential throughput in cafeterias:

1 **Service time**: the time it takes each customer to pass along or by the counter and reach the till point.
2 **Service period**: the time the cafeteria is actually serving.
3 **Till speed**: the time it takes for each customer to be billed and payment taken.
4 **Eating/seating time**.
5 **Seating capacity**.

The main criterion is seating capacity. The speed required in the queue is determined by the seating capacity and the average seating time.

For example, if there are 186 seats and the till speed is nine customers per minute, it will take 20.66 minutes to fill the cafeteria. If the customers' seating time is 20 minutes, then the cafeteria will be filled just after the first customers are leaving. A faster till speed will mean that the last customer through the till will have nowhere to sit. Too slow a till speed will mean the cafeteria is not being fully utilised. For one till, four to six people per minute is a maximum.

Assuming the service period is to be one hour, this cafeteria will be able to provide service as follows:

- 55 minutes (60 minutes less 5 minutes service time) x 9 (people per minute till speed) = 495 people.
- The cafeteria would need to be open for 1 hour 20 minutes (1 hour service period and 20 minutes for the last person to finish eating).

To calculate the seating capacity of a cafeteria required to serve 200 people in one hour, with a service time of 5 minutes and an average seating time of 20 minutes:

Example 1

All customers will need to be served in:

$$
\begin{array}{rl}
& 60 \text{ minutes (opening time)} \\
- & 20 \text{ minutes (seating time)} \\
- & \underline{5 \text{ minutes (service time)}} \\
& 35 \text{ minutes (service period)}
\end{array}
$$

The number of seats required will be:

$$\frac{200 \text{ (people) x 20 (minutes seating time)}}{35 \text{ (minutes service period)}} = 114.25 \text{ seats}$$

There will need to be 115 seats in the cafeteria.

The till speed will need to be:

$$\frac{115 \text{ (seats)}}{20 \text{ (minutes seating time)}} = 5.75 \text{ people per minute}$$

Example 2

If the seating time is reduced to 15 minutes then all customers will need to be served in:

```
   60 minutes (opening time)
–  15 minutes (seating time)
–   5 minutes (service time)
   40 minutes (service period)
```

The number of seats required would then be:

$$\frac{200 \text{ (people) x 15 (minutes seating time)}}{40 \text{ (minutes service period)}} = 75 \text{ seats}$$

This is 40 fewer seats than required in Example 1, which represents a considerable saving in seating provision.

Till speed will reduce to:

$$\frac{75 \text{ (seats)}}{15 \text{ (minutes seating time)}} = 5 \text{ people per minute}$$

Hence the service speed will also reduce which may mean a saving in staffing.

Generally, if the seating time is greater than the service period, then the actual number of seats will need to equal the total number of customers. If the eating time is less than the time it takes to serve all the customers then the number of seats may be less than the actual number of people to be served. However, the queue may need to be staggered to avoid excessive waiting before service.

Customer throughput in single point service operations

Customer throughput in single point service operations may be determined by looking at the records of till transactions. The increase or decrease in the service that is required is provided for by increasing or decreasing the number of till points available at different times (or in the case of vending, additional machines). If seating areas are provided then similar calculations as for cafeterias (see above) can be carried out. The percentage of the customers using the seating facilities will also need to be known.

Customer demand in specialised service

For hospital and airline tray methods there is a limitation on the number of customers that can be accommodated in beds or in aircraft seats. For other forms of specialised service methods there are records or estimates of potential take-up of services in specific locations, such as hotel rooms, lounges and home delivery.

Daily duty rota

The object of a duty rota is to ensure that all the necessary duties are covered in order that efficient service may be carried out. The exact nature of the duty rota will vary according to the type of establishment, the duties to be performed, the number of staff, staff time off and whether a split/straight shift is worked. Figure 12.1 gives an example of a daily duty rota for pre-service duties for a table service operation and shows how they may be allocated.

Waiter	3.6.14	4.6.14	5	6	7	8	9	10	11	12	13	14	15	16.6.14	Task No.
A	1	11	10	9	8	7		6	5	4	3	2	1		1. Menus
B	2	1	11	10	9	8		7	6	5	4	3	2		2. Restaurant cleaning
C	3	2	1	11	10	9		8	7	6	5	4	3		3. Linen
D	4	3	2	1	11	10		9	8	7	6	5	4		4. Hot plate
E	5	4	3	2	1	11	CLOSED	10	9	8	7	6	5	CLOSED	5. Silver
F	6	5	4	3	2	1		11	10	9	8	7	6		6. Accompaniments
G	7	6	5	4	3	2		1	11	10	9	8	7		7. Sideboard
H	8	7	6	5	4	3		2	1	11	10	9	8		8. Dispense bar
I	9	8	7	6	5	4		3	2	1	11	10	9		9. Stillroom
J	19	9	8	7	6	5		4	3	2	1	11	10		10. Miscellaneous
K	11	10	9	8	7	6		5	4	3	2	1	11		11. Day off

Figure 12.1 Example of a daily duty rota

A duty rota also provides the basis for staff training. Detailed lists are drawn up for all the tasks and duties that must be covered. These task and duty lists will also identify the standards that are to be achieved for the operation.

Staff training

Training may be defined as the systematic development of people. The general objectives of training are to:
- increase the quantity and quality of output by improving employee skills
- reduce accidents
- increase the return to the employee in personal rewards, such as increased pay, recognition and other benefits which the employee wants from the job
- make the operation more profitable by reducing the amount of equipment and material required to produce or sell in a given unit
- make it possible for the supervisor to spend less time correcting mistakes and more time in planning
- minimise discharges because of inadequate skills
- improve morale and achieve a more satisfactory working environment
- enable new employees to meet their job requirements and enable experienced employees to accept transfers, adapt to new methods, increase efficiency and adjust to changing needs
- encourage willingness, loyalty, interest and the desire to excel.

Terms used in staff training

Job
All the tasks carried out by a particular employee in the completion of prescribed duties, within the setting of a particular working environment.

Job analysis

The process of examining a job to identify its component parts and the circumstances in which it is performed. This would normally require an examination of:

- the *purpose* of the job – what it exists for and what key results are expected from it
- the *setting* of the job – the physical, organisational and social conditions of the job
- the main *tasks* that have to be performed in order to achieve the results – what the employee does
- the *resources* or facilities available to the employee – what people, equipment, services, etc., he or she can call upon.

Job description

A broad statement of the purpose, scope, duties and responsibilities of a particular job. This would normally include the following:

- job title
- purpose and scope of job
- to whom responsible
- place of work
- for whom responsible
- main duties
- main characteristics and working conditions
- key performance measures.

Task

An identifiable element of a job, by means of which a specific result is achieved.

Task identification

The process of identifying, listing and grouping the tasks that make up a job.

Task analysis

The detailed and systematic examination of the skills used by an experienced worker in performing a task to the required standard.

Job specification

A detailed statement of the tasks involved in a job, the standards required and the corresponding knowledge and skills involved.

Syllabus

A statement of what a trainee needs to learn, based on the comparison between the job specification and his or her present knowledge and competence.

Training programme

A broad outline of training that indicates the stages or sequence of the training and the time allowed for each part.

Training manual

This is a guide for the training of staff and trainees that specifies the points to be covered in training, standards to be achieved, methods of instruction to be used, equipment and materials required, forms and records to be kept and any tests or targets which have to be achieved. These manuals are sometimes called 'Standards of Performance Manuals'.

Training programmes and the role of the supervisor

The advantages of clear and thorough training programmes include:

- identification of standards of performance required
- improved ability of staff
- a means of measuring ability
- more efficient working
- clearer responsibilities for staff.

The role of the supervisor in training is to:

- ensure that staff are competent to carry out the duties required of them
- ensure that legal and company requirements are met (for example, no staff under 18 to work with dangerous machinery)
- develop and train staff as required
- develop existing staff to train others
- identify training needs of staff, now and in the future
- develop the necessary skills to achieve the list of advantages of well-produced training programmes described above.

What is a training need?

A training need is present when there is a gap between:

- the knowledge, skills and attitudes displayed by people in their jobs, and
- the knowledge, skills and attitudes needed for them to achieve the results the job requires, both now and in the future.

Identifying training needs

In order to systematically determine what the training needs of the operation are, it is necessary to find specific answers to the questions listed below.

Present needs

The first action is to examine the current staffing position and determine where the immediate training needs are. This includes consideration of the following:

Staffing

- What staffing does the establishment currently have?
- Where do they fit in?
- How long do they stay and why?
- Where do they come from?
- How are they chosen?
- How many new people are recruited and how often?

Agreed job descriptions

- What do the members of staff do in theory and in practice?
- Do they know what they have to do?

Standards and performance

- What results and standards are expected from the staff?
- Are the members of staff aware of these requirements?
- How well do they meet the requirements?
- What prevents these requirements from being met?

Present training
- How do members of staff currently learn their jobs and from whom?
- How well do they learn?
- How quickly do they learn?

Key problems
- Are there any special difficulties:
  ○ in the skills people have to learn
  ○ in the circumstances under which they work
  ○ in organising training?

Resources
- What training facilities exist within or outside the organisation that can be used or developed?

Future needs
Any change brings a training need with it. It is therefore necessary to ask questions in order to find out what future training will be needed, for instance:

Normal staff changes and development
- What is the age range of the staff?
- What posts are likely to have to be filled due to:
  ○ retirement
  ○ normal replacements
  ○ transfers?
- Is anyone earmarked for promotion?
- What potential for promotion is there?
- What plans are there for craft or other trainees?

Other changes
- What plans, if any, are there for:
  ○ expansion
  ○ new equipment
  ○ new working methods?
- How will existing jobs have to be altered to meet these changes?
- What further training will existing staff need?
- Will new staff be required?

Induction training
Induction training must be given to all new members of staff and should cover such things as:
- health, safety and security policies and procedures
- company employment policies and procedures (related to grievance, disciplinary, sickness, holidays, periods of notice, etc.)
- organisation of working department including duties of colleagues
- other departments – their role and responsibilities
- where things/people are
- duty rota.

Planning training

The contents of this book are based upon an operations hierarchy which is used to identify tasks and duties in food and beverage service operations. These tasks and duties are summarised in the Master Reference Chart shown on pp.ix–xi. This identification of tasks and duties forms the basis of the content of this book.

For individual operations a similar list of tasks and duties can be drawn up that are specific to that particular operation. The set of tasks and duties, when compiled, are then analysed to identify specific knowledge, skills and attitudes required for each task. In other words, each task and duty is defined and standards of performance identified. Existing members of staff are then assessed against these criteria. The gaps are the training needs and plans should then be drawn up to carry out the training that is required.

12.5 Food and beverage pricing

Relationship between revenue, costs and profits

For a foodservice operation there is a relationship between the costs of running the operation, the revenue that is received and the profit that is made. In foodservice operations there are three elements of cost:

1 **Food or beverage costs**: often called cost of sales.
2 **Labour**: wages, salaries, staff feeding, uniforms.
3 **Overheads**: rent, rates, advertising, fuel.

There are also two types of profit:

1 **Gross profit**: total revenue less cost of sales.
2 **Net profit**: gross profit less both labour costs and overhead costs.

In foodservice operation sales or revenue is always equal to 100 per cent. Therefore, the relationship between the elements of costs and profits in foodservice operations may be seen as shown in Figure 12.2.

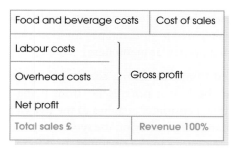

Figure 12.2 Summary of the relationship between revenue, costs and profits in foodservice operations

Thus all elements of cost and profits in a foodservice operation are always calculated as a percentage of the total sales figures. This is different to many retail operations, where the cost of sales figures are taken as 100 per cent, so the gross profit percentage is then worked out as a percentage of the cost price.

> **Note**: In kitchen operations gross profit is sometimes called kitchen percentage or kitchen profit.

Price, cost, worth and value

Price is that element of the *meal experience* that also relates to value. Price is also directly related to profitability. However, price is also flexible and can be changed relatively easily, thereby changing value perceptions and possibly changing profitability.

Although values are attached to various food and beverage products because of the perception of the customer needs they can satisfy, the ability to realise those goals is dependent on the customer's ability to pay. But this is not just about having the required amount of money. Customers also make choices by considering their view of the relationship between price, cost, worth and value:

- **Price:** the amount of money required to purchase the product.
- **Cost:** includes in addition to price the cost of not going somewhere else, the cost of transport and time, the cost of potential embarrassment, the cost of having to look and behave in a required manner and the cost in terms of effort at work to earn the money to pay the required price.
- **Worth:** a perception of the desirability of a particular product over another in order to satisfy a set of established goals.
- **Value:** a perception of the balance between worth and cost.

Good value for a food and beverage operation is where the worth is perceived as greater than the costs, and poor value is where the costs are perceived as greater than the worth.

Prices should always be set in relation to the quality and value perception that operators want the customers to have. A high-priced product might be perceived as either good quality or a rip-off, and a low-priced product as poor quality or good value, indicating that it is more than just the cash price that determines value, but rather the price and the other costs relative to the perceived worth.

It is good practice to establish a price range within which the customer will be prepared to pay. The foodservice operator can also establish the price range within which the operator is prepared to offer the food and beverages and other services. The overlap is the range available to the foodservice operator to work within. Setting prices within ranges, which the consumers will pay, should also be undertaken with reference to the particular market segment and type of operation. Market research can determine a range within which families travelling on motorways, for example, are prepared to stop and pay for food and drink, and will also be able to determine a price range for a particular menu item.

The information to be gained from researching customers' attitudes and behaviour towards price will always show that the lowest price is far from being the only consideration for customers. The importance that a customer attaches to the five elements of the *meal experience* (see Section 1.3, p.10) will change depending on the type of experience they are undertaking at the time. Thus the importance of price to the customer for different experiences also changes, as indicated in Table 12.4.

Table 12.4 Possible meal experience factor rankings for different meal experiences

Type of meal experience	Possible ranking of meal experience factors
Night out	Atmosphere Food and drink Service Price Cleanliness and hygiene
Gourmet event	Food and drink Service Atmosphere Cleanliness and hygiene Price
Cheap meal	Price Food and drink Cleanliness and hygiene Service Atmosphere
Civic banquet	Service Atmosphere Food and drink Cleanliness and hygiene Price

Pricing policies

Various pricing methods are available to foodservice operators, but whichever methods are used, the foodservice operator should always have a clear pricing policy or objective in mind. These pricing objectives might include the following:

- **Sales volume maximisation:** the pricing objective is to achieve the highest sales possible.
- **Market share gain:** the objective is to increase the number of customers relative to the total possible market and the competition.
- **Profit maximisation:** the pricing objective is to achieve the highest profit possible.
- **Market penetration:** the pricing objective is to move from a position of a zero or low market share to a significant market share.

Once a clear pricing policy has been established, the pricing methods most suitable can be drawn; this is often a combination of a range of the various pricing methods.

Pricing methods for foodservice operations

Pricing methods used by operators vary in their appropriateness and sophistication. The main pricing methods for foodservice operations are described below.

Cost plus

This is the most common method. The ingredient cost is established – not always very accurately – and the required profit (referred to as gross profit) is added. The result is a selling price that gives the operator the required profit for that dish (although it should be noted that this required profit would only be realised when that dish is actually sold).

This method is attractive because of its simplicity but it ignores price sensitivity and demand (price is a determinant of demand) and that value for money must be factored into the pricing decision. It also makes the assumption that the required profit can be established by making it a set percentage of the selling price (often between 65 and 75 per cent); fails to account for different restaurant types and different menu categories; and does not take into account that each dish/beverage is only part of a collection of items purchased to produce the *meal experience*. Where this method is applied, differentiated percentages are used so that low cost starter items earn proportionately more gross profit than higher cost main course items.

Prime costing methods

These methods attempt to factor in the labour cost of a dish, and *actual* cost pricing attempts to include fixed and variable costs as well as labour. These additional costs are also established as a percentage of the final selling price (e.g. labour at 25 per cent and variable costs at 10 per cent). These methods are flawed in the same way as *cost plus*: labour is a factor related to the time needed to prepare a dish, not to the value of the ingredients used to prepare it; no account is taken of volume of business or item popularity in assessing the labour content of a dish, therefore not taking into account economies and diseconomies of scale. Allocating fixed and variable costs to each menu item should at least be related to the volume of each dish sold rather than a fixed percentage figure to be used for each menu item.

Backward pricing

This attempts to match costs to a price previously established for a desired potential market. This market-driven approach – which is not really backwards – is a good starting point in new product development but it is still difficult to establish the necessary gross profit, ingredient and labour costs. Care must also be taken to avoid the problems of using percentages. However, identifying what the customer is prepared to pay for a particular product and investigating whether the operation can provide the product, profitably, at that price may avoid an operation being created that is never going to be profitable.

Rate of return pricing

This method tries to establish price based on a forecast of sales and costs and may be used to produce a break-even matrix for the operation. This approach may help give a guide to the price range but will not in itself establish individual selling prices.

Profit-per-customer pricing

This establishes the total profit required and allocates this to a forecast demand resulting in an average profit per customer. This 'profit' is then added to the material and/or other costs to produce a selling price for each dish. Again, this may be used to produce a break-even matrix, but caution should be exercised because profit is a factor of demand, which is a factor of price, which is a factor of demand, and so on. However, as with *backward pricing* described above, relating the required profitability of an operation to a given level of demand and within a price range that the customer is likely to pay can be used to determine whether the operation can in fact ever be successful.

Elasticity pricing

This asks how sensitive a market is to price changes. In order to determine menu prices the operator will try to determine the effect a price change may have on demand. It should be remembered that it is possible to increase demand and profitability through price decreases. It is very difficult to predict market responses to price changes, but considering elasticity may inform the pricing decisions.

Competition pricing

This is copying the competitors' price. However, there is no guarantee that the cost structure of any competitor offering a similar product will be similar, so a particular market price may produce higher or lower profits. Copying the competition may also take the form of discounting, premium promotions, happy hours, special meals, free wine and children's toys. All of these are short-term tactics, which can lead to increasing costs and fierce price-based competition.

12.6 Food and beverage revenue control

A control system covering the sale of all food and beverages in a foodservice operation is essential to maximise returns. The type of control system used will vary from one operation to another.

In a large establishment a control and accounts department will be in overall charge of the efficient running and working of the control systems used. In a smaller establishment this may be managed by an assistant manager, who will personally carry out the necessary daily and weekly checks. All control systems should be as simple as possible, making it easier for the food and beverage service staff to operate, and for the control and accounts department staff to check for any errors and omissions and have them rectified.

Purpose of a revenue control system

A control system essentially monitors areas where selling takes place.
- There must be efficient control of all food and beverage items issued from the various departments.
- The system should reduce any pilfering and wastage to a minimum.
- Management should be provided with any information they require for costing purposes and so that they may estimate accurately for the coming financial period.
- The cashier should be able to make out the customer's bill correctly so that the customer is neither overcharged nor undercharged.
- The system should show a breakdown of sales and income received in order that adjustments and improvements may be made.

The main control methods in use in foodservice establishments are:
- Order taking methods (see Section 6.3, p.215).
- Billing methods (see p.404).
- Sales summary sheets (see p.413).
- Operational statistics (see Section 12.8, p.423).

The process of food and beverage revenue control is summarised in Figure 12.3. This chart is based upon the triplicate method for food and the duplicate method for the dispense bar. The chart indicates that all top copies go to the dispense points (bar, kitchen) and follows the flow of information through until top and second copies are matched up by control.

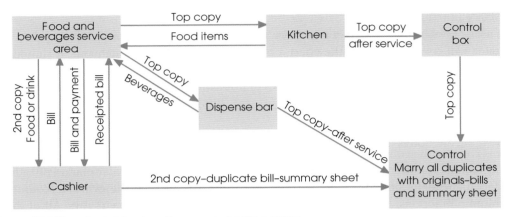

Figure 12.3 Flow chart of food and beverage checking system

Billing methods

The seven basic billing methods are described in Table 12.5.

Table 12.5 Billing methods

Method	Description
Bill as check	Second copy of order used as bill
Separate bill	Bill made up from duplicate check and presented to customer
Bill with order	Service to order and billing at same time, for example bar or takeaway service methods
Pre-paid	Customer purchases ticket or card in advance, either for specific meal or specific value
Voucher	Customer has credit issued by third party for either specific meal or specific value, for example a luncheon voucher or tourist agency voucher
No charge	Customer not paying – credit transaction
Deferred	Refers to, for example, function catering where the bill is to be paid by the organiser, or customers who have an account

Note: All billing methods are based upon these seven concepts. The main systems used to support these methods and the different payment methods are described below.

Bill as check

When a customer requires the bill, the waiter checks everything is entered on the duplicate copy of the food and drink check and then totals the bill. It is then presented to the customer. One of two methods of payment may now occur. The customer may pay at the cash desk on the way out, or pay direct to the waiter who will give any change if payment is made by cash. The cashier usually keeps a copy of the bill on payment and the customer gets a receipt and a copy of the bill if requested.

Depending on the system used, a waiter may enter the details of their bills from the stubs on their check pads into an account slip. This account slip plus the stubs and payments received are then passed on to the control and accounts department who match them all up.

If the waiter makes out and presents the bill to the customer, who then pays the cashier on leaving the establishment, then the cashier will draw up a daily summary or analysis sheet. This shows the daily takings and also an analysis sheet showing each individual waiter's takings.

Control is effected by the accounts department matching up the checks used to order food and drink from the bars, stillroom and kitchen against the bills issued by each waiter.

Separate bill

This billing method is usually run with the duplicate or triplicate checking system.

On receiving the duplicate copy of the food check from the waiter, the cashier opens a bill according to the table number on the food check. All the sets of manual bills are serial numbered for control purposes. The number of an electronic bill is recorded as it is opened. The cashier enters the items ordered onto the bill together with the prices, as checks are received from the food or wine waiters. When this is done the bill and duplicate checks are pinned together (with electronic systems only the checks are pinned together) and may be placed into a special book or file that has its pages numbered according to the number of tables in the foodservice area. As further checks are received the items are entered onto the bill and the checks then stored with the others for that table.

When the customer requests the bill, the waiter must collect it from the cashier who must first check that all items are entered and priced correctly and then total it up. The top copy of the bill is presented to the customer, on a side plate and folded in half, or in a bill folder. On receiving the necessary payment from the customer, the waiter returns the bill and payment to the cashier who will receipt both copies of the bill and return the receipted top copy plus any change to the waiter. The waiter then returns this to the customer. The receipted duplicate copy with the duplicate checks pinned to it is then removed from the special book or file and put on one side until service is completed.

Bill with order

This billing method may take a variety of forms depending upon the requirements of the establishment and the level of management control information required. See also 'Menu order and customer bill' and 'Single order sheet' (Section 6.3, p.215).

This type of billing may also be used in bars where the customer's order is rung up as requested on a pre-set (electronic) keyboard. Here, each key relates to a specified drink and its cost. A visual display unit (VDU) shows the customer the order as it is rung up and the prices being charged. When the order has been completed, the total sum owing is displayed. On receipt of cash for the order dispensed, the VDU displays the change to be returned to the customer. A receipt or itemised bill can be printed out for the customer if required.

This system speeds up the process of billing to the customer and allows specific control over payment received, change given where appropriate, and all stock items held.

Pre-paid

This billing method happens when pre-payment is required for a specific occasion or event. The organiser must determine the exact number of customers prior to the event. Upon arrival at the event, admission and/or the receipt of food or beverages is obtained by the customer handing in a ticket or card.

Voucher

This method involves a customer being issued credit by a third party. This could be by his or her employer, in the form of a luncheon voucher. A luncheon voucher can be exchanged for food and non-alcoholic beverages to the maximum value indicated on the voucher. Should the goods requested come to less than the sum shown on the voucher, no cash may exchange hands to make up the difference to the purchaser. However, should the cost of the goods requested exceed the sum shown on the voucher, then the customer must pay the difference to the supplier of the goods.

Other types of credit vouchers may be issued to a specific value, to be given in exchange or part exchange for goods or services received. The supplier of the goods or services then uses these credit vouchers as the basis of the claim for the payment owing from the employer, firm or agency that issued them.

No charge

If no charge is to be made to a customer receiving goods or services, he or she should be asked only to sign for the goods and services received and the bill should then be sent to the firm or company supplying the hospitality. In some instances the customer will be required to show some type of official form or letter authorising the provision of the service. This method of billing is also used if the establishment, for whatever reason, decides not to charge the customer. This is called 'comping'. The procedure is the same but in this case the bill is sent to the person who authorised the comping.

Deferred/account billing

In deferred or account billing a service has been requested by an individual, firm or company, which has been confirmed and taken place. The bill for the total services provided is then sent after the event to the organising person or body for payment. Payment in this manner often relates to special party bookings or function catering. This method of payment is also available to customers who have accounts with the establishment, where an invoice for payment is sent to the customer, usually once a month. In these cases the customer is normally presented with the bill to sign, before the bill is sent to the control department for adding to the customer's account. This arrangement is similar to those for the resident guests of an hotel.

Systems for revenue control

The four basic methods for order taking are shown in Table 6.1 (p.215). The seven basic methods of billing are shown in Table 12.5 (p.404). The systems that are used to support the various order taking and billing methods are summarised below.

● **Manual systems**: using hand-written duplicate or triplicate checks for ordering from kitchen and bar and for informing the cashier. Often used with a cash till or cash register. This system is found in many high class restaurants and in popular catering.
● **Pre-checking system**: orders are entered directly onto a keyboard that then prints each order check with a duplicate and retains a record of all transactions. The keyboard may be pre-set or pre-priced. This system may be found in many full-service restaurants and in popular catering.

- **Electronic cash registers**: allows for a wider range of functions including sales analysis. ECRs may be installed as standalone or linked systems. These systems are found in store restaurants, cafeterias and bars.
- **Point-of-sale control systems**: have separate keyboard terminals in the various service areas, which are linked to remote printers or visual display units (VDUs) in the kitchen, bar, etc. The terminals can be fixed or set in docking stations for hand-held use. In hotels, this equipment may also be linked to the hotel accounting systems. This system is also found in many modern restaurants.
- **Computerised systems**: enable a number of serving terminals, intelligent tills and remote printers to be controlled by a master unit compatible with standard computer hardware. Depending on software, the functions may also include a variety of performance measures such as planning and costing, sales analysis, gross profit reporting, stock control, re-ordering and forecasting, VAT returns, payroll, staff scheduling and account information. These systems are often found in hotels, fast food and chain restaurants.
- **Satellite stations**: remote terminals linked by telephone to a central processor to enable sales performance to be analysed (usually overnight) and reported back. These systems are found in fast food and chain restaurant operations.

Electronic point-of-sale control (EPOS)

The more sophisticated of the systems (point-of-sale, computerised and satellite) provide for increasingly efficient service at the point of sale, as well as improving the flow and quality of information to management for control purposes. The advantages will vary from one system to another, but may be summarised as follows:

- **Fewer errors**: sales information entered will be more accurate because mistakes in the sequence of entries required for a particular transaction are not permitted. Automatic price look-up or pre-set keys are available rather than the potentially less reliable manual entry.
- **Faster processing**: transactions can be processed more quickly and this may be achieved by:
  - ○ automatic reading of price tags using a hand-held wand or moving the item over a fixed reader set in a counter top
  - ○ single key entry of prices
  - ○ eliminating any manual calculation or handwriting by the assistant.
- **Training time**: may be reduced from days on the conventional cash register to hours with the electronic systems. This is because many systems have a sequencing feature, which takes the user through each transaction step by step, giving instructions on a VDU.
- **Instant credit checking**: a customer's credit rating can be checked by having terminals compare the account number with a central computer file or through online connections to card providers.
- **Detailed management information**: electronic systems provide more direct information in a computer-readable form. This improves both the detail and quality of computerised stock control and accounting systems and makes them more economic for relatively small establishments.
- **Additional security features**: includes such things as:
  - ○ locks which permit the ECR to be operated only by authorised personnel and totals that can only be altered and reset by supervisors and managers
  - ○ not disclosing at the end of the day the sum of the receipts that should be accounted for.

- **Advanced calculating facilities**: systems can be programmed to calculate the total price when a number of items of the same price are purchased, there are a number of items at various prices or if VAT has to be added.
- **Improved printouts**: in terms of quality and the amount of information contained on the customer's receipt. This may also include facilities where:
  - receipts may be overprinted with sales and VAT
  - both alphabetic and numeric information can be presented in black and white or colours
  - the receipt can contain the names of the goods purchased as well as, or instead of, a simple reference number.
- **Improved appearance**: modern systems are styled to fit in with the decor of modern foodservice environments.

Individual foodservice operators will determine which system best suits their needs and gives them the information they require.

Figure 12.4 Electronic point-of-sale billing and payment system

Maintaining a payment point

Before the start of service the cashier should have made all relevant checks and have the required materials to hand. Each establishment will have its own procedure but it will generally include the following:

- Check the float: if it is incorrect follow the company procedure.
- Ensure the cash drawer is properly organised with notes and coins in the relevant compartments.
- Ensure there are enough credit/debit card vouchers, till rolls, promotional items, bill folders, stapler or paper clips and pens, etc.

The cashier's duties for table and assisted service may include:

- issuing and recording of check books
- maintaining cash floats
- preparation of customer bills
- maintaining copies of the food and wine orders together with the bills in case of server or customer queries
- counter-signing spoilt checks
- receiving payments (which may include cash, credit card and cheque payments as well as luncheon vouchers or other forms of pre-paid voucher)
- receiving all unused checks back
- ensuring payments are balanced with manual or electronic sales summaries
- delivering the reports and payment to the control department.

In some operations the individual servers may take payments. Cashiers on cafeteria checkouts may have similar duties but excluding the tasks involving checks.

Where services are provided to residents in hotel lounges and in room service, payment might not be taken at the same time. Therefore, all bills must be signed by the resident concerned to show he or she has received a particular service. When a resident signs a bill the waiter must ensure the correct room number is obtained so that the charge can be made on the right bill. These bills should then be immediately passed to the control and accounts department. It is their job to ensure that the bills are posted onto the guest's account. In this way all residents' bills are kept up to date and all services provided are charged for.

Figure 12.5 Example of a bill

Methods of payment

There are various ways of making payment for goods or services received, some of which have already been described in the section Billing methods (p.441). The main methods of payment are described below.

Cash

The amount of cash received by the operator should always be checked in front of the customer and when change is given it should be counted back to the customer. Any notes received by the operator should be checked to ensure they are not forgeries. An itemised and receipted bill should always accompany the change.

Cheque

The use of cheques is declining. The acceptance of cheques is now mostly restricted to the payment of invoices, for example for monthly accounts. For payments in food and beverage operations, the acceptance of a cheque is dependent on the policy of the establishment and is most often limited to known regular customers. If cheques are being accepted then the operator receiving the cheque should make sure:

- it is dated correctly
- it is made payable to the correct firm or company
- the correct amount is filled in
- it is signed by the person indicated on the cheque.

It is also normal practice for some additional form of identification to be required such as a credit or debit card. In this case the credit or debit card must be in date and the signature on the cheque must be the same as that on the credit or debit card. In the case of a debit card, the bank sort code and account number should also be the same.

Credit cards/debit cards/charge cards

- **Credit cards**: allow customers to spend up to a pre-determined limit. The customer receives a statement of payments at the end of each month, which he can then pay off in full or in part. Interest is charged on any remaining balance.
- **Debit cards**: used in a similar way to a credit card but the amount due is immediately deducted from the customer's bank account. Examples include the Switch and Connect cards.
- **Charge cards**: work in a similar way to credit cards but the customer is invoiced once a month. The account must then be paid up in full. Examples include the American Express and Diners Club cards.

On receipt of a credit, debit or charge card the operator should check that it is still valid by looking at the dates on the card. There are now two systems for accepting payments with these types of cards: signature verified and chip and PIN.

Signature verified

This is a manual system in which the validity of the card is checked, often through an online or dial-up connection to the card issuer, by passing it through an electronic card reader. Once verified, the details of the transaction are printed in the form of an itemised bill, which the customer is then asked to sign. A copy of this itemised bill is given as a receipt. Some establishments also make out a sales voucher. The customer is then requested to sign the voucher after which the operator should check the signature with that on the card. The customer receives a copy of the voucher as a receipt.

Chip and PIN

Chip and PIN means that the customer enters their PIN (personal identification number) into a keypad when they use a credit, debit or charge card for face-to-face transactions in shops, hotels or restaurants.

Receiving chip and PIN payments

- The POS (point-of-sale) terminals provide step-by-step instructions to complete a transaction.
- First the transaction total is displayed on the POS terminal display.
- The customer is then asked for their card.
- In most cases the customer will hand the card to the member of staff, but sometimes customers may be asked to insert the card into the reader themselves.
- The chip and PIN card is inserted into the reader.
- Once the card is verified, the customer is asked to enter their PIN.
- The machine will then check the PIN number entered against the PIN held on the chip in the card.
- Customers *must* enter their own PIN – it is not secure for a member of staff to do it and customers are required not to reveal their PIN to anyone.
- If the customer says they cannot remember their PIN, then they may be allowed to sign the payment slip in the traditional way (depending on establishment policy). If this does happen, pay particular attention to the card and signature.
- The prompts on the POS terminal screen are followed and the payment is processed.
- The card is then removed from the card reader.
- The receipt is issued and the receipt and the card are returned to the customer.

Payment in restaurants

There are two ways of dealing with payments in restaurants:
1 The customer is asked to come to the cash desk or workstation to complete the payment transaction there – some customers may prefer this.
2 A hand-held self-powered terminal is taken to the customer at their table.

Figure 12.6 Hand-held credit/debit card payment terminal with printer

Locked PIN

If the customer enters the wrong PIN three times in a row, the card will become temporarily unusable. The POS terminal prompt will indicate whether payment on this card can be made using signature or whether the customer needs to provide a different method of payment. Customers can unlock their PIN:

- by contacting their card issuer – contact numbers are on the back of most cards or on statements
- by using the unlock PIN facility available on most cash machines.

People with disabilities

The procedures for taking payment are generally the same as described above. However, some additional considerations are given below.

- Offer to assist when needed and most importantly exercise patience to ensure that the customer has enough time to complete a stress-free transaction.
- Make sure all customers, including those in wheelchairs, can easily reach the desk or table to sign the bill or to access the PIN pad.
- Follow the terminal prompts – some cardholders may have chip and signature cards instead of chip and PIN cards. Chip and PIN terminals will recognise this type of card and automatically ask for a signature.
- Encourage, or help, the customer to pick up the PIN pad from the cradle if appropriate.
- Suggest that the customer shields the PIN pad from other customers as they enter their PIN.

Declined transactions

Procedures for declined transactions are the same for any credit card/debit card/charge card payments, whether signature verified or chip and PIN. Where the card is declined, always ask for an alternative method of payment.

Travellers' cheques

These may be issued by either a travel agent or bank in the traveller's own country. They may be issued in sterling, US dollars, Euros and other currencies.

The travellers' cheque must be signed once when issued and again when used to pay for something or when exchanging for cash. The rate of exchange will be that at the time of the transaction.

All travellers' cheques come in different values and this value is guaranteed as long as the two signatures match. When a payment is made by travellers' cheque the customer must:
- date the cheque or cheques required
- make them payable to the establishment concerned
- sign the cheque or cheques for a second time in the appropriate place.

The cashier will then:
- match the two signatures
- ask for other identification to check the two signatures against, such as the customer's passport
- give change where needed in the currency of the travellers' cheque.

Vouchers and tokens

Vouchers, such as Luncheon Vouchers, may be offered in exchange for food in those establishments that accept them. The vouchers have an expiry date. Should food be purchased above the value of the voucher, the difference must be paid for in cash.

Tokens might be exchanged for specific meals or for certain values. If food purchased is more than the value of the token then the difference is again paid in cash. No change can be given for purchases valued at less than the token being exchanged.

Dealing with discrepancies

When dealing with cash, do not allow anyone to interrupt you during the transaction or get involved with the counting of money as this will only lead to confusion.
- Always double check cash received before placing it in the till and any change before giving it out.
- If you make a mistake always apologise and remain polite. If you feel you cannot deal with a situation ask for assistance from your supervisor or manager.
- Bank notes should be checked for forgeries and if found to be fake then they must not be accepted. You should explain why you cannot accept them, advising the customer to take the note to the police station.
- If credit card fraud is suspected the credit card company may request that the card be retained. Suggest to the customer that they contact the company to discuss the matter. You may wish to offer the use of a telephone with some privacy.

Sales summary sheets

Sales summary sheets are also known as restaurant analysis sheets, bill summaries or records of restaurant sales. They provide for:
- the reconciliation of items with different gross profits
- sales mix information
- records of popular/unpopular items
- records for stock control.

There are many different formats for sales summaries, which are often electronically produced. Depending on the needs of the establishment, the information often includes:

● date
● address of food and beverage outlet (if more than one exists)
● period of service
● bill numbers
● table numbers
● number of covers per table
● bill totals
● analysis of sales, e.g. food, beverages, or more detailed, such as menu and wine and drink list items
● various performance measures (see p.460/426)
● cashier's name.

They may also include individual staff or till sales breakdowns.

Consumption control

In food and beverage service areas there may be food and beverage items displayed on:

● cold tables
● buffets
● carving trolleys
● sweet trolleys
● liqueur trolleys
● food and beverage counters.

A consumption control method is used for these services that identifies the number of portions or measures issued to the area. Following service, returns are deducted and the final total equals the consumption. The consumption is then checked with actual sales to identify shortages/surpluses. This method of control is also found in room and lounge service. An example of a consumption sheet is shown in Figure 12.7.

Consumption Control Sheet			Date: 22/05/2014		Service period: Luncheon	
Item	Portions issued	Portions returned	Portions consumed	Billed portions	Difference +	-
Fruit salad	24	6	18	15		3
Gâteau	20	5	15	14		1
Flan	30	10	20	16		4

Figure 12.7 Example of a completed consumption sheet

The system of beverage control is basically the same as for food. However, for beverages the cellar is the focal point for the storage of alcoholic and non-alcoholic liquor.

Cellar storage

Beers

The factors that determine good beer cellar management are:

- good ventilation
- cleanliness
- even temperatures of 13–15 °C (55–58 °F)
- avoidance of strong draughts and wide ranges of temperatures
- on delivery, all casks should be placed immediately upon the stillions
- casks remaining on the floor should be bung uppermost to better withstand the pressure
- spiling should take place to reduce any excess pressure in the cask
- tappings should be carried out 24 hours before a cask is required
- pipes and engines should be cleaned at regular intervals
- all beer lines should be cleaned weekly with a diluted pipe-cleaning fluid and the cellar floor washed down weekly with a weak solution of chloride and lime (mild bleach)
- beer left in pipes after closing time should be drawn off
- returned beer should be filtered back into the cask from which it came
- care should be taken that the cellar is not overstocked
- all spiles removed during service should be replaced after closing time
- all cellar equipment should be kept scrupulously clean
- any ullage should be returned to the brewery as soon as possible
- re-ordering should be carried out on one set day every week after checking the bottle stocks of beers, wines, minerals, etc.
- strict rotation of stock must be exercised, with new bottle crates or cases being placed at the rear and old stock pulled to the front for first issue.

Wine

Wines should ideally be stored in a subterranean cellar, which has a northerly aspect and is free from vibrations, excessive dampness, draughts and odours. The cellar should be absolutely clean, well ventilated, with only subdued lighting and a constant cool temperature of 12.5 °C (55 °F) to help the wine develop gradually.

Wines should be stored on their sides in bins so that the wine remains in contact with the cork. This keeps the cork expanded and prevents air from entering the wine – a process that quickly turns wine to vinegar. Wines are also stored on their sides with the labels uppermost as this ensures they can be easily identified, the label is protected from the base surface of the bin and any sediment is always located on the side of the bottle away from the label. This approach is also used for wines with alternative stoppers such as screw tops. White, sparkling and rosé wines are kept in the coolest part of the cellar and in bins nearest the ground (because warm air rises). Red wines are best stored in the upper bins. Commercial establishments usually have special refrigerators or cooling cabinets to keep their sparkling, white and rosé wines at serving temperature.

Other drinks

Spirits, liqueurs, squashes, juices and mineral waters are stored upright in their containers, as are fortified wines. The exceptions are port-style wines, which are destined for laying down, and these are treated as for wines above.

Determining stock levels

All the individual outlets within an establishment such as the lounge, lounge bar, cocktail bar, saloon bar, brasserie, dispense bars and floor service should draw their stock on a daily or weekly basis from the cellar. Each outlet will hold a set stock (or 'par stock') of liquor, which is sufficient for a service period or for a day or week. The level of the par stock will be determined mainly by the amount of storage space available in the service areas and also taking account of the expected sales demand. At the end of this service period each individual outlet will requisition for the amount of drink consumed in that one service period, day or week, thus bringing their total stock back up to the par stock level.

For the establishment as a whole, the central stock levels that are required in order to meet expected sales demand may be determined by using past sales data. A useful formula is:

$$M = W\ (T + L) + S$$

Where:
- M is the maximum stock level
- W is the average usage rate (over the review period)
- T is the review period (time interval between orders)
- L is the lead time (time it takes for the order to arrive)
- S is the safety stock (buffer or minimum stock level)

For example:

W = 24 bottles per week
T = 4 weeks
L = 1 week
S = 1 week's usage of 24 bottles

Therefore:

M = 24 x (4 + 1) + 24 = 144 bottles

Minimum stock (buffer or safety stock) may also be calculated as follows:

L x W = 1 x 24 = 24 bottles

ROL (re-order level) may also be calculated as follows:

$(W$ x $L)$ + S = (24 x 1) + 24 = 48 bottles

The same basic approaches can be applied for all types of alcoholic and non-alcoholic beverages, whether based on purchasing units such as bottles above, or quantities such as litres/gallons.

Using this approach can enable foodservice operations to determine the stock holding that will meet the needs of the expected demand, while at the same time minimising the amount of capital tied up in the stock being held. Good stock control can also be supported by the application of a 'just in time' (JIT) approach to purchasing. JIT involves only ordering stock as required in order to meet forecasted demand, rather than holding unnecessarily high stock levels, just in case.

Beverage control procedures

In any foodservice establishment where income is received from the sale of wine and drink, a system of control and costing must be put into operation. The system used will depend entirely on the policy of the establishment. Some or all of the books listed in Table 12.6 may be necessary, depending upon the requirements of the particular foodservice operation.

Table 12.6 Books used in beverage control

Book	Used to record
Order book	Orders made to suppliers
Goods inwards/goods received book	Goods received from suppliers
Goods returned book	Goods that are sent back to suppliers
Returnable containers book	Returnable containers sent back to suppliers
Cellar ledger	Stock movement in and out of the cellar
Bin cards	Stock of individual lines in the cellar
Requisition book	Restocking orders for individual service areas
Daily consumption sheets	Usage of stock in individual service areas
Ullage book	Breakage, spillage and wastage
Off-sales book	Items sold at the off-sale prices
Transfers book	Movement of stock between different service areas

Although referred to as books here, most modern-day systems are computer-based. However, the basic processes are the same whatever the method being used to record the data.

A summary of the basic steps in bar and cellar control is given in Figure 12.8.

Determine establishment stock levels

Order from suppliers

Goods inwards

Goods returned

Cellar Stock Ledger

Bin Cards

Issues against Requisitions to :

Lounge Bar   Cocktail Bar   Saloon Bar   Brasserie   Dispense Bar   Room Service

Individual Bar Stock Book

Ullage Books

Off-sales Books

Transfer Books

Daily Consumption Books

Check consumption aginst levels

Figure 12.8 Summary of basic steps in bar and cellar control

Order book

The cellar person is responsible for purchasing all alcoholic and non-alcoholic drinks needed to maintain the level of stock in an establishment. The order should be written in duplicate on an official order form. The top copy is then sent to the supplier and the duplicate remains in the order book for control purposes when the goods are delivered. In some instances there may be three copies of the order sheet. If so, they are distributed as follows:

- **Top copy**: supplier.
- **Duplicate copy**: control and accounts department.
- **Third copy**: remains in the order book.

Goods inwards/goods received book

All deliveries should be recorded in full in the goods received book. Each delivery entry should show the following:

- delivery note/invoice number
- name and address of supplier
- order number
- date of delivery
- list of items delivered
- quantity
- unit
- item price
- discounts if applicable
- total price.

When the goods are delivered to an establishment they should be accompanied by either a delivery note or an invoice. Whichever document it may be, the information contained should be exactly the same, with one exception: invoices show the price of all goods delivered whereas delivery notes do not. The goods delivered must first be counted and checked against the delivery note to ensure that all the goods listed have been delivered. The cellar person may carry out an extra check by checking the delivery note against the copy of the original order in the order book. This is to ensure that the items ordered have been sent, in the correct quantities, and that extra items have not been sent which were not requested on the order sheet, thereby incurring extra cost.

Goods returned book

Records of any returns made to suppliers are recorded in the good inwards book or in a separate goods returned book. This may also include records of returnable containers such as kegs, casks and CO_2 cylinders, or these may be recorded in a separate returnable containers book.

Cellar stock ledger

The cellar stock ledger (Figure 12.9) is an essential part of beverage control and may be used as either an extension of, or in place of, the goods received book. It therefore shows movement of all stock into the establishment and issues out to the bars or dispensing points. All movement of stock in and out of the cellar is often shown at cost and selling price.

| Stock item _____ | | | | |
| Stock/bin number _____ | | | | |
Date	Received	Issued	Total stock	Unit price

Figure 12.9 Stock ledger

Bin cards

Bin cards (Figure 12.10) are used to indicate the physical stock of each separate stock line held in the cellar. The movement of all stock in and out of the cellar should be recorded on each individual bin card.

Every time an item is received or issued it must be entered on the corresponding bin card and the remaining total balance shown. Thus, the bin cards should show, at any given time, the total amount of each particular line currently held in stock.

The bin cards are also often used to show the maximum stock and minimum stock levels, thus providing a guide to the cellar person when re-ordering. The minimum stock indicates the re-order level, leaving sufficient stock in hand to carry over until the new delivery arrives. The maximum stock indicates how much to re-order and is determined by such considerations as storage space available, the turnover of a particular item and, to some extent, by the amount of cash available within the establishment budget (see Determining stock levels, p.416).

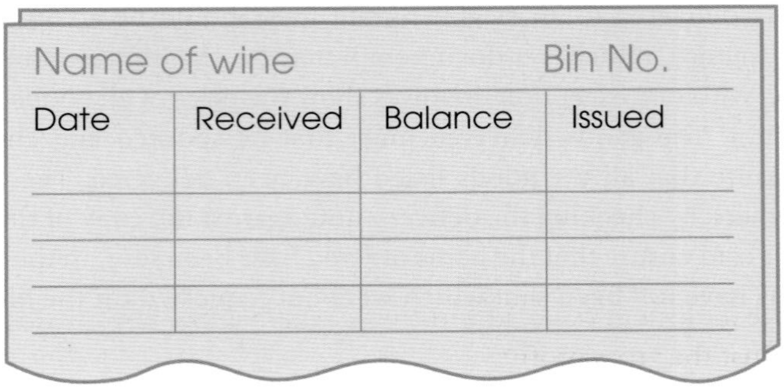

Figure 12.10 Bin card

Requisition

Each unit dispensing alcoholic beverages should use some form of requisition to draw items from the cellar. These requisitions may be controlled either by colour or serial number, and are normally in triplicate. The copies are sent as follows:

- **Top copy**: to the cellar.
- **Duplicate copy**: to the beverage control department.
- **Triplicate copy**: used by each unit to check its goods when they have been received from the cellar.

The following information is listed on the requisition:

- name of the dispensing unit
- date
- list of items required
- quantity and unit of each item required
- signature of the authorised person who may both order and receive the goods.

The purpose of the requisition is to control the movement of items from the cellar into the dispensing unit and to avoid too much stock being taken at one time, thus overstocking the bar. The level of stock held in the bar is known as 'par' stock. The amount ordered on the requisition each day should bring the stock back up to par. The amount to re-order is determined by taking account of the following equation:

Opening stock + additions (requisition) – closing stock = consumption (the amount to re-order, each item to the nearest whole unit).

No items should be issued by the cellar person unless he or she receives an official requisition form, correctly filled in, dated and signed by a person in authority from the department concerned. The cellar person should have a list of such signatures and should not issue any stock unless a person on the list signs the requisition sheet. To aid the cellar person, all requisitions should be handed into him or her at a set time each day, when all issues will be made. In certain instances, however, depending on the organisation of an establishment, it may be necessary to issue twice per day, once before opening time in the morning and again before opening time in the evening.

Ullage book

Each sales point must have a ullage book for recording the amount of beer wasted in cleaning the pipes, broken bottles, measures spilt or anything that needs a credit.

Off-sales book

The off-sales book contains a record of the number of bottles, whether beers, spirits or wines, sold at off-sales prices and the difference in price between the off-sales price and the on-sales price (this is the price if the item was sold within the establishment by measure). This difference will be allowed against the gross profit.

Transfer book

With multi-bar units it is necessary to minimise the movement of stock between bars with different prices otherwise this can create shortages. If this does happen then all such stock movements must be recorded in a transfer book.

Daily consumption sheet

The daily consumption sheet lists all of the sales in an individual service area, such as number of spirit measures, number of bottles of wine or beers by quantity. This information is then used to calculate what receipts should have been received for the items used.

Name of drink	Bin no.	Opening stock	Received	Total	Closing stock	Consumption	Price per visit	£

Figure 12.11 Daily consumption sheet

Beverage gross profit

An analysis of non-alcoholic and alcoholic beverage sales and the stock held allows for two performance measures to be obtained:
- the gross profit
- the overage or shortage of the estimated monetary revenue and stock in hand.

The data can then be analysed to identify the reasons for any variations in beverage gross profit.

Calculating gross profit

Gross profit is determined by deducting the beverage cost from the sales. It is essential that a physical alcoholic beverage stock be taken at least on a monthly basis, and more often if it is felt necessary.

To determine the overage or shortage it is necessary to estimate how much money should have been taken during a given period of time, based on the consumption at selling price. The consumption must be priced out bottle-by-bottle, keg-by-keg.

For example, a bar has sold 12 x 75 cl bottles of whisky (which sells at £2.70 per 25 ml measure), 6 x 75 cl bottles of sherry (at £2.50 per 50 ml measure) and 5 kegs (9 gallons each) (selling at £2.50 per pint):

Whisky: 12 x 30 measures x £2.70 = £972.00

Sherry: 6 x 15 measures x £2.50 = £225.00

Kegs: 5 x 72 pints x £2.50 = £900.00

(Note: Keg = 9 gallons x 8 pints = 72 pints)

Estimated takings = £2,097.00

Actual cash takings = £2,184.26

Surplus = £87.26

£87.27 is 4.16% of estimated takings

Variations in beverage gross profit

The relative proportion of wines, beers and spirits that have been sold will often help to explain why a certain month's gross profit is low (a lot of beer sold) or high (more spirits have been sold). There are, however, other reasons for a high or low gross profit:

- Under-ringing and keeping the difference, for example by ringing perhaps £0.50 instead of £1.50, whereby the bar loses a £1. The cash register should be sited so that both the customer and the management are able to check visually the amount being keyed or rung up.
- Too many 'No sales' on the till roll may give a clue to shortages. It is not always possible to prohibit the use of the No sale key altogether. Therefore, the till roll should be examined each time it is removed so that excessive use of the No sale key may be queried at the time.
- The till roll itself can be very revealing. It is sometimes found that there are a lot of very small sales recorded or that the average sale is lower than usual or lower with one operator than with another. Such indications can be taken as evidence that there are potential problems.
- Working with the till drawer open. If the till is not set on closed drawer then it is possible to give change without keying in, or ringing the amount up.
- Failing to ensure that all off-sales are kept apart from the bar where measures are sold, and a separate stock used. All off-sales should be entered into a separate book. The difference between the bar measure prices and the off-sales prices will be needed by the stock taker.
- Letting bar staff cash up could lead to the balance of the receipts being made to fit the expected sales recorded.
- Lounge sales or sales at a table away from the bar may also be vulnerable. The till ticket provides one simple method of control: If each waiter is provided with a float and has to pay for drinks at the time of collecting, then they will have a ticket to present to the customer. The customer then knows that the money has gone into the till and this gives the customer confidence in the establishment. The other advantage is that, unless there is collusion, the bar staff will not overcharge the waiter or under-ring the transaction. Even though this is a simple method of control it is still open to abuse. Staff have been known to use the same chit twice, but only if they are able to get drinks without paying for them.

An efficient manager will ensure that the receipts are counted first and then the till is read rather than reading the till first and then checking the receipts. In busy bars it is good practice to collect most of the receipts before the end of a session, leaving a temporary receipt in the drawer.

The use of electronic equipment may help to reveal that losses have taken place, but it will not in itself prevent them. Most electronic equipment is designed primarily to facilitate the analysis and recording of sales. Such equipment may, for example, provide automatic pricing for up to 1000 items, including for instance a half-pint and pint of beer, whisky, gin, gin and tonic, and thereby greatly reduce the likelihood of miscalculation and make under-keying/under-ringing easier to detect.

12.8 Performance measures

Sales mix

Sales mix figures may be taken from a sales summary sheet (see p.450) and shown in a simple report, as in Table 12.7, and with an application of percentages as shown in Table 12.8.

Food and drink sales may be broken down further to provide sales mix data. This not only reconciles sales of items with differing gross profits but also provides information on:
- popular/unpopular items on the menu/drinks lists
- records for stock control, for example to help predict future demand
- changes in customers' interests
- where profits/losses are being made.

Table 12.7 Simple sales report

Service	Total	Food	Liquor
	£	£	£
Lunches	190	110	80
Dinners	180	100	80
Snacks	115	115	–
Daily total	485	325	160

Table 12.8 Application of percentages

Service	Total		Food		Liquor	
	£	%	£	%	£	%
Lunches	190	39	110	58	80	42
Dinners	180	37	100	56	80	44
Snacks	115	24	115	100	–	–
Daily total	485	100	325	67	160	33

(Figures have been rounded)

Cost percentages

All costs such as cost of sales, labour or overheads can be classified in relation to sales. Thus cost of labour for example:

$$\text{Labour costs as a percentage of total wages cost} = \frac{\text{Department labour cost}}{\text{Total wage cost}} \times 100$$

$$\text{Labour costs as a percentage of sales} = \frac{\text{Labour cost}}{\text{Revenue}} \times 100$$

These calculations of labour costs are summarised in Table 12.9.

Table 12.9 Labour cost percentages

Sales		Direct labour costs	% of total labour costs	% of department sales
Food	£125	£35	78%	28%
Liquor	£60	£10	22%	17%
Total	£185	£45	100%	24%

By using a similar approach, all costs (food, drink, labour or overheads) can be attributed to a return in revenue.

> **Note**: Sales in foodservice operations are always equal to 100 per cent and all cost and profits are calculated as a percentage of the sales figures. The relationship between costs and profits in foodservice operations is summarised in Figure 12.2 (p.436).

Index of productivity (alternative method of showing labour costs)

The index of productivity is calculated by dividing the total sales figure by the total labour costs (including any staff benefit costs).

The index of productivity will vary according to the type of operation. For example, a popular catering operation should have a high index of productivity, as the labour costs should be relatively low, whereas a restaurant with a high ratio of staff to customers should have a relatively low index of productivity. As payroll costs can be controlled, and should be related to the forecasted volume of business, a standard index of productivity can be established over time to measure how accurately the two elements are related.

Seat turnover

Seat turnover is a pointer to efficiency. It shows how many times a seat is being used during a service period. An example of the report can be seen in Table 12.10. Seat turnover is calculated by dividing the number of covers served by the actual number of seats available per service period. For example:

- in a snack bar the seat turnover might be four to five times per service period
- in an expensive restaurant the seat turnover might be once per service period.

In operations where customers do not occupy specific seats (such as in cafeterias or takeaway operations) the customer throughput is calculated by the number of till transactions per service period (e.g. lunch) or time period (e.g. per hour).

Table 12.10 Example of seat turnover calculation

Service period	No. of covers served	No. of seats available	Seat turnover
Lunch	60	80	0.75 times
Dinner	85	80	1.06 times

Average spend per head/average check

The average spend per head is a calculation of the average amount spent per person during a service period. It is calculated by dividing the total sales by the number of people or covers served. This performance measure is useful in restaurants where the total number of customers (covers) is known.

The average check is a calculation of the average spend per order taken, during a service period. It is calculated by dividing the total sales by the number of orders taken. This performance measure is useful in bars or takeaway operations where the actual number of customers is not known. An example of both of these calculations is shown in Table 12.11. Working out these performance measures assists in the interpretation of sales figures. For example:
- If revenue goes up from one trading period to the next, is this due to higher selling prices or more customers being served or the same number of customer spending more?
- If the revenue reduces from one trading period to the next, is this due to fewer customers being served or to the same number of customers spending less?

Table 12.11 Example of average check and average spend per head calculations

∘	Total revenue	No. of orders taken	Average check	No. of covers served	Average spend per head
	£				£
Food	490	16	30.62	48	8.54
Beverages	280	13	21.54	39	7.18
Overall	770	29	26.55	87	8.85

These data can also be used to calculate the average number of customers in a group. This is calculated by dividing the number of covers served by the number of orders taken. Using the data in Table 12.11 for food sales, this would be:
- 48 covers served, divided by 16 orders taken = an average of 3 persons in each group.

Sales per seat available

Sales per seat available shows the sales value that can be earned by each seat in a restaurant, coffee shop, etc. It is used for comparison of different types of operation as well as a record of earnings per seat over a period of time. It is calculated by dividing the sales figures by the number of seats available in the dining area for specific service periods.

Sales per square metre

An alternative method of comparison between establishments is to calculate the sales per square metre or per foot. This is particularly useful in bars or takeaway operations where earnings per seat cannot be calculated. It is calculated by dividing the total sales by the square meters of the service area, for a specific service period.

Stock turnover

The rate of stock turnover gives the number of times that the average level of stock has turned over in a given period. It is calculated as follows:

$$\text{Rate of stock turnover} = \frac{\text{Cost of food or beverage consumed in specific period}}{\text{Average stock holding (food or beverage) at cost}}$$

The average stock holding is calculated by taking the opening stock value, adding the closing stock value and dividing by two. High stock turnover should be expected in a restaurant using predominantly fresh foods. Low stock turnover indicates usage of convenience food. Too high a turnover indicates potential problems through panic buying and lack of forecasting. Too low a turnover indicates that capital is being tied up in unused stocks.

Annex A: Glossary of cuisine and service terms

This annex gives a selection of classic and other cuisine and service terms and their definitions. Many cuisine terms are derived from the classic European cuisine. French terms are mostly used because it was in France that cuisine terms were codified through, for instance, the development and publication of the *Le Répertoire de la Cuisine*. This is much the same as the use of Italian terms for music (musical terms being codified in Italy), French terms in ballet (dance terms being codified in France) and English being the international language for aviation traffic control.

A

à la in the style of, for example: à l'Anglaise (English style); à la Française (French style); à la Maison (style of the house)

à la broche cooked on a spit

abats offal, the internal organs of meat and poultry, e.g. heart, kidneys, liver

accompaniment condiment or seasoning offered to a customer to add to and improve the flavour of a dish

aceto vinegar (Italian), e.g. Balsamico

achar Indian pickle

acidity indicates tartness in foods and beverages

Advocaat liqueur made up of brandy, egg yolks, caster sugar and vanilla flavouring; Dutch in origin

agneau denotes lamb on the menu

agrodolce sweet and sour

aiguillettes long, thin, vertically cut strips of meat or poultry

ail garlic

aïoli garlic mayonnaise from Provence. Used with cold fish dishes and as a salad dip, e.g. crudites

ajo blanco purée sauce of garlic and almonds (Spanish)

al dente cooked until firm and crunchy (pasta/vegetables)

ale general term covering all forms of brewed beer

allumette cut into matchstick shapes

amaretti macaroons (Italian), almond flavoured

amontillado medium dry sherry, classified as a fortified (or liqueur) wine

amuse-bouche small savoury snacks served pre-hors d'oeuvres

anchoide Provençal paste-sauce of garlic, anchovy and olive oil

Angostura bitters proprietary brand of aromatic bitters used as a flavouring in drinks, e.g. pink gin

anguille eel

antipasti starters other than pasta and rice dishes (Italian)

apéritif drink served prior to a meal in order to stimulate the appetite

arborio rice short, fat-grained Italian rice used for risotto

Armagnac quality brandy made in the Armagnac district of France

aroma indicating smell, scent or fragrance and often alluding to wine

arroser to baste

arrosto roast (Italian)

arugula salad leaf similar to rocket with a sharp peppery flavour (Italian)

aspic clear savoury jelly used in the decorating of joints of cold meat

assiette platter or dish

assiette anglaise plate of cooked meats

au bleu a method of cooking trout. When applied to grilled steaks it indicates 'very underdone'

au four baked in the oven

au gratin topped with breadcrumbs and grated cheese and browned under the grill

au jus with cooking liquors or gravy

au naturel uncooked or in its natural state

au sec until dry

auslese German wine label term indicating specially selected bunches of late picked grapes, high in sugar content, that make a sweet dessert wine

B

baba yeast sponge or bun that may be soaked in flavoured syrup to moisten, e.g. Baba au rhum

babaganoush aubergine purée (Middle Eastern meze dish)

Bacardi proprietary brand of white rum originating from Cuba

back of house work areas not seen or used by customers, e.g. stillroom, linen room, floor pantry

bagel ring-shaped roll with a tough, chewy texture

baguette long, stick shaped loaf of French bread

bain-marie hot water bath or well in which smaller containers may be set in order to cook food items slowly or to keep them warm/hot in readiness for service

baklava Turkish and Greek sweet made from filo pastry, chopped nuts and honey

ballotine meat, fish or poultry, boned, stuffed and rolled

balsamic vinegar Italian sweet wine vinegar; the finest being made in Modena in Northern Italy

balthazar equivalent of 16 standard size 75cl bottles of sparkling wine

bard (barder) to cover or wrap poultry, game or meat with a thin slice of fat bacon so that it does not dry out during roasting

baron double sirloin of beef or the saddle of lamb/ mutton with the legs attached, e.g. baron de boeuf rôti

barquette boat-shaped tartlette case

basil flavouring herb; goes well with tomatoes

basmati rice aromatic, long-grained rice used in Indian cuisine, e.g. Biryani

baste to spoon over liquid during cooking, e.g. hot fat over a joint

baton stick-shape cut of root vegetables

bavarois Bavarian cream – a sweet custard made with eggs, cream and gelatine and served cold

bayleaf used fresh or dried to flavour various dishes such as casseroles; also found in a 'bouquet garni'

beard (ébarber) to remove the beard from oysters, mussels, etc.

béarnaise hot sauce offered with fish and grilled meats, made from beaten egg yolks and reduced wine vinegar and flavoured with tarragon

Beaujolais fruity and light French red wine from the Beaujolais region of France

beaum measure used for sugar boiling

béchamel basic white sauce that is made from a white roux and seasoned hot milk. May be used as a thickening agent in cream soups or extended into other derivative sauces, e.g. mornay, moutarde

beer term broadly covering lagers, ales and stouts. An alcoholic beverage made from fermented malted barley or other cereals and flavoured with hops

beignets deep-fried fritters (assorted fruits cooked in batter) or doughnuts

belacan south-east Asian fermented shrimp paste

bercy a white wine-based sauce for fish

bergamot orange scented herb, native to America, giving a distinctive flavour to Earl Grey tea; also used in sweet and savoury dishes and in tisanes

beurre blanc light emulsion sauce of white wine, vinegar, shallots and butter

beurre fondu melted butter with lemon juice added and heated until golden brown before use

beurre maître butter with lemon juice and chopped parsley added; used to garnish
d'hôtel some fish and grilled meat dishes

beurre manié butter and flour kneaded together and used to thicken soups and sauces

beurre noisette golden brown butter that may have a little lemon juice added to take away the greasiness and add bite

bhaji vegetable deep fried in gram flour batter (Indian)

bianco medium sweet type of white/golden vermouth

bien cuit degree of cooking of a grilled steak – well done

billfold style of wallet used for presenting the bill to the host and returning the receipted bill and any change

bind (lier) to thicken soups and sauces with eggs, cream, etc. To mix pasta, chopped meat, vegetables, with sauce

biryani long grained rice, spiced and coloured yellow with saffron. An oven baked rice to accompany meats (Indian)

bisque thickened shellfish-based purée soup, usually with tomato and cognac, e.g. Bisque d'homard (lobster)

bistro small informal restaurant, bar or nightclub

bitters alcoholic spirits, flavoured and of different strengths, e.g. Angostura bitters, Campari, Fernet Branca and Underberg

blanc water to which flour has been added and used to keep vegetables white when cooking, e.g. celery

blanch (blanchir) placing briefly in boiling water or hot fat/oil and then draining. Also allows part cooking without colouring

blanquette thickened white stew of lamb, veal, rabbit or white fish thickened with egg yolks and cream

blini small, thick, buckwheat flour savoury pancake. Accompaniment to caviar (Russian)

boeuf French menu term for beef

boeuf Stroganoff thin strips of beef in a thick creamy sauce with mushrooms, tomato, onion, seasonings and flavoured with dry white wine, lemon juice and tarragon

boeuf braised, marinaded beef casserole made from braising steak, flavoured

bourguignonne with red wine and garnished with button onions and mushrooms, lardons of bacon and heart-shaped croûtons

bollito misto mixture of boiled meats

Bolognaise savoury meat sauce made from lean minced beef, demi-glace (a half glaze basic brown sauce), red wine, onion, tomato and seasonings including garlic

bombe an ice cream dessert made by using two different types of ice cream mixtures

bonito flaked dried tuna used to make Japanese broths and essential for 'dashi', a Japanese soup stock

bonne femme mushroom garnish for fish, with onions and bacon for chicken

bonne-bouche small savoury bite, often in a vol-au-vent case

bordelaise rich brown sauce flavoured with red wine

borlotti dry speckled haricot bean used in dips and salads

Bortsch rich duck flavoured consommé of East European origin

bouchées small sweet or savoury puff pastry bites, being a minature version of a vol-au-vent

boudin French version of the British black or white pudding with the black containing pigs' blood while the white may have chicken, veal or pork

bouillabaise Mediterranean fish soup made by the stewing method with the most popular version coming from Marseilles

bouillon unclarified meat or vegetable stock

bouillon, court made up liquor for cooking (poaching) fish. Seasonings may include sliced root vegetables, peppercorns, bayleaf, rosemary and condiments

bouquet aroma or smell, e.g. of an improving wine

bouquet garni bundle of herbs such as parsley, thyme, bay leaf and peppercorns used to flavour stews, casseroles, stocks and sauces

bourbon American whiskey made from a fermented cereal (maize) base

bourride garlic flavoured fish stew from the Provence region of France

braisé French menu/cookery term denoting 'braising' of a joint or portion of meat

braising pan (bisière) covered cooking dish

brandy spirit distilled from wine using the 'pot still' method

brasserie small restaurant and bar where food and drinks are served. French in origin

breadcrumb (paner) to cover a piece of fish, meat, poultry, etc. with breadcrumbs after first dipping it in seasoned flour, then in beaten egg or melted butter

breathe to allow a wine to come into contact with the air upon removal of the cork, which then enhances the bouquet

brioche soft, light textured roll or bun made from eggs, butter, flour and yeast

brochette, en indicates grilling on a skewer, e.g. kebab, which is Turkish in origin and often served on a bed of braised rice

brodo Italian term for stock, a base ingredient in soups, sauces and casseroles

broyer to crush or grind finely

brunch late morning meal that often replaces both breakfast and lunch

brunoise a name used to describe vegetables, ham or chicken cut into tiny dice

bruschetta toasted or baked slices of bread, oiled and sprinkled with herbs and served as an appetiser

brut Champagne/sparkling wine label term indicating very dry

bulgur part-cooked cracked wheat

Burgundy wine producing region of France, also a smooth, soft, dry red wine from that same region

busboy/girl American term indicating a person who carries out clearing duties in a food and beverage service area and also used as a general term meaning waiter or server

C

caffeine bitter white alkaloid found in tea, cocoa and coffee and used as a stimulant

Cajun French/American cuisine where the key ingredients used are capsicum, onion, celery and peppers

calamari French menu term for squid and classified as a mollusc

canapés small pieces of bread, usually toasted and of varying shapes, or dry cracker/water biscuits, covered with a variety of savoury items and then served as appetisers

cane spirit clear spirit distilled from sugar cane, e.g. rum

cannellini beans creamy white kidney beans, having a slightly fluffy texture and mainly used in Italian cooking

cannelloni type of pasta shaped in large rolls, normally stuffed with cheese, meat and minced vegetables, covered with a cheese sauce and then baked in the oven (Italian)

cannoli Sicilian pastry tubes filled with ricotta cheese, chocolate and candied peel

canteen style of restaurant found in a school, hospital or industrial catering where the style of service is usually self-service. This term may also indicate a temporary or mobile eating place set up in an emergency

Cantonese form of cuisine usually found in westernised restaurants and is one of the five main styles of Chinese cuisine

capsicum peppers, either sweet or hot, available in many colours and sizes

carafe form of glass bottle or jug used for the service of wine or water at the table. May also be defined as a decanter

caramel sugar heated until browned, also known as Black Jack

caramelise (carameliser) to line a mould thinly with caramel sugar, or to coat fruit with, or dip it in, cracked sugar. Also to slowly brown sugar or foods such as onions and carrots over heat

carbonara spaghetti sauce of egg, bacon and parmesan

carbonnade beef braised in beer and brown stock and seasoned with garlic

carciofo globe artichoke

carpaccio originally thin slices of raw red meat, now also applied to fish

carpet bag steak fillet steak, filled with oysters, then sealed and grilled

carré French menu term indicating the 'best end' of lamb which is made up of all the lamb cutlets

carte du jour card or menu of the day

carte, à la menu where all dishes are individually priced and often cooked or finished to order

cassata ice cream dessert made up of layers of different flavoured ice creams, usually three, and mixed with glace fruits flavoured with liqueur

casserole, a style of stew cooked in a casserole dish

casserole, dish fireproof earthenware dish, round or oval in shape, with a lid

Cava term used to indicate Spanish sparkling wines made by the traditional method

caviar roe of the female sturgeon and named after the species of sturgeon that provides it, e.g. Sevruga or Beluga

cayenne hot red pepper derived from a species of powdered capsicum. An accompaniment with oysters and smoked salmon

célestine strips of savoury pancake; a garnish found in consommé

centilitres hundredths of a litre of liquid

chafing dish style of frying pan used on a flare lamp for cooking at the table or to maintain the warmth of food

champignons French menu term for mushrooms

chantilly whipped cream with sugar and vanilla

chapatti thin flat cake of coarse unleavened bread, Indian in origin. Accompanies various curries

char grill cooking food on a grill which has coke or coals over an artificial electric or gas heat source

charcuterie cold, cooked and cured meat products, especially pork, such as pâtés, hams, sausages and bacon

chard spinach-like leaves with thick, white edible ribs

charlotte moulded dessert of pastry cream, custard, mousse or puréed fruit

charsiu Chinese glazed pork fillet

chartreuse herb-flavoured, brandy-based liqueur

chartreuse, en feathered game served with cabbage

Chateaubriand double fillet steak cut from the head of the fillet of beef

chaudfroid sauce for cold buffet work; a jellied brown or white sauce used as an aspic to decorate and garnish cold meats and fish

chemiser to line a mould

chermoula Moroccan fish marinade

chervil green leafed herb used in seasoning, especially in French cuisine, with a flavour similar to anise (aniseed)

chèvre goat's milk cheese

chiffonade salad leaves (lettuce) or vegetables, cut in fine shreds, used in prawn cocktail or as a vegetable dish, e.g. chou (cabbage)

chilli con carne stew of minced meat, normally beef, chillies and purple kidney beans. Mexican in origin

chilli sauce mainly a Chinese-made hot sauce, offered with Chinese-style foods

Chinese green teas most familiar as the teas served in Chinese restaurants. The tea leaves are unfermented and produce a very pale drink with a mild and fruity flavour

chine backbone of beef, lamb, pork or venison with meat attached

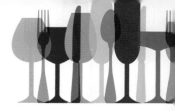

Chingkiang dark rice wine vinegar of Chinese origin and similar to Balsamic

chinois conical strainer (also known as Chinese Hat)

chioca yams

chives herb (fresh chopped)

choisum Chinese greens with yellow flowers

chop suey Chinese-style dish consisting of small pieces of chicken or meat cooked with bean sprouts and other vegetables and served with a savoury rice

chorizo spicy pork meat and fat sausage, flavoured with garlic, paprika and pimento and of Spanish origin

choucroûte see 'sauerkraut' – pickled cabbage

choux pastry for sweet fillings; used for éclairs and profiteroles

chow mein Chinese dish made up of varying combinations of stewed meat and vegetables and served with fried noodles

chowder creamy thick soup or stew made from shellfish, especially clams, and vegetables, e.g. Clam Chowder

chutney generic name for Indian sauces. Common varieties are sweet mango or hot mango, also Piccalilli and the proprietary Branston pickle. Indian chutneys may be used for Tandoori and other Indian dishes, while other chutneys may accompany cold meats or cheeses

ciabatta broad, white Italian bread, made with wheat flour and yeast

cilantro term used for coriander in the USA and Canada

citron French menu term for lemon

civet game stew, usually related to hare

clafouti baked batter tart usually filled with cherries

claret traditionally a red wine from Bordeaux, the wine producing region in France

clarified impurities removed from butter, stock, soup or jelly

cloche dish cover (usually bell-shaped) with a handle at the top, used to cover food and keep it hot until served at the table

cloud ears form of dried Chinese mushroom used in soups, fish and chicken dishes

clouted (orange) an orange studded with cloves, as used in mulled wine

coat (napper) to cover a dish or sweet entirely with a sauce, a jelly or a cream. To mask, to dip

cocotte small, round, fireproof, earthenware dish for cooking an egg, e.g. oeuf en cocotte. Also used to describe a larger oval casserole with a lid for slow cooking chicken, ragoût (brown stew,) etc.

Cognac quality brandy from the Cognac region of south-west France

compôte fruit poached in a sugar/fruit syrup and recognised as stewed fruit

concassé roughly chopped (tomato), having many uses in French cuisine, e.g. sauces, stews, salads, garnishes

condé cold sweet made up of poached fruit (pears) on a creamed rice base

condiment seasoning offered to a customer to give added flavour/contrast to a dish served, e.g. salt and pepper, horseradish sauce

confit virtually boneless meat (game, duck, goose or pork) cooked slowly in their own juices and fat

confiture French menu term for jam

consommé clear soup made from beef or chicken stock and may be served hot or cold, with various garnishes added

coque, à la soft boiled in its shell, e.g. eggs

coquilles Saint-Jacques scallops

coral roe or eggs of some shellfish

corbeille denotes a 'basket', usually of fresh fruit and nuts and offered as an alternative to the sweet course

cordial fruit-based, sweet, non-alcoholic drink. Also term for concentrated fruit squash, such as lime cordial

coriander sometimes known as Chinese parsley, this herb has a fresh taste, similar to orange and is an important ingredient in curry

corkage charge made for opening and serving bottles of wine brought into a restaurant by customers

corked spoilt wine due to a faulty or mouldy cork, or because of bad storage

cos lettuce sometimes called romaine lettuce, this has long, slender, crisp but coarse leaves and is mainly used in salads and for garnishing

cotechino Italian in origin, this is a sausage made with lean and fat pork, white wine and spices and is often served hot with beans

coulis purée of fruit or vegetable, used to garnish and decorate

courgette British term for a 'baby' or miniature marrow. Called 'zucchini' in America and often termed 'Italian squash' in Italy

court bouillon seasoned poaching liquid, usually for fish

couscous cereal processed from semolina into tiny pellets and originating in North Africa

couvert a cover; number of guests at a function; a place setting for a guest for a set meal; a place setting for a specific dish ordered

couverture confectioner's chocolate which may be sweet or semi-sweet and used in baking, coating, ornamental work and sauce making

cover charge an additional charge added to the customer's bill

crème Anglaise rich custard sauce, of pouring consistency, to accompany a sweet

crème brûlée thick, smooth and rich custard with a covering of caramelised sugar

crème fraîche thick cream that has had a 'culture' added to it. Available either plain or in varying fruit flavours

crème pâtissière custard or pastry cream, thickened with flour or other starch

crêpe thin pancake with sweet or savoury filling

crevettes French menu term for shrimp

croissant crescent-shaped roll, made from a yeast-based Danish pastry dough

croquettes minced fowl, game, meat, fish, mashed potato or vegetables bound with a sauce, seasoned and shaped like a cork, then flour, egg and bread crumbed and deep fried

cross-contamination transfer of bacteria to food from another food, equipment or work surface

crostini bread canapés, see 'canapés'

croustades deep, scalloped, tartlet cases with either sweet or savoury fillings

croûte bread or pastry crust

croûtons fried bread used as a garnish, cut into small cubes for soups and some salad dishes, e.g. Caesar salad; also cut into a variety of fancy shapes for other dishes, e.g. heart-shaped croûtons

crudités served as an appetiser and made up of small pieces (batons) of vegetable, such as carrot and courgette, with an accompanying savoury dip

crumb down to brush debris (crumbs) from the tablecloth between courses

crustacean shellfish having a segmented body and limbs, e.g. lobsters, crabs, shrimps, crayfish, Dublin Bay prawn

cuisine minceur cooking method where low calorie ingredients are used to replace traditional rich foods of the French cuisine

Cumberland sauce sweet and sour sauce, with orange and lemon juice and zest, redcurrant jelly and port amongst its ingredients. Used as accompaniment for cold game dishes and charcuterie

D

dacquoise layers of meringue with whipped cream or butter cream and fresh berries

daikon large, white radish, sometimes called the Japanese pickled radish and often eaten with fish. Can be grated and used as a garnish

dariole small, tin-lined, cylindrical-shaped mould made from copper or aluminium, having sweet or savoury items baked in it, e.g. crème caramel

darne thick slice from a round fish, including the central bone

dashi Japanese soup stock made from bonito flakes and konbu seaweed and combined with 'miso' to produce miso soup

daube, en method of cooking meat (stews of beef or mutton) very slowly in the oven, in a hermetically sealed dish (daubière) to preserve its full flavour

dauphinoise sliced potatoes baked in cream (or milk and cheese), seasoned with nutmeg and garlic

decant to pour a wine or other liquor, slowly, off the sediment in its container with the aid of muslin or filter papers

deglaze dissolve caramelised sediment in a roasting pan by adding wine or stock

dégorger to soak fish or sometimes vegetables to remove impurities

délice French menu term denoting a trimmed and folded fillet of fish, e.g. Délice de sole

demi-glace refined Espagnole (basic brown sauce). Smooth glossy sauce of pouring consistency used as base for other sauces, soups and stews

demi-tasse half-cup (espresso coffee cup)

dépouiller to remove skin or scum formed on top of liquid

dessert fresh fruit and nuts served from the fruit basket, but nowadays it also means the choice of sweets available from the menu

dessert wine style of sweet wine, e.g. Sauternes, Muscat, Auslese; often offered with the dessert (sweet) course

devilled – à la diable applied to fried or grilled fish or meat prepared with the addition of very hot condiments (cayenne pepper) and sometimes a highly seasoned and spiced sauce

dhal thick purée of lentils offered as an accompanying dish with curry

digestif any alcoholic liquor served as an after dinner drink, e.g. liqueurs, brandy, port

dim sum Chinese meal consisting of a variety of hot snacks

donburi Japanese dish of a bowl of rice topped with leftovers

dorer egg wash pastry or bread goods with yolk of egg beaten with water. Some bread goods may be brushed with milk

du jour French menu term literally translated as meaning 'of the day', e.g. carte du jour, which lists an establishment's daily menus

Dubarry garnished with or containing cauliflower

dum Indian method of steaming, especially for pilau rice

dumb waiter indicates either the sideboard found in a food service area or the small lift that sends food from the kitchen to the dining room or to hotel floors

duxelles finely chopped mushrooms and shallots, sweated in butter and used as a stuffing or flavouring in sauces or as a garnish

E

earthenware type of strengthened china much used in the hospitality industry

elver young eel

embrocher to place on a spit for spit roasting or on skewers for grilling or frying

en cocotte cooked in a round, earthenware dish. May be egg (oeuf en cocotte) or meat (pot-roasted)

en papillote French menu term indicating fish or meat baked in a greaseproof bag in the oven

endive vegetable with a slightly sharp taste used in salads or braised; known in Britain as chicory and endive in France and America

Entrecôte steak of beef coming from the boned out sirloin (contrefilet de boeuf)

entrée meat dish served with a sauce and made up of small cuts of butcher's meat or poultry, frequently served as a main course, e.g. garnished cutlets, sweetbreads

entremets sweet course on the everyday menu and includes a selection of mainly cold sweets and a limited number of hot dishes

escalopes thin slices of flattened and boneless veal, beef or pork. Veal escalopes come from the fillet or cushion of veal, pork from the fillet or boned out pork loin and beef from the boned out sirloin

étuver method of simmering food very slowly in butter, or very little liquid, in a closed casserole, e.g. Chou étuvée

Evian brand of sparkling spring water from France

F

falafel rissoles made from dried broad beans, shallow fried and served with a piquant sauce

faraona Italian term for guinea fowl with a slight tanginess of game, reminiscent of pheasant. May be roasted, braised or casseroled

farce cuisine term for a savoury stuffing

fennel bulbous leafstalk which can be used raw with salads or braised whole and served as a vegetable, sometimes with a cheese sauce. The aniseed tasting leaves are traditionally used with fish dishes while the aromatic dried seeds of the fennel plant are used in fish dishes, curries and apple pie

fenugreek seeds of this plant are ground and used as a spice in curries and chutneys. Associated mainly with Indian cuisine

fettuccine thin ribbons of pasta similar to tagliatelle, available in a green and white version, the green being mixed with a spinach purée

feuillantine puff pastry strips brushed with egg, sprinkled with sugar and baked

feuilletage puff pastry used to produce savoury and sweet dishes, e.g. vol-au-vent, bouchées, tranche, cream horns and many others

feuilleté triangle-shaped puff pastry case

fèves broad beans, often served bound in a cream sauce

filet mignon comes from the fillet of lamb and is also used to indicate a small round fillet steak cut from the whole beef fillet

filo pastry thin and crisp paper-like pastry, used in the making of sweet dishes, mince pies, fruit filled filo pastry cases, etc.

fine champagne one of the best styles of Cognac and indicative of quality

fines herbes mixed herbs. The traditional French blend being chives, tarragon, parsley and chervil finely chopped together

flageolet small, pale-green kidney bean

flambé to cook or finish cooking a dish at the table and then 'flaming' it by pouring a spirit or liqueur over, e.g. brandy, rum

fleûrons crescents and other fancy shapes of baked puff pastry used to garnish a variety of dishes such as entrées, poached fish and shellfish dishes

float sum of money of varying denominations placed in a till prior to service commencing

flûte stemmed glass with a tall but narrow bowl and used in the service of sparkling wines. The shape assists in retaining the sparkle (effervescence) of the wine

focaccia flat, round, flavoured Italian bread

foie de veau French menu term denoting calves liver and may be served with onions (Lyonnaise) or with bacon (au lard)

foie gras liver of specially fattened geese, either served as a piece or used to make a pâté

forestière garnished with mushrooms

fortified wine wine whose alcoholic strength is increased by the addition of alcohol, usually brandy, e.g. sherry and port. Called liqueur wine in the EU

four, au baked in an oven

frappé chilled, e.g. melon frappé or crème de menthe frappé

French dresssing made from oil and usually wine vinegar or lemon juice and seasonings. Mustards and herbs may be added. Used to dress salads

friandises another name for petit four and offered at the end of the meal with coffee. See also 'petit four' and 'sweetmeats'

fricassée white stew in which poultry, pork, veal or rabbit is cooked in a thickened sauce throughout the cooking period

frittata flat, unfolded omelette

froid cold. Applies to any item of food or liquor served cold or chilled

fromages, assortis French menu term meaning assortment of cheeses

frost to decorate a glass by dipping its rim in lemon juice and then caster sugar that may be coloured. Applicable to certain cocktails

fruits de mer fruits of the sea. French menu term indicating an assortment of sea foods

fumé denotes smoked when used on the menu, e.g. Truite fumé

fumet stock from fish, meat, game or poultry and the basis for sauces, stews, soups, etc.

funghi Italian term for wild mushrooms, the cep being the most well known and is a quality tasting mushroom eaten widely in Europe

fusil sharpening steel

G

gailan Chinese spring greens

galangal root spice related to the ginger family, used in Thai cuisine and has a faint flavour of camphor. Available in root or powder form and is used in the Far East in curries and in Malay dishes

galantine cold dish of poultry or meat, boned, stuffed, braised in concentrated stock and then coated with aspic and garnished

galette flat, round, sweet or savoury cake or biscuit

ganache cake filling or topping made from couverture and whipping cream and may also be used for warm piping or cold modelling

garnish any ingredient which decorates, accompanies or completes a dish. Many dishes are identified by the name of their garnish, e.g. chicken Maryland (corn fritters, sautée banana, grilled bacon rolls and tomatoes), horseradish sauce would be offered separately

gastrique caramelised sugar and vinegar mixture used to flavour sauces

gâteau usually a rich sponge cake that may be decorated and flavoured in a wide variety of ways, e.g. Gâteau Moka (coffee gâteau); certain gâteaux do not have sponge bases, e.g. Gâteau MacMahon (shortbread base) or Gâteau St Honoré (puff pastry and choux pastry base)

gazpacho cold soup of puréed tomato, cucumber, onion, red pepper and garlic. Sometimes garnished with croûtons

gelato soft whipped ice cream (Italian), available in a variety of flavours

genoise very rich and light sponge cake made from equal quantities of egg, caster sugar and soft white flour, plus a small quantity of melted butter

Gentlemen's Relish proprietary brand of anchovy paste, butter, herbs and spices. Used mainly as a spread, often on canapés

ghee Indian term denoting clarified butter and is the yellow liquid left when the sediment has been removed

gibier game, e.g. pheasant, partridge, grouse

ginger spicy root used in many forms, ground ginger being the most common but pickled whole ginger may also be found, the former offered with melon and the latter used with sushi

glacé French menu term for ice cream

glaze (glacer) to dust a cake or sweet with icing sugar and brown under a grill; to simmer vegetables

that are cut into fancy shapes in butter until they have a glossy coating; to give meat a glossy appearance by frequent basting; to give cold dishes, cakes and sweets a shiny appearance by coating with aspic or jelly that is on the point of setting

gluhwein spicy mulled wine served hot, the main ingredients being red wine, caster sugar, lemon, orange, nutmeg, cinnamon and vanilla sticks

gluten protein substance found in cereal grains, mainly wheat, and used as a flour substitute

gnocchi farinaceous (pasta) type dish, made from a starch base that may be flour, semolina, potatoes or maize flour. Italian in origin

gomme syrup white sugar syrup used as a flavouring ingredient in certain cocktails, e.g. whisky sour and in fruit cups

gosht Indian term indicating meat

gougère ring of choux pastry with savoury filling, often cheese

goujons French menu term denoting thin strips of fillet of fish, e.g. goujons de sole, prepared by dipping in seasoned flour, beaten egg and breadcrumbs (pané), then deep fried

goulache casserole of stewing meat, either beef, veal, lamb, pork or mutton and onions, flavoured with paprika and tomato

grana grating cheese

gratin, au a dish that has been sprinkled with grated cheese, possibly mixed with breadcrumbs and a little

butter, and then browned under a grill or in a hot oven. May also simply mean a sweet or savoury dish that is browned under a grill

gravadlax/gravlax raw salmon cured in sugar, salt, pepper and dill

gremolata combination of lemon zest, parsley, garlic, tomato concassé and seasoning used to garnish osso buco (knuckle of veal casserole)

griottines morello cherries, usually preserved in alcohol

grissini long, thin and crisp bread sticks offered as alternatives to rolls (Italian)

gros sel coarse or rock salt, this is a less refined salt than table salt. Offered with boiled beef and also widely used in table grinders

guacamole spicy avocado sauce with tomato, onion, hot green chilli, cilantro (the fresh leaves of the coriander plant), lemon juice and cream added to the mashed flesh of the avocado

guéridon trolley or service side table on which food is served or prepared and cooked at the customer's table

gumbo spicy casserole of seafood and vegetables, including okra (thickening agent). In the USA this term applies to any dish incorporating okra as one of its ingredients

gurnard small round salt water fish known as the 'sea robin', e.g. Red gurnard and Ray gurnard; may be braised or baked

H

HACCP Hazard Analysis Critical Control Point, a food safety self-inspection system

hacher French term meaning to mince or finely chop meat such as stewing beef, e.g. hachis de boeuf (savoury beef mince)

haggis traditional Scottish dish made of oatmeal, chopped offal of either a sheep or calf and seasonings and boiled in the stomach lining of the animal

halal meat killed and prepared according to Muslim law

Haldi Indian term for turmeric. See 'turmeric'

halloumi goats milk cheese

hang to keep freshly killed meat or game in a cool place and exposed to the air, for a period of time, until it becomes more tender and improves in flavour

harissa red chilli paste of medium strength that has been seasoned with cloves of garlic, coriander, cumin, caraway seeds and dried mint, used in the North African dish of couscous and also in Moroccan cuisine

harusame transparent, rice-flour noodles

hash browns dish of American origin made up of puréed potato and onion, bound with egg, shaped and fried

haute cuisine originally a French term meaning highest standard of cooking and service

Hawthorn strainer essential piece of equipment in the cocktail bar and used in conjunction with the Boston shaker and bar mixing glass when making cocktails

hock English name for German wines produced in the vineyards along the banks of the river Rhine

hoisin sauce made from soy, flour, vinegar, garlic, sesame, salt and pepper

Hollandaise egg yolk and butter-based sauce. This or one of its derivatives may be offered with grilled steaks, e.g. sauce béarnaise

Hollands A Dutch style of gin made from malted barley and rye and double distilled in a pot still. Often sold in stone bottles

homard lobster

homardine white wine sauce finished with lobster butter and garnished with diced lobster

hors d'oeuvre an appetizer or starter; may be hot or cold

horseradish sauce hot-tasting sauce made from the horseradish root. Often needs cream adding. Traditional accompaniment with roast beef and

chicken Maryland and also for cold smoked fish dishes when creamed down

house wine red, white or rosé wine recommended by the establishment as being acceptable to the average palate and sold at a modest price. May be served by the glass, half bottle or bottle and sometimes by the carafe

---

Indian pickles unsweetened hot pickles, featuring limes, mango, brinjals, etc. An accompaniment for Indian (and other) savoury dishes

infuse to soak ingredients, e.g. herbs, tea leaves, in liquid to impart flavour

insalata indicates salad, either served as a dish in its own right or used as a garnish to decorate a particular dish (Italian)

Irish coffee liqueur coffee made using Irish whiskey, sugar and floating double cream over the surface

---

J

jaggery unrefined sugar

jalousie baked pastry tart topped with latticed pastry strips

jambonette ham and pork sausage-like dish

jambonneau small leg – applied to poultry

jardinière matchstick-shape cut of spring vegetables, used as a garnish or as a vegetable dish

Jasmine tea Chinese green tea scented with jasmine flowers

Jeroboam large bottle holding the equivalent of four standard size (75 cl) bottles

joue beef or pork cheek

jugged hare traditional hare dish made with red wine marinated hare cooked in a casserole with a little red wine, vegetables and seasoning added to this and its blood being added at intervals to flavour and thicken the sauce

julienne foods, especially vegetables, cut into fine, even strips

jus juice, e.g. fruit juice or juice extracted from roasted meats

jus lié thickened gravy

K

kasundi hot Indian pickle featuring chopped mango. Accompaniment for Indian (and other) savoury dishes

kebab Turkish term equivalent to the French 'en brochette' meaning grilling on skewers

kedgeree savoury dish of cooked rice mixed with hard-boiled egg, smoked fish (usually haddock) and may be flavoured with either turmeric or saffron

ketjap manis thick and sweetened derivative of soy sauce and the main condiment in the Far East and China; used in place of salt

khao niao glutinous rice from Thailand which, when boiled, becomes sweet and sticky and is used mainly in confectionery and baking

khoresh meat stew with fruit and nuts

khoshaf macerated dried fruit salad containing apricots, raisins and almonds

kilojoule (kj) the metric measure of the 'energy' contained in food

knead (fraiser) to work dough on a pastry board or marble slab with the ball of the hand

kohlrabi turnip/cabbage style vegetable that is either purple or green in colour and has a swollen, edible stem with a delicate turnip flavour; boiled or grated and used in salads

konafa Turkish pastry which resembles shredded wheat

korma mild, spicy, meat casserole that is cooked in a rich coconut sauce and originates from northern India

Kosher meat killed, and food prepared and served according to Jewish dietary laws

kulebyaka Russian salmon and rice pie

kulfi Indian ice cream made from reduced milk

kway teow Malaysian flat noodles

L

lady's fingers originating from Africa and indicates okra or gumbo. Used to thicken soups and stews and also eaten as a vegetable

lager bottom fermented beer

laifen type of Chinese tubular noodles

lait, au denotes 'with milk' as in café au lait

laksa noodle and seafood soup from Malaysia

langouste denotes a crawfish and is almost the size of a lobster but clawless. Prepared and cooked like lobster and classified as a crustacean

langoustine scampi, classified as a crustacean. See 'scampi'

lard (larder – piquer) to draw strips of larding bacon through the middle of a piece of meat by means of a larding tube (larder). To lard the surface by means of a larding needle (piquer)

lardon strip of bacon or pork fat that may be used to enhance the flavour of raw meat during its cooking process and also used as a garnish in salads and with vegetables

lasagne large flat pieces of ribbon pasta made with whole wheat dough or with the addition of puréed spinach (lasagne verdi)

légume vegetable with seeds in a pod, such as peas, broad beans, mange tout and lentils

lentil type of bean, rich in protein and the basic ingredient of dhal (a side dish to curry). Also produces a thick soup

levin starter dough made from live yeast and flour

linguini pasta cut into long and very thin, flat strands

liqueur sweetened and flavoured spirit, sometimes termed a digestif

loin joint of meat, either lamb, pork or veal, that may be boned, seasoned, rolled and tied and stuffed if required. All regarded as first class roasting joints

lumpfish roe eggs of the lumpfish and often referred to (incorrectly) as caviar, available in both orange and black varieties. Usually from Iceland

lyonnaise sauce sauce of chopped onions sautéed in butter with wine vinegar and demi glace

lyonnaise, à la denotes a garnish or sauce of onions, e.g. pommes lyonnaise or foie de veau sauté, sauce lyonnaise

M

macaroon chewy almond flavoured biscuits made with caster sugar, egg whites and ground almonds and sometimes coconut

macchiato extra strong espresso coffee served with a dash of cold milk

mace outer covering of nutmeg

macédoine small, evenly cut dice of vegetables or fruit, e.g. macédoine de légumes

macerate to pickle briefly, to steep, to soak or to souse

magret boneless breast of the mallard duck

maître d'hôtel herb butter containing parsley and lemon juice and served with grilled

butter meats

malt cereal grain, the best is barley, soaked in water to germinate and then dried by hot air. The duration and intensity of this drying process (kilning) produces different coloured malts, from pale malt to black malt. The degree of kilning determines the type of beer to be produced, e.g. pale malt makes pale ale

mancha powdered green tea

mandolin manual vegetable slicer

mange tout thin, flat, green pea that is eaten whole after topping, tailing and cooking

mantecato the action of beating butter and Parmesan into risotto (Italian)

marbling fat deposited within muscle tissue

marinade seasoned liquid used for flavouring and tenderising raw fish, meat poultry and game

marinate to soak fish, meat, poultry and game for a short while to improve flavour and make more tender, in a marinade

marjoram perennial seasoning herb with a very delicate flavour and very similar to oregano. Appears in many French and Italian dishes, especially tomato-based sauces

marmite, petite beef and chicken flavoured clear soup (consommé) and also the name given to the container in which the soup is served

marron chestnuts that may be eaten raw, roasted, boiled or preserved in sugar and then glazed in syrup, e.g. marron glacé

Marsala fortified (or liqueur) wine from Sicily, classified as a dessert wine and used mainly in cooking

Martini brand of Vermouth, which is an aromatised wine that has been fortified. May be red, white or rosé and dry or sweet (Bianco)

masalas aromatic spice blend originating from India and known as masalas, it may be mild or strong. Ingredients of the blend may include pepper, ginger, turmeric, coriander, cumin, clove and chillies, e.g. garam masala

matelote French freshwater fish stew made with red or white wine

mayonnaise made from a combination of oil and egg yolks, flavoured with vinegar, herbs and seasonings. An accompaniment for cold poached fish and salads and provides a base for other sauces such as tartare sauce

meat glaze (glace de viande) boiled down bone broth of marrow bones, etc., and reduced to the thickness of jelly. Used for glazing cooked meats to improve appearance and flavour

médaillon small round cut of meat that may also be termed a 'rosette' and is cut from the boned out, rolled and tied loin of lamb. Often sautéed

melba toast very thin, curled toast, made either by splitting toasted bread, after removing the crusts and toasting the untoasted sides or from toasting very thin sliced bread

membrillo quince paste

mesquite tree from America, the wood of which is used for barbecuing

méthode Champenoise process by which French Champagne is made

meunière menu term that denotes shallow fried, e.g. filet de plie meunière

mignonette coarsely crushed peppercorns

mille-feuille gâteau puff pastry cake filled with jam and whipped cream and decorated on the surface with fondant

millet a grain native to Africa and Asia

mineral water water containing various minerals and said to promote health. May be still or sparkling

minestrone Italian soup containing a wide variety of assorted vegetables, vermicelli and herbs in a meat or vegetable broth

minute steak thin, tender steak, often cut from the sirloin and sometimes termed an Entrecôte minute. May be fried or grilled, but very quickly (for a minute) to seal the outsides without overcooking the interior

mirepoix garnish of diced, browned onions, carrots, celery and bacon, with various herbs and used to flavour stocks, soups, sauces and stews

mirin sweet Japanese rice wine, used in sukiyaki and Japanese sauces

mise-en-place French term meaning 'to put in place'. Refers to preparation beforehand, this includes all the tasks that have to be completed to get a food service area or kitchen ready for service

miso salted and fermented soy bean paste available in red or yellow, enhances the taste of many dishes

mitsuba Japanese green leaf used as a herb

mizuna salad leaf with a peppery flavour

mocha Arabica type of coffee bean. Produces a very strongly flavoured coffee. Originally from the old port of Mocha in Yemen

moelle beef marrow

monté to enrich by incorporating butter, egg yolks, cream

morilles edible fungus with a delicate flavour and sometimes termed the sponge mushroom, picked fresh during spring and early summer

mornay cheese sauce, normally made with milk and with dried mustard added to improve flavouring, e.g. Choufleur mornay

mortadella large Italian sausage that has been lightly smoked. The ingredients may consist of pork, garlic and seasonings

Moselle lively and crisp-tasting white wine produced in the vineyards lying along the banks of the river Mosel in Germany

moule French menu term denoting a mussel that may be steamed open and served in the half shell. Classified as a mollusc. Best known for its use in the classic dish moules marinière

moussaka dish of Greek origin, made of minced lamb or mutton, aubergine, tomato, onion, garlic and seasonings with a topping of cheese sauce and baked

mousse light and fluffy mixture, which is usually sweet to the palate and served cold, e.g. mousse aux frais (strawberry mousse)

mousseline light fish or meat purée strained extra fine and mixed with cream. Sauce mousseline is a derivative of sauce Hollandaise, having whipped cream added to the basic sauce, and is served with poached fish or vegetables

muddle cocktail-making term that indicates a number of ingredients being crushed together in the bottom of the bar mixing glass using the flat end (muddler) of the bar mixing spoon, e.g. mint and caster sugar

mulled wine red wine slowly heated, with sugar, citrus fruits and spices added to the liquor. Served hot

murgh Indian term for chicken

muselet wire muzzle used to clamp the cork of a bottle of sparkling wine securely in place

mushimono Japanese cuisine term for steaming a food item

mustard (English) generally the hottest. Available as a powder for making up or as a proprietary bottled sauce. May accompany roast beef, boiled beef, grills, cold meats and pâtés. Also used as an ingredient in dressings, e.g. vinaigrette

mustard (other) wide variety including French, au poivre, vert, Bordeaux, Meaux, Dijon, Douce, German (senf). Used with cold meats, grills and dressings

N

naan flat, but puffy and light leavened bread that may accompany curry

nage, à la cooked in a court bouillon

nam pla Thai fish sauce

nam prik Thai chilli sauce

nantua crayfish sauce

nappé to mask or coat evenly with a sauce or jelly, e.g. aspic used in cold buffet work

naturel, au in its natural state, e.g. plain boiled without additional flavouring, ingredients or garnish

navarin brown lamb or mutton stew with vegetables and potatoes

neat term relating to liquor and meaning undiluted, e.g. neat rum

niçoise French salad dish that traditionally includes green beans, tomatoes, potato, tuna, anchovies, olives and garlic

nimono Japanese cuisine term indicating a simmering technique

nip small measure, legally recognised, and usually of spirits, e.g. nip of whisky (25 ml or 50 ml)

noisette small cut of meat from the rib, usually lamb

nori thin, black seaweed sheets used in wrapping sushi; a Japanese sweetened vinegar rice

nose combination of the aroma and the bouquet of a wine when wine tasting

nouvelle cuisine form of French cooking that promotes lighter alternatives to replace the very rich dishes of the traditional classic French cuisine

O

oeuf en cocotte egg baked in its own dish (cocotte) in a bain-marie in the oven

oeuf mollet soft boiled and shelled egg, the boiling time being five minutes

offal the organs of animals, e.g. heart, liver, brains, kidneys, tongue, tail, tripe and sweetbreads

olive oil oil made from olive pressings and which is cholesterol free. Used in dressings

olives black or green fruit lightly pickled in brine. Used as an appetiser and also as a garnish for food and drinks

on-the-rocks poured over a quantity of cubed ice, e.g. scotch on-the-rocks

oregano perennial seasoning herb similar to marjoram that blends well with oil and vinegar salad dressings, French, Italian and Greek dishes and

tomato-based sauces

osso buco knuckle of veal casserole stewed in a dry white wine, tomato and vegetable sauce flavoured with garlic, chopped parsley, basil and thyme and traditionally served with rice

Ouzo aniseed flavoured spirit of Greek origin and similar to Pernod, coming under the heading of pastis (aniseed or liquorice flavoured spirits)

oyster shellfish usually eaten raw, the best coming from Colchester and Whitstable, and may be served either hot or cold. Classified as a mollusc

Oyster cruet group of accompaniments offered with oysters and comprises of cayenne pepper, peppermill, Tabasco sauce and chilli vinegar

oyster sauce brown sauce used in Chinese cuisine for flavouring various dishes

P

paella rice dish flavoured and coloured with saffron, containing chicken, shellfish, various vegetables including peas, pimento, garlic sausage, chopped garlic and seasonings. Cooked in chicken stock

pak choi Chinese white cabbage – classified as a brassica, this plant does not form a 'heart' and appears very similar to leaf spinach. Eaten raw in salads, but may also be stir fried with rice

pakora Indian term indicating a deep fried vegetable fritter

panada dough used to bind forcemeat that is made from flour, milk or water, eggs and butter

pancetta streaky bacon (Italian)

panée food item dipped in seasoned flour, egg and breadcrumbs, then either shallow or deep fried

paneer fresh milk curds used in Indian cookery

panna cotta cooked, rich, cream Italian dessert, similar to bavarois, the consistency of which is similar to a sauce sabayon

papillote paper wrapping to contain aroma and flavour when cooking meat or fish

pappardelle long, flat egg noodles with a crimped edge

paprika powdered mild, red spice produced from dried and ground sweet peppers (capsicum), giving an appealing flavour to food as well as a deep red colour, e.g. Hungarian goulash. Used as a garnish on and in seafood cocktails

parboil to partially cook in boiling liquid

parfait enriched ice cream made from a caster sugar, egg yolk and double cream base

Parma ham delicate tasting, cured Italian ham, served with salads or as a starter dish, e.g. melon and Parma ham

Parmesan very hard dry cheese of Italian origin. Used in Italian cooking and may be grated or shredded to accompany minestrone and for pasta dishes

passato puréed and sieved or strained

pasta pastes made from Durum wheat semolina flour in a variety of shapes and dried, e.g. macaroni, spaghetti, vermicelli, noodles, lasagne and ravioli

pastilla traditional Moroccan dish of pigeon pie in egg, lemon and onion sauce sweetened with almonds in pastry layers covered with cinnamon and sugar

pastis aniseed or liquorice flavoured alcoholic beverage such as ouzo and Pernod

pâté de foie gras made by blending together a fine paste of fattened goose livers and decorating/garnishing with truffles. See 'foie gras'

pâté maison pâté particular to the establishment (house) and made according to the chef's recipe

paupiettes thin slices of meat or fish filled with forcemeat (sausage meat stuffing) then rolled up, tied and braised in the oven. Usually of beef , veal or sole, e.g. paupiettes de boeuf braisés

pave a special cut of rump steak that is leaner and less sinewy than a traditional rump cut

Pavlova meringue cake filled with whipped cream and topped with fruit and may be served with a fruit coulis, e.g. raspberry

paysanne vegetables cut into small, very thin slices the size of a 1p piece and used as a garnish, e.g. consommé paysanne

peach Melba sweet dish of peaches, vanilla ice cream and a raspberry sauce (coulis). Decorated with whipped cream

pecorino ewe's milk cheese

peperonata pepper and vegetable stew (Italian)

peppercorns green are usually pickled in brine and soft. Used in various food dishes. White and black peppercorns may also be used. The black variety are generally used in peppermills for the table and sometimes mixed with white

pepperoni dry Italian sausage that is made up of coarsely chopped pork and beef and strongly seasoned with ground red pepper and other spices. Commonly used on pizzas

persillade chopped parsley spiked with crushed garlic

petit four wide variety of tiny, fancy, oven-cooked cakes or biscuits, but now used to also mean fruits dipped in chocolate or sugar syrups or other sweetmeats made up of such things as marzipan, ice cream, stuffed dates and fruits, shortbreads, etc. Offered with coffee and sometimes termed friandises

piatto plate or dish (Italian)

piccalilli mixed pickle in thickened, spiced sauce (predominantly turmeric and sugar). Accompanies cold meats, ploughman's lunch and light cold snacks. Also seen on the buffet

piccata Italian term denoting an escalope

pieds de mouton sheeps' trotters

pilaff dish of spiced rice braised in the oven and garnished with prawns, chicken livers, ham, mushroom or chicken. Literally translated, pilaff means braised savoury rice

pilau Indian version of pilaff and usually includes chicken, mutton or goats meat or a mixture of these and is well seasoned

pimento large, sweet red pepper

pimentón Spanish spice similar to paprika and made from the Spanish pepper which, in its fresh form, is more well known as the red stuffing inside green Spanish cocktail olives

pipe to force a soft mixture or dough through a forcing bag containing a plain or fancy nozzle. In liquor terms it also relates to a cask holding 523 litres (115 gallons) of port

piquant denotes spicy, sharp, appetising, a sharp flavour, a bite to the sauce or dish, e.g. sauce piquante (a combination of shallots, capers, gherkins, wine vinegar and fines herbes added to demi-glace)

piquer food items studded with fat, garlic, truffle, cloves, etc.

piri-piri hot chilli sauce of Portuguese/African origin. Accompanies chicken, prawns and crayfish

pirozhki small savoury pastries

pitta bread of Greek origin, sometimes called 'pocket bread' as it can be split open and filled. It is a double-layered bread that is flat and round or oval in shape

plancha, à la grilled on a griddle

poach (pocher) to simmer dishes in a mould in a bain-marie until done or to cook food in water that is kept just on boiling point (simmering), without actually letting it boil, e.g. oeuf poché

poêler to casserole in butter, in a covered dish, with the absolute minimum of liquid added together with diced root vegetables and is sometimes known as a pot roast. Used only for the better cuts of meat and poultry

point, à denotes medium degree of cooking of a grilled steak

polenta maize flour which is ground from Indian corn and can be eaten either as a type of porridge or used to garnish fish and meat dishes

pomme de terre potato

pont-neuf puff pastry filled with frangipane cream and macaroons. Pommes pont neuf are large, thick, deep fried, chipped potatoes

poppadum very fine, thin and crisp wafer-like pancake, made from lentil flour, deep fried or grilled and served with curry

pot roast joint of meat baked in the oven with stock and vegetables, in a covered pan or casserole dish. See 'poêler'

pot still traditional still used to distil cognacs, armagnacs, dark rums, tequila, calvados and malt whisky. The spirit is distilled in batches

pot-au-feu French dish of meat and vegetables cooked in stock – the broth is eaten first followed by the meat and vegetables as a main course

poulet French menu term for chicken, e.g. poulet rôti à l'Anglaise

poussin baby or young (spring) chicken weighing from 450–900 g (1–2 lb), that may be roasted, grilled, sautéed or baked. It is usual to serve one to a portion

praline almonds, sometimes with hazelnuts added, caramelised in sugar, then crushed and added to a variety of sweet dishes

preserves assorted jams that may be offered at either breakfast or afternoon tea, e.g. strawberry, raspberry, cherry, plum, marmalades

Prosecco term now used to indicate Italian sparkling wines

profiterole cold sweet dish of small choux pastry buns filled with whipped cream and coated with chocolate, either fondant or couverture

prosciutto Parma ham originating from Italy. A raw, delicate tasting cured ham that is sliced very thinly. See also 'Parma ham'

provençal sauce of tomatoes, onions and garlic sautéed in olive oil

Provençale, à la provincial or regional way or style and generally accepted as meaning cooked with garlic, onions and tomatoes

pumpernickel dark brown or black rye bread that may be used as a base for canapés

punch alcoholic beverage made from a wine base with spirits, liqueurs, fruit juices, lemonade, tisanes and fruit syrups added to enhance the taste. Can also be flavoured with spices, such as cloves, cinnamon and nutmeg and citrus fruits. Sometimes served hot

punt hollow found in the base of some wine bottles which strengthens the bottle, especially if a secondary fermentation takes place in the bottle itself, e.g. Champagne

purée to finely mash or pass food through a sieve or a thickened variety of soup, namely a purée

 Q

quail small game bird that may be roasted, grilled or sautéed. Often serve two birds per portion

quenelles oval-shaped. Also indicates light oval-shaped dumplings, made from various types of fine forcemeat, such as veal, chicken, game and fish, which are poached

quiche flan case filled with a savoury egg custard plus other added ingredients, such as vegetables, mushrooms and bacon

quince hard, yellow and acid tasting Asiatic fruit, with a delicate scent, which when cooked turns pink and is mainly used in preserves

R

râble French menu term indicating the saddle, and usually of hare

rack (of lamb) menu term indicating a joint made up of the lamb cutlets – a best end (the ribs) – usually roasted, e.g. carré d'agneau rôti

ragoût thick and rich brown stew/casserole of meat, usually beef or lamb and cooked with root vegetables, e.g. ragoût de boeuf

ragu basic meat sauce for pasta

raita yoghurt-based side dish of Indian origin

ramekin small earthenware, individual, circular baking dish holding one portion

rang French term indicating the team or brigade of food service staff and their level of authority within that team, e.g. commis de rang

rapini member of the broccoli family with a bitter, assertive flavour

rare degree of cooking of a grilled steak meaning underdone

Ras-el-hanout Moroccan spice mix used to flavour rice, couscous, and 'tagines', the slowly cooked stews common to Morocco

ratatouille Provençal vegetable stew of diced aubergine, tomato, courgettes, red and green peppers, onions and garlic, cooked in olive oil

ravioli small meat or vegetable filled pasta squares (Italian)

réchaud spirit lamp used for cooking at the table and to keep food warm

réchauffé reheated dish made with previously cooked ingredients

reduce to add wine or other liquid to the pan residue and simmer down to a desired consistency to concentrate flavours

rémoulade cold mayonnaise-based sauce containing capers, gherkins, anchovy essence, parsley and fines herb for flavouring

rillettes shredded belly of pork cooked in its own fat, mixed until smooth and potted. Sometimes has goose or rabbit added. French in origin

ripieno Italian stuffing

ris de veau calves sweetbreads that are pale in appearance and delicate in taste, coming from the thymus glands found in the neck and heart of young animals and are braised, fried or sautéed

risotto savoury rice containing vegetables, such as finely chopped onions, and a bouquet garni for flavouring, cooked in chicken stock

roast (rôtir) roast meat, poultry or game and vegetables, e.g. potato, parsnips

roe fish eggs, the soft herring roe having a creamy, smooth texture and is served as a savoury dish or garnish. Smoked cod's roe is used for taramasalata which is of Greek origin

romesco Catalonian sauce of tomato, almond, sherry, garlic and paprika

rösti grated and fried potatoes

roti of Indian origin and denoting bread. Usually a circular, flat unleavened bread similar to chapati

rôti French menu term indicating a roasted item, e.g. côte de porc rôti

rouille Provençale sauce made from pounded chillies, garlic and breadcrumbs (or cooked potatoes) blended with olive oil and fish stock. Accompanies boiled fish and fish soups such as bouillabaisse. If served with chicken bouillabaisse then chicken stock is used to make the sauce

roulade stuffed roll of food that may be sweet or savoury, e.g. thin slice of meat stuffed and rolled – paupiette de boeuf, or a thin, flat sponge spread with jam and whipped cream and rolled Swiss roll style

roux mix of flour and butter cooked together slowly until white, blonde or brown in colour and used to thicken soups and sauces

royale, à la French menu term denoting a garnish for a soup, e.g. consommé royale (diced savoury egg custard)

rye cereal used in the making of bread and also used in its fermented form in the making of American whiskey

S

sabayon French term meaning a dessert sauce and used to thicken, enrich and improve the appearance of various dishes. Together with Marsala and caster sugar produces the Italian sweet zabaglione

sablé French shortbread

sachertorte rich chocolate cake, coated in ganache with apricot jam

saffron spice used for flavouring, produced from the stigmas of the crocus. Colours food bright yellow and is a key ingredient in paella, bouillabaisse and the liqueur Chartreuse

saké originating from Japan, this is a slightly sweet, colourless rice beer, usually served warm but may also be served chilled

salamander grill with top heat and used for browning and cooking

salami strongly seasoned sausage of Italian origin and served cold. Made from beef, pork and pork fat and seasoned with garlic and pepper, often used for antipasto and in hors d'oeuvres

salmis game birds and ducks, skinned and boned after roasting, placed in a rich, brown, red wine flavoured sauce and served as a game stew

salpicon mixture of foods cut into a small dice, bound with a sauce and used as a filling, e.g. salpicon de volaille (salpicon of chicken)

salsa Mexican in origin but nowadays means an uncooked tomato-based relish flavoured in varying degrees by onion, cilantro and chillies

salsify white root vegetable with oyster-like flavour

sambal sharp, spicy and vinegary sauce or chutney of raw vegetables or fruit, used as a relish or in cookery. Comparable to chutneys in Indian cuisine

samosa small, pastry-coated food item with a spicy meat or vegetable filling and deep fried

sansho prickly ash powder sprinkled on grilled meat

sashimi Japanese origin, this term indicates sliced fish eaten raw

satay cubes of fish or meat on a skewer and grilled over a charcoal grill, served with a thick peanut flavoured sauce

sauce gribiche cold sauce, mayonnaise based and mixed with capers, gherkins, hard-boiled egg whites and seasonings

sauerkraut (choucroûte) pickled, finely shredded white cabbage served hot with bacon and sausages. National dish of Germany and Alsace in France

sauté shallow fry in butter, with a little oil added, to a golden brown colour

sauter quick cooking process, to brown quickly in a sauté or frying pan, or toss in fat anything that requires quick cooking at considerable heat

sauteuse shallow pan with sloping sides and a lid, in which food may first be fried and then braised

savarin circular yeast sponge cake, often soaked in a rum-flavoured syrup and filled with fresh fruit salad, e.g. savarin au fruits

scampi recognised in Britain as the Dublin Bay prawn, in America as the saltwater crayfish and occasionally known as langoustine

schnitzel thin slice of veal or chicken. A breaded veal cutlet, e.g. wiener schnitzel

score parallel cuts made on the surface of food items

sea salt a salt derived from evaporated sea water. Used as a seasoning, especially with boiled beef. Also used in table grinders

sec degree of sweetness of Champagnes and sparkling wines or the amount of sugar they contain; here it means medium sweet

sekt quality German sparkling wine produced by the Charmat method (secondary fermentation in a sealed tank)

sepia cuttlefish, prepared like calamari (squid), either sautéed whole in oil or stuffed and poached while the legs are blanched and stewed

service cloth cloth approximately the size of a table napkin, used by food service staff as a protection against heat and to assist in handling equipment and in the service of food

shaoxing an amber-coloured rice wine

Sherry fortified (or liqueur) wine, having a grape spirit (brandy) added to improve the alcoholic content; made from white grapes

shiitake dark brown Japanese mushroom that has a distinctive earthy flavour and is used for garnishing and flavouring

shish kebab term of Turkish origin indicating small pieces of meat, usually fillet of lamb, interspersed with button mushrooms and grilled on a skewer. May be accompanied by a Madeira sauce

shooter layered cocktail consisting of alcoholic liquors of varying densities, the heaviest lying at the base of the glass and the lightest on the top. Also known as the rainbow cocktail or pousse café and served in an Elgin-shape liqueur glass

short (of pastry) having a high fat content

shred (émincer) to cut meat or vegetables into thin slices or strips

sichuan peppercorns fragrant Chinese seasoning from a plant unrelated to pepper

skim to remove impurities and fat from the top of soups and broths by using a skimming ladle

skorthalia garlic sauce of Greek origin

smorgasbord term of Scandinavian origin which indicates a self-service buffet. In Scandinavia this may take the form of quite a substantial meal of several courses, offering a varied number of dishes such as salads, cheeses, pâtés, cold meats and almost always includes dishes of herrings

smorrebrod open or Scandinavian sandwich. Various breads, wholemeal, rye, pumpernickel, bread rolls and white and brown sandwich bread are used for these sandwiches, onto which selected food items, meats, soused fish, meat and fish pastes, salami and salad are placed

soba noodles, Japanese in origin, made of white wheat or golden buckwheat and accompanied by nori (seaweed) and horseradish

soffritto a sauce/stew base of fried diced vegetables and sometimes pancetta (streaky bacon)

sorbet soft fruit flavoured water ice, sometimes flavoured with liqueur or wine and served as a sweet dish or between courses to cleanse the palate

soubise smooth onion pulp served with a variety of meat entrées

soufflé sweet or savoury baked pudding made with whipped egg whites

soy bean round bean, rich in protein and used to make tofu (unfermented bean paste); can be cooked fresh or dried in stews

soy sauce key ingredient of East Asian cuisine, and in particular Chinese and Japanese cuisine, enhancing many dishes, e.g. soups, stews and sauces. Made from soy beans, the Japanese equivalent is shoyu

spaetzele (spaetzeli) Swiss and Austrian paste speciality made by pressing an egg noodle dough through a colander and simmering it in salt water

spare ribs rib bones of beef or pork, marinated and then baked or grilled

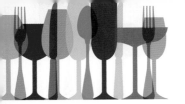

spatchcock young game bird or chicken that is split open down the backbone and flattened, then fried or grilled

spirits overall term for all distilled alcoholic liquors, the most common of which are whisky, brandy, gin, vodka and rum

split drink term indicating a bottle size. Usually a small or half bottle (285 ml) of a sparkling drink such as tonic, soda or lemonade

spring roll pancake-type roll of Chinese origin, filled with minced meat and vegetables and deep fried

spumante Italian wine label term denoting sparkling

station refers to the sideboard (or workstation) from which the food service team work together with the group of tables they are responsible for serving

still equipment used to produce spirits, either the pot still or the continuous still, e.g. brandy distilled from wine in copper pot stills

stillroom area in the back of house that provides those items, both food and beverages, not provided by the key sections of the kitchen or bars

still-set traditional commercial installation consisting of a water boiler and bulk storage containers for coffee and hot milk. The latter is steam heated and a steam injector will also be attached

stir fry the East Asian process of preparing food by cooking over a very fast and high heat

stockfish dried salt cod, braised, stewed, fried and eaten raw in salads. Also pounded to make a savoury paste or butter used in pâtés

stout strong dark beer with a smooth, malty flavour and creamy consistency and brewed from a very dark roasted malt

strudel fruit dessert made of either a puff pastry or filo pastry case filled with various mixtures of fruit and served hot or cold

sugar syrup sweet liquor of sugar and water boiled together; when used as an ingredient for cocktails it is termed gomme syrup

sumac Middle Eastern spice, the berries being deep, brick red when dried. Used whole or ground and may be sprinkled on fish, added to salads and used to season kebabs

suprême denotes cuts from the wing or breast of poultry and feathered game. Also indicates a cut of fish on the slant and free from bone

sushi Japanese sweetened vinegar rice and toasted nori sheets (a tissue-thin Japanese seaweed used as a wrapping) are key ingredients in sushi. Other fillings may be spinach, mushrooms or pickled ginger

sweetmeat sugar-coated confection, e.g. small fancy cake, and may also take the form of crystallised fruits. Also see 'petit four'

syllabub rich dessert dish of sweetened cream and lemon juice, flavoured with sweet white wine and brandy, served well chilled in a glass

---

T

tabasco hot, spicy and pungent Indian pepper sauce, two key ingredients of which are vinegar and red peppers. Used largely in Creole cooking. May accompany oysters, clams and other seafood

tabbouleh salad of bulgur wheat mixed with tomatoes, onion, lemon juice, mint and parsley

tagliolini thin noodles. Italian in origin

tahina crushed sesame seed paste, widely used as a flavouring in Middle Eastern and Latin American cuisine

tamarind fruit pods of an African tree that may also be found in India. Pods contain a very sour juice used in some Indian curries. Fruit of the tamarind tree is dried and ground and used in flavouring curries

tandoor open topped clay oven originating in Northern India

tandoori food that has been cooked in a charcoal fired tandoor, e.g. tandoori chicken

tannin obtained from the pips and stalks of grapes during the wine-making process and acts as a preservative, especially in red wines. Is also the brown colouring of tea

tapenade paste of capers, black olives, anchovies, garlic and often tuna

taramasalata Greek in origin, a dish made from dried, salted and pressed roe of mullet or cod, seasoned with garlic, lemon juice and olive oil to form a pink, creamy paste

tarka Indian method of tempering spices in hot oil

tarragon flavouring herb with long, narrow, green leaves and found in fines herbes, sauce béarnaise, poached fish and chicken dishes

tartare cold mayonnaise-based sauce with finely chopped capers, gherkins and fines herbes added. Served with deep fried fish

tartare, steak minced raw fillet of beef mixed with parsley, capers, gherkins, finely chopped onion and seasonings and served cold

tarte tatin French apple tart baked upside-down

tartufo Italian term for truffle, an edible fungus; see truffle

T-bone steak (porterhouse) steak on a T-shaped bone that is cut from the fillet end of a sirloin of beef. Includes both the fillet and the sirloin of beef

tempura seafood and vegetables dipped in batter and deep-fried

tequila Mexican spirit distilled from the fermented juice (pulque) of the agave plant

teriyaki fish or meat marinated in teriyaki which is a mixture of mirin (sweet Japanese rice wine), Japanese soy sauce and chicken stock

terrine mixture of meat, fish or vegetables and seasonings in a lined dish that is cooked, cooled and served cold in a terrine – an oblong, straight-sided cooking utensil with a close fitting lid

tian shallow gratin of chopped vegetables

tikka marinated pieces of fish, meat or poultry. Indian in origin, e.g. tikka masala (aromatic spice blend). Also see 'masalas'

timbale half conical tin mould. The dish is cooked and served in this single portion mould. Usually fish, meat, rice or vegetables in a sauce, or fruit with Chantilly

tisane all forms of herbal teas containing no caffeine or tannin and consumed either cold or hot, e.g. mint, rosehip and lemon

tofu a highly nutritious unfermented bean paste made from soy beans; Japanese in origin

tokay Hungarian sweet white wine, available in three styles, the most well-known of which is probably tokay aszú

torte German for a round, rich, layer cake or flan, decorated and divided into portions. Contains nuts, cream and fruit or jam

tortilla Mexican round, flat, unleavened pancake made from cornmeal, filled with beans or meat and a sauce. Served hot

tostada Spanish for toast

tournedos fillet steak cut in round, neatly trimmed portions from the heart of the fillet of beef

toxin poisonous substance, secreted by certain organisms

tranche length of puff pastry, with a puff pastry wall either side and often with a fruit filling. Served hot or cold, e.g. tranche aux pommes (apple)

trenette long, flat pasta; another name for linguini

trifolato method for sautéing vegetables in oil, garlic and parsley

tripe lining from the first and second stomach of oxen. The classic dish is stewed tripe and onions

tronc collection of tips received by food service staff

tronçon portion of flat fish cut across the body, on the bone, e.g. tronçon de turbot

truffle edible fungus found underground near the roots of oak or beech trees. The Périgord black from France and the Piedmontese white from Italy are noted for their taste and scent. The black truffle is used as a decorative garnish in pâté and aspic dishes; the white truffle is grated raw on salads, risotto, pasta and egg dishes. The word is also used to indicate a round chocolate

truss to bind or truss poultry or game birds for cooking, giving them a better shape

tuile crisp biscuit, traditionally flavoured with almond

tureen deep, covered dish from which soup is served when working from the guéridon. The tureen may be large enough for one portion only or for a number of portions

Turkish coffee traditionally made in a long handled container called an ibrik. A dark, very strong but sweet coffee served in small cups

turmeric mild peppery spice, bright yellow in colour and used in many curry mixtures. Called haldi in India and obtained from the root stems of a plant belonging to the ginger family. The stems are dried and then ground producing the powder called turmeric

tutti frutti confection, especially ice cream, mixed with a variety of diced candied fruits and Italian in origin

U

udon very narrow, ribbon-like, Japanese white wheat noodles served in hot soups and mixed meat and vegetable dishes

Underberg proprietary brand of German herb-flavoured bitter with a brandy base

underliner an underplate. Plate or flat with a napkin, doily or dish paper on it placed underneath another dish or accompaniment

univalve mollusc with a shell consisting of one valve, e.g. snails, clams

V

vacherin sweet dish made up of meringue, fresh soft fruit such as raspberries or strawberries, whipped cream and a fruit coulis

veal meat of a calf, the French menu term being veau, e.g. escalope de veau. Also see 'escalopes'

vegan strict vegetarian and one who consumes no animal products at all

vegetarian person who does not eat either fish or meat, but may eat eggs and dairy products

velouté rich, smooth, white sauce made from white stock, a white (blond) roux and seasonings. The style of velouté relates to the variety of stock used: fish, veal, mutton or chicken; also used to indicate a soup made in the same way

verjuice sour grape or crab apple juice used in place of vinegar

vermicelli very thin pasta style noodles, Italian in origin and often used to garnish soups. Capellini is the finest ribbon pasta

vermouth fortified and flavoured wine. Three main types are bianco, rosso (Italian) and white dry (French)

vichyssoise thick potato and leek soup, garnished with chives and usually served cold

viennoiserie yeast dough bakery products

vierge whipped butter or olive oil, seasoned with salt, pepper and lemon juice and served with vegetables

vinaigrette combination of oil and vinegar or lemon juice with seasonings. May also include mustard and herbs. Used to dress salads

vindaloo very hot, sour curry sauce from southern India and spiced and flavoured with vinegar, e.g. chicken vindaloo

voiture term for a trolley used in the food service area, for the purpose of hors d'oeuvre, sweets, cheeses, liqueurs, carving, etc.

vol-au-vent round or oval, open baked, puff pastry case being a large edition of a bouchée and filled with savoury items such as chicken, mushroom or asparagus, each bound with a thick, creamy sauce

W

waiter's friend corkscrew, bottle opener and small penknife blade combined and safely carried in the pocket so that it is available at all times. Also called a wine knife

wakame Japanese seaweed with a mild flavour and a pleasant green colour. Popular in salads, added to pickles and sprinkled over rice dishes

wasabi Japanese horseradish, the root being similar to the common horseradish. Has a fierce aroma and biting taste. Comes in green paste or powder form. Used as a condiment and with sushi and other Asian dishes, particularly Japanese sashimi

whitebait very small young fish of the herring family, deep fried, eaten whole and best in the spring and summer

wok large basin-shaped frying pan that concentrates the heat in a small area. Used in East Asian cuisine, especially for stir fry dishes

won ton wrappers of Chinese noodle paste similar to ravioli

Worcestershire sauce maceration of blend of spices and fruit in vinegar and used as accompaniment and as flavouring; often known by the brand name 'Lea and Perrins'

Y

yakimono Japanese method of grilling and pan frying

yellow bean sauce made from fermented and puréed yellow soy beans that are highly nutritious

yum neau yum is a form of cooking unique to Thailand, involving searing sirloin steak in a steak and spice combination to produce a hot and sour flavour and then tossed with a salad of cucumber, tomato, onion, coriander and fresh chillies

yuzu Japanese citrus fruit

Z

zabaglione light and creamy sweet dish made by whipping together egg yolk, caster sugar and Marsala (dark, sweet, fortified wine from Sicily), accompanied by sponge finger biscuits

zahtar Lebanese seasoning of thyme, salt and sometimes sumac

zest outer skin of citrus peel, without the oils it produces and the pith; obtained by rubbing on a fine grater

zucchini American term, known in Britain as courgette. A baby or miniature marrow

Annex B: Cocktails and mixed drinks recipes

The list of cocktails and mixed drinks below is mainly drawn from the official listings of the International Bartenders Guild (IBA). Other recipes are drawn from United Kingdom Bartenders Guild (UKGB).

When making cocktails and mixed drinks it is important to check the definition for permitted alcoholic liquor measures for your country, including any licensing restrictions on sales to minors.

Examples of glasses for the service of cocktails are shown in Section 3.11, Figure 3.12, p.87).

Whisk(e)y cocktails	Ingredients	Methods
Highball	5.0 cl whiskey Dry ginger ale	Place ice in the Highball glass. Add the whiskey and stir to chill well. Add the dry ginger ale to taste. Decorate with a twist of lemon peel
Highland Fling	5 cl Scotch whisky 2 cl dry vermouth 6 dashes orange bitters	Pour all ingredients into a mixing glass filled with ice. Stir. Strain into a cocktail glass. Garnish with a twist of orange
Manhattan	5 cl rye whiskey 2 cl red vermouth 1 dash Angostura bitters	Pour all ingredients into mixing glass with ice cubes. Stir well. Strain into chilled cocktail glass. Garnish with cocktail cherry
Dry Manhattan	Substitute dry vermouth for 3.0 cl sweet vermouth	Garnish with a thin twist of lemon or an olive
Mint Julep	6 cl Bourbon whiskey 4 fresh mint sprigs 1 teaspoon powdered sugar 2 teaspoons water	In a Highball glass gently muddle the mint, sugar and water. Fill the glass with cracked ice, add bourbon and stir well until the glass is frost. Garnish with a mint sprig
Old Fashioned	4.5 cl bourbon or rye whiskey 2 dashes Angostura bitters 1 sugar cube Few dashes plain water	Place sugar cube in Old-fashioned glass and saturate with bitters, add a dash of plain water. Muddle until dissolved. Fill the glass with ice cubes and add whiskey. Garnish with orange slice and a cocktail cherry
Rusty Nail (or Kilt Lifter)	4.5 cl Scotch whisky 2.5 cl Drambuie	Pour all ingredients directly into Old-fashioned glass filled with ice. Stir gently. Garnish with lemon twist
Whiskey Collins	4.5 cl American rye whiskey 2 teaspoons caster sugar 3.0 cl lemon juice soda water	Collins is a sour served on the rocks in a Collins (or Highball) glass and topped with soda water. Garnish as a sour but add straws

Whisk(e)y cocktails	Ingredients	Methods
Whiskey Sour	4.5 cl bourbon whiskey 3.0 cl fresh lemon juice 1.5 cl Gomme (sugar) syrup	Dash egg white (optional: if used shake a little harder to foam up the egg white). Pour all ingredients into cocktail shaker filled with ice. Shake well. Strain in cocktail glass. If served 'On the rocks', strain ingredients into Old-fashioned glass filled with ice. Garnish with half orange slice and maraschino cherry
	Variations: *Gin Sour, Bourbon Sour, Rum Sour* (dark rum), *Scotch Sour, Daquiri Sour* (light rum)	

Gin cocktails	Ingredients	Methods
Dry Martini (Gin and French)	6.0 cl gin 1.0 cl dry vermouth	Pour all ingredients into mixing glass with ice cubes. Stir well. Strain in chilled martini glass. Squeeze oil from lemon peel onto the drink, or garnish with olive
Sweet Martini	6.0 cl gin 1.0 cl red vermouth	Basic method as above and for a sweet martini garnish with a maraschino cherry
	Variation: *Vodka Martini*	Replace gin with vodka
Gibson	6.0 cl gin Dash of dry vermouth	Pour the gin into a mixing glass with ice. Add the dry vermouth and stir. Strain into a cocktail glass. Garnish with a white pearl onion in the drink
Gin Fizz	4.5 cl gin 3 cl fresh lemon juice 1 cl Gomme (sugar) syrup 8 cl soda water	Shake all ingredients with ice cubes, except soda water. Pour into Highball glass. Top with soda water. Garnish with lemon slice
	Variations: *Golden Fizz*, same as Gin Fizz plus egg yolk; *Royal Fizz*, same as Gin Fizz plus whole egg; and *Silver Fizz*, same as Gin Fizz plus egg white only	
Pink Gin	5 cl gin 2 dashes Angostura bitters	Always serve it ice cold Pour the gin and bitters into a mixing glass with ice. Stir with a bar spoon. Strain into a cocktail glass
Singapore Sling	3.0 cl gin 1.5 cl cherry liqueur 0.75 cl Cointreau 0.75 cl DOM Bénédictine 12.0 cl pineapple juice 1.5 cl lime juice 1 cl grenadine 1 dash Angostura bitters	Pour all ingredients into cocktail shaker filled with ice cubes. Shake well. Strain into Highball glass

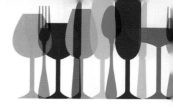

Gin cocktails	Ingredients	Methods
John Collins	4.5 cl gin 3 cl fresh lemon juice 1.5 cl Gomme (sugar) syrup 6 cl soda water	Pour all ingredients directly into Highball glass filled with ice. Stir gently. Garnish with lemon slice and maraschino cherry. Add a dash of Angostura bitters (Note: Use Old Tom Gin for Tom Collins)
White Lady	4 cl gin 3 cl Triple Sec 2 cl fresh lemon juice	Add all ingredients into cocktail shaker filled with ice. Shake well and strain into large cocktail glass

Brandy cocktails	Ingredients	Methods
B & B	3.0 cl brandy 3.0 cl DOM Bénédictine	Pour brandy into a brandy balloon and gently float the Bénédictine over a bar spoon onto the top of the brandy
Between the Sheets	3 cl white rum 3 cl cognac 3 cl Triple Sec 2 cl fresh lemon juice	Pour all ingredients into shaker with ice cubes, shake, strain into chilled cocktail glass
Blue Lady	3.0 cl cognac 3.0 cl Blue Curaçao 3.0 cl lemon juice 1 egg white	Put all the ingredients together into a cocktail shaker with ice. Shake vigorously. Strain into a cocktail glass
Brandy Alexander	2.0 cl brandy 3.0 cl fresh double cream 3.0 cl brown Crème de Cacao	Put all ingredients into a cocktail shaker with ice and shake well. Strain into a chilled cocktail glass. Sprinkle the surface with fresh ground nutmeg
Sidecar	5 cl cognac 2 cl Triple Sec 2 cl fresh lemon juice	Pour all ingredients into cocktail shaker filled with ice. Shake well and strain into cocktail glass

Rum cocktails	Ingredients	Methods
Bacardi classic	4.5 cl Bacardi white rum 2 cl fresh lime juice 1 cl grenadine	Pour all ingredients into shaker with ice cubes, shake well, strain into chilled cocktail glass
Cuba Libre	5 cl white rum 12 cl cola 1 cl fresh lime juice	Build all ingredients in a Highball glass filled with ice. Garnish with lime wedge
Daiquiri	4.5 cl white rum 2.5 cl fresh lime juice 1.5 cl Gomme (sugar) syrup	Shake and strain all ingredients into a cocktail glass

Rum cocktails	Ingredients	Methods
Frozen Daiquiri	As above with the addition of one scoop of ice cream	Pour all ingredients into blender with crushed ice. Blend until slushy and smooth and pour into chilled goblet
Mojito	4 cl white Cuban rum 3 cl fresh lime juice 6 mint sprigs 2 teaspoons white sugar soda water	Muddle mint springs with sugar and lime juice in a Highball glass. Add splash of soda water and fill glass with cracked ice. Pour rum and top up with soda water. Garnish with spring of mint leaves and lemon slice. Serve with straws
Pina Colada	3 cl white rum 9 cl pineapple juice 3 cl coconut milk	Blend all the ingredients with ice in an electric blender, pour into a large goblet (sometimes called a Hurricane glass) and serve with straws. Garnish with a slice of pineapple with a cocktail cherry

Vodka cocktails	Ingredients	Methods
Black Russian	5 cl vodka 2 cl coffee liqueur	Pour the ingredients into the Old-fashioned glass filled with ice cubes. Stir gently
White Russian	As above but add 3.0 cl fresh cream	As above then float fresh cream on the top and stir gently
Bloody Mary	4.5 cl vodka 9 cl tomato juice 1.5 cl lemon juice 2 to 3 dashes of Worcestershire sauce tabasco celery salt pepper **Variations**: To make tomato juice spicier, add salt, pepper and Worcestershire sauce to taste Any of the following may also be added to enhance flavour: dash of Tabasco, fresh lemon juice, pepper from the peppermill or cayenne pepper Garnish may also be varied by the use of a stick of celery, carrot stick or a wedge of lemon	Pour all ingredients into Highball glass and stir gently, garnish with celery and lemon wedge (optional)
Cosmopolitan	4.0 cl Citron vodka 1.5 cl Cointreau 1.5 cl fresh lime juice 3.0 cl cranberry juice	Shake all ingredients in cocktail shaker filled with ice. Strain into a large cocktail glass. Garnish with lime slice
Harvey Wallbanger	4.5 cl vodka 1.5 cl Galliano (to float on drink) 9 cl orange juice	Pour vodka and orange juice into a Highball glass filled with ice. Stir gently and float Galliano on top. Garnish with orange slices and cherry

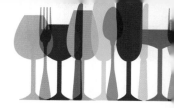

Vodka cocktails	Ingredients	Methods
Kamikaze	4.0 cl vodka 2.0 cl Cointreau 2.0 cl lemon juice	Add all ingredients into cocktail glass shaker filled with ice. Shake well and strain into cocktail glass. Garnish with a lime wedge and stirrer
Mai-Tai	4 cl white rum 2 cl dark rum 1.5 cl Orange Curaćao 1.5 cl Orgeat syrup 1 cl fresh lime juice	Shake and strain into Highball glass. Garnish with pineapple spear, mint leaves and lime peel. Serve with straw
Moscow Mule	4.5 cl vodka 12 cl ginger beer 0.5 cl lime juice, fresh 1 slice lime	Combine the vodka and ginger beer in a Highball glass. Add lime juice. Garnish with a lime slice
Salty Dog	4.0 cl vodka 10.0 cl grapefruit juice	Shake vodka and grapefruit juice in cocktail shaker. Strain into a salt rimmed Highball glass filled with ice
Sea Breeze	4.0 cl vodka 12.0 cl cranberry juice 3.0 cl grapefruit juice	Build all ingredients in a Rocks glass filled with ice. Garnish with lime wedge
Sex on the beach	4.0 cl vodka 2.0 cl peach schnapps 4.0 cl cranberry juice 4.0 cl orange juice	Build all ingredients in a Highball glass filled with ice. Garnish with orange slice
Screwdriver	5 cl vodka 10 cl orange juice	Pour all ingredients into a Highball glass filled with ice. Stir gently. Garnish with an orange slice
Vodkatini	9.0 cl vodka 2 dashes extra dry vermouth in a small bitters bottle	Place a cocktail glass in the freezer before using. Pour the vodka into the glass. Splash the vermouth on top of the vodka. Garnish with a twist of lemon or an olive

Tequila cocktails	Ingredients	Methods
Margarita	3.5 cl tequila 2 cl Cointreau 1.5 cl freshly squeezed lime juice	Pour all ingredients into shaker with ice. Shake well and strain into a cocktail glass rimmed with salt (For a Fruit Margarita – blend selected fruit together with the ingredients in the recipe above)
Tequila Sunrise	4.5 cl tequila 9 cl orange juice 1.5 cl grenadine	Pour tequila and orange juice directly into Highball glass with ice cubes. Add a splash of grenadine to create chromatic effect (sunrise), do not stir. Garnish with orange slice and cherry

Wine based cocktails	Ingredients	Methods
Kir	9 cl dry white wine 1 cl Créme de Cassis	Pour Créme de Cassis into glass, top up with white wine
Mulled Wine (Serves 20)	2 bottles of Burgundy or Rhône red wine ¼ bottle dark rum ½ bottle Dubonnet ½ bottle drinking water Whole orange studded with cloves (clouted) 2 cinnamon sticks 25 g (1 oz) sultanas 2 lemon halves 5 g (¼ oz) mixed spice 1 x 400 g (1 lb) jar of clear honey	Heat the clouted orange for 10 minutes in the oven to bring out the flavour. Tie the mixed spices in a muslin bag to prevent clouding the wine. Place all of the ingredients with the exception of the rum into a large pot. Hold some of the honey back so as to be able to adjust the flavour later. Place the pot on a low heat and stir occasionally. Bring the mixture almost to boiling point but do not allow it to boil. When ready to serve add the rest of the honey to taste. Finish with the rum just before serving into small Paris goblets. Sprinkle a little grated nutmeg onto the top of each drink

Champagne cocktails	Ingredients	Methods
Bellini	10 cl Prosecco 5 cl fresh peach puree	Pour peach puree into chilled flûte shaped Champagne glass and add sparkling wine. Stir gently Variations: Puccini (fresh mandarin juice); Rossini (fresh strawberry puree); Tintoretto (fresh pomegranate juice)
Black Velvet	Guinness Chilled dry Champagne	Half fill the glass with Guinness and top up with the chilled dry Champagne. Sometimes served in silver tankards
Bucks Fizz	10.0 cl well chilled Champagne 5.0 cl fresh orange juice	Prepare in a flûte-shaped Champagne glass by pouring in the fresh orange juice first and topping up with the well-chilled Champagne. Decorate with a curl/twist of orange peel
Champagne Cocktail	9.0 cl chilled Champagne 1.0 cl Cognac 2 dashes Angostura bitters 1 sugar cube	Add dash of Angostura bitters onto sugar cube and drop it into champagne flûte. Add Cognac followed by pouring gently chilled Champagne. Garnish with orange slice and maraschino cherry
	Note: This cocktail may be made with any sparkling wine but should then be called by the name of the wine used and not Champagne Cocktail as the name Champagne is protected	
Kir Royale	9.0 cl dry Champagne 1.0 cl Crème de Cassis	Place the Crème de Cassis in a chilled flûte-shaped Champagne glass. Add the well-chilled Champagne. Do not stir

Other cocktails	Ingredients	Methods
Americano	3.0 cl Campari 3.0 cl red vermouth A splash of soda water	Mix the ingredients directly in an Old-fashioned glass filled with ice cubes, add a splash of soda water and garnish with half orange slice
B52	2.0 cl Kahlua 2.0 cl Bailey's Irish Cream 2.0 cl Grand Marnier	Layer ingredients one at a time starting with Kahlua, followed by Bailey's Irish Cream and top with Grand Marnier. If allowed in the establishment, light the Grand Marnier and serve while the flame is still on, accompanied with a straw on side plate
Egg-Noggs	5.0 cl cognac or other brandy or whisky or gin, etc. whole egg caster sugar to taste nutmeg	Place the ice, whole egg, two teaspoons of caster sugar and the alcohol into a cocktail shaker and shake vigorously. Strain into a cocktail glass and sprinkle with the grated nutmeg. Named according to the alcohol used
Golden Dream	2 cl Galliano 2 cl Triple Sec 2 cl fresh orange juice 1 cl fresh cream	Pour all ingredients into shaker filled with ice. Shake briskly for few seconds. Strain into chilled cocktail glass
Grasshopper	3.0 cl Créme de Cacao (white) 3.0 cl Créme de menthe (green) 3.0 cl fresh cream	Pour all ingredients into shaker filled with ice. Shake briskly for few seconds. Strain into chilled cocktail glass
Negroni	3.0 cl gin 3.0 cl sweet vermouth 3.0 cl Campari dash of soda water	Pour all ingredients directly into Old-fashioned glass filled with ice. Stir gently. Garnish with half orange slice
Pimms	5.0 cl Pimms No 1 cup 9.0 cl lemonade/tonic water/ginger ale	Pour Pimms into a Worthington or Highball glass. Add ice and top up with lemonade or alternatives. Decorate with slice of apple, orange, lemon, lime and a twist of cucumber peel. Alternatively just use mint leaves. Stirrer and straws are optional
Round the World	3.0 cl banana liqueur 3.0 cl Scotch whisky 0.5 cl Cointreau 0.5 cl orange cordial orange slice	Put the banana liqueur and whisky into a shaker with plenty of ice. Add Cointreau and undiluted orange cordial. Shake and strain into a cocktail glass. Add orange to garnish and serve
Sherry Cup	5.0 cl dry sherry 9.0 cl medium cider fresh sliced unpeeled cucumber	Use very chilled ingredients. Put sherry into a Highball or Worthington glass and top up with cider. Garnish with freshly cut unpeeled cucumber slices

Non-alcoholic cocktails*	Ingredients	Methods
Fruit Cup	3.0 cl orange juice 3.0 cl grapefruit juice 3.0 cl apple juice lemonade/soda water	Pour all ingredients, with the exception of the lemonade/soda, onto ice in a glass jug. Stir well to blend and chill. Add sliced fruit garnish. Top up with lemonade or soda water. Serve well chilled in Highball or Worthington glasses
Pussyfoot	15.0 cl orange juice 3.0 cl fresh lemon juice 3.0 cl lime cordial 0.5 cl grenadine 1 egg yolk soda water 2 dashes grenadine	Place all ingredients with the exception of the soda water on ice into a cocktail shaker. Shake vigorously to blend well together. Strain over crushed ice into a Collins glass. Top up with the soda water. Add straws
Saint Clements	4.5 cl orange juice 4.5 cl bitter lemon	Mix the orange juice and bitter lemon on ice in a Worthington glass. Stir well to blend. Garnish with a slice of orange and lemon
Shirley Temple/Roy Rogers	9.0 cl ginger ale 0.5 cl grenadine	Place ice in a Highball glass and add grenadine. Pour in the chilled ginger ale. Decorate with full fruit garnish and add straws
	Variations: Ginger ale and fresh lime juice or ginger ale and lime cordial to taste	
Tropicana	7.0 cl pineapple juice 7.0 cl mango juice 3.0cl coconut milk	Mix the well chilled ingredients on crushed ice in a Slim Jim glass and serve with straws

* Non-alcoholic cocktails are often now referred to as Mocktails

Annex C: Cigars

Where cigars are served, it is often the sommelier's responsibility to sell these to the customer. However, some restaurants now discourage the sale of cigars. In addition, in many countries smoking bans now preclude the smoking of tobacco products in enclosed areas.

The Havana is regarded as the best of all hand-made cigars, to be savoured like a rare wine. The Jamaican cigars come a close second but are milder than Havana and much less expensive. Nowadays, cigars are also made in other countries including the USA, Puerto Rico, the Philippines, Japan, the Dominican Republic and the East Indies.

Table C.1 Cigar terms

Binder	A single leaf of tobacco that is wound around the filler of the cigar to hold it together
Bunch	The term usually applied to the construction of the cigar when it consists of the binder tobacco wrapped around the filler leaves
Curing	The process of drying the moisture out of newly harvested tobaccos
Filler	The blended tobaccos, which form the inner core of the cigar. The filler is the most important part of the cigar as it is responsible for most of the flavour and smoking quality
Long filler	Those fillers whose tobaccos run the entire length of the cigar. Long fillers are found in only the better cigars
Shapes	Cigars are made in a variety of shapes and sizes to suit the individual's preferences for taste and style. Many smokers select different shapes for different times of the day
Wrapper	The outer covering of the cigar is an important part of the cigar's flavour and smoking quality. The various shades of wrapper are: Claro (light, golden brown), Double Claro (the result of picking the leaves before reaching maturity), Candela (light green), Colorado (reddish mid-brown), Maduro (darkest) and English Market Selection/Natural (lighter in colour than Maduro).

There are classic measurements for cigars, which many cigar makers attempt to follow. However, the size of a cigar, when indicated by a name only such as Corona or Robusto, is not an indication of a universal standard. Cigars are now categorised by length and Ring Gauge (also spelt Ring Guage), which is measured in multiples of 64ths of an inch. A cigar with a 52 Ring Gauge, for example, measures 52/64ths of an inch in diameter. A Ring Gauge of 50 x 6 is 50/64ths of an inch in diameter by 6 inches long. If the Ring Gauge is stated 6 x 50 it is still 6 inches long and 50/64ths of an inch in diameter. Some examples of cigars are show in Table C.2

Table C.2 Examples of cigar types and sizes

Type	Length in inches	Length in mm	Ring gauge
Torpedo and Pyramides	6–9	152–228	50–58
Belicoso	5–6	127–152	50–55
Robusto	4½–5	115–127	50–55
Hermoso	5	127	48
Double Corona	7½–8	190–203	47–52
Grand Corona and Montecristo A	9¼	235	47
Churchill	7	178	46–50
Corona Gorda	5½–6	140–152	46–48
Lonsdale Corona	6½	165	32
Corona Grande	6	152	42
Corona	5	127	40–43
Petit Corona	5	127	40
Perla	4	102	40
Tres Petit	4½	115	40
Corona Culebras	5¾	145	39
Especial	7½	190	38
Long Panatela	7	117	35–39
Demi Tasse	4	102	30–39
Panatela	4½	114	26–33

Storage

A fine cigar should be kept at between 15.5 °C and 18 °C (60 °F and 65 °F) and between 55 per cent and 60 per cent relative humidity, with as little variation as possible. A cigar will pick up any smell or moisture in the air, or dry up and smoke like tinder.

When there is regular turnover, the best presentation and method of keeping cigars is in a humidor (see Figure C.1). This is a polished box with half a dozen sections, each holding a different size and type of cigar. On the inside of the lid is a pad which is kept damp, but not wet, to maintain the humidity.

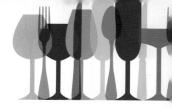

Figure C.1 Example of cigar presentation box – humidor (image courtesy of Hunters and Frankau)

Where there is little turnover of cigar sales then the safest way to keep cigars in good condition is to buy and offer them for sale in tubes. These tubes are hermetically sealed and cigars stored in this way will retain their good condition for a long time.

Whether a cigar is stored in a tube, humidor or specially made box, all such containers are either made with, or lined with cedar wood. This is done because the aroma of cedar blends well with cigars and, as cedar wood is porous, it allows the cigar to breathe. A free circulation of air around these boxes is essential.

Selection and smoking

- Cigar boxes should be opened carefully with a blunt instrument.
- To extract a cigar, press the rounded head and the cigar will tilt upwards for easy extraction.
- Cigars should not be handled before selection. Rolling a cigar near the ear, sometimes called 'listening to the band', says nothing at all about the cigar and simply damages it.
- The appearance of a cigar should be smooth, firm and even to the touch. It should always be the same size and colour as its partners in the box. The wrapper (outer leaf) should have a healthy glow to it and the open or cut end should be smooth and even.
- The band or identification tag should only be removed if the customer requests it. If it is to be removed it should be done carefully as moving it up and down can damage the cigar. Even if peeled off gently, it can still rip the tobacco leaves.
- When cigars are not pre-cut a V-shaped cigar cutter is required to cut the end, thereby facilitating maximum free draught and ease of smoking. Do not make a small hole with a match or cocktail stick, as this will leave a moist tar concentrate, which imparts a very bitter flavour as the end of the smoke is approached.
- To light a cigar use the broad flame of a long match, a cedar wood spile, or a gas lighter, rotating the cigar to achieve even burning and periodically moving the cigar through the air to encourage burning.

Index

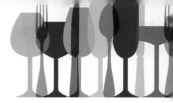